P9-CEM-327

A. JEYARATNAM WILSON
DENNIS DALTON
editors

THE STATES OF SOUTH ASIA

PROBLEMS OF NATIONAL INTEGRATION

essays in honour of W. H. Morris-Jones

C. HURST & COMPANY, LONDON

First published in the United Kingdom by
C. Hurst & Co. (Publishers) Ltd.,
38 King Street, London WC2E 8JT

ISBN 0-905838-69-6
Printed in Great Britain

CONTENTS

W. H. MORRIS-JONES:
A BIOGRAPHICAL NOTE

W. H. Morris-Jones's life has rested on four geographical nodal points: Wales, England, India, Italy. Wales was where he started from and from where in spirit he never moved. England is where he was educated and taught and wrote. India was to him a leading revelation, a challenge and a joy, an all-absorbing field. Italy is where he found his life's companion and, with that, a family and another home.

Morris-Jones comes from middle-class stock in rural Wales — small farmers and small shopkeepers, his father's side in Carmarthenshire in South Wales, his mother's on the coast and by the mountains of Merioneth in the North. There were the occasional teachers and preachers and one of the latter was a scholar whose work on the Welsh Bible brought him renown.

For all these relatives Welsh was the language of worship, of business and of the hearth. But Morris's father had been despatched at the age of ten to live for four years with cousins who had emigrated to northern Argentina in the 1870s. The father's formal education was affected but he acquired Spanish and even after his return found employment with the River Plate Trust Loan and Agency Company in the City of London. It was at one of London's Welsh chapels just before World War I that the senior Morris-Jones met his future wife who had come to receive a teacher's training. Morris-Jones (senior) was however soon called to army service in 1914; he survived several of the more gory battles.

During one of the elder Morris-Jones's periods of leave from the fighting in Flanders, he married. W. H. Morris-Jones was born on 1 August 1918 in his father's home in Carmarthen where his mother had gone to live. Within just over a year his father had been demobilised, resumed his job and found a place for his family to live in Finsbury Park. Morris's introduction to English took place in an informal kindergarten; it seems to have taken him by surprise, for on being fetched on the first day he presented to his mother a little girl companion, explaining that she was strangely unable to understand a word of his Welsh!

The family soon moved to an outer suburb, Hendon, and there Morris lived during school and university. He recalls those as contented years without undue drama. At University College School, Hampstead, he made reasonable progress, varying between delight in English and Maths and misery in Physics and Chemistry. Outside school he wandered with friends over the nearby still country fields, became a proseletysing evangelical and tried to write plays and compose pop music of a very sentimental kind. Only the first of these enthusiasms endured. His plays and songs were politely rejected and with the study of economics in the sixth form religion gave way to a curiosity about socialism through some reading of Stafford Cripps. Such changes made him restless and he declared a wish to leave school to become a journalist. His father dealt with this threat to his dreams of a university education for his son by arranging for him to be interviewed for a place at the London School of Economics and to be persuaded by a Welsh newspaper man that journalism could best follow some degree course in economics and politics.

Morris therefore began his studies at LSE attending, at the tender age of 17, lectures by Laski, Robbins, Tawney, Herman Finer, Evan Durbin, Smellie, Eileen Power, Hayek and so on. The excitement was intense and he was soon busily engaged in political activity in the united socialist party and only a little later in the communist group within it. Meetings of one sort or another — student union, party, cell, clique and Marxist theory classes — were daily time-consuming. Demonstrations and marches — for the Republican Government in Spain, against British imperialism in India ('Amery Must Go!'), for better pay for bus drivers, against appeasement of the fascist dictators — were less frequent but even more absorbing of energy. At the same time student leaders stressed that red students had to be the best students. Morris and his fellow-students probably made up for fewer library hours than some by more intense discussion among themselves, trying to construct Marxist critiques of all that they encountered. It worked: those of the Left got a disproportionate share of the Firsts (including Morris). Not less important, they experienced exhilarating intellectual exchanges and a sense of intimate comradeship which extended from late night smoke-filled committee meetings to long trekking holidays in the hills of England and the French Alps.

Nevertheless, when Morris obtained in 1938 an award to begin post-graduate work at the School, he began a process of withdrawal from activism. Still, he chose as his research subject the work of William Thompson, an Irish Ricardian economist who anticipated some of Marx's analysis, but he pulled out of committees and cut down on demonstrations. Towards the end of the first year, Morris had become as uneasy about his subject as Robbins, his supervisor, had become about his equipment for the task. He also felt the need for some change of scene. When he was offered a research award at Christ's College, Cambridge, he readily accepted, though by then war clouds were thickening fast. He kept to the same period but left Marxist economics for the fascinating but unmanageable comparison of the political ideas of Coleridge, John Henry Newman and F. D. Maurice.

By the time Morris went up to Christ's, war had formally begun. Almost worse for him, L.S.E., from which he wanted a rest, were to move up to Cambridge 'for the duration of the emergency'. Morris buried himself in his books and produced wildly ambitious fragments for his patiently tolerant supervisor, Ernest Barker. So long as the war remained 'phoney' it was possible to work. But by the summer of 1940 — most dramatically when a load of weary survivors from Dunkirk collapsed on the secluded lawns of the college court below his study window — Cambridge had become unpalatably unreal and Morris knew that in any case he would soon be 'called up' for one of the armed services.

Residual left ideas caused Morris to view the war as less than wholly worthy: Chamberlain was not to be trusted and a 'deal' with Hitler to turn Germany eastwards seemed very possible. With some indifference, therefore, Morris accepted his father's advice to opt for the Indian Army. The father was probably thinking in terms of his son's survival but he wisely used the argument that this would at least give him access to a civilisation he might otherwise never encounter. While waiting for the call-up Morris lived in dingy rooms in London and worked as a reporter for Tom Harrison's *Mass Observation*. By the end of 1940, Morris was accustomed to nights in air raid shelters, his parents had been evacuated from London and his Hendon home had been bombed.

Before sailing from the Clyde on a grey, icy day in January 1941 Morris had located a Cambridge student of like political persuasion and they had, during two dreadful weeks in Aldershot barracks, got to know two other university men. The four huddled together to give themselves solace against the several unknowns. The seemingly unending journey — a huge convoy played hide-and-seek with German submarines in the North Atlantic and briefly put in at Freetown, Durban and Mombasa before reaching Bombay in March; the incredible boredom and discomfort of army routines on an overcrowded troopship; the touchingly quaint ideas of the retired Indian Army officers who were to prepare them for the role of defenders of the Raj; the terrifying naivety of the bulk of the cadets, straight from school; the now tolerant, now bullying behaviour of British regular army sergeants who were their immediate masters — with all these the new recruits sought to cope through private jokes, long bouts of bridge and the reading and re-reading of the few books they had been able to take with them.

India made its impact — but by stages. The army was a world complete in itself and only gradually did the country and people come into view, partly of course through the Indian soldiers themselves. After periods of training and of managing (or, rather, mis-managing) mules on the North-West Frontier, Morris was posted to South India to run a supply depot, guarding the large petrol store, keeping weevils out of the rice and *atta* and buying up fresh produce from canny local contractors. It was during this period that the impact of the 'Quit India' movement obliged him to take notice of the local political scene. Morris decided to send up reports containing analysis and assessment. G.H.Q. concluded that he was better at politics than at store-keeping; from then on his work consisted partly in relating to newspaper editors, who in effect became his first tutors in Indian politics, partly in editing magazines for distribution in several languages to Indian soldiers.

When the war in Europe ended, Laski asked Morris if he would be interested in standing as a Labour candidate in the coming elections. But Morris was by then in love with India and did not want to leave. This nevertheless obliged him to think of the future. Daringly, Morris asked *The Times* if they could use him in India; they would give him a trial under their man in Delhi but if he passed the test they could give no undertaking to keep him in India. Morris peeped at Indian universities but was not reassured. When he was eventually released in 1946, he settled for returning to England, hoping for some way of keeping India in his life. He had no idea how or how soon this would happen.

Encouraged to apply for a vacancy as Assistant Lecturer at L.S.E., Morris seized the chance, the more readily because Indian politics was agreed upon as an area of specialisation. The transition into academic life was easy because L.S.E. was warm and familiar and Indian politics was in his bones. Within six months he was asked by Cripps and Attlee to join Mountbatten's staff for the final stages of the transfer of power — an experience on which he has written elsewhere.* There were other visits to India in those years, notably a full year which followed his marriage in Italy and culminated in his first child and his first book.

To leave L.S.E. was difficult and when he did so in 1955 it was to move as far away as was possible within England, to Durham. Constructed at the same time as London University, this was the reply to that latter, the Godless creation of early nineteenth-century modernity. Nestling by the Cathedral and occupying the Castle, it was in every sense a far cry from L.S.E. But the city was beautiful and the University was full of promise, very small but with a firm grip on standards and goals. For Morris the challenge was exciting and the period of his stay was one of glorious but well-considered expansion. Within eleven years the tiny Department of Social Studies numbering

* 'The Transfer of Power, 1947: a View from the Sidelines', *Modern Asian Studies*, 16, 1 (1982), 1–32.

W.H. MORRIS-JONES

five teachers had grown to a staff of nearly forty organised in a Faculty of Social Studies comprising departments of Economics, Politics, Sociology, Economic History and Law but still primarily operating joint honours degrees. Durham was kind to Morris and enabled him to continue his work on India through further research visits and periods of teaching in Chicago and Berkeley. In this setting of achievement Morris's family too grew with two further children.

The decision to return to London was taken against calls from Australia and elsewhere in Britain. From one of the latter he was told that they could offer 'slavery at the centre compared to freedom at the periphery' of the Institute of Commonwealth Studies in Russell Square. The years since 1966 have never seemed to be at a periphery, for Russell Square was the centre of a satisfying world; alas, freedom too was limited, for all too soon the financial blizzard swept in and a struggle for survival was on. But there were good friends, a sense of a worthwhile job to do and some further writing as creative as he could make it. And to more of India there was added the delight of getting to know Sri Lanka, Jamaica, Malaysia and, briefly, Ghana.

As Morris says, 'the prospect now returns to the opening lines of this piece. For, in retirement, I shall continue to divide my time and thoughts between each of the four points of my soul's compass.'

March 1982 THE EDITORS

in consultation with W. H. Morris-Jones

INTRODUCTORY NOTE

South Asia presents a mosaic, a congeries of artificial administrative entities left by a departing power. Before independence in 1947, India was one state, only to become two with the creation of Pakistan. Even while this happened, the future of India was threatened by the lapse of British paramountcy. In 1971, Pakistan became two states with the secession of its east wing and the birth of the Republic of Bangladesh. It is not possible to say what is yet in store for the weakened new state with its lack of political skills. There are other breakaway movements in India and Sri Lanka.

How long will the fragile unity last? What are the impediments to national unity? Can political secession be contained by constitutional designs that can satisfy the aspirations of discontented groups? To what extent does the presence of the two super-powers, as well as interest in the region on the part of Britain and the People's Republic of China, prevent further balkanisation or maintain greater coherence? Can India play a role which can fortify the *status quo*? Or will India itself suffer disintegration with the collapse of a centralising leadership? From still another perspective, can a viable political alternative to centralised government emerge in South Asia short of balkanisation or disintegration? Can there be a legitimate basis for a highly decentralised system of government in India, Pakistan, Bangladesh and Sri Lanka?

Our contributors have endeavoured in various ways to answer these questions. Exactly for this purpose we divided the volume into three sections with a view to detecting the various strands in the historical process. In a span of some thirty-five years, from 1947 to 1982, many events have invaded the scene to raise doubts as to the validity of historical or political predictability. Nevertheless there are continuing trends which make it possible to identify the future of national integration in the states of the subcontinent.

The first section looks at the subcontinent as a whole while examining the scenario of the individual states — Pakistan, India, Sri Lanka — at independence. The second probes into the dynamics of political integration and disintegration as states become formalised and their élites and counter-élites take responsibility for their destinies. The causes of national breakdowns are investigated. The essay on India deals with the philosophical aspects of that country's political paradigm. The third section is an attempt to look into the future, indicating weaknesses in the political systems of the new states. It seeks to explain how and why some of their explosive political problems are being dealt with in a particular way. The political processes of the states of the subcontinent are naturally the focus of attention of super-powers and major powers. Their future will depend on the degree and kinds of outside intervention and non-intervention. The concluding essay takes these factors into account and weighs a range of prospects.

The contributors to this volume have known Wyndraeth Humphreys Morris-Jones since 1947. They have gratefully acknowledged their debt to him, being only too aware of the fact that the directions in the study of South Asian politics had already been mapped out for them by the '*guru*'. Morris-Jones would scoff at that appellation. Yet there is a sense in which the term is particularly appropriate. Whether in a classroom in Chicago, a lecture hall in London, or at a chance meeting in Delhi, Morris-Jones can be counted on to liberate the learning process from two of its worst enemies: the impersonal and the abstract. Colleagues and students alike consistently delight in his bag of tricks: lectures laced liberally with idiom, metaphor, symbol and anecdote; conversation enriched by incisive understatement and unfailing wit and, above all, his writing with its elegance of style and a touch of poetry. We could not have asked for more and, in whatever way we received it, his wisdom made its impact. Like the effect of a good *guru*, his insights entered our consciousness and an authentic closeness of spirit formed. How he could have managed to do this with so many scholars is a wonder; this volume is one attempt to pay tribute to the fact that it happened. We, the contributors, consider it most appropriate to have written these essays around a theme in which Professor Morris-Jones still continues to make his impact on the thought-processes of scholars working on the politics of the subcontinent.

A. JEYARATNAM WILSON

DENNIS DALTON

NOTES ON CONTRIBUTORS

PAUL R. BRASS, M.A., Ph.D. (Chicago), is Professor of Political Science and South Asian Studies at the University of Washington, Seattle. He is the author of *Factional Politics in an Indian State: the Congress Party in Uttar Pradesh* (1965), *Radical Politics in South Asia* (with M. F. Franda, 1973), *Language, Religion, and Politics in North India* (1974) and of numerous articles and contributions on Indian politics in various journals and books. He has visited India many times since 1961 for field research and travel.

DENNIS DALTON, M.A. (Chicago), Ph.D. (London), is Professor of Political Science at Barnard College, Columbia University, New York. He taught at the school of Oriental and African Studies, University of London, for four years. He has been researching for the last twenty years on modern Indian political thought and has published numerous articles on the ideas of M. K. Gandhi, M. N. Roy, Swami Vivekananda, Sri Aurobindo, and J. P. Narayan. He is concerned with an analysis of dominant themes that have emerged from the theories of these and other Indian thinkers in the last hundred years.

C. R. DE SILVA, Ph.D. (London), is Associate Professor of History at the University of Peradeniya, Sri Lanka, where he has been Dean of the Faculty of Arts and Director of its Ceylon Studies Seminar. He was a Calouste Gulbenkian Fellow in 1970 and 1976 and Hallsworth Research Fellow at the University of Manchester in 1982. He is the author of *The Portuguese in Ceylon 1617–1638* (1972), and has published numerous articles on the politics and history of Sri Lanka.

K. M. DE SILVA, Ph.D. (London), holds the chair of Sri Lanka History at the University of Peradeniya, Sri Lanka. He has been Smuts Fellow in Commonwealth Studies, Cambridge (1968–9), Visiting Fellow of Clare Hall, Cambridge (1968–9), a Commonwealth Visiting Professor at the University of Manchester (1976–7) and a member of the University Grants Commission of Sri Lanka since 1979. He was a member of the Presidential Commission on Development Councils (Sri Lanka) during 1980–1. He is editor-in-chief of the University of Sri Lanka, *History of Ceylon* and managing editor of *The Ceylon Journal of Historical and Social Studies*. He is the author of *Social Policy and Missionary Organizations in Ceylon, 1840–55* (1965) and *A History of Sri Lanka* (1981). He edited and contributed chapters to the University of Ceylon, *History of Ceylon*, vol. III: *1900–1948* (1973) and *Sri Lanka: a Survey* (1976), and has contributed numerous articles on Sri Lanka's history and politics to various journals. He is currently working on a study of ethnicity and national development in Sri Lanka.

TALUKDER MANIRUZZAMAN, Ph.D., is Professor of Political Science at the University of Bangladesh. Previously he was Professor and Chairman, Department of Political Science, University of Rajshahi. He is the author of *The Politics of Development: The Case of Pakistan, 1947–1958* (1971), *The*

Bangladesh Revolution and its Aftermath (1980), *Group Interests and Political Changes: Study of Pakistan and Bangladesh* (1981). He has contributed to N. T. Uphoff and W. F. Ilchman (eds.), *The Political Economy of Development* (1972) and to P. R. Brass and M. R. Franda (eds.), *Radical Politics in South Asia* (1973) and has published extensively in Indian, Bangladeshi and international journals.

JAMES MANOR is Lecturer in Politics at the University of Leicester, England, and Editor of the *Journal of Commonwealth and Comparative Politics*. He holds degrees from Yale University and the University of Sussex and has taught at the Chinese University of Hong Kong, the University of London and Yale University. He is the author of *Political Change in an Indian State: Mysore, 1917–1955* (1977), *Utopia and the Main Chance: Bandaranaike and Ceylon* (forthcoming) and (with Marcus Franda and Bhabani Sen Gupta) *India: Dilemmas of Representative Government* (forthcoming). He is co-editing, with Walter Hauser, *Two Faces of India: Bihar and Karnataka.*

ROBIN J. MOORE, Ph.D., D. Litt. (London), is Professor of History, Flinders University of South Australia, and has been a Lecturer in the Modern History of South Asia at the School of Oriental and African Studies, University of London (1964–71), Smuts Fellow in Commonwealth Studies, Cambridge (1974–5), Visiting Fellow, Wolfson College, Cambridge (1974–5), Resident Scholar, Rockefeller Foundation, Bellagio (1975), Australian Vice-Chancellors' Committee Asian Fellow (1979) and Chapman Visiting Fellow in Commonwealth Studies, University of London (1980–1). He is the author of *Sir Charles Wood's Indian Policy, 1853–66* (1966), *Liberalism and Indian Politics 1872–1922* (1966), *The Crisis of Indian Unity, 1917–40* (1974), *Churchill, Cripps and India, 1939–45* (1975) and editor of *Tradition and Politics in South Asia* (1979). He has contributed to C. H. Philips and M. D. Wainright (eds.), *The Partition of India* (1970); A. G. L. Shaw (ed.); *Great Britain and the Colonies 1815–65* (1970); D. A. Low (ed.); *Congress and the Raj* and C. C. Eldridge (ed.); *British Imperialism in the Nineteenth Century* (1981); and edited South Asia and Burma entries for A. J. P. Taylor and G. M. D. Howat (eds.), *A Dictionary of World History* (1973). He has published numerous articles on Indian history and politics in international journals, completed a monograph on 'The Parting of the Ways: The Attlee Government and the Indian Problem' and is currently working on a book *A Study of Lord Curzon and the Imperial Idea*.

ATAUR RAHMAN, M.A. (Dacca), Ph.D. (Chicago), is Associate Professor of Political Science and Director of the Centre for Policy Research, University of Dacca, Bangladesh. He was formerly Research Director, Ministry of Foreign Affairs, Government of Bangladesh. He held research fellowships from the Ford Foundation, the Brookings Institution and the University of Chicago, and is author of *Pakistan and America: Dependency Relationships*. He has contributed to Raju G. C. Thomas (ed.), *The Great Power Triangle and Asian Security* and has published extensively on the politics, economy and foreign policy of Bangladesh.

M. RASHIDUZZAMAN, M.A. (Dacca), Ph.D. (Durham), is Associate Professor in Political Science at Glassboro State College, Glassboro, New Jersey. He has been Associate Professor of Political Science, University of Dacca (1967–70), Bangladesh; Provost, University of Dacca (1969–70); Visiting Associate Professor, University of Virginia (Spring 1972); Visiting Fellow (1970–3) and a Research Associate, Southern Asian Institute, Columbia University, since 1973. He has served on the editorial boards of *The Journal of Commonwealth Political Studies* and *South Asia*. He has also been a consultant at Bangladesh Public Administration Training Complex (1979), a project leader of a survey on rural leadership and population control in Bangladesh (1977–9), and a project leader for the Government of East Pakistan's study of local councils (1965–7). He is the author of *The Central Legislature in British India 1921–47* (1967), *Pakistan: a study of Government and Politics* (1967), *Politics and Administration in the Local Councils: A Study of Union and District Councils in East Pakistan* (1968), *Village Government in East Pakistan: A Study of Union Boards and Union Councils* (1967), and numerous articles in international journals on the political problems of Pakistan and Bangladesh. His monograph *The Political Inheritance of Bangladesh: a Study of Parties and Politics* will be published shortly.

DR LEO E. ROSE is Editor of *Asian Survey* and Lecturer in Political Science at the University of California, Berkeley. He has published extensively on South Asian international and regional relations and on the politics and foreign policies of the Himalayan states. Currently, he is working on a study of Indian and Pakistani decision-making in the 1971 Bangladesh war and on Kashmiri state politics. Dr Rose was the recipient of the Hildegarde Millar Award in International Relations and a Sherman Fairchild Distinguished Scholar grant.

LLOYD I. RUDOLPH, Ph.D. (Harvard), is Professor of Political Science and the Social Sciences at the University of Chicago. With Susanne Hoeber Rudolph he is the co-author of *The Modernity of Tradition: Political Development in India* (1967) and *The Regional Imperative* (1981), and has contributed chapters to numerous books and articles to a wide variety of international scholarly journals.

SUSANNE HOEBER RUDOLPH, M.A., Ph.D. (Radcliffe College), is Professor of Political Science and the Social Sciences at the University of Chicago. Besides her books with Lloyd I. Rudolph, she has also co-authored with him *Education and Politics in India* (1981), and contributed chapters to books, and articles to a variety of international scholarly journals.

KHALID B. SAYEED is Professor of Political Studies, Queen's University, Kingston, Ontario. He obtained degrees from Madras University, the London School of Economics and Political Science, and McGill University. He has taught in Indian and Pakistani universities, at the University of New Brunswick, at Duke University (as a Visiting Associate Professor) and McGill University (as a Visiting Professor). He also served as United Nations adviser in development administration to the Plan Organization, Government of

Iran. He is the author of *Pakistan the Formative Phase* (1960 and 1968), *The Political System of Pakistan* (1967), *Politics in Pakistan: The Nature and Direction of Change* (1980), numerous articles in encyclopaedias and journals, and chapters in edited works.

HUGH TINKER is Professor of Politics, University of Lancaster, England. He served in the Indian Army and civil administration (1941–6), and was successively Lecturer, Reader and Professor at the School of Oriental and African Studies, University of London (1948–69); Director, Institute of Race Relations, London (1969–72), and Senior Research Fellow, Institute of Commonwealth Studies, London (1972–77). He participated in the Indo-British Exchange at Poona in 1979. His books include *South Asia: a Short History* (1966), *India and Pakistan: a Political Analysis* (2nd edn, 1967), *Separate and Unequal: India and the Indians in the British Commonwealth* (1976), *The Banyan Tree: Overseas Emigrants from India, Pakistan and Bangladesh* (1977), *Race, Conflict and the International Order* (1977) and *The Ordeal of Love: C. R. Andrews and India* (1979). He is currently working on a volume of documents on *The Transfer of Power in Burma*.

A. JEYARATNAM WILSON, Ph.D., D.Sc. (Econ.) (London), is Professor of Political Science, University of New Brunswick. He was Professor of Political Science, University of Sri Lanka (1969–72); he was also a Leverhulme Research Scholar, London School of Economics and Political Science (1955); Research Fellow in Politics, University of Leicester (1964–5); Research Associate, McGill University (1970–1); Simon Senior Fellow, University of Manchester (1971–2); Senior Research Associate, Columbia University (1977) and Senior Associate Member, St. Antony's College, Oxford (1977). He is the author of *Politics in Sri Lanka* (1974 and 1979), *Electoral Politics in an Emergent State: the Ceylon General Election of May 1970* (1975), and *The Gaullist System in Asia: the Constitution of Sri Lanka 1978* (1980).

SUSILI WILSON, B.A. (Ceylon), Postgraduate Diploma in Librarianship (Ceylon), A.L.A., worked as a librarian in the University of Ceylon, Peradeniya, and later in the Government of Sri Lanka's Industrial Development Board. She is presently a librarian at the library of the University of New Brunswick.

SOUTH ASIA AT INDEPENDENCE: INDIA, PAKISTAN AND SRI LANKA

Hugh Tinker

When independence came to South Asia it came both unexpectedly and after long anticipation and delay. For a quarter of a century, Gandhi and other Congress leaders had called for the early attainment of *Swaraj*: and this concept was accepted — certainly from 1929 onwards — as 'complete freedom from British dominion and British imperialism'.[1] The British response to this demand was lukewarm. When the Secretary of State for India announced in August 1917 that the goal for India was 'the progressive realisation of responsible government', this was hailed as 'the most momentous utterance ever made in India's chequered history'. Yet, in reality, the commitment was hedged around with every kind of qualification. The Preamble to the 1919 Government of India Act laid down that 'The time and manner of each advance can be determined only by [the British] Parliament, upon whom responsibility lies for the welfare and advancement of the Indian peoples.'[2] Safeguards: this was what Parliament was concerned about: safeguards for the Muslims, safeguards for the Princes, safeguards for Indian defence and all the time, of course, safeguards for the British. The Indian public was lectured on the virtues of delay. The Simon Commission admonished: 'Indian political thought finds it tempting to foreshorten history, and is unwilling to wait for the final stage of a prolonged evolution. It is impatient of the doctrine of gradualness.'[3] And so, the transfer of power was doled out spoonful by spoonful. Indian attempts to hasten the process by direct action, Civil Disobedience, *Satyagraha*, were not very productive (some argue that they were counter-productive). The Raj was still secure. The Indian Army was still 'loyal', administrators and police (Indian as well as British) did their duty with alacrity. Thousands might obey Gandhi's call to defy the Raj, but their destination was the jailhouse. And Gandhi's weakness (which was also his strength) was that he did not hate the British; he loved them, and only wanted to arouse them to their moral obligation to their Indian fellow-citizens.[4]

India requires first consideration because Ceylon (Sri Lanka) advanced at a pace largely determined by India.[5] The 'model colony' was administered by a different Whitehall department, but developments in India had immediate repercussions, both in the politics of the island and in Whitehall. However, in 1929, Ceylon took a massive constitutional leap — far ahead of India, and far ahead of many Western countries — when the franchise was extended to the entire adult population. This leap took place not because it was demanded by the political leadership of Ceylon, but because the visiting Donoughmore Commission decided that, in the absence of a national movement, political consciousness must be stirred by the extension of the franchise to a much wider electorate. A particular member of the Commission, Dr Drummond Shiels, persuaded the Colonial Secretary, Sidney Webb, that there was no point in limiting the vote to a narrower base. The rising leader of the Ceylonese élite, D. S. Senanayake, asked for the exclusion of certain potential voters from the franchise, and at his prodding the Governor suggested imposing limitations, but the British government went ahead. Three years later, Senanayake was modestly asking for 'complete control over the internal affairs of the island'.[6] Ceylon was back in the wake of India's political demands.

And so South Asia hastened slowly towards self-government. What seemed like a major step forward in India, with the introduction of full provincial self-government in 1937, was lost when the Congress withdrew from the constitutional experiment on the outbreak of war. Twenty years after the 'August declaration', India and Ceylon were still firmly under British control. Nehru later admitted that he had not expected to see independence during his lifetime; Gandhi declared that he would have to live 125 years in order to witness *Swaraj*.

There was one feature of political life upon which Indians and British seemed agreed: that the country was moving towards a growing national consciousness: it was a 'Nation in Making'.[7] Earlier, British writers had questioned whether India would ever be unified: it was much more like a multi-national Europe than a distinct nation.[8] Indians of all political persuasions resented this charge, seen as yet another attempt to 'Divide and Rule'. That India was a nation, or a nation in making, was accepted and assumed by all. Out of many statements we could select, let us take one by a literary man, with no stake in active politics — a Tamil professor, working in Bombay, K. R. Srinivasa Iyengar:

> India may be really a huge country, but geographically and culturally she is one; India may speak a multitude of different tongues, but her heart is sound and her soul is one. The fact of Indian unity is a positive faith with most Indians and it does not require any logical or material corroboration from statistician or propagandist.[9]

This sense of nationhood was acknowledged by the British rulers, whether gladly or reluctantly:

> The unity imposed upon India by the external forces of Great Britain is today

reinforced by an increasing sense of Indian nationality . . . Whatever may be its shortcomings and however distasteful some of its manifestations, it appears to be the one force in Indian society today that may perhaps contain within itself the power to overcome the deep and dangerous cleavages which threaten its peace . . . Nationalism is a force with immense power for good or evil, and the task in the future is to utilise that force for constructive ends.[10]

Yet these assumptions were openly challenged by the leaders of India's largest minority, the Muslims. Their spokesman, Jinnah, insisted that not one but two nations existed in India: a notion that Gandhi (whose own son was temporarily converted to Islam) regarded as preposterous. Yet, from the enunciation of the demand for separate Muslim states at Lahore in 1940 to its ultimate realisation, Pakistan, took only seven years; despite relentless and unremitting opposition from Congress and the scepticism — indeed, incredulity — of the British. The accepted concept of an Indian nation had to bow to the unaccepted admission of another nation rooted in the widely separated territorial strongholds of the Muslim community. Nehru and many other Congress leaders never did accept the legitimacy of Pakistan: sooner rather than later, they believed, the Indian Muslims would return to the Indian fold.

In India, the struggle for independence involved a considerable degree of political mobilisation. Those Indian writers who articulated the nationalist concept of a Freedom Struggle exaggerated the total involvement of the Indian people in the struggle. There was still a 'loyalist' (pro-British) element at every social level. Protest was much more intense in the cities than in the countryside; those with some degree of education were much more aroused than the illiterate; certain areas were much more politically conscious than others — notably the 'Hindi Heartland' (U. P., Bihar, and what is now Madhya Pradesh) and the Gujarati country, with Bengal generating an explosive and incalculable nationalism all its own. But whatever reservations one may express, the extent of the participation of Indians in the national struggle remains impressive.

Nothing like this occurred in Ceylon, where the politics of co-operation flourished to the very end. Political activity remained the exclusive preserve of an élite (despite the introduction of full adult franchise), and only about one per cent of the population played any part, however minimal, in the political bargaining. How far, then, did a consciousness of Ceylon as a nation begin to emerge? Well, it was an island, like Britain or Japan. Its whole economy was dependent upon the export of certain primary products; its cosmopolitan upper middle class seemed to share the same set of values: 'On the eve of the transfer of power in Sri Lanka few if any of her leaders reflected on the nature of the polity they had inherited from the British. When they stopped to think of it at all they tended to turn back to the Kandyan kingdom . . . and looked upon themselves as its heirs . . . They regarded Sri Lanka as first and last a nation-state — which it no doubt was — but forgot that it was also a state-nation created by the British out of what they had conquered from the Dutch.'[11]

In retrospect, the whole movement towards independence has an air of inevitability. To anyone under the age of fifty-five in 1980, what seems extraordinary is that a small nation on one side of the world should ever have presumed to control the destiny of an empire on the other side of the world. Yet, at the time, imperial rule did seem almost immutable. When the Round Table Conference was convened in London in 1930, one delegate — the erstwhile revolutionary, Mohammad Ali — addressed the conference chairman, Lord Sankey, thus: 'My Lord, Divide and Rule is the order of the day: we divide, and you rule.' The British might make tactical concessions, but time and again a 'soft' period of nationalist pressure and British retreat was followed by a 'hard' period of nationalist collapse and the assertion of British control.

There were three massive attempts to force the British to relinquish power in India: the campaigns led by Gandhi in 1920–1, 1930–1, and 1942. Each campaign ended in defeat. It might have seemed as though the British could impose their own timetable for a transfer of power, a timetable which could, conceivably, take up most of the twentieth century. In November 1942, Winston Churchill declared that 'he had not become His Majesty's First Minister in order to preside over the liquidation of the British Empire': yet, within five years, the brightest jewel in the imperial crown had been relinquished. Ceylon, Burma and Palestine-Israel followed immediately after.

This massive demission did not flow from the Labour government's ideological objections to empire but from the realisation that Britain could not afford the military investment required to preserve the Indian Empire. The generals told the Cabinet that four or five extra British army divisions would be needed to maintain internal security in India, while the Viceroy, Lord Wavell, added that if the decision to stay were taken, it would only make sense if Britain planned to stay for another twenty years.[12] And so the British government was reduced to announcing that power would be transferred in India, come what may, by a definite date (June 1948), even though it was unclear to what authority (or authorities) power would be transferred. This was the dénouement to the assertion of the 'responsibility' of parliament for determining constitutional advancement. Its last act was to pass the necessary enabling legislation in double-quick time.

The escalation of Ceylon's claims from the level of internal self-government to that of independence flowed from the acceptance by the

British Cabinet of Indian independence: and also from the unexpected leap forward taken by Burma (conceded 'Full Independence within one year' in January 1947). Senanayake, as Leader of the State Council, argued that unless his moderate policies were seen to pay dividends, his adversaries would insist that independence could only be obtained by civil disobedience or rebellion. His bluffing persuaded the British Government, and an announcement that Ceylon would receive 'Fully responsible status' followed.[13]

One key feature of the transfer of power in India remained uncertain almost to the last moment: would power be transferred to a united India or to 'Hindustan' and 'Pakistan'? The Muslim League had demonstrated an ability to bring about near-chaos in the Punjab and in Calcutta. Nehru and his supporters were totally committed to a united, secular India and (as he constantly emphasised on public platforms) prepared to fight the British to obtain this goal. However, under pressure from Sardar Patel and the right wing, and in the absence of a strong lead from Gandhi, Nehru acquiesced in the division of India.[14]

It is a strange paradox that although both Congress and League had established their unchallengeable sway over Indian politics by mobilising mass support on the streets and in the polling booths, when the final decisions were made, they were made by so few individuals. Within the Congress, the younger, militant leadership, with Jayaprakash Narayan at their head, were effectively by-passed and neutralised. J. P. demanded that Congress organise for war against the British, rather than accept partition. His words were ignored. The Congress President, Abul Kalam Azad, afterwards complained bitterly that his attempts at compromise were thrust aside. Gandhi withdrew from Delhi, departing to a remote corner of rural Bengal to bring peace to its strife-ridden villages: he hoped to find the answer to the Pakistan demand in Noakhali, declaring, 'The moment I find it I will announce it to the world.' But he did not find it. In the end, the Congress decision to accept partition was left to Nehru and Patel alone.

Without question, the success of the Pakistan demand was due to one man, M. A. Jinnah, whose strategy was masterly: giving a little here and there when put under pressure but never losing sight of the goal. It was his tragedy that his untimely death removed the main hope of realising the Pakistan dream in a constitutional reality.[15] Similarly, the unexpected acceleration of Ceylon into independence was almost entirely the work of Don Senanayake; although he was assisted by two shrewd advisers, Sir Oliver Goonetilleke and Sir Ivor Jennings. Ostensibly withholding co-operation from the commission of inquiry sent from London (headed by Lord Soulbury), he nevertheless masterminded the whole inquiry, steering the commission towards making the recommendations he wanted (as Soulbury later partially acknowledged).[16]

Independence came to South Asia at the end of a protracted debate in which the issues were exhaustively considered. The situation was dramatically different fifteen years later when the British colonies in Africa casually obtained their independence as the result of the 'Winds of Change' in the Conservative leadership.[17] Yet, as we see, there was something almost accidental in the *timing* and in the *manner* of South Asia's independence, although its leaders would have indignantly repudiated such a suggestion. To them, independence was the just reward of a Freedom Struggle by a national Freedom Movement. This interpretation was accepted by the Western scholars, who were predominantly liberal, and many of them American — seeking to empathise on behalf of 'the First New Nation' with the first among the new nation-states of Asia. Thus, the accepted version was that all classes in South Asia had participated in the fight for independence, bringing about a 'revolution', a new world for the new states.

By comparison with the easily obtained independence which most of Africa received, the accepted version was right, relatively. But, of course, the struggle by the Congress bears no comparison with that of the peoples of Algeria or Vietnam. To a considerable extent, independence came because British belief in empire was exhausted and the post-war British Labour government (unlike the post-war leftist government in France) was ready to recognise the new reality.[18] Because the struggle for independence was believed to be more vigorous, more radical, more revolutionary than it really was, the *dynamic* of independence was exaggerated in contemporary estimations, and the political dynamic of the leaders and the movements was also exaggerated.

Throughout South Asia, the political leaders who took over the new regimes were moderate constitutionalists; men whose outlook was largely westernised and secular and whose social origins were upper middle class, with a heavy emphasis upon professional and intellectual values. It was therefore not surprising that their commitment to government by parliament, and to law enacted by legislatures and applied by a qualified judiciary was strong and sincere. The top leaders were largely supported by political parties and groups whose outlook was not so consistently westernised and constitutional — and yet who were distinctly more conservative and non-revolutionary.

If we draw up a short-list of the top South Asian leaders, it reads something like this: for India, Gandhi, Nehru, Patel; for Pakistan, Jinnah and Liaqat Ali Khan; for Ceylon, D. S. Senanayake and S. W. R. D. Bandaranaike. Of these seven men, only one (Senanayake) did not receive higher education in England, either in the Inns of Court or at Oxford or Cambridge. As it happened, he was perhaps the most committed of them all to the English style of political institutions.[19]

With growing Third World disillusionment and dismay in the 1970s at the failures of democratic institutions, the idea then gained ground that Western political models were foisted upon the new states to their detriment. As one writer, B. K. Nehru, concludes: 'History has no example of any country raising itself from poverty to prosperity while suffering the disabilities of a liberal democratic system.'[20] In the case of South Asia, the evidence actually suggests that the British political masters stoutly resisted any notion of transplanting a parliamentary system on the Westminster model in South Asia. John Morley's disclaimer is well known: 'A parliamentary system in India is not at all the goal to which I would for one moment aspire.'[21] The Montagu-Chelmsford Report, also, sought out means of introducing 'responsible government' other than through a parliament. It was the Indian political élite who insisted that any alternative would be second-best. The Simon Commission raised doubts as late as 1930:

> The Governor-General's Executive Council in the next stage of India's constitutional development cannot, in our judgment, be 'responsible' to the Indian Legislature in the same sense as a British Cabinet is 'responsible' to the British Parliament . . . It has struck us as remarkable that it should be so commonly assumed in India that the development of responsible government must take place on purely British lines . . . Our own view is that, until the provinces of India have established themselves . . . as self-governing units, the ultimate form which the Central Government of India will take cannot be finally determined . . . The utmost, therefore, that can be done now is . . . to recognise that the British system is not the only model . . . The ultimate form which the Government of India will take cannot possibly be precisely determined in present circumstances.[22]

The most striking attempt to wean Asians from their yearning for Westminster was made under the constitution which Ceylon received as a result of the Donoughmore Report. Instead of Parliament, Cabinet and Parties, Ceylon was provided with committee government (though it has to be conceded that the model was that of the London County Council!). Systematically, Senanayake and his associates stretched the Donoughmore constitution until it did yield Cabinet government in a parliamentary setting. At the next round of reforms, Ceylon returned thankfully to the Westminster model.

Asian voices had been raised in warning against acceptance of Western models as the basis for Asian self-government. One Indian leader of a far from revolutionary standpoint, C. R. Das, declared in 1922:

There is all the difference in the world between *Swarajya* (self-rule) and *Samrajya* (rule of the country) . . . No system of Government which is not for the people and by the people can ever be regarded as the true foundation of Swaraj . . . How will it profit India if in place of the white bureaucracy that now rules over her there is substituted an Indian bureaucracy of the middle classes?[23]

The most powerful of these dissenting voices was, of course, that of Gandhi, who urged the peoples of India to rediscover their future from their past. India had evolved a unique form of politics, he believed; government rooted not in power and authority but in local society, the rural community. 'Society based on non-violence can only consist of groups settled in villages in which voluntary co-operation is the condition of dignified and peaceful existence,' he declared. 'The nearest approach to civilisation based on non-violence is the erstwhile village republic of India.'[24] Contemplating the Western model, he concluded: 'The European democracies are to my mind a negation of democracy.'[25]

Influential Muslims also spoke out against the false goals offered by the West. A theologian, Maulana Abul Ala Maududi, was a consistent critic of the basic beliefs of Western democracy. Islam, he insisted, is

the very antithesis of secular Western democracy. The philosophical foundation of Western democracy is the sovereignty of the people. Lawmaking is their prerogative . . . Islam . . . altogether repudiates the philosophy of popular sovereignty and rears its polity on the foundations of the sovereignty of God and the viceregency [*Khilafat*] of man.[26]

Maududi opposed the formation of Pakistan, arguing that the *millat*, the people of the faith who inhabited India, must not be divided — with some belonging to the new state and some remaining in India. But (as we have noted) Pakistan was not created by Islamic theologians; it was the creation of a man, Jinnah, whose opposition to an India dominated by Congress was really an opposition to what he saw as a Hindu theocracy. Similarly, the new India, though venerating Gandhi, was not prepared to believe in his vision of an India revitalised by its ancient tradition. South Asia moved on to embrace the English parliamentary system because it really did not believe that there was a viable alternative.

'Nehru's government inherited its ethics and morality from the national movement; its structure, style and appearance of infallibility from the British Raj.' So B. N. Pandey begins his account of Nehru's stewardship after independence.[27] There was the strange spectacle of *khaddar*-clad figures moving into the viceregal and gubernatorial palaces which had been the symbol of British might and majesty. There might be orange juice in place of the whisky, but most of the pomp of the Raj was preserved. President and governors wore Gandhi caps, but the aides and attachés who surrounded them were uniformed in scarlet and gold and other gorgeous colours. Unceremoniously, the statues of British viceroys were taken down from their pedestals, but the statues of Indian proconsuls — Patel, Pant, Rajagopalachari — were soon to replace them. Fortunately, the bizarre proposal that Gandhi's statue should replace that of George V in the central site on Kingsway (Rajpath) was not adopted, although, as Dr. Pandey observes, 'Gandhism was placed on a pedestal from whence it could inspire, but not interfere with, the affairs of state.'[28] The first demonstration that Gandhism was safely relegated to its pedestal came with the fashioning of the Indian Constitution.

The principal architect of the constitutional structure was Sir B. N. Rau, an anglicised jurist and civil servant, although Dr. B. R. Ambedkar the Law Minister, with his Columbia Ph.D., played an energetic part in steering the drafts through the Constituent Assembly. Most political elements in India, from Left to Right, regarded a parliamentary form of government as the only suitable democratic form.[29] The main divergence was provided by the Gandhian concept of community co-operation conducted in a spirit of agreement, even unanimity. This was defined as *Panchayat Raj*, 'the rule of the village sages', as contrasted with government from above, *Sarkar*. Dr Ambedkar totally rejected the *panchayat* idea: 'I hold that these village republics have been the ruination of India . . . What is the village but a sink of localism, a den of ignorance, narrow-mindedness and communalism? I am glad that the Draft Constitution has discarded the village and adopted the individual as the unit.'[30]

Such Gandhian elements as remained in the Constitution were largely embedded in Part IV, 'Directive Principles of Policy', which B. N. Rau referred to as 'moral precepts', but which others dismissed as 'solemn promises and pious platitudes'.[31] Thus, Article 40 declared: 'The State shall take steps to organise village panchayats.' Article 43 laid down: 'The State shall endeavour to secure . . . a decent standard of life . . . and in particular the State shall endeavour to promote cottage industries.' Gandhian objectives were restated in 'Western' or 'modern' terms. Thus, Article 47: 'The State shall regard the raising of the level of nutrition . . . and the improvement of public health as among its primary duties and . . . shall endeavour to bring about prohibition of the consumption . . . of intoxicating drinks.' Or, Article 48: 'The State shall endeavour to organise agriculture and animal husbandry on modern and scientific lines and shall . . . take steps for . . . prohibiting the slaughter of cows.'

The most ambitious provision in the Constitution might be ascribed to Gandhi's own crusade, or might be seen as part of the liberal, democratic ethos which in general pervaded the Constitution. This was

Article 17, which declared: '*Untouchability* is abolished, and its practice in any form is forbidden. The enforcement of any disability arising out of *Untouchability* shall be an offence.' It was really more in consonance with Western approaches to social reform via legal enforcement, than through Gandhian soul-force, that the Constitution tackled this problem.

The one feature of the Constitution which was vigorously debated, and which at one time divided the legislators into two opposing groups, was the question of language. Gandhi had insisted that India must shake off the bondage of the English language and demonstrate its unity through a national language, acceptable to both Hindus and Muslims: the lingua franca termed 'Hindustani'. The constitution-makers started with this proposition but it was steadily eroded. On one side, the Hindu traditionalists successfully pressed the substitution of Hindi in its Sanskritic, Devanagari form.[32] On the other side, the opponents of Hindi succeeded in maintaining the status of English, as a temporary all-India language: which in time was to become a permanent all-India language.[33]

The constitutional debate on language included a provision (Article 351) which appears to hold open the door of compromise: 'It shall be the duty of the Union to promote the spread of the Hindi language, to develop it so that it may serve as a medium of expression for all the elements of the composite culture of India and to secure its enrichment by assimilating . . . the forms, styles and expressions used in Hindustani and in the other languages of India.' Here was the consensus view stated again: subsequent events were to demonstrate that Gandhian faith in harmony and unanimity was less compelling than the determination of regional and religious power-groups to maximise their own interests.

When all was concluded, one Congress leader, Sampurnanand (then Premier of Uttar Pradesh) declared: 'Our constitution is a miserable failure. The spirit of Indian culture has not breathed on it . . . It is just a piece of legislation, like, say, the Motor Vehicles Act.'[34] Nevertheless, the Indian Constitution was to endure, surviving its suspension on many occasions as well as drastic amendments during the Emergency. The Constitution symbolises the duality of the Indian political culture. Respected and accepted by judges, lawyers, professors and other westernised professional people, it makes no impact upon the masses, except when one of its provisions bears unexpectedly upon them.[35] The greatest gap between Constitution and people is seen in relation to Untouchability, where popular practice is almost totally unaffected by its directives.

From time to time, Gandhism was brought down from the pedestal. One major move was the introduction of the *Panchayati Raj* programme in the late 1950s and '60s. There were Gandhian features, such as the assumption that the village was a corporate community with a corporate will, corporate needs, and a capacity for corporate action. Experience was to demonstrate the obvious divisions in the contemporary village between the 'Haves', the prosperous (so-called 'progressive') farmers, and the 'Have-Nots', poor peasants and the landless. The councils called into being to administer *Panchayati Raj* were urged to choose their members by a process of consensus. Substantial rewards accrued to villages where the councils were formed on a basis of 'Unanimity', that is, without recourse to competitive elections. This idea was soon abandoned as it became obvious that the *Panchayati Raj* elections were stirring up the realities of contemporary rural life, with caste rivalries and personal and factional rivalries providing the nexus for a relentless struggle for local power. So intense were these local conflicts that a later investigation into the *Panchayati Raj* programme — the Mehta Report (1978) — recommended taking decision-making from the local level and giving policy implementation to bodies dominated by officials at the District level. Gandhism gave way to bureaucracy, to the *Sarkar*.

The last and most pathetic evocation of Mahatma Gandhi was made in the revolt led by Jayaprakash Narayan against the Indira Gandhi system. J. P. invoked the Mahatma's appeal to idealism: he called upon the students to give a year of their lives to the service of India. J. P.'s campaign brought on the Emergency. It also provided the dynamic for the Janata Party which in February 1977 appealed to the people of India to reject the Indira Gandhi system. Confounding all predictions, Janata won the election. In the moment of victory, J. P. (like his teacher, Gandhi) declined to assume power: but he led the newly-elected Janata M.P.s to Gandhi's memorial at Rajghat and administered an oath to them in which they pledged to dedicate themselves and their service to a new kind of politics. Within two years, by their internecine feuding and fighting, the Janata leaders had destroyed their own government and their own mandate. Disgusted by their gross betrayal, the Indian people turned to the only viable alternative: Mrs Indira Gandhi.

And so India by-passed the Gandhian heritage which had made its struggle for independence unique. When Gandhi was shot, Nehru told India: 'The light has gone out of our lives and there is darkness everywhere.' The light has, indeed, been dimmed; though who can know whether one day it will blaze forth again? India after independence still had Nehru: he was to symbolise his country in its achievement in the first decade and also, perhaps, in awareness of growing limitations, as development faltered and an enemy threw down the frontier defences. However, Nehru gave India nearly two decades of stability. 'His stature in the nation is reflected in his standing in the Lok Sabha, which he can dominate almost at will . . . But the Prime Minister's dominance is by no means absolute; it is tempered by a subtle and perhaps unconscious amenability to the will of the House — and particularly to the submerged but powerful opposition within the Congress Party.' So concluded the perceptive man from *The Times*.[36] Nehru dominated India; but he did not challenge those forces which might have unseated him; he knew that he depended upon them. Big business, capitalist farmers: what place had they in a socialist society? They had a key place in the Congress Party.

Neither did Nehru question the continuing relevance of the pillars of the Raj, which the British had set up — the bureaucracy, the police and the army — when he fashioned his new India. In his indictment of British rule, Nehru especially let himself go on the subject of the Old Indian Civil Service — 'mediocrity', 'dull routine', 'self-satisfied and self-sufficient, narrow and fixed minds, static in a changing world' — the invective flows on. Of all those in the I.C.S., Nehru most disliked its Indian members, *plus royaliste que le roi* (rather overlooking the ample representation of the Nehru clan in that service).[37] Yet, when independence came, Nehru yielded to the persuasion of Patel and others and agreed to the rights and privileges of the 'Twice Born' being entrenched in the constitution.

Nehru's criticism of the Indian Army which the British had fashioned was equally pungent: of the Indian King's Commissioned officers, trained at Dehra Dun, he observed: 'They are very smart on parade . . . But I sometimes wonder what purpose this training serves . . . Infantry and cavalry are about as much use today as the Roman phalanx.'[38] Again, although he did not — as Patel did — actively intervene to preserve the morale of the armed forces inherited from the British, he accepted the continuation of the British style, undiluted. Nehru had sprung to the defence of the Indian National Army officers, who had hoped to defeat the British in battle, when they were put on trial at the Red Fort, but the former I.N.A. leaders (even though trained at Sandhurst or Dehra Dun) were carefully excluded from the post-independence regular army.[39]

Nehru had obtained ample personal experience of the police forces of the Raj; for he had always been the first to confront their *lathis*. Again, he made no attempt to alter police methods or functions (even though they bungled so badly in failing to protect Gandhi from assassination).[40] The security forces were soon engaged in a full-scale operation of repression on the orders of Nehru and Patel. In Telengana and what was soon to be Kerala, a peasant revolt against the landlords achieved widespread success. The army sent in 50,000 or 60,000 troops, supported by armed police and the village soviets were liquidated at the cost of 4,000 killed and 10,000 arrested. There was no room for militant peasant power in the new India.

The acceptance of these pillars of the British Raj as the main pillars of Congress Raj contributed much to continuity, to institution-building, to the strengthening of the national superstructure. On both sides there was a remarkably smooth adjustment towards establishing a viable working relationship. The army was soon tested in the imbroglio in Kashmir and acquired a popular esteem which is a little curious in view of its traditions: a mixture of British regimental customs and the semi-feudal *Sahib-Jawan* relationship, stemming from Rugby School and from Rajasthan. Soon the *Jawans* were as much idolised by Indian journalists as they had been by their British officers, and even those mercenaries the Gurkhas were given an honoured place in the new folklore! The bureaucracy did not acquire the same glamour, but its importance in the new India of 'development' was as great (or greater than) before. Despite the massive increase in the activities of government, the élite cadre — the Indian Administrative Service, successor to the I.C.S. — remained relatively small (between two and three thousand) and retained much of the old *esprit de corps*. However, a different bureaucratic role emerged as the politicians made it clear that they were the bosses and the job of the civil servants was to implement *their* instructions as *they* required, not to implement some Olympian ideal of service to the state. Most senior officials got the message; the few who did not soon disappeared from the scene.[41]

The Indian Army and the I.C.S. might be given respect, even admiration, by the erstwhile Freedom Fighters; probably no-one felt much regard for the police, yet their powers were preserved and even strengthened. During the Second World War, the British had created special armed units of constabulary, maintained as reserves to back up the provincial police in an emergency. The armed police reserves were now steadily expanded, and under Indira Gandhi were to become the main central security force. Similarly, the powers which the British had assumed to detain political prisoners without trial (powers they only used in extreme emergency) were continued under Congress Raj, and were now widely used as a routine measure against political 'extremists'.

If the new India preserved the authoritarian instruments of British rule it also cherished those features which had developed from the liberal, law-enhancing aspect of British rule. The press remained free and relatively unafraid of pressures from above. The higher judiciary maintained the tradition of independence and distance from the executive arm. The universities continued to uphold the practices — and among the older institutions, the standards — of their original English model: the University of London.[42] It all ensured that there was no breakdown, as British prophets of doom had anticipated, and indeed provided a launching pad for the development decade which followed after independence.

The perpetuation of so many institutions of foreign origin, and the failure to preserve the Gandhian legacy, meant that indigenous custom and practice had to find its own level in an environment partially alien. Primordial loyalties shape the whole working of local and regional politics: even big city politics has been shaped upon traditional, rustic, preindustrial lines (as in the rise to power of *Shiv Sena* in Bombay).

It has been argued that 'modern' (i.e. Western) and 'traditional' (i.e. Indian) politics interact, and give life and meaning to Indian democracy.[43] However, to transpose what Arnold Toynbee (and Jesus Christ) suggested was a 'source of disharmony', one may expect trouble if one attempts to put old wine in new bottles.[44] Toynbee was analysing the impact of new ideologies and new economic forces upon old institutions (new wine in old bottles): we are concerned with old ideologies and traditional economic and social forces adapting to new institutions. Will this impact create radical change in the old ideologies and social forces? At the time of independence, observers expected Hinduism and caste to be transformed by the working of democratic institutions. Thirty years later, it seemed much more clear that the democratic institutions had been remoulded by religion and caste.

However, the traveller to Delhi, arriving in the early 1980s after a thirty-five-year interval, would find the political scene very similar. A strong prime minister presides, invulnerable to any would-be challenger. The Congress Party enjoys a two-thirds majority in parliament (though it is scarcely the same Congress as that of the old Freedom Fighters). The Supreme Court interprets the constitution, with only a very subtle regard for political realities. The civil servants arrive in New Delhi's palatial offices to a leisurely, but not unmeaningful day's work. The English-language newspapers deliver verdicts upon the questions of the hour with a *gravitas* long lost by the London *Times*. And, a few miles beyond New Delhi's endless avenues, the dust of the real India, the old India, ascends over the toiling bullocks and buffaloes and their drivers.

The traveller entering Pakistan after the same thirty-five-year interval would discover little that was familiar. Few of the hopes of 1947 have been realised; and few of the questions demanding answers in 1947 have yet been resolved. The moderate constitutionalists who straddled the political scene after Partition have departed, and can never be restored. We saw that India's constitutional debate ended in westernised, liberal, juridical solutions, with the Gandhian philosophy reduced to no more than the icing on the cake. The constitutional debate in Pakistan has never really ended, because never properly begun, and no lasting constitution has been found. Paradoxically, the constitution which survived longest was the revised version of the 1935 Government of India Act which was adopted as a temporary formula to legalise Pakistan's transition into independence. The various constitutional phases may be listed thus:

1. 1947–56: Government of India Act (9 years)
2. 1956–8 : first constitution (2½ years)
3. 1958–62: interregnum (3½ years)
4. 1962–9 : second constitution (7½ years)
5. 1969–72: interregnum (2½ years)
6. 1972–7 : third constitution (5 years)
7. 1977–??: interregnum

Thus, Pakistan has experienced longer periods of *interim* government, within an imperial frame, or martial law administration, than it has spent under constitutional forms of government: and if we recall that the second, Ayub Khan constitution was virtually imposed upon the country (though ratified by the Basic Democrats), then the contrast becomes even sharper.

If India relegated Gandhian political philosophy to the pedestal, Pakistan really had no ideological inspiration to accept or discard. The principal inspiration for the Pakistan dream was provided by the poet Iqbal. His Islamic ideology was infused by a mild, westernised liberalism. He reassured the Hindu population of a future Pakistan: they should not 'fear that the creation of autonomous Muslim states will mean the introduction of a kind of religious rule in such states', and to his fellow-Muslims he declared: 'The claim of the present generation of Muslim liberals to re-interpret the foundational legal principles [of Islam] in the light of their own experience and the altered conditions of social life is, in my opinion, perfectly justified.'[45] In his inaugural speech to the hastily assembled legislators of the new Pakistan, Jinnah went even further in emphasising the secular, non-dogmatic character of the new state: 'Work together in a spirit that every one of you, no matter what is his caste, colour or creed, is first, second and last a citizen of this State with equal rights, privileges and obligations . . . You will find that in the course of time Hindus would cease to be Hindus and Muslims would cease to be Muslims; not in the religious sense . . . but in the political sense as citizens of the State.'[46]

Even if Jinnah had lived long enough to guide his country towards an acceptable constitution, it is impossible to believe that his followers would have swallowed the idea of a secular state in which there happened to be more Muslims than Hindus; indeed, it made nonsense of the 'Two Nations' philosophy. But how far was the new state to accept democratic principles? And if this meant 'One Man, One Vote,

One Value', would East Pakistan with its substantial Hindu minority have majority status in the overall system? If Islam was to have a recognised place in the political framework, did this imply that the politicians must defer to the *Ulama*? These vexed questions were to hold up the realisation of a constitution until 1956. In the process, Pakistan was to have its first taste of martial law in the disturbances in 1953 over the agitation to exclude the Ahmadiya community from the brotherhood of Islam (it was left to Bhutto to declare that the Ahmadis were non-Muslims: one of his many populist gestures). In the same year, Pakistan experienced its first taste of the many coups to come later: the prime minister, Nazimuddin, was sent packing in the wake of the anti-Ahmadiya riots, although he enjoyed a clear majority in the legislature. Soon after, the masterful Governor-General, Ghulam Mohammad, dissolved the Constituent Assembly, and the Supreme Court validated the dissolution with learned legal precedents culled from medieval England.

Doubting whether the politicians could, any longer, 'deliver' firm government, the Governor-General invited the Commander-in-Chief, General Ayub Khan, to take over the reins of power.[47] He was not yet prepared to accept the responsibility, and so parliamentary government staggered on. Increasingly, those in office were not the lawyer-politicians who had followed Jinnah in his Pakistan demand but great landlords who had been loyal supporters of the British Raj: men like Sir Firoze Khan Noon.[48] Their role as *Ji Huzoors* (Yes Sir stooges) had not equipped them to manipulate an unruly political charade. Real power was being exercised by the top civil servants. Whereas in India the I.C.S. and their successors had to learn to accommodate their political masters, in Pakistan the administrators were still the masters. Ghulam Mohammad was a civil servant; his successor as Governor-General and first President was another administrator, Iskander Mirza. It was he who in October 1958 decided that it was time to bring the parliamentary charade to a close.

The Civil Service of Pakistan (C.S.P.) adhered even more closely to the I.C.S. pattern than did the Indian Administrative Service. This was not surprising. Many more British officials stayed on in Pakistan than in India. After Partition, the governors of every province except one (Sind) were British, as were about 28 per cent of the top bureaucrats, although there was a fairly rapid run-down of these ex-colonial officials, and by 1954 only 6 per cent of the C.S.P. cadre were still British. The C.S.P. training academy at Lahore was run entirely on former lines, with a British director until 1960, when a Pakistan ex-I.C.S. officer took over: a man known to his colleagues as 'the last of the British'![49] Dinner-jackets were still worn.

However, increasingly the C.S.P. came to resemble a Mughal

rather than a British administrative concept. At the lower levels of the British-Indian administration there were officials notorious for strong-arm methods: *zoolm* and *zabardasti*, in the eloquent Urdu idiom. But the I.C.S. deliberately distanced themselves from an open display of force. In the 1942 Congress rebellion ('Quit India'), a district officer who strode around with a revolver on waist and a big stick in hand was rather a figure of fun to his colleagues. Increasingly, after Partition, the C.S.P. officers in the districts themselves employed harsh, even terroristic methods against the people — usually, when incited by one of the landlord political bosses. The I.C.S., whether British or Indian, had eschewed all forms of corruption and nepotism (except, perhaps, the most subtle and indirect), although corruption may have flourished up to administrative levels just below theirs. After Partition, abuse of power was practised by C.S.P. officers; and the many dismissals for corruption by no means checked the disease. The top administration became riddled with cliques and factions, competing for power and influence. Criticism of the top bureaucrats was voiced in the press and by urban intellectuals, but the increasing failure by the politicians to govern meant that the bureaucrats were consolidating an impregnable position. When, at last, the populist premier Z. A. Bhutto abolished the C.S.P. in 1973, he virtually pulled the rug out from under his own feet.

During the early years, the Pakistan Army was a national rather than a political institution. Yet almost immediately it was called upon to compensate for political shortsightedness: as in bringing relief to thousands of refugee immigrants, and in trying to restore the debacle in Kashmir. The first overt political action — the abortive Rawalpindi conspiracy, hatched by dissident senior officers — served to discourage any shift towards political involvement. Yet the collapse of political will in the face of the anti-Ahmadiya agitation, leaving to the army the task of going into Lahore and other cities to restore order, indicated that the army *was* involved in politics. Within five years, the army *was* politics.

The officers of the new army of Pakistan were westernised, members of the urban élite (though a few came from rural 'yeoman' stock, and a handful were from the landlord aristocracy). During the first decade, the army was a modernising force: the early reforms carried through by Ayub Khan involved modernising Islamic law and practice regarding marriage and divorce. But despite the massive American military investment in Pakistan, a switch to American military hardware, and exposure of many Pakistani officers to American training techniques at Fort Bragg and elsewhere, the army increasingly identified with the quasi-military regimes of Turkey, Iran and the conservative Arab states. Gradually, the Islamic tone — at first merely formal, even nominal — began to permeate the upper echelons (as it always had the rank and file). In the two wars with India, the invocation of Allah became almost deafening. It was not until General Zia ul-Haq rose to the top that the process reached its climax. Significantly, General Zia had been attached to the Jordanian Army and was decorated by King Hussain for his part in the suppressions of 'Black September'.

The movement towards Islamic orthodoxy was unplanned and uncertain. The first President, Iskander Mirza, showed almost open contempt for the mullahs. Ayub Khan treated religious issues cautiously, realising their explosiveness. His shortlived successor, General Yahya Khan, almost reverted to the Mirza mode. It was left to Z. A. Bhutto, the son of a Hindu mother, to try to exploit 'Islamic Socialism' while defying the injunctions of Islam in his personal life. At last, in General Zia, there emerged a leader who actually *believed* in the Islamic code. But still, Zia is aware that to concede the last word on policy to the *Ulama* is to abdicate power. The dilemma that Jinnah side-stepped in his attempt to exploit Islam, while remaining uncommitted, still therefore remains unanswered.

The whole trend towards an Islamic polity in Pakistan represents the impact of popular consciousness upon élite control. It is the masses who are the believers, and their true leaders are lower-middle-class religious teachers and zealots who have virtually no place in the upper echelons of politics, the bureaucracy or the army. Jinnah aroused the masses in the last days of British rule with the cry 'Islam in Danger'. It was their response, turning the streets of Calcutta and Lahore to rivers of blood, which made Partition inevitable. Thereafter, the élite eschewed this inflammable element, although the one populist leader — Bhutto — again tried to exploit Islamic sentiment. General Zia, lacking any popular appeal, attempts to strike the same note. If ever a charismatic religious leader of Ayatullah status emerges in Pakistan, it will be hard for anyone to stand against him.

Sri Lanka has also experienced the explosive effects of populist religion in politics. Ceylon had to await a 'delayed-action' independence. The moment when the Duke of Gloucester congratulated the people of Ceylon on their new status (in February 1948) was one of the non-events of all time. For ten years previously, Ceylonese politicians had managed affairs, and their directives had been implemented by sagacious Ceylonese officials. What was now different? Under the Defence Agreement, the Royal Navy still occupied the magnificent base at Trincomalee and the R.A.F. still ran the main aerodrome. The last British Governor became the first Governor-General: and he was replaced by the obliging Lord Soulbury who did not depart till 1954. The British Crown was still the symbol of sovereignty. Nearer to hand,

British tea estates provided the backbone for the island's economy. What did independence mean, other than trips to London for the Commonwealth Prime Ministers' Conference and a vote for Ceylon in the United Nations?

When Bandaranaike broke with Senanayake and the United National Party to seek power through his Sri Lanka Freedom Party, he declared that he intended to take politics from the 'Somebodies' and transfer it to the 'Nobodies'. His approach was to appeal to the rural Buddhist Sinhalese voters, telling them that the Christian and Tamil Hindu middle class had excluded them from power. The 1956 election saw the radical monks in the market place, calling on the people to vote S.L.F.P. and calling on the S.L.F.P. to restore Sri Lanka to its former Buddhist glory. Subsequent changes were cosmetic rather than fundamental, and those who interpret the 1956 election as a massive turning-point, bringing the revolutionary change which independence had passed by, surely exaggerate.[50] The attempted insurrection of 1971 was another turning-point which somehow did not turn. The hollowness of the 1956 change, from the 'Somebodies' to the 'Nobodies', is symbolised by the failure to alter Ceylon's anachronistic status as a Dominion headed by a Governor-General representing the Crown. Bandaranaike obtained the agreement of the Commonwealth prime ministers to Ceylon becoming a republic: but this was not implemented because he lacked the necessary two-thirds majority for constitutional change. It was only after Mrs Bandaranaike's massive victory in 1970 that she was at last able to bring in the republic under the 1972 Constitution.

Sri Lanka, like Pakistan, eventually abolished the élite civil service structure inherited from the British, although in the first decade after independence the civil servants — with Goonetilleke as their patron — continued to govern. The army had no great tradition, as in India, and fulfilled no special role in the State. Senior military officers were suspected of plotting a coup, and some were punished. Even the insurrection of 1971 did not enhance the army's standing. Without the two pillars of the Raj which survived, however altered, in India and Pakistan, Sri Lanka has looked elsewhere for institutional underpinning. Although the two major parties — U.N.P. and S.L.F.P. — have alternated in power with absolute regularity (a phenomenon seen nowhere else in the Third World) party organisation has remained rudimentary and the parties have not become national institutions as the Congress did in India. Parliament is respected, and consciously adheres to the Westminster model.[51] The English-language press has been an unrelenting critic of Left-wing government follies, though less stern about Right-wing shortcomings. When all is said, the main element in government has continued to be the 'Somebodies', and Mrs Bandaranaike eventually relied almost exclusively upon a small circle of close relatives. J. R. Jayewardene was only on the edge of the magic circle, and he seems conscious of the importance of giving government deeper roots among the people. Perhaps Sri Lanka may find its independence revolution sometime in the 1980s.

Gandhi once observed that 'One may judge a nation by the way it treats its minorities.'[52] We will close this survey by considering how far India, Pakistan and Sri Lanka have succeeded in transforming the vague assumptions about national cohesion with which they entered independence into coherent nation-building policies and beliefs. We saw how Hindi, North-Indian sub-nationalism was aroused over the language question. However, after intense regional pressures developed, acceptable formulae were evolved. It helped that there is no majority for any one language. There is also no majority for any one caste. 'India is a land of minorities,' observed the Simon Commission.[53] The absence of an identifiable, dominant group has meant that all groups have had to learn to trade with each other. Bazaar politics may not be politics at its most edifying. It has certainly assured democratic politics; for all (or almost all) must feel they obtain some gain, however small.

One community has been largely excluded from this bargaining process of all the minorities: the Muslims. Their political future was not resolved by the creation of Pakistan: thirty-five years on, there are as many Muslims in India as there are in Pakistan (former West Pakistan). Except for a few with impeccable nationalist backgrounds, taken into government and politics as tokens of India's secularism, the community remains outside the national mainstream. Hugging its memories of past greatness, the Muslim community seems unwilling to discard the cultural heritage which is its only protection. Non-Muslims seem unable to accept that Indian Muslims are truly 'loyal'; all are suspected as covert Pakistanis. Periodically, communal tension explodes into communal riot. The Indian genius for what Nehru called 'absorption, synthesis' has been baffled in this one area.

Pakistan, despite its relative religious homogeneity, has been unable to build a genuine Pakistani consciousness. Language and regional cultures have proved stronger than the unifying Islamic, Perso-Urdu culture of an élite. The alienation of the Bengalis and the bloody birth of Bangladesh signified the final breakdown of Jinnah's vision of a homeland for the Muslims of India. In Bangladesh, religious nationalism uneasily clashed with regional nationalism: the first to feel the misery of being a minority in their adopted homeland were the persecuted Muslim Biharis. In what was the 'new', truncated Pakistan, regional and linguistic differences escalated to the point that critics began to refer to the troubles in Baluchistan as 'Pakistan's Vietnam'. Fortunately (or unfortunately), real and imagined external threats restrained the divided tribal and linguistic groups from open conflict.

Sri Lanka demonstrated that national consciousness would be formed not on 'Inclusive' but on 'Exclusive' concepts of belonging. The Tamil tea-estate workers of Indian ancestry were immediately defined as non-belongers.[54] For a time, linguistic rivalries were masked by the shared middle-class use of English and by a vague, nationalistic reference to *Swabasha* ('Our Own Language') as the goal. When Bandaranaike decided to play the Sinhalese card in the political game, the Ceylon Tamils — whose history on the island stretches back 2,500 years — found themselves isolated as non-belongers. Like the Indian Muslims, they were increasingly suspected of giving their allegiance to another country — South Indian Tamilnadu. After two decades of alienation, it seems that they may find an acceptable place in Jayewardene's Second Republic. But concessions which are acceptable to an older generation are rejected by the new militant 'Panthers'.

And so, thirty-five years after independence, it seems that the countries of South Asia are still 'Nations in Making'. It is still not clear what will be the dominant influences which will determine their destiny. Will it be a resurgence of religious populism? Will it be through the evolution of democratic institutions, assimilated to indigenous cultural norms? Or will the authoritarian institutions, adapted and developed by the Raj, be further adapted to indigenous authoritarian rule? Writing in 1980, the last alternative seems the most probable. But let us remember what has become of the expectations of thirty years ago which went along with independence, and await with reasonably open minds the final outcome.

NOTES

1. As claimed by Jawaharlal Nehru at the Lahore Congress which defined independence (Purna Swaraj) as the goal: B. N. Pandey, *Nehru*, London, 1976, p. 142. However, Gandhi was still satisfied with Dominion Status as late as 1939: S. R. Mehrotra, *The Commonwealth and the Nation* (Delhi, 1978), 105.
2. See *Report of the Indian Statutory Commission*, vol. I, pp. 1–2. Cmd. 3568, 1930 (hereafter: I.S.C.)
3. I.S.C. I, 466.
4. For many examples of Gandhi's affection for Britain, see the present writer's *The Ordeal of Love: C. F. Andrews and India* (Delhi, 1979): e.g. Gandhi to Andrews (15 June 1933) 'You must be silently and imperceptibly permeating the best English minds with the truth that is in you. All this will tell in the end' (p. 265).

5. Though perhaps we need not go as far as Sir Emmerson Tennent (Colonial Secretary, Ceylon, 1846–51) who, comparing Ceylon's administration with that of India, observed: 'Like the miniature oak which the Chinese can raise in a flower pot, the dwarfed plant had every characteristic of the great tree, except its strength and solidity' (J. E. Tennent, *Ceylon*, London, 1859, vol. I, 173).
6. Tinker, *Separate and Unequal: India and the Indians in the British Commonwealth* (London, 1976), 116–21.
7. The title which the veteran nationalist, Surendranath Banerjea chose for his autobiography, *A Nation in Making* (Calcutta, 1925; new edn, 1963).
8. For British arguments that India was a continent not a country, see the present writer's 'Is There an Indian Nation?' in Philip Mason (ed.), *India and Ceylon; Unity and Diversity* (London, 1967.)
9. K. R. Srinivasa Iyengar, *Literature and Authorship in India* (London, 1943), 9: in his introduction, E. M. Forster declares 'Something is in progress behind the mouthings of the politicians and the rustling of the newspapers' (p. 8).
10. I.S.C., II, 12.
11. K. M. de Silva, 'Discrimination in Sri Lanka', in W. A. Veenhoven (ed. in chief), *Case Studies on Human Rights and Fundamental Freedoms* (The Hague, 1976), vol. III, 81.
12. Nicholas Mansergh (ed.), *The Transfer of Power*, 1942–7, vol. VII, 'The Cabinet Mission', see especially 'Report by chiefs of Staff on military implications of proposed courses of action' (p. 893). In addition, six British brigades would be required to replace Indian troops in Burma and Malaya.
13. *Separate and Unequal*, 305–7.
14. In the second volume of his biography, *Jawaharlal Nehru* (London, 1980, p. 14), Sarvepalli Gopal relates that, at the end of 1946, Nehru told a French journalist 'Remember: one, India will never be a Dominion, two, there will never be a Pakistan, three, when the British go there will be no more communal trouble.' Characteristically, the introspective Nehru recalled his hollow prophecy to the same journalist a year later.
15. Near the end of his life, when someone praised the contribution of the Muslim League in winning Pakistan, Jinnah replied: 'Don't talk to me about the Muslim League. I and my stenographer created Pakistan.' (This anecdote was told me by ex-president Iskander Mirza, but others also claim to have had the same experience).
16. In his Introduction to B. H. Farmer, *Ceylon: A Divided Nation* (London, 1963).
17. This dismissal of Black African Freedom Movements should not ignore the contribution of 'Mau Mau' in Kenya to accelerating the transfer of power from white to black leadership, while the guerrilla war in Rhodesia, particularly the Z.A.N.U./P.F. campaign, certainly forced a myopic white minority government to recognise that the twentieth century had caught up with them.
18. Indira Gandhi is, perhaps, one South Asian leader prepared to see the Transfer of Power in perspective. In his latter years, Clement Attlee

devoted a lot of his time to Toynbee Hall in East London (where, he had been a settlement worker as a young man). After his death, Toynbee Hall appealed for funds to establish a worthy memorial. The High Commissioner for India in London put up a proposal for an Indian Government contribution on what he considered an appropriate scale. Mrs Gandhi insisted that the Indian gift must be much more generous, adding: 'After all, *he gave us our freedom.*'

19. The 'Freedom Movement' in Ceylon was so undeveloped that the country went into independence with only a nominal party organisation — the United National Party. Senanayake requested the help of a Labour peer, and former M.P., to advise on organisation: see *Separate and Unequal*, 425.
20. *Third World Quarterly*, vol. I, no. 2, (1979). This led to a reply in the next issue (vol. 1, no. 3, July 1979) by W. H. Morris-Jones: 'The West and the Third World: Whose Democracy, Whose Development?' In this he argues that democracy provides the most hopeful prospect for the improvement of the lot of the impoverished masses.
21. Speech of 17 December 1908: see the present writer's *South Asia: a short history* (London, 1966), 165.
22. I.S.C., II, 143.
23. Prithwis Chandra Ray, *Life and Times of C. R. Das: the story of Bengal's self-expression* (London, 1927), 111–13.
24. Quoted in the present writer's 'The Village in the Framework of Development', in R. Braibanti and J. J. Spengler (eds.) *Administration and Economic Development in India* (Durham, N. Carolina, 1963), 96.
25. Quoted by Joan Bondurant, *Conquest of Violence: the Gandhian Philosophy of Conflict* (Berkeley: University of California Press; revised edn 1965), 174.
26. Quoted by E. I. J. Rosenthal, *Islam in the Modern National State* (Cambridge University Press, 1965), 138.
27. B. N. Pandey, *Nehru*, 293.
28. Ibid., 294.
29. Granville Austin in *The Indian Constitution: cornerstone of a nation* (Oxford 1966, 40) points out that these included M. N. Roy's 'Radical Humanists' and the Hindu Mahasabha.
30. Quoted in the present writer's 'Tradition and Experiment in Forms of Government', C. H. Philips (ed.), *Politics and Society in India* (London, 1963), 157–8.
31. Ibid., 158.
32. When Nehru received a copy of the Sanskritised Hindi version of the Constitution he complained that he 'did not understand a word of it'. Granville Austin, 282.
33. Still, in 1980, the highly competitive entrance examination for the prestigious Indian Administrative Service and Indian Foreign Service can only be taken in English.
34. *Politics and Society in India*, 159.
35. Far too often, the Constitution has failed to protect the weak and those who do not conform. Articles 21 and 22 state that 'No person shall be deprived of his life or personal liberty' and 'Every person who is arrested

and detained in custody shall be produced before the nearest magistrate within 24 hours' and 'No law providing for preventive detention shall authorise the detention of a person for a longer period than 3 months.' Thousands have been held, without recourse to a magistrate, without trial, and without limit to their time in jail: both under Mrs Gandhi and under the Janata government.

36. *The Times*, 1 December 1960: 'Free Translation of Westminster'.
37. Jawaharlal Nehru, *An Autobiography* (London, 1936; 1942 edn), 439–44.
38. Ibid., 448.
39. Some I.N.A. personnel were recruited into the civil police, where they formed a disruptive — indeed mutinous — element. They did not last long. Some ex-I.N.A. officers were taken into the Indian Foreign Service, where they readily donned the diplomatic mask.
40. Manohar Malgonkar, *The Men Who Killed Gandhi* (Delhi and London, 1978). Although obvious clues were presented to the police before the event their actions were so dilatory that one ponders over the suggestion that the murder of Gandhi (like that of President Kennedy) was committed with the foreknowledge of people in power.
41. As, for example, did N. B. Bonarjee, Chief Secretary of U.P. at independence, who was soon at odds with his political bosses. His autobiography, *Under Two Masters* (Calcutta, 1970) is a superbly literate self-analysis by an Indian trained in the British tradition.
42. A sad example of the dominance of the nineteenth-century English model is provided by Visva-Bharati at Santiniketan. Rabindranath Tagore founded his international university as 'the playground of my own spirit'. It was to bring together India's traditional culture and international scholarship, with special emphasis upon the arts, music, and literature. Most of the teaching was to be in Bengali; there were to be no formal exams and degrees. After Tagore's death, the enterprise languished. The state assumed financial responsibility and control. Gradually, Visva-Bharati took on all the attributes of a standard university. As Chancellor, Indira Gandhi appointed a special commission to recommend how it might be restored to Tagore's original conception. But it does not appear that they were able to succeed.
43. See Lloyd and Susanne Rudolph, *The Modernity of Tradition: political development in India* (Chicago, 1967). A cogent expression of a similar view is offered by W. H. Morris-Jones, 'India's Political Idioms' in C. H. Philips (ed.), *Politics and Society in India*.
44. Arnold Toynbee, *A Study of History*, abridgement by D. C. Somervell (London, 1947), part IV, 'The Breakdowns of Civilizations', ch. XVI, 'Failure of Self-Determination' (pp. 279–307).
45. Rosenthal, op.cit., 197, 207.
46. Quoted (at greater length) in 'Tradition and Experiment in Forms of Government', in *Politics and Society in India*, 161.
47. According to Ayub Khan in his autobiography, *Friends Not Masters* (London, 1967), 51–3.
48. The shift in power from one group to another is well described by S. J.

Burki, *Pakistan Under Bhutto, 1971–1977* (London, 1980), 17–18, 24–6, etc.

49. Ralph Braibanti (ed.), *Asian Bureaucratic Systems Emergent From the British Imperial Tradition* (Durham, N. Carolina, 1966), 244–57.
50. K. M. de Silva calls the 1956 election 'a watershed' (op.cit., 85).
51. On the only occasion on which this writer met Mr J. R. Jayewardene — at the Institute of Legal Studies, London University — he was much concerned to ferret out some ruling by the Speaker during Sir Robert Peel's premiership which appeared especially relevant to him.
52. The sentiment is not original. Tolstoy and J. S. Mill said much the same and so did Socrates.
53. I.S.C., II, 22.
54. The troubles of the 'Indian Tamils' are discussed by the present writer in *The Banyan Tree: Overseas Emigrants from India, Pakistan and Bangladesh* (London, 1977), ch. 2, 'Permanently Second Class Citizens'.

THE HISTORICAL ORIGINS OF SOME OF PAKISTAN'S PERSISTENT POLITICAL PROBLEMS

Khalid B. Sayeed

There have been three major climacteric military coups in Pakistan. The first one, in 1958, had been preceded by minor civil-military coups in 1953 and 1954.[1] In the second, which took place in 1969, a government dominated by the military was overthrown by the military because the outgoing Ayub Khan had been unable to control civil and regional unrest. In the third military coup in July 1977 we witnessed the overthrow of a government dominated by Z. A. Bhutto, whose party had obtained an overwhelming majority in the recently held elections but who had been accused of having rigged the polls.

What emerged during 1977–80 was not only the continuation of a military regime drawing whatever political support it had in the provinces and in the districts through civil and military officials; but also the country was confronted with certain perennial problems, with the difference that they had become even more menacing and intractable. Historical evidence suggests that the rallying cry of Islam was a vital factor which contributed to the creation of Pakistan; yet, more than thirty years after the establishment of the state, Pakistanis have not yet reached a clear and democratic consensus as to the kind of Islamic political system that they should set up. An attempt will be made here to explore and analyse in the light of some new evidence the precise role the Islamic factor played in overcoming the opposition of an important group like the pro-British Unionist Party in the Punjab and in establishing a decisive edge over the anti-British, pro-Congress, and Pakhtun-supported Khudai Khidmatgar in the North-West Frontier Province (N.W.F.P.).[2] Since we are tracing the origins of some of the political problems of Pakistan as it exists today, we shall exclude from the scope of our analysis East Bengal or East Pakistan, even though the latter was a part of Pakistan until December 1971.

Pakistan, particularly since 1953, because of its membership of U.S.-sponsored defence pacts, has created the impression of being a protectorate or the most allied ally of the United States. Again, new historical evidence suggests that the popularity of Muhammad Ali Jinnah and the Muslim League had attracted the attention of American military officials in the early 1940s and that they were fully aware of the military and strategic importance that Indian Muslims were likely to play in any global strategy. We have also tried to establish historical continuity between the concerns of Sir Robert Sandeman and other British officials in consolidating their position in Baluchistan and the North-West Frontier to counter a possible Russian invasion of India and the current American and Western concerns over Soviet ambitions to establish their presence in the Indian Ocean.

Economic development based on capitalist lines has often encountered considerable opposition in Pakistan. It has generated both class and regional conflicts. In addition, there is the regional discontent in the strategic Pakhtun and Baluchi areas of the N.W.F.P. and Baluchistan. There is also discontent in Sind. These ethnic and regional problems have become more alarming because of the Soviet incursion into Afghanistan and the threat which such an incursion poses to Pakistan's security and integrity. Faced with these threats and given the nature of its polity, Pakistan has sought the protection of powers like the United States and China without at the same time provoking Soviet wrath.

It is our purpose here to establish a link between the civil-military complex[3] that rules Pakistan and the kind of colonial regime that Pakistan inherited from the British. The military regime that took power in Pakistan in 1967 perceives the same threats to Pakistan's security as its colonial predecessors. And the way the regime mobilises political support to maintain its hegemony and pursue its economic, strategic and foreign policy objectives is more or less the same as that followed by its colonial predecessor, the British Raj.

When Pakistan came into being in August 1947, Jinnah became the first Governor-General and Liaquat Ali Khan the first Prime Minister under the adapted Government of India Act, 1935. What kind of a political change did this represent? It was certainly not a social revolution because there was no element of 'the coincidence of societal structural change with class upheaval'. It was not even a political revolution of any radical kind because, although the colonial rulers had departed, the state structures had not been transformed.[4] Could it be said that even though the dominant governmental structures like the military and the civil service did not change, yet evidence that Muslim nationalism lay at the roots of Pakistan meant that the promise and the potential for societal self-transformation was there? The goals of an Islamic polity had neither been clearly defined nor agreed upon, yet the term 'Islamic' suggested that the goals were going to be different — leading to, perhaps, different basic structures and patterns of behaviour.

In the present author's earlier works, *Pakistan: the Formative Phase* (1960 and 1968) and *The Political System of Pakistan* (1967), it was argued that Muslim separatism leading to the creation of Pakistan could not be explained exclusively as an outcome of the British policy of 'divide and rule'.[5] This Muslim separatism had been reinforced by Hindu communalism generated by the activities of certain upper castes who tended to dominate the economic life of urban and rural areas. In addition to these factors, it was also emphasised in those works that there was something positive and perennial in the Islamic political doctrines which created among Muslims a yearning for a separate political identity. Others have pointed out that behind these transient manifestations there lay certain economic forces which could best be explained by analysing the semi-feudal mode of production that the British had resurrected and maintained particularly in areas like Punjab, Sind, Baluchistan and the North-West Frontier Province, which constitute Pakistan today. Wilfred Cantwell Smith, probably concerning himself more with the urban forces, offered another explanation:

> They have said that Muslims and Hindus are so different that they cannot live together in one state. What they have meant is that the Muslim bourgeoisie and the 'Hindu' bourgeoisie are so competitive that they cannot both own the banks and industries, run the commerce, do the professional and other jobs, in one capitalist state.[6]

Later Smith admitted that he was swept off his Marxist feet by the 'mood of vibrant stamina and creativity of Pakistan in the initial years' and that his youthful work was based on 'inadequate understanding of Islam and also the crucial role played in history by ideological and moral factors'.[7]

The Islamic Appeal and the Success of the Muslim League in Punjab

The vibrant stamina and religious fervour generated by Islam had always been there. It had to be aroused to a critically high political pitch. In order to do this, Muslims needed political craftsmanship, organisation and leadership, and these crucial variables were supplied by Jinnah. The British had been able to keep the potential for unity and political action that lay in Islam virtually in a state of disarray both in the Punjab and in the North-West Frontier Province. This was no accident or mere stroke of good fortune. It was a result achieved through deliberate design and policy.

In order to see how all these factors were grappled with and utilised, one has to see with what disadvantages Jinnah started his campaign for gaining political power and ascendancy among the Muslims of the Punjab. As a political leader, he had to make the best 'of every inimicable occasion'. Even before the Muslim League launched its election campaign for the 1937 provincial elections in the Punjab, Jinnah must have been aware of the enormous hold that the triumvirate of the deputy commissioner, the landlord and the *pir* (spiritual guide) exercised over Muslims living in the rural areas. He is reported to have remarked in 1932: 'The Muslim camp is full of those spineless people, who whatever they may say to me, will consult the Deputy Commissioner about what they should do.'[8] Why were these influential district leaders so amenable to the influence of the deputy commissioner? This was because the deputy commissioner exercised both police and political powers in the districts. He had influence over the landlord, the *sajjada nashin* (hereditary custodian of a shrine or tomb) and the *pir*. In some areas the landlord and the *sajjada nashin* tended to be the same person. The autonomy enjoyed by the landlord in such a society was not all that great because in many areas he was totally amenable to the influence and power of the government as exercised by the deputy commissioner.

In the 1937 provincial elections in the Punjab, the Muslim League won only one out of eighty-six Muslim seats, whereas the Unionists, supported by the triumvirate, won not only the majority of the seats in the provincial assembly (96 out of 175) but also the bulk of the Muslim seats. Muslim political and religious organisations in the urban areas led by the *ulama* of the Deoband School or those belonging to the Ahrar groups were avowedly anti-British and pro-Congress. There were also urban Muslim Leaguers concentrated in Lahore who were led by Muhammad Iqbal. All these urban Muslims were averse to the idea of any Muslim organisation co-operating too closely with the Muslim Unionist Premier of the Punjab, Sir Sikander Hyat, and his government. Jinnah had to bide his time. He knew he could not take on the Muslim Unionists in a straight confrontation, particularly in the rural areas where their influence over both land and the religious shrines could not be challenged easily. Therefore, he urged leaders like Iqbal to be patient until he prepared the soil in such a way that their ideas and his message of national unity would reap a rich harvest. To Iqbal he wrote: 'I want to pull them [Muslims] up step by step and before making them run I want to be sure they are capable of standing on their own legs.'[9] Jinnah had been in Indian politics for a long time and had watched the *Khilafat* movement. Therefore, he must have been aware that Muslims were extremely receptive to the idea of national unity when called upon to close ranks in the name of Islam. So was the powerful Sir Sikander Hyat aware that in spite of Jinnah's present weakness, his latent and potential power was considerable. In 1941 Sir Sikander Hyat was reported to have told a British official 'that unless he walked warily and kept on the right side of Jinnah, he would be swept away by a wave of fanaticism and, wherever he went, would be greeted by the Muslims with black flags.' Penderel Moon was not convinced at that time. 'Subsequent events suggest that his reading of the situation was more correct than mine.'[10]

We need to consider two questions at this stage. What were the kinds of political, administrative and religious institutions that the British had patronised and reared in the rural areas of Punjab? How were these citadels of the British power structure in the rural areas overwhelmed or outflanked by the Pakistan movement? As we have suggested earlier, the British power in the districts in the first instance rested on the deputy commissioner and his revenue and police officials. This aspect of British power is fairly familiar. As for the power and influence of the *pir*, again much has been written by British writers like Sir Malcolm Darling.[11] We have also drawn on such works and extended the analysis to cover the post-Partition period.[12] Where some path-finding work has been done is by David Gilmartin, particularly in the way he has analysed the role that the *sajjada nashins* played first in supporting the British Raj and the Unionist Party and later in supporting the Pakistan movement.[13] Gilmartin has tried to show how some of the British officials went out of their way to confer the status of the landed gentry on some of the *sajjada nashins*.[14] Since the source of the religious authority of the *sajjada nashins* was based more on heredity than on piety, it meant that the government as represented by the deputy commissioner had considerable say in the matter of which of the disputed claimants to the guardianship of the shrine would be recognised as the officially accepted *sajjada nashin*. The fact that the *sajjada nashins* were recognised as agriculturalists meant that their lands could not be alienated under the Land Alienation Act of 1900. The British also made the hereditary custodians of shrines (*zaildars*) honorary magistrates and district board members. As regards the Cardezi families associated with a shrine, the *Multan Gazetteer* said: 'They are all thoroughly loyal.'[15] Of another leading custodian of a shrine the *Multan Gazetteer* declared: 'The present Makhdum, Khan Bahadur Makhdum Murid Hussain, has precedence over all other unofficial Viceregal Darbaris in the district and is thus the premier peer of Multan. He possesses land in various parts of the district . . . As guardian of the shrine of the saint Bahawal Haqq he is venerated by Muhammadans of the south-west of the Punjab and of Sind.'[16]

Gilmartin argues that even though these *sajjada nashins* tended to support the British-backed Unionist Party government, significant sections among the *sajjada nashins* had stemmed from the nineteenth-century religious revival in rural Punjab. The Chishti *pirs*, who belonged to this tradition, were never enthusiastic in their support of the Unionists, although Gilmartin admits that most of them were not able to resist government pressures. However, what made them more determined, particularly in the districts of west Punjab, to come out in support of Jinnah was the emergence of the Pakistan movement in the 1940s. According to Gilmartin, it was the custodians of famous shrines like those of Tonsa, Golran, Alipur, Sialsharif, and Jalalpur, who played a decisive role in helping the Muslim League to win the Punjab Legislative Assembly elections of 1946.[17] However, he does not give enough credit to Jinnah and the Muslim League for having in the first instance created the political climate when it had become increasingly difficult for Muslims to oppose the Muslim League campaign for Pakistan. Such an opposition would have resulted in the persons concerned being dubbed as anti-Muslim and anti-Islamic. We must also remember that the sweeping power of the Islamic tide was such that even some of the *ulama* in the urban areas of both the Punjab and the U.P., who had hitherto been opposed to the Muslim League, felt in duty bound to support and work for the demand of Pakistan.

What is also missing in the evidence that Gilmartin has marshalled to establish his thesis that the *sajjada nashins* played a vital role in determining the Muslim League victory in the provincial elections of 1946 is an analysis of the 1946 election results, particularly of the rural constituencies of the western Punjab. We would like to fill this important gap. A broad analysis of the 1946 election results suggests that the Muslim League victory, though impressive, was by no means overwhelming in all the districts. The constituencies where the Muslim League won by a margin of 50 per cent or more were Jhelum, Pind Dadar Khan, Chakwal, Gujar Khan, Rawalpindi East, Mianwali North, Montgomery, Okara, Dipalpur, Jhang East (acclaimed), Jhang Central, Jhang West, Lodhran, Mailsi, Khanewal, Kabirwalla, Muzaffargarh North, and Dera Ghazi Khan North.[18] Gilmartin indicates that in constituencies like Jhelum, Rawalpindi East, Montgomery, Okara, and Dipalpur the support provided by the *pirs* and *sajjada nashins* played a decisive role. Our analysis of election results also confirmed this finding in the sense that the majority in these districts was overwhelming, with the exception of Dipalpur where the majority was just about 50 per cent. What is still awaited is a content analysis of the kind of speeches and electoral tactics of the *pirs* and *sajjada nashins*. In constituencies like Shahpur, Sargodha, Attock South, Mianwali South, Multan, Alipur, and Dera Ghazi Khan Central, the Unionist Party won. In Attock North, the Unionist Party won by acclamation. There were other constituencies where either the election results were close, or the Muslim League won by a minority with the total vote of the opposition parties being high.[19]

What needs to be emphasised is the role of political craftsmanship and coalition building that Jinnah exercised in snatching his victory for Pakistan from a highly complex and confusing situation. The clarion call for Islamic unity, the role of *sajjada nashins, pirs,* landowners, students, and the Muslim League organisation all played their respective parts, but none by itself would have been adequate. The skill involved in combining all these factors, a sense of timing and leadership were just as vital if not more so. If one analyses the Islamic variable, one finds that Jinnah was bringing together the *ulama* from the urban areas of the Punjab and other Indian provinces along with the *pirs* and *sajjada nashins* from the rural areas of the Punjab in launching his electoral assaults on the Unionist power bases in the Punjab. Over these two layers of Islam stood the liberalism of Jinnah. R. W. Sorensen, an acute British observer of the Indian scene, referred to Jinnah as 'a sword of Islam resting in a secular scabbard'.[20] In spite of his advocacy of the two-nation theory, his liberalism had not become quite extinct, for in his first address to the Constituent Assembly, he declared: 'You will find that in course of time Hindus would cease to be Hindus and Muslims would cease to be Muslims, not in the religious sense, because that is the personal faith of each individual, but in the political sense as citizens of the state.'[21]

In the first euphoria after the establishment of Pakistan, the volcanic forces latent in the urban areas and particularly the *ulama* could be persuaded to wait until the constitutional blueprint of the state emerged. In any case the founders thought that they could be kept under control by the steel framework that Pakistan had inherited from the British. Thus, even after the anti-Ahmadi religious disturbances of 1953 in the Punjab had set at naught the entire law and order machinery, the Court of Inquiry established to enquire into these disturbances wrote: 'And it is our deep conviction that if the Ahrar had been treated as a pure question of law and order, without any political considerations, one District Magistrate and one Superintendent of Police could have dealt with them.'[22] In these Punjab disturbances of 1953 and later in the anti-Ayub demonstrations of early 1969, in the anti-Ahmadi demonstrations in Lahore and Lyallpur of 1974, and in the anti-Bhutto demonstrations of 1977, the religious factor was ever present in varying degrees of virulence. And Pakistan's rulers found that such disturbances could not be controlled even by the military. What has become clear over the years is that the same Islam which had been used to rally the faithful in the struggle for Pakistan could not also serve as an opiate to create political quiescence among the masses. No solution to the problem of what crucial or fundamental role Islam should play in the constitutional and political system of Pakistan has yet emerged. Should it provide merely a broad set of principles to guide the legislators and the policy-makers or should it embrace and inspire every important social and individual behaviour?

The thin layer of westernised or liberal politicians who stood above the thick layer of also westernised but much more powerful civil servants and military officers had inherited the tradition of using Islam as a manipulative and mobilising political force. The Muslim League organisation and that of other political parties, including the powerful and better organised Pakistan People's Party, never developed sufficiently deep grassroots either at the rural or urban level to integrate Islamic practices and institutions with the needs and imperatives of either political or economic development. The result was that the masses at the urban and the rural level remained captives of the exploitative practices and rhetoric of the *ulama*, the *mullahs*, and *sajjada nashins*. This explains why there have been so many social eruptions of a religious nature led by religious leaders.

Continuing Strength of Pakhtun Ethnic Consciousness

Pakistani leaders all the way from Jinnah to Bhutto must have been aware of the continuing ethnocentric and centrifugal pull that Pakhtun regionalism represented long before partition. The famous Pakhtun poet, Khushhal Khan Khattak, had lyricised the fierce independence of the Pakhtuns in their defiance of the mighty Mughals. Aurangzeb, who was widely venerated in Muslim circles in India both for his piety and his attempts to Islamicise the Mughal empire, was denounced by Khushhal Khan Khattak as a tyrant. The fact that considerable numbers of Pakhtuns were sceptical about the claims of Pakistan emerging as an Islamic state dedicated to the public well-being of the Muslim citizens should not have come as a surprise to Pakistani ruling circles.

The Pakhtuns had found in Khan Abdul Ghaffar Khan their most outstanding leader to articulate both through struggle and institution-building their native independence and defiance of British rule. Through his social service and political organisation, the *Khudai Khidmatgar* (servants of God), and through his emphasis on creating a stronger sense of Pakhtun consciousness and solidarity, he had reached out not only to the Tribal Areas inhabited by the Pakhtuns in the north but has also forged close political links with the Congress organisation in India. His efforts bore fruit in the way the Congress with its hardcore support from the *Khudai Khidmatgars* won decisive victories in the two provincial elections of 1937 and 1946 in the N.W.F.P. In the election of 1937, even though the Congress won only fifteen out of thirty-six Muslim seats, the Muslim League had not been able to win even one seat. In 1946, even after the Muslim League had launched its campaign for the establishment of Pakistan, it failed to win any significant support in the Pakhtun areas of the N.W.F.P. The total vote polled by the League was 147,880, whereas the League's opponents polled 208,896 in Muslim constituencies. It should also be noted that in the Pakhtun areas the Congress won sixteen out of the twenty-two seats. The contrast with the Punjab was striking. In the 1946 elections, the Muslim League in the Punjab was arrayed against the pro-British Unionists and used the Islamic appeal to topple a well-entrenched political party. In the Frontier, the Muslim League and the British worked against the Congress and were defeated in the 1946 elections.

It was significant that the British had also used the Islamic appeal to undermine the political support that Khan Abdul Ghaffar Khan and his *Khudai Khidmatgars* ('servants of God') or the Congress had created both in the Tribal Areas and in the Settled Districts. Sir George Cunningham, who was governor of the province both during the pre-Partition and post-Partition periods, in a policy note dated 23 September 1942, wrote: 'Continuously preach the danger to Muslims of connivance with the revolutionary Hindu body. Most tribesmen seem to respond to this.'[23] It looked as if British officers like Cunningham and others, through their years on the Frontier and their mastery of the Pushtun language and culture, knew the Pakhtuns so well that they (non-Muslims themselves) were confident of skilfully using the Islamic appeal through the *mullahs*. Thus, the Cunningham papers, referring to the period 1939–43, stated: 'Our propaganda since the beginning of the war had been most successful. It had played throughout on the Islamic theme.'[24] The *mullahs* could be pressured into issuing *fatwas* (decrees) against every enemy of the British government. Such *fatwas* were issued not only against the Germans, the Italians and the Russians but also against the 'idolatrous' Japanese. The underlying tone of all this propaganda was also anti-Congress. Sir George Cunningham, in a personal note to the author, wrote that in 1942 the Afridis passed a solemn resolution at a big *jirga* (council of tribal leaders) in Tirah that any Afridis joining any political party from India would be put to death.

The British used a combination of repression and propaganda against the Pakhtun leaders, but it looked as if such tactics resulted in further hardening Pakhtun resistance. The Muslim League relied primarily on the Islamic appeal. Particularly at the time of Partition, the point that was hammered home was the question of how a predominantly Muslim community like the Pakhtuns could align itself with a Hindu-dominated India which, to make matters worse, did not even occupy territories contiguous to the Pakhtun areas. Even though the Muslim League had lost the 1946 elections, it launched a civil disobedience campaign against the Congress government in the Frontier. Even the hitherto conservative League leaders courted arrest. In addition, there was Hindu-Muslim communal rioting in Peshawar. The Muslim League wanted to create the impression that it was no longer an organisation of the big and prosperous pro-British Khans. Qaiyum

Khan, who had joined the Muslim League and become the leader of the party, was also arrested. Writing to Jinnah from prison, he said: 'No one can now say that the Leaguers here are incapable of sacrifices.'[25] This indicated how moribund the Muslim League organisation had been in the N.W.F.P. and how hastily it had been changed for purposes of organising the civil disobedience movement and later the Referendum campaign.

The factors that helped the Muslim League to win the Referendum of July 1947 were the Islamic appeal, the growing Hindu-Muslim conflict in the subcontinent, and the boycott of the Referendum by the Frontier Congress and the *Khudai Khidmatgar*. This boycott was reflected in the returns for only 50.99 percent of the eligible electorate of the N.W.F.P. took part with 289,244 expressing their support for Pakistan and 2,874 for India. In the Referendum, in all only 292,118 people had participated out of a total electorate of 572,799. Even in the provincial elections of 1946, the number of voters polling in Muslim constituencies alone was 356,776. Thus, it can be argued that the Muslim League position in the Frontier was even weaker than it was in the Punjab. Opposition anchored in Pakhtun regional and ethnic consciousness was even more difficult to overcome than the opposition of landowners and the *pirs* in the Punjab.

It seemed that even the British governor, Sir George Cunningham, had a far better knowledge of the Frontier situation than Muslim League leaders like Jinnah and Liaquat Ali Khan. In a secret note that he sent to Jinnah in 1948, Cunningham wrote:

> What I have been striving for, for some years past, is to get the good right-wing members of the old Congress party to join up with all those elements — Khans, professional men, villagers etc. — who used to oppose Congress and are now united under the Muslim League. Reduced to simple terms, that would nowadays mean a junction of Khan Sahib (whom I take as a typical and good example of the old Congress partyman) with Abdul Qayum. I believe Khan Sahib himself could be got to do this today, but for the influence of A.G.K. and Qazi Ataulla (particularly the latter).[26]

The key men who could have brought about a long-term settlement of the Frontier problem were Jinnah and Khan Abdul Ghaffar Khan.[27] No two men could have been more different from one another, and the twists and turns of politics had widened the chasm. One was licking his wounds and the other sat supreme in the hour of his triumph in Karachi. The loser had to be realistic and the victor had to be magnanimous. Unfortunately, neither displayed these qualities in full measure. Jinnah made overtures for a reconciliation but later insisted on Abdul Ghaffar Khan's joining the Muslim League. To the latter, this would have constituted not only an admission of defeat, but abject surrender to men who had won Pakistan without making too many sacrifices.[28]

Even under the *Quaid-i-Azam* (Jinnah), the governors of Sind and the N.W.F.P. were instructed to dismiss ministries which had majority support. Later, perhaps, Governor-General Ghulam Muhammad could also justify his dismissal of the Nazimuddin ministry in 1953 and even the dissolution of the constitutent assembly in 1954 by citing the precedents of dismissals of provincial ministries enjoying majority support in their assemblies on instructions from the *Quaid-i-Azam*.[29] After the dismissal of the Khan Sahib ministry in the Frontier in 1947, Khan Abdul Qaiyum Khan was installed as the chief minister. In spite of the restraining influence of Governor Cunningham, Qaiyum Khan unleashed a reign of repression throwing most of the Pakhtun leaders, including Khan Ghaffar Khan, in jail. Khan Abdul Ghaffar Khan later pointed out that out of the eighteen years he spent in Pakistan, fifteen were in jail. This bitterness and animosity between the central government and the Pakhtun leaders continued through the 1950s, '60s and '70s. The entire period was marked by the same inability and lack of statesmanship that the founders had displayed in accommodating the regional demands of the Pakhtuns within a flexible federal framework.

Under Bhutto, the same trends continued with the dismissal of provincial governments both in Baluchistan and the Frontier and the continued incarceration of Wali Khan, the son of Ghaffar Khan, who had emerged as the leader of the Pakhtuns. Wali Khan represented both the landowning and the middle-class urban groups in the Frontier and preferred the Frontier's economic development under a private sector dominated by Pakhtun professionals and industrialists to it being dominated by the Punjabi capitalists. The latter, he charged, had been the result of economic development under central control. Thus, the conflict between Bhutto and Wali Khan could not be characterised purely as a regional conflict or a conflict between the centre and the regions. Another way of viewing this conflict is that members of the same landowning or business class were in conflict with each other for certain economic resources and job opportunities. It is possible that in the future, with a gradual awakening of class consciousness among the poorer peasants and landless labourers as well as among the industrial labour force, in Pakistan, these classes may develop common interests which would cut across regional lines. One can see how difficult it would be for some of these classes to think purely in regional or ethnic terms because there are significant movements and migrations taking place across regions. Large numbers of Baluchi workers and landless labourers have moved out of Baluchistan and are living in Sind. Similarly, the largest urban concentration of Pakhtuns is in Karachi which has over 700,000 Pakhtuns.

The Pakhtun and Baluchi Borderlands and Western Strategic Interests

The Soviet incursion into Afghanistan which started in December 1979 has shocked the Americans, and their old fears of the Russian desire to seek access to the Arabian Sea and the Indian Ocean have been aroused. President Carter's national security adviser, Zbigniew Brzezinski, referred to documentary evidence which established such Russian strategic objectives clearly. It has been reported that while ransacking the German Foreign Office archives at the end of the Second World War, the British and the Americans found a clear statement of the conditions which Russia demanded from Germany in November 1940 for participation in a projected Four Power Pact with the three members of the Axis. These conditions were 'the establishment of a base for land and naval forces of the U.S.S.R. within range of the Bosphorus and the Dardanelles by means of a long-term lease' and the recognition of 'the area south of Batum and Baku in the general direction of the Persian Gulf . . . as the centre of the aspirations of the Soviet Union.'[30] The American fear is that the Russians by moving massively into Afghanistan are going for the jugular by threatening their very lifeline, namely, the uninterrupted supply of oil from the Middle East. American and British perception of Russian strategic objectives and their determination to safeguard their interests are by no means of recent origin. Similarly, Western strategists have always taken the view that the borderlands of Pakistan, namely, Baluchistan and the N.W.F.P., would constitute the first line of defence against Russian attempts to penetrate these vital areas.

It was clear from the pronouncements of the early architects of British policy that the primary purpose of pacifying and controlling the tribal areas of Baluchistan and the Frontier was the safeguarding of specific British imperial interests. An officer who served on the Afghan Boundary Commission discerned that the feared Russian invasion of India might be launched via Herat and Khandahar in Afghanistan and follow its further course through Baluchistan.[31] Sir Robert Sandeman, in his memorandum 'On British Relations with the Waziri and Other Frontier Tribes' (1890), observed:

> All military experts, however, without exception, declare it to be necessary to secure Afghanistan from Russian aggression in British interests and for the defence of India . . . The policy which I advocate has given us Baluchistan, the position at Quetta and on the Khojak, in Zhob, and on the line of the Gumal . . . If we knit the frontier tribes into our Imperial system in time of peace and make their interests ours, they will certainly not oppose us in time of war, and as long as we are able and ready to hold our own, we can certainly depend upon their being on our side.[32]

There is a clear continuity in the perceptions and policies of the

Sandeman era all the way down to the present phase when the American or Western strategic concerns seem to run along parallel lines. The resurrection of the decaying feudal and tribal institutions by the British were accompanied by the special protection that the agricultural tribes in the Punjab received under the Land Alienation Act of 1900. One of the main purposes of the Act was to protect the lands of the Muslim peasants and landlords against the ever-present threat of foreclosures that hung over their heads in the event of non-payment of their debts to the moneylending urban interests. This measure as well was an integral part of the overall policy to create a sense of security and satisfaction with British rule in north-western India which the British thought was likely to receive the brunt of a Russian attack. We have also referred to the systematic propaganda that the British carried out in the Frontier during the 1930s and '40s when they used Islam and the *mullahs* to create among the Frontier tribes certain attitudes of hostility towards the Germans, the Italians, the Japanese and the Russians.

At the time of Partition, British military officers were quite concerned about the defence capabilities of the proposed state of Pakistan. A note prepared by the Deputy Chief of the General Staff of Field-Marshal Sir Claude Auchinleck, who was then Commander-in-Chief of the British Indian Army, observed:

> They [advocates of Pakistan] will refuse to consider the situation in terms of any threat from a first-class power or in terms of armoured forces or air offensives. They will regard their defence problem in terms of some local third-class war which will be settled one way or another with infantry and artillery.[33]

Auchinleck expressed equally disquieting views about the matter when he pointed out: 'It must be concluded that the provision of adequate insurance in the shape of reasonably good defensive arrangements for Pakistan would be a most difficult and expensive business, and that no guarantee of success could be given.'[34]

According to the popular view, American interest, particularly a desire to forge closer links with Pakistan, started in the early 1950s. Similarly, it is widely believed that the Americans, particularly under Democratic administrations, have always been favourable towards India and have viewed the development of Pakistan as a separate state with some misgivings. Dr Betty Unterberger, who has examined the American archives relating to American attitudes towards India during the Second World War, has given us certain insights and information which are considerably at variance with popular beliefs.[35] Quoting a report prepared by the Military Intelligence Division in the State Department, Unterberger points out that the American military intelligence officers in India believed that Muslim soldiers were deeply loyal to Jinnah and opposed to Gandhi's Quit India movement. Even though leading American diplomats and military observers were not well disposed to Jinnah's Pakistan scheme, yet they were appreciative of his leadership in dissuading Muslim civilians and soldiers from participating in the Congress civil disobedience movement.[36] Winston Churchill, in a letter to President Franklin D. Roosevelt, observed: 'We must not on any account break with the Moslems who represent 100 million people and the main Army elements on which we must rely for the immediate fighting.'[37] While confirming this position, Ambassador W. Averell Harriman reported to the U.S. Secretary of State that because of the important role that Muslims were playing in the defence of India, Prime Minister Churchill had made it clear that he would not 'take any political step which would alienate the Muslims.'[38]

It is in the 1950s that we see the culmination of these concerns and strategic interests when Pakistan became a member of the U.S.-sponsored and -supported defence pacts, the Central Treaty Organization and the Southeast Asia Treaty Organization. It was no accident that General Ayub Khan, who had spent his formative years as an officer of the British Indian Army, became the most ardent champion of Western and American interests in the area. He argued that the role of being the protector and promoter of Western interests that the British Indian Army had fulfilled would henceforth be played by the Pakistan Army. In July 1958 he put forward the idea of 'lend-lease' which he defined as 'We provide the manpower and you provide us with the means to do the fighting.'[39] Addressing the U.S. Congress in 1961, he declared: 'The only people who will stand by you are the people of Pakistan.'

Even though Pakistanis later became sceptical and apprehensive about American willingness to come to the rescue of Pakistan if its security were threatened by either India or the Soviet Union, yet there is some evidence to suggest that the American administration under President Nixon did put pressure on the Soviet Union to dissuade India from launching any military action against West Pakistan in December 1971 when it had succeeded in defeating the Pakistani forces in East Pakistan. It seemed that when India was likely to make such a move, the Chinese were willing to go to the military assistance of Pakistan, and this might have provoked a Soviet attack against China. It was at this critical juncture that Nixon, without informing either his Secretary of State or Secretary of Defense, sent a message to the Soviet Union warning: 'I cannot emphasize too strongly that time is of the essence to avoid consequences neither of us wants.'[40] Commenting on Mrs Gandhi's offer of an unconditional cease-fire with Pakistan on the Western front, Henry Kissinger observed:

There is no doubt in my mind that it was a reluctant decision resulting from Soviet pressure, which in turn grew out of American insistence, including the fleet movement and the willingness to risk the summit . . . It was also Chou En-lai's judgment, as he later told Bhutto, that we had saved West Pakistan.[41]

Unfortunately, the Pakistani leaders have followed the tradition of concentrating heavily on military means to protect their frontiers. Even though they profess to develop Pakistan into an Islamic polity based on social and regional justice, to date they have tended to follow the British pattern of political management and manipulation of the Baluchi and Pakhtun tribes. There is no doubt that it is an extremely difficult task, but not even a beginning has been made to create a situation in which the government of Pakistan would pay equal attention to the political and federal solution so that the Pakhtuns and the Baluchis would feel that in defending Pakistan they would also be defending their own regions and homelands. In an interview General Zia acknowledged that in Baluchistan 'the ground is ripe for seeds of subversion, because of deprivation and lack of resources.'[42]

The simple and clear conclusion that emerges from our analysis is that the excessively centralised and colonial bureaucratic model has become increasingly dysfunctional to the needs and political realities of Pakistan. Ever since its establishment Pakistan, except on brief occasions only, has relied primarily on the colonial and coercive political and bureaucratic apparatus under which the pace and direction of change is dictated from the top. In the colonial, bureaucratic model, contact with the district or grassroot base was there, but in this dialogue there was very little response and mostly direction and coercion from the top. What we have witnessed in Pakistan is a growing groundswell internally and increasing penetration and pressure from external sources. A new constitutional apparatus with new political structures and more sophisticated political skills is needed. Of this the Pakistani rulers seem to be dimly aware. But it is too much to expect from the bureaucratic and military élites to have the experience or imagination to develop the urgently needed new constitutional and political apparatus.

NOTES

1. In 1953 the Nazimuddin ministry, which enjoyed majority support in the constituent assembly, was dismissed by Governor-General Ghulam Muhammad and in 1954 the constituent assembly itself was dissolved. In both these actions the Governor-General was supported by the civil services as well as the military.

2. For a further analysis, see Khalid B. Sayeed, *Politics in Pakistan: The Nature and Direction of Political Change* (New York: Praeger, 1980), ch. 1.
3. Every time the military seized power in Pakistan it relied on the civil services to run the day-to-day administration, particularly during the earlier coups of 1958 and 1969. Even though a number of civil servants were dismissed by the military regime, yet it could not be said that the military had established their outright domination in policy-making or administration. For matters relating to economic policy making, the military relied on the technical skills of the civil service. And even for law and order problems in the districts, the military relied on the administrative and political skills of the deputy commissioners. Therefore, what emerged in each of these periods was a civil-military complex. Later, when the C.S.P. was abolished during the Bhutto period and the power of the civil service had been undermined, the military became even more powerful. Particularly under the present military regime, the military penetration of the civil service structure has become much more extensive. However, it cannot be said that even in the new situation civil servants, particularly those who have risen from C.S.P. ranks, have lost much of their influence in areas relating to economic and foreign policy.
4. Theda Skocpol, *States and Social Revolutions* (Cambridge University Press, 1974), 4.
5. Khalid B. Sayeed, *Pakistan The Formative Phase* (Oxford University Press, 1968) and Khalid B. Sayeed, *The Political System of Pakistan* (Boston: Houghton Mifflin, 1967).
6. Wilfred Cantwell Smith, *Modern Islam in India* (Lahore: Ripon, 1947), 331.
7. Wilfred Cantwell Smith, *Islam in Modern History* (Princeton University Press, 1975), 210 and 211.
8. A. H. Albiruni, *Makers of Pakistan and Modern Muslim India* (Lahore: Ashraf, 1950), 209.
9. *Dawn*, 25 December 1955.
10. Penderel Moon, *Divide and Quit* (Berkeley: University of California Press, 1962), 38.
11. Sir Malcolm Darling, *Rusticus Loquitur* (Oxford University Press, 1930), and Sir Malcolm Darling, *Punjab Peasant in Prosperity and Debt* (Oxford University Press, 1932).
12. Khalid B. Sayeed, *Politics in Pakistan: The Nature and Direction of Political Change*, op.cit., ch. 2.
13. David Gilmartin, 'Religious Leadership and the Pakistan Movement in the Punjab', *Modern Asian Studies*, 13, 3 (1979).
14. Ibid., 495.
15. *Punjab Gazetteer, VII, Multan District 1923–24*, Part A (Lahore: Government Printer, Punjab, 1927), 108.
16. Ibid., 109.
17. Gilmartin, op.cit., 512–14
18. My analysis is based on a summary of the Punjab elections which are to be found in the India Office Library, London, in the series *Transfer of Power*, vol. L/P & J/8/472, folios 8–16.

19. Ibid.
20. Reginald Sorensen, *My Impression of India* (London: Meridian Books, 1946), 109.
21. *Constituent Assembly (Legislature) of Pakistan Debates*, vol. 1, no. 2. (11 August 1947), 18–20.
22. *Report of the Court of Inquiry Constituted under Punjab Act II of 1954 to Enquire into the Punjab Disturbances of 1953* (Lahore: Government Printer, 1954), 387.
23. *Cunningham's Diary "C", November 1939–May 1943*. It may be noted that these citations from Cunningham's Papers are from the same papers as are to be found in the India Office Library. Our references, however, are different because our citations are from the papers which are in our possession. In these citations we are following the titles as given by Sir George Cunningham.
24. Ibid.
25. *Quaid-i-Azam Papers. Muslim League Leaders'/Workers' Correspondence*. File 324, 19.
26. *Cunningham Papers. Note on the N.-W. Frontier Province*. Sent to Jinnah on 8 May 1948, 2.
27. In this section I have drawn freely on my article, 'Pathan Regionalism', *The South Atlantic Quarterly*, LXIII, 4 (Autumn, 1964), 497–8.
28. *Adalat-i-Aliya Men Khan Abdul Ghaffar Khan Ka Bayan*, (Lahore: Abdul Salam Nadwi, 1956). 17–18.
29. Chaudhri Muhammad Ali was a witness to a bizarre scene on the eve of the dissolution of the constituent assembly in Governor-General Ghulam Muhammad's house: 'There I saw a strange spectacle. Ghulam Muhammad was sitting on a sofa, flushed in face. He was flanked by Ayub Khan and Iskander Mirza. In front of him was Bogra like a cowering captive. Ghulam Muhammad had a pistol in his hand and was severely reprimanding him saying that he had betrayed him despite the fact that he had made him the Prime Minister. Ghulam Muhammad insisted on dismissing the Constituent Assembly.' Chaudhri Muhammad Ali, *The Task Before Us* (Lahore: Research Society of Pakistan, 1974), 297.
30. Cited in Khalid B. Sayeed, 'The Arabs and the West', *Behind the Headlines*, XVII, 3 (Sept. 1957), 1–2.
31. Lieutenant A. C. Yate, *Travels with the Afghan Boundary Commission* (Edinburgh and London: Blackwood, 1887), 433 and 440.
32. Thomas Henry Thornton, *Sir Robert Sandeman: His Life and Work* (London: John Murray, 1895), 358–9.
33. John Connell, *Auchinleck* (London: Cassell, 1959), 877.
34. Ibid.
35. We are grateful for this information to Dr Betty M. Unterberger who has done this research. For details, see her paper, 'American Views of Jinnah as the Founder of a State', presented to the Association for Asian Studies, 1977. See also Unterberger's contribution to A. H. Dani (ed.), *World Scholars on Quaid-i-Azam M. A. Jinnah* (Islamabad: Quaid-i-Azam University, 1980).
36. Unterberger, 'American Views of Jinnah as the Founder of a State', 8.

37. Ibid., 9.
38. Ibid.
39. General Muhammed Ayub Khan, 'Strategic Problems of the Middle East'. *The Islamic Review* (July–August 1958), 12.
40. Henry Kissinger, *White House Years* (Boston: Little Brown, 1979), 910.
41. Ibid., 913.
42. *The Economist* (29 January–1 February 1980), 46.

INDIA IN 1947: THE LIMITS OF UNITY

Robin J. Moore

Perspectives

As time gives perspective to the partition of the Indian sub-continent in August 1947, the limits of the unity that were then achieved will probably be related to the history of imperial expansion and control. Apprehensive of external aggression and inconvenienced by unstable indigenous regimes, the British steadily extended their empire to the geographical limits of the sub-continent. At the end of the empire the territories that seceded from British India were (save East Bengal, which could not have seceded alone) among those last annexed — Sind, West Punjab, Baluchistan and the North-West Frontier Province (N.W.F.P.) — while the Pakistan movement itself was first spearheaded from the last of the princely states to be seized, the Kingdom of Oudh. The failure of the Congress national movement to achieve in the dissident areas the dominance that it established almost everywhere else is usually explained simply in terms of the Hindu-Muslim conflict. An analysis of the interaction between the survival of parochial Muslim socio-political structures and the Raj's post-mutiny reliance upon traditional forms of social control is overdue. At the same time, the outstanding problem of national integration around the time of Independence was the assimilation of the princely states, themselves survivals explicable in terms of Britain's need after 1857 to buttress up its direct rule of the provinces with princely alliances.

In the twentieth century the necessities of imperial rule gave the territories of the Muslims and the Rajas a disproportionate importance. During a period of avowed devolution of power upon responsible provincial governments, the princes enjoyed imperial support without obligation to introduce comparable reforms. When modest central reforms unlikely to win Congress support were contemplated, a special effort was made to retain the collaboration of the Muslims by the creation of Sind province, the enhancement of the N.W.F.P.'s status, the perpetuation of communal electorates in the Punjab and Bengal, and the concession of one-third of the seats in the putative all-India federal legislature. The relaxation of imperial control in the provinces, while it remained tight at the centre, enabled Muslim politicians to consolidate their provincial bases without challenge from the national level. Assuredly, Congress strategies contributed to the failure of Britain's two major attempts to set up constitutions for a united India, but under the India Act of 1935 the princes were given a veto on the development of a central government for the sub-continent, and by the Cabinet Mission scheme in 1946 the Muslims were enabled to defeat the creation of a fully representative Indian Constituent Assembly.[1]

Seen thus, the limits of unity that India achieved under the terms of the final transfer of power seem impressive, and the terms themselves acquire particular interest.

The Deal for Dual Dominionhood[2]

The signal for the break-up of imperial India was Clement Attlee's announcement on 20 February 1947. Unless the Constituent Assembly became fully representative and formed a constitution by June 1948, H.M.G. would

> have to consider to whom the powers of Central Government in British India should be handed over, on the due date, whether as a whole to some form of Central Government for British India, or in some areas of the existing Provincial Governments, or in such other way as may seem most reasonable and in the best interests of the Indian people.[3]

The Congress leaders welcomed this irrevocable decision to quit and assumed that in the absence of representatives from the non-Congress areas the Constituent Assembly would proceed to make a constitution that would embrace all areas of India willing to accept it. Nehru was sanguine:

> This may result in the Indian Union being first established for the whole of India except Bengal, the Punjab and Sind. Of course the Union constitution will apply to or rather be open to all; but those Provinces may not choose to adhere to it. If so, the second question that arises is that those parts of Bengal and Punjab which are fully represented in the Constituent Assembly (Western Bengal and Southern Punjab) should be parts of the Union. That means a partition of the Punjab and Bengal. It is unlikely that Jinnah or the Muslim League will agree to this truncated Pakistan. . . . They will thus have to make a choice ultimately between this and joining the Indian Union possibly on special terms. In other words, the position of Bengal and Punjab in such an event approximates to that of an Indian State.[4]

Nehru anticipated the continuation of the Cabinet Mission scheme so that willing areas could form a Union of India. The states would either enter the Assembly and help devise arrangements for joining the federation, or reach 'particular arrangements' with the Union on, he assumed, a subordinate basis.

This was to reckon without the determination that now possessed

Jinnah and the League, whose experience during the previous year's unsuccessful negotiations for groups of Muslim provinces within the Union had steeled them to seek security in a separate sovereign nation, however small. Jinnah had called for 'direct action' in August 1946, and the 'Calcutta killing' had ensued. The next month, with the lapse of the Defence of India Rules that suppressed private armies, the ranks of the Muslim League National Guards rapidly rose to some 91,500 men, now subordinated directly to the League's central leadership.[5] The Guards, who were pledged to 'strive for the achievement of Pakistan and for the freedom and glory of the Muslim nation', were, in the words of the Assistant Director of the Intelligence Bureau, 'put . . . on a war footing.'[6] The Hindu Rashtriya Swayamsevak Sangh (R.S.S.) and the Sikh Akalis were of a similar size. By January 1947 the Guards were parading the streets of Lahore in military uniform, and towards the end of the month the Punjab Coalition (Unionist-Akali-Congress) ministry declared them and the R.S.S. unlawful. When the Guards defied the ban and it was withdrawn the ramshackle coalition of Muslims, Sikhs and Hindus collapsed. On 2 March the Premier resigned. The League's leader in the Assembly was asked to form a government but he could not secure the numbers. As disorder spread and Governor's rule became imminent, Vallabhbhai Patel noted that Attlee's statement 'for the present, has resulted in our losing the Punjab'.[7] Still, like Nehru, he remained confident of eventual unity:

> Before next June [1948] the Constitution must be ready and if the League insists on Pakistan the only alternative is the division of the Punjab and Bengal. They cannot have Punjab as a whole or Bengal without civil war. I do not think that the British Government will agree to division. . . . They will not help the minority in securing or maintaining division, and a strong Centre with the whole of India except East Bengal and a part of the Punjab, Sind and Baluchistan, enjoying full autonomy under that Centre, will be so powerful that the remaining portions will eventually come in.[8]

Early in March the Congress Working Committee passed resolutions that defined its policy in the aftermath of Attlee's statement. They called for the partition of the Punjab between its Muslim and non-Muslim areas. While they hoped for the entry of all provincial and state territories into the Constituent Assembly, they accepted that its work was 'essentially voluntary'.[9] There must be 'no compulsion', and provinces and parts of provinces must be free to accept, by the choice of their own people, whether to join the Union. At the same time, during the transitional period of constitution-making, and pending the transfer of power, the Interim Government must be recognised as a fully responsible Dominion Government with the Viceroy as its constitutional head. Dominion status was to be a device for an interim transfer of power under the existing constitution. Thereby, the Interim Government, with Nehru as Prime Minister and Congress predominant, would preside over the process of constitution-making, the partition of provinces, and the secession of dissident areas. At that moment Congress did not press this demand for full power during the interim period. Lord Wavell's departure was imminent and discussions must be held with Lord Mountbatten as the Viceroy sent out to achieve a 'New Deal' for winding up the Raj.[10] For the moment, too, although the League had launched civil disobedience movements in the N.W.F.P. and Assam, their Congress governments remained in control.

On 8 April Nehru outlined the Congress approach to the transfer of power in an interview with Mountbatten. He emphasised that a constitution should not be imposed on any area against its will and that provinces and partitioned provinces should be free to join Hindustan, Pakistan, 'or possibly even remain completely independent.'[11] This was no prescription for fragmentation, for 'the whole thing revolved around having a strong centre . . . and for that reason [he] would favour making a statement soon and transferring power to Provinces while there was still time for [Mountbatten] . . . to help in the early stages of negotiations at the Centre.' The reference to a Dominion-Status Interim Government was clear enough, but Mountbatten regrettably overlooked it when he commended Nehru's principle of partition by self-determination to his staff as the basis of planning.[12] The staff proceeded to work up 'Plan Balkan', which, thus unhappily named, was brought before a conference of the provincial Governors in mid-April.[13] It provided for self-determination by provinces, and the partitioning of provinces, which could be members of Hindustan or Pakistan or independent from both — prior to the concession of Dominion status. The Governors generally approved the Plan. Their discussions suggested that the Plan might yield a very small Pakistan indeed. Though strongly challenged by the League, the Congress government of the N.W.F.P. might still be returned if an election were held in the near future, as the Governor wished, to resolve prevailing tensions. In Bengal, the essentially League ministry had construed Attlee's statement as foreshadowing a transfer of power to an independent province. The Governor preferred that outcome to a partition that would separate out the 'rural slum' of East Bengal, an unattractive prospective partner for West Pakistan. Mountbatten warned of the 'Balkanisation' of India by self-determination, but he also spoke of the feasibility of a minimal Pakistan, resembling an Indian state and including only West Punjab and Sind (and with the choice of not taking over the deficit Frontier Province).[14]

In mid-April Mountbatten achieved a minor victory when he induced Gandhi and Jinnah to issue a joint appeal to end the communal violence that was becoming endemic. But the Congress leaders grew increasingly restive at the League's persistent resort to direct action for political advantage. On 20 April, Patel reminded Mountbatten that though he had completed one month in office, 'bestiality' prevailed as the League sought to capture the Punjab, N.W.F.P. and Assam.[15] Soon afterwards he complained that Mountbatten was neither prepared to govern firmly himself nor allow Congress to take over.[16] When 'Plan Balkan' finally issued from Mountbatten's staff at the end of April and Nehru saw that it provided for fresh elections in the N.W.F.P., he called the Congress Working Committee (C.W.C.) into session to take stock. Tension was exacerbated on 30 April by Jinnah's release of a press statement attacking the partition of Bengal and the Punjab as a 'sinister' Congress device and calling for his full six-province Pakistan.[17]

On 1 May the C.W.C. reiterated its acceptance of the principle of partition by self-determination. However, its main emphasis, as expressed in a letter in which Nehru conveyed its opinion of the Plan, was on an orderly transfer of power.[18] The C.W.C. accepted the Cabinet Mission scheme and its Constituent Assembly in their entirety, whereas the League had rejected them and resorted to violence. Since Attlee's statement, the League had attempted by large-scale violence to overthrow provincial governments, even after the Gandhi-Jinnah appeal. 'Every proposal . . . must be viewed in this context.' If policy were to be influenced by terrorism, then the inevitable result would be civil war. Yet in the N.W.F.P. Mountbatten now proposed to yield to violence. The C.W.C. would resist any such proposal to end a duly constituted provincial government and call elections in response to terrorism.

The C.W.C., with Gandhi in attendance, considered the N.W.F.P. and the general political situation on 1, 2, 4, 5 and 7 May. Although no minutes of proceedings are extant, it is clear that the big three, Gandhi, Nehru and Patel, agreed on an immediate showdown. The Congress demand was put by Nehru to Mountbatten personally at Simla on 8 May, by Gandhi in a letter to Mountbatten written on that day, and by Patel in a press release next day.[19] There were individual differences but the approach was essentially the same. Power should be demitted to the Central Government on a Dominion status basis forthwith. The provinces should not be asked to decide their future until the Constituent Assembly had formed a constitution. Then provinces and part provinces should be free to leave the Union and a referendum might be held in the N.W.F.P. The demand was a restatement of the policy that Congress had adopted in response to Attlee's announcement and the unrest that followed it in the Muslim provinces: a strong Indian government at the Centre to preside over the peaceful preparation of an all-India constitution by the Constituent Assembly and the subsequent secession by self-determination of dissident areas.

Much has been made of Nehru's explosion when, on 10 May, Mountbatten showed him the plan for the transfer of power in the form that the British Cabinet had finally approved. There is no doubt that Nehru had seen the full draft of the Plan on 30 April and approved its underlying principle of partition by self-determination — indeed, his own proposals of 8 April had embodied it. However, he did not read the Plan closely enough to realise that the context for the application of the principle had been changed. Instead of a strong Indian Centre presiding over the secession of dissident areas once the Assembly had prepared a constitution, the Plan envisaged that provinces would choose whether to be partitioned, and whether to join Hindustan, Pakistan, or remain independent, prior to the constitution-making process. Moreover, after Nehru had seen the draft Plan, it had been altered by Mountbatten so as to enhance the possibility of an independent united Bengal, and by H.M.G. so as to emphasise the freedom of provinces, sub-provinces and states to choose complete independence.[20] The dangers of 'Balkanisation' had, as Nehru saw, been immeasurably increased. The contrasting approaches of Congress and the British only became clear amid the flurry of discussions at Simla and the exchange of cables with Whitehall from 11 to 13 May.

Although on 11 and 12 May Mountbatten was disposed to accept the Congress scheme for an immediate demission of power to a Dominion status Interim Government, he was pulled up sharp by Lord Ismay, his chief of staff, who had taken the Plan to London. Ismay's cables emphasised that such an approach would be in breach of past parliamentary assurances that the Muslims would not be subjected to the will of the majority.[21] From the wreckage of 'Plan Balkan' and the Congress plan Mountbatten, aided by his Reforms Commissioner, V. P. Menon, now struck with Nehru the deal that was to become the 3 June plan for an immediate transfer of power to two Dominions.[22] For the sake of a final settlement of Muslim claims, the Congress accepted the cession by self-determination of the Muslim majority areas. Congress would lose to Pakistan the areas of Sind, Baluchistan, West Punjab, East Bengal and the N.W.F.P. (despite later backsliding in an attempt to secure its separate independence). But the possible loss of the whole of Bengal was averted and an assurance of Dominion status for the rest of British India within weeks was secured.[23]

Congress had long accepted that unity could not be imposed and that Muslim India must eventually choose to remain in a Union or secede to form Pakistan. It had hoped that, given a favourable sequence of events, the Constituent Assembly might be able to attract the Muslim areas by constitutional concessions. With the deterioration of communal relations in March and April, the possibility receded steadily. At the end of April Nehru still believed that 'sooner or later India will have to function as a unified country', but he recognised that 'perhaps the best way to reach that stage is to go through some kind of a partition now.'[24] At Simla V. P. Menon urged him to accept a quick partition in order to avert the further spread of communal bitterness and to prepare for later reunification.[25] Under the dual Dominions deal there were to be a common Governor-General for India and Pakistan and a Joint Defence Council. Mountbatten himself believed that Pakistan would be scarcely viable, a very poor country with the burdensome Frontier Province and East Bengal, and he expected that it would accept international representation by India or Britain, except in the United Kingdom, the United States and some Muslim countries.[26] The Simla deal averted the fragmentation of British India, drawing the limits of unity by restricting the options of Muslim majority areas to membership of India or Pakistan.

The Problem of the Princes[27]

Probably the main attraction of the deal to Congress was that it promised to banish the spectre of princely Ulsters. It is likely that the primary significance of the deal will come to be seen as its preparation for the integration of the 562 princely states within the two Dominions, and that Mountbatten's viceroyalty will be assessed mainly in terms of his contribution to that process. On the eve of the deal, the Congress leaders appreciated that as Governor-General of an Indian Dominion, Mountbatten would be most useful in negotiations with the princes.[28] In his letter to Mountbatten on 8 May, Gandhi condemned the 'vicious doctrine' of the 'intransmissibility of paramountcy' — the non-transferability of the Crown's relations with the princes to a successor Indian government.[29] That day, too, Patel was writing of the states as one of the 'outstanding' problems demanding an immediate settlement of 'the shape of things . . . for purposes of transfer of power'.[30] In discussions with V. P. Menon and Krishna Menon at Simla, Nehru revealed that his acceptance of Dominion status rested heavily upon his expectation of Mountbatten's helpfulness with the princes. On 9 May he expressed to V. P. Menon the hope that paramountcy might be transferred in respect of defence, foreign relations and communications.[31]

Policy and protest proceeded from the 'Memorandum on States' Treaties and Paramountcy' that the Cabinet Mission released in May 1946.[32] It was the work of Sir Stafford Cripps, supplemented by some suggestions from Sir Conrad Corfield, Political Adviser to the Crown Representative. It spoke of an interim period between the British Indian parties' acceptance of a plan and the final transfer of power. During the interim period the states might participate in the process of constitution-making by joining the Constituent Assembly. Whether they did so or not, they would surely wish to strengthen their position by ensuring that their administration conformed to the highest standard and by placing themselves 'in close and constant touch with public opinion in their state by means of representative institutions'. During the interim period, too, they must negotiate with British India over the future regulation of matters of common concern, especially in the economic and financial field. As such negotiations might still be incomplete by the time of the transfer of power, standstill agreements between the states and the new British Indian governments would be necessary. The states were assured that the British Government would not and could not 'in any circumstances transfer paramountcy to an Indian Government'. The rights surrendered by the states to the paramount power would return to the states. When British India became fully self-governing H.M.G. would cease to be able to exercise the powers of paramountcy, which must then lapse:

> Political arrangements between the states on one side and the British Crown and British India on the other will thus be brought to an end. The void will have to be filled either by the states entering into a federal relationship with the successor Government or Governments in British India, or, failing this, entering into particular political arrangements with it or them.

Official action pursuant to the Memorandum was the responsibility of Corfield. His predecessor wrote of him:

> He is a very able person indeed, but his cast of mind is for these days excessively conservative. He has been all his life in Indian states and has imbibed, perhaps too successfully, the Princely point of view.[33]

His actions reveal a passion for legal correctitude (not always matched in his later reflections by factual exactitude). In mid-December 1946 he called the Residents into conference on the retraction of paramountcy. Although the Cabinet Mission scheme had not secured the agreement of the Indian parties, the Constituent Assembly had met and the princes had set up a Negotiating Committee to discuss terms for the entry of the states. At the same time, an Interim Government with Congress and League members had been formed. Corfield knew and approved of Lord Wavell's 'Breakdown Plan', then under discussion in London, which provided for a full British withdrawal by 31 March 1948, preceded by a phased geographical withdrawal of British civil and military administration.[34] Corfield might well assume that the 'interim period' had begun. On 16 December he told the Residents:

What we contemplated was the gradual reduction of paramountcy intervention *pari passu* with a gradual increase in states' freedom, so that the smallest possible vacuum remained at the end of the interim period when paramountcy would lapse.[35]

The retraction of paramountcy was to be hastened. Residents were to encourage the establishment of states' constitutions that would obviate the need for action by the paramount power.

The conference anticipated Attlee's February statement that during the period up to the transfer of power 'the relations of the Crown with individual states may be adjusted by agreement.'[36] Mountbatten's instructions, too, empowered him to negotiate such adjustments. They enjoined him to persuade rulers 'to progress rapidly towards some form of more democratic government', and to 'assist the States in coming to fair and just arrangements with the leaders of British India as to their future relationships.'[37] On 26 February Corfield furnished Wavell with a memorandum for the Secretary of State on the 'contraction of paramountcy' and proposed a Residents' conference in April to discuss it.[38] The memorandum, which was sent next day, sought the Secretary of State's approval for the contraction of paramountcy so that action could be taken to bring about the maximum devolution by the end of 1947.[39] Thereby, 'alternative arrangements may have a chance of functioning before paramountcy as a system finally disappears.' Lord Pethick-Lawrence agreed to this approach. The December Residents' conference had 'tackled the question in a businesslike and realistic fashion'.[40] Yet while the Viceroy should secure the 'greatest practicable devolution', he should avoid 'any step which would prejudice the future unity of India in regard to defence and communications'. The object was 'to enable states to stand on their own feet to encourage them to stand together but to do everything to encourage them to co-operate to the full with British India'. In particular, negotiations on matters of common concern should be pressed forward to avoid an administrative vacuum at the transfer of power. On 21 March, Pethick-Lawrence followed up with a cautious letter to Mountbatten, fearing that the approved contraction might precipitate the 'premature withdrawal' of political officers.[41] He requested monthly reports from the Political Department on the princes' steps to integrate their rule with the will of their subjects and with the future structure of British India. Corfield advised that the April Residents' Conference would produce a programme of contraction. He added: 'I fear that any tendency to delay withdrawal [of political officers] will defeat the very object at which we are aiming, namely to make the States stand on their own legs.'[42] Only physical withdrawal would stir the princes to action. Moreover, as political officers withdrew, his department would progressively become unable to report as Pethick-Lawrence requested. On 5 April Mountbatten replied to Pethick-Lawrence in these terms.[43] On 8–9 April the Residents' Conference at Delhi concerted a program for the withdrawal of Political Agents by the autumn and of Residents by the end of the year, and the completion of the Political Department's main duties by March 1948, three months before the transfer of power deadline.[44] In sum, the progressive contraction of paramountcy would mean the substantial transfer of power to the princes some months ahead of the due date for British India.

At the mid-April Governors' Conference, Mountbatten 'handed round' the text of Attlee's instructions to him and unveiled 'Plan Balkan'.[45] The latter provided for the states to become independent on the transfer of power and to negotiate freely with any confederation of provinces that might emerge. In the course of discussion on the wisdom of according provinces the choice of separate independence, Corfield argued that as the states were to have the choice it ought to be extended for the sake of consistency. Ismay argued that the option of independence flowed logically from Attlee's statement. The Plan that Ismay took to London on 2 May reaffirmed that His Majesty's Government (H.M.G.) policy towards the states remained unchanged. Paramountcy would lapse and all rights surrendered to the paramount power would return to the states. They were free to negotiate with the British Indian successors whatever association was in the best interests of their people.

Corfield has written that he was now anxious to clear the programme of contraction with the Secretary of State (Lord Listowel):

> Mountbatten was too busy negotiating with the Congress and Muslim League leaders to give any attention to the States' problem, so I gladly accepted the offer to accompany Ismay to London when he was taking to the cabinet Mountbatten's final plan. . . . As regards this plan, all I wanted to do was to make sure that the cabinet memorandum of May 1946 was referred to and endorsed.[46]

The Plan did not then refer explicitly to the Memorandum, and Corfield may have feared that Mountbatten would succumb to Congress pressure on the problem of the princes. On 18 April Nehru, as president of the All-India States' Peoples' Conference (A.I.S.P.C.), virtually a Congress subsidiary, attacked the princes for their reluctance to join the Constituent Assembly without assurances on their privileges.[47] Their 'shopkeepers' mentality' would alienate both British India and their own subjects. Those who did not join the

Assembly should be regarded as 'hostile' states and be made 'to bear the consequences of being so regarded'. Nehru referred bitterly to the Political Department, which was acting secretly and mysteriously, without the knowledge of the Interim Government, and 'dividing the country not into one or two parts but into one hundred or more'. Patel shared his contempt for the Political Department.[48]

In London Corfield secured a specific reference to the Memorandum in the Plan, which now became far more precise about the states:

> Some may confirm their wish to proceed with framing a constitution in the existing Constituent Assembly. Some may wish to join any other Constituent Assembly that may be established. Some may wish to stand out independently, either singly or jointly, as is open to the Provinces. But, whatever their decision, all will require to enter upon negotiations for new agreements, especially in the economic and financial sphere, on the lines contemplated in . . . the Cabinet Mission's Memorandum. . . .[49]

On 9 May, in a discussion with Listowel on the progressive retraction of paramountcy, Corfield won assent to the 'policy of withdrawing first Political Agents and then Residents, leaving by about March 1948 no more than a nucleus at Political Department headquarters'.[50] Corfield 'made it clear that Pandit Nehru disliked this procedure of retraction, and argued that since the structure of paramountcy was built up between the states and the Governor-General in Council, the successor Indian Government[s] should inherit the whole nexus of agreements with the States.' It was 'agreed that this argument was fallacious' for 'the agreements were between *the Crown* and the States'. It was not possible to legislate for the transfer of the Crown Representative's authority to a successor-government but only for the abolition of the Crown Representative, thus voiding paramountcy and any agreements between the Crown and the states. New arrangements between the parties were necessary. With the disappearance of the Crown Representative, the British High Commissioner might possibly exercise some residual functions in relation to the states. He would do so as an intermediary not between the states and the successor-governments but between H.M.G. and the states. It was clearly contemplated that some states might decline to join any Constituent Assembly. Corfield returned to India to put the retraction of paramountcy into effect.

Meanwhile the situation underwent a dramatic change. On 10 May, when Mountbatten showed him the Cabinet's revise of the Plan, Nehru alleged that it represented a Balkanisation of India. The states were practically encouraged to stand out of the Indian Union, the larger ones to become allies of Britain, playing off Pakistan against the rest of British India. Mountbatten advised Listowel that Nehru intensely disliked the passage in the Plan relating to the states. 'We must preserve the position of the states but at the same time we cannot avoid giving a lead to the Princes.'[51] The deal that Menon drafted and Nehru approved gave the following 'lead':

Some of the states are already participating in the deliberations of the existing Constituent Assembly. H.M.G. hope that all others will join either the existing Constituent Assembly or the new Constituent Assembly [of Pakistan].[52]

Mountbatten's deal with Nehru was for *dual* dominionhood, which involved Mountbatten in exerting his influence to ensure the integration of the states in India or Pakistan. During meetings with the India Committee of the Cabinet in May, he was insistent that the prospect of direct relationships between the Crown and independent states would encourage the 'disintegration of India'.[53] The states 'must be told that their relations with the Crown will have to be through one or other of the Governors-General.'[54] On 24 May the Committee accepted that H.M.G.'s 'prime object should be to facilitate the exclusive association of the states with one of the new Dominions.' However, it also accepted that if a state ultimately stood aside from both then H.M.G. would have to consider separate relations with it.

The 3 June statement as finally issued merely remarked cryptically that the policy of the Cabinet Mission Memorandum 'remained unchanged'.[55] Corfield might feel justified in contracting paramountcy. Yet Mountbatten had authority to 'lead' the princes into the Dominions; he would be in breach of his understanding with Nehru if he failed to do so, and Congress might well refuse to endorse the deal. The relations of the states with the Dominions would depend not upon the execution of a clearly avowed policy but upon the ability of the disputants to impose their interpretations of the flexible Memorandum. The situation produced tensions between Corfield and Mountbatten, the Political Department and the Congress, the princes and Congress, H.M.G. and the Opposition, and even, to a mild degree, between Mountbatten and H.M.G. The reduction pursuant to the 3 June statement of the interim period to ten weeks made this last phase in the long transfer of power the most critical one for Indian unity. The maximization of the limits of unity may be analysed by considering in turn the emergence of policies for, first, the retraction of paramountcy and the negotiation of administrative continuity; secondly, the definition of the states' status in relation to the new Dominions; and, thirdly, H.M.G.'s relations with states that declined association with the Dominions consistently with that definition.

A de Facto Policy of Unification

Nehru had no sooner accepted the 3 June statement than he resumed his attack on the lapse of paramountcy and the Political Department's preparations for it. On 4 June he complained to Mountbatten that the demolition of the Political Department's machinery for regulating relations with the states would provoke administrative chaos.[56] The Department had handled not only the Crown's relations with the princes but also all-India arrangements between the Government of India and the states, which were vital to the integrity of British India. To confer independence on the states would prejudice the defence and internal administration of India as a whole. Just as the Raj had once articulated relations throughout India essential to its wellbeing, so too must an Indian Dominion now. On 5 June, at a meeting of the Congress and the League leaders with Mountbatten, Nehru emphasised the need for machinery to co-ordinate the Dominions' relations with the states and complained of the Political Department's sabotage of existing arrangements.[57] On 6 June Mountbatten discussed the complaint at a meeting of Corfield, Ismay, Sir Eric Miéville (Principal Secretary to the Viceroy), and representatives of the states, and he relayed a suggestion of Nehru's that upon the transfer of power, representatives of the government of India should be sent out to the residencies to maintain relations on matters of common concern.[58] The meeting was in 'complete disagreement' with the proposal. Some states and groups of states had already arranged to send representatives to the Indian Dominion, and they would no doubt feel that the despatch of central agents to them bespoke the transfer of paramountcy. At a meeting with the Indian leaders on 7 June Mountbatten said that he would write to the states, giving them the choice of sending representatives to the Dominions or receiving agents.[59]

On 9 June Nehru urged Mountbatten to set up a department of the Government of India to deal with matters of common concern with the states.[60] The Political Department was 'functioning without any consultation with the Government of India'. Regardless of paramountcy, the Government was 'concerned with its numerous relations with the states', and it was 'extraordinary and highly improper for the Political Department . . . to liquidate itself and . . . all our relations with the states without reference to us'. Such behaviour was 'unconstitutional' and many things that were being done for the disposal of property, buildings, records and staff were open to challenge in a court of law. The same day C. Rajagopalachari published an article in the same vein in the *Hindustan Times*. He had already sent the gist of it to Cripps: 'Paramountcy came into being as a fact and not by agreement, and on Britain's withdrawal the successor authorities must inherit the fact along with the rest of the context.'[61] Irrespective of relations between prince and Crown, existing relations between the states and British India involved matters of continuing common concern, including civil and criminal administration, railways, posts and telegraphs, currency, defence and external affairs. Cripps disagreed: relations between British India and the states were a function of those between the Crown and the states; they had always been constitutionally distinct from the relations of the executive government of British India, though until 1935 the Crown had employed the Governor-General in Council as its agent. The Cabinet Mission's Memorandum was right and paramountcy must lapse: 'It is a case for co-operation and goodwill on the administrative level in the first instance . . . and cannot be settled on a legalistic basis.'[62] Cripps emphasised that the Memorandum had envisaged standstill agreements as necessary to administrative continuity.

Although there had been no open breach with Mountbatten, Corfield now decided to seek early retirement. He must have felt that they were, in H. V. Hodson's words, 'pulling in different directions'.[63] Whereas he was trying to set the princes on their feet by mid-August, so that they might subsequently negotiate their future relations with the new Dominions from a position of strength, Mountbatten was committed to leading them into a Constituent Assembly by then. On 9 June Mountbatten wrote to Listowel that Corfield's daughter was to be married in London on 5 August and that he wished to take leave from 23 July preparatory to retirement.[64] These facts are at odds with Corfield's published account of his departure, which he associated with a conflict over an issue that had yet to arise.[65]

On 10 June Nehru and Patel raised with Mountbatten the validity of the Government of India's existing contractual arrangements with the states after the transfer of power.[66] Mountbatten agreed to raise the question, together with that of standstill agreements, at a meeting of Indian leaders scheduled for the 13th. Nehru also condemned the proposed restoration of power to the princes, and threatened to 'encourage rebellion in all states' that stood out of the Assemblies. Next day the Standing Committee of the A.I.S.P.C. declared that when paramountcy lapsed sovereignty would reside in the states' peoples. It demanded the transfer of the Political Department and its agencies to the Government of India, or, alternatively, the creation of a new department to receive the properties, records and staff of the Political Department and its Agencies and Residencies.

At the 13 June meeting of Mountbatten, Corfield and the Indian leaders, Nehru charged Corfield with 'misfeasance' (the improper performance of a lawful act) in the progressive retraction of paramountcy.[67] Corfield was on sure ground, for he had acted with the blessing of the Crown Representative and the Secretary of State and consistently with the Cabinet Mission's Memorandum. While Nehru could assert that the document contained no reference to the ultimate independence of a state, Corfield could answer that neither did it require a state to enter a Constituent Assembly; provision was made for 'particular political arrangements', which implied 'autonomy'. In later years Corfield was to argue that while he had thought independence 'impractical' in the long run, the 'threat' of it was a legitimate lever for states to use during negotiations with the successor-governments, which the Memorandum certainly expected to continue beyond the transfer of power into a period of standstill agreements.[68] It might be added that the dual nature of the transfer raised the question of choice for states contiguous to both Dominions and for those with rulers of a different religion from that of most of their subjects. Mountbatten intimated that his plans envisaged the subordination of the states and he produced a document that offered them the choice of sending representatives to a Dominion or receiving agents. When Nehru pressed for a central department, Mountbatten conceded that he could not prevent the Dominions establishing new departments. He proposed the creation of a 'States Department' forthwith. It would have sections for each of the Dominions, which, according to the decision of individual states, would either send or receive agents. The States Department began work on 1 July, with V. P. Menon as its secretary and Patel in charge.[69]

The contentious meeting of 13 June also agreed on the despatch to all Residents of a Political Department letter setting out a formula for standstill agreements.[70] All states (some only after bargaining) accepted agreements covering matters of common concern, especially economic and financial arrangements, with the new Dominions for a period of two years from the lapse of paramountcy, and pending the negotiation of new agreements.[71] Despite the insistence by H.M.G. that all agreements between the Government of India and the states were aspects of paramountcy and must lapse with it, nevertheless the Independence Act, in deference to Congress pressure, provided for agreements to continue until they were denounced by one of the parties or superseded.[72]

The States Department and the standstill agreements ensured administrative continuity, but the status of the states *vis-à-vis* the Dominions remained to be defined. Essentially to accommodate the Muslim provinces, the Cabinet Mission scheme had adumbrated a federation for three subjects only, Defence, External Affairs and Communications. The states might enter a Constituent Assembly on this understanding or, alternatively, enter into 'particular political arrangements' with the Union for such matters. The 3 June deal went further, by opening the way to Dominion governments with wide powers, so that states might well recoil from their Constituent Assemblies. As the deal was to be implemented through the constitutional machinery of the 1935 Act, it is not surprising that the Act should also have been adapted in order to allay princely apprehensions. The Act had provided for the states' incorporation in an all-India federation through the negotiation of an instrument of accession. In June 1947 it was realised that, pending the Dominions' preparation of constitutions, the princes might be invited to accede for only the Cabinet Mission's three Union subjects. Nehru had been contemplating such an interim arrangement since March, and on 9 May he suggested a transfer of paramountcy thus limited. At the beginning of June Sir Walter Monckton (Hyderabad's adviser) was led to believe that Nehru was privately suggesting a limited accession but that he would interpret the three subjects formula widely.[73] On 10 June Mountbatten put it to Nehru and Patel that the princes were understandably frightened off by the departure from the Cabinet Mission's Plan Union, only to be assured by Patel that the central powers would only be enlarged with the princes' consent.[74] On 17 June, when the jurist and constitutional adviser to the Nawab of Bhopal, Zafrullah Khan, voiced the princes' fears at a meeting with Mountbatten, the Nawab and Monckton, Mountbatten himself stated that the Congress would accept the states' accession on the basis of the three subjects only.[75] It was indeed the case that on 6–8 March and 1 May the C.W.C. had resolved upon acceptance of the Cabinet Mission scheme 'in its entirety'. The 3 June deal involved a reaffirmation of the acceptance of the Mission's Memorandum. The three subject accession was thus implicit in the deal, by which Nehru enlisted Mountbatten's best efforts to effect the transfer of paramountcy 'in every sense except the legalistic' (in Lumby's phrase).[76] Rather too much has been made of Menon's averred conversion of Patel to three subject accession as late as July, and Nehru's subsequent acquiescence.[77] However, they may well have found difficulty in convincing their party colleagues of the wisdom of this apparently generous invitation to the princes, which Patel delivered publicly on 5 July.

Mountbatten construed his role as 'going into battle' with Congress on behalf of the princes.[78] He argued, more as tactics than by conviction, that by holding Congress to the acceptance of a three subject accession he was preserving the internal autonomy of the states. By using his influence as Viceroy to lead them into the Dominions he was securing a better bargain for them than if they were to negotiate individually and from isolation after the lapse of paramountcy, when, as constitutional Governor-General, he would be obliged to accept such action as his ministers found necessary. Nehru had foreshadowed rebellions of the states' peoples against non-acceding princes. The Indian Union 'could never agree' to a state becoming independent,

> which means having external relations and the power to declare war or peace and controlling its defence and communications. . . . The facts of geography cannot be ignored and the dominant power will necessarily exercise certain control over any state which does not choose to come into the Union.[79]

Some princes appreciated Mountbatten's intervention to secure the three subject arrangement as completely transforming their future prospects, which the cruel logic of *realpolitik* threatened to blight.[80] Others saw matters differently. On 11 July the States Department listed the accession scheme on the agenda for a meeting of states' representatives on 25 July, at which Mountbatten would employ his redoubtable talents of persuasion. He was to achieve a diplomatic triumph. But this is to cast ahead, as Mountbatten was casting ahead of H.M.G. in his intimations of the post-paramountcy international status of non-acceding states.

Very early in his viceroyalty Mountbatten learned that some princes wanted the status of separate Dominions, among them Bhopal, Travancore and Hyderabad. Bhopal, Chancellor of the Chamber of Princes, was evidently disappointed when Mountbatten told him on 1 June that Dominion status was not available to any state that sought independence from India and Pakistan. Mountbatten refused, consistently with H.M.G.'s policy of 24 May, to answer or refer questions about H.M.G. entertaining relations with such a state after 15 August. Nevertheless, on 4 June Bhopal declared that he would pursue independence and a week later Travancore and Hyderabad followed suit. In mid-July the learned Dewan of Travancore, Sir Ramaswami Aiyar, contended that the three-subject accession scheme violated Britain's earlier assurances that state relations with the successor-governments were a matter of negotiation.[81] Accordingly, after paramountcy lapsed, independent Travancore would negotiate with the Dominions about foreign relations, defence, and communications. Junagadh state, in Kathiawar, protested similarly against the 'altogether extraordinary and unexpected' revival of the scheme of federal accession.[82] The states had not been consulted about it and the Cabinet Mission's Memorandum had not mentioned it. The scheme denied states the choice whether to join a Union or merely seek 'particular political arrangements' with it. Accession during the interim period would cost a state its freedom to stand out once the Dominion's constitution was made.

The main critic and ultimate test of British policy was Hyderabad. Even before Attlee's February statement, Monckton (who was in touch with Jinnah through Bhopal) was testing the possibility of

Conservative party support for appeals by Jinnah and the Muslim princes for separate membership of the Commonwealth. In mid-January he was in touch with the chief creator of the 1935 Act, Sir Samuel Hoare (by now Lord Templewood), and 'much encouraged' by their measure of agreement. He wrote:

I think what the Muslims would like to know is that if Jinnah came out with a declaration that they want to stay within the Commonwealth — a policy in which the most important Princes would in due course join — they would receive a substantial measure of support from responsible opinion in England. After what you said last night I feel I can give that assurance. Do you think I can assume that RAB [Butler], Anthony [Eden] and Bobbity [Lord Cranborne — later Salisbury] will take the same line?[83]

Templewood's astonishing reply seems to mock the self that had once defied the diehard and Churchillian cries of 'sham' when he toiled indefatigably to bring the putative all-India federation on to the statute book:

I would say [publicly] that our great achievement in India has been the creation of a united and peaceful sub-continent. It has, however, become quite obvious that this unity depended on the British mediatory influence and that, when once this influence is withdrawn, it becomes an artificial sham [*sic*]. This being so, it is better that the fundamental division in India should be recognised in a peaceful and constitutional manner rather than be accepted at the end of a period of chaos and civil war.[84]

He believed such a statement would carry great weight in England and he authorised Monckton to confide his views to Bhopal. He offered to meet Monckton to prepare a campaign before Monckton went out to India in April. In mid-January, too, Monckton was lobbying Lady Mountbatten.[85]

Within days of his arrival in India on 22 March, Mountbatten was approached by Bhopal about dominionhood, which, he confided, was also Jinnah's object for Pakistan. Mountbatten trod warily, offering encouragement in neither case, for although he passionately favoured Commonwealth membership for India, it must be for all of India, and he played his cards astutely to that end. Until the Simla deal he confided doubts about Congress intentions in his reports home, and, in consequence, on 10 May Attlee requested an appraisal by the Chiefs of Staff of the military and strategic implications of Dominion status being accorded to part only of the sub-continent, for example West Pakistan, Bengal, and a seaboard state such as Travancore.[86] On 12 May the Chiefs of Staff reported in favour of Dominion status in all three cases.[87]

Since late in 1945, landlocked Hyderabad had been seeking access to a port.[88] In April 1947 Monckton was in touch with Templewood about the acquisition of port facilities at Marmagao, in Portuguese Goa, with a rail link to be built from the state to the sea. The businessman Sir Alexander Roger was employed as an intermediary, but Monckton himself seems to have visited Portugal in April. He was keeping Templewood informed so that the latter could 'give our enterprise a fair wind when you pay your visit to Lisbon later in May'.[89] However, on 3 May he wrote from Viceroy's House in New Delhi that as the whole Indian situation was 'tense and anxious', Templewood should stay out of the Portuguese negotiations.[90] As a guest and friend of Mountbatten's, he had been shown his notes and plans and been enlisted to help secure the entry of all India to the Commonwealth.[91]

Monckton was chagrined at the dual Dominions deal and the exclusion thereby of separate dominionhood for Hyderabad. On 7 June he wrote a 'Note on the Position of Hyderabad' and on the 9th sent it to Ismay, intimating that he wished to avoid ventilating the grievance through political channels in England.[92] The note acknowledged Mountbatten's success with the British Indian leaders, but criticised his failure to consult Hyderabad's representatives until 3 June. The Congress represented the states as an 'anachronistic heritage to be pressed or cajoled, whether they wish it or not, into the pattern which British India has chosen'. In fact they had a living culture of their own, and were, in many cases, as well administered as the provinces. They accounted for over a third of the area of the sub-continent and a quarter of the population. If they were 'fairly treated', many of them had a 'sounder hope of survival than the brittle political structure of the Congress party after they . . . attained independence'. Hyderabad had a population larger than that of any of the existing Dominions and its area was as large as France; it had been a faithful ally for a century and in two world wars. Yet it was denied association with the Commonwealth except through India or Pakistan. For the Nizam to join India would be political suicide. He wanted to remain in the Commonwealth, whereas Congress would be eager to leave it, and he could not understand Britain's denunciation of his treaties. Monckton concluded: 'I think this is rather a shameful performance. How ready we are to appease our enemies at the expense of our friends.' Yet another letter that he wrote at this time reveals that he remained sanguine of Hyderabad's survival.[93] As Britain would not be present to protect Hyderabad it was necessary not to antagonise the Union of India, but 'if we go warily we shall very likely outlast them.' Jinnah would support Hyderabad if it stood firm, while Corfield, who had 'fought a really noble battle for us', had prepared standstill agreements that could endure for two or three years. If H.M.G. would maintain relations with Hyderabad, then Pakistan would recognise it, as would

Egypt and Saudi Arabia. 'Then we can think concretely of U.N.O. and we may well get our Dominion Status in the end.'

For such hopes to have foundation Hyderabad would require direct relations with H.M.G. after paramountcy lapsed. On 14 June, in the wake of the Nizam's declaration of intended independence and amid condemnation of it by Congress leaders, Monckton advised Ismay that he must return home to press the case.[94] On the 17th, when Mountbatten saw Monckton, Bhopal and Zafrullah Khan together, he emphasised that 'Congress would never have accepted the plan [of 3 June] if there had been more than two Dominions; they had even refused to allow Bengal to vote for independence and separate Dominion status to avoid partition.'[95] Nevertheless, Monckton persuaded Mountbatten to recommend that H.M.G. clarify its intended relations with states that joined neither Dominion. Ismay and Miéville drafted a parliamentary question and answer for the purpose. Monckton wrote to R. A. Butler to ask him whether he would put the question to the Under-Secretary of State for India, and Mountbatten, then in Kashmir, surprisingly commended the reply: on the lapse of paramountcy, states were free to join the Dominions of India or Pakistan or become separate autonomous units, and H.M.G. would not refuse direct relations with those taking the latter step.[96] Monckton confided to R. A. Butler, Templewood, Lord Cranborne and Brendan Bracken that Travancore, Bhopal and Jinnah all supported the proposal.[97] He also had in mind the possibility of Hyderabad securing dominionhood if India left the Commonwealth once it had made its constitution. Listowel recognised that the proposed answer went beyond the India Committee's position of 24 May — the discouragement of post-paramountcy relations with the states unless they ultimately became unavoidable. On 26 June the Committee adopted his advice to postpone parliamentary comment until the second reading of the Independence Bill in a fortnight's time.[98] Mountbatten responded to Monckton's evident disappointment by asking Ismay to refer Hyderabad's claim to Mr W. H. Morris-Jones, recently arrived Constitutional Adviser to the Viceroy. Morris-Jones disagreed with Monckton that Hyderabad had a valid claim to the perpetuation of its place in the Empire.[99] Its present place arose solely from its relation with the paramount power. The relationship had been based on political power and the withdrawal of that power would be a political fact. The right of parliament to terminate paramountcy was beyond doubt. The Independence Act would thus wipe clean the slate of British relations with Hyderabad. The location of Hyderabad precluded the possibility of direct relations without the Indian Dominion's concurrence, for they would be 'most improper' and contrary to the spirit of relations with the Dominions.

On 5 July the India Office cabled to Corfield that during the second reading debate the Government would admit the possibility of a state that did not join a Dominion upon the lapse of paramountcy securing relations with foreign powers through H.M.G. on a temporary basis.[100] Menon cabled the reply: to give any inkling of the possible recognition of the states' independent status would exacerbate the problem of securing their adherence to the Dominions.[101] Now that the Mountbatten-Congress deal over three-subject accession had become public, Menon was on firm ground. On 8 July Listowel told Mountbatten that there would be no statement on the international position of the states during the Commons debate.[102] The same day Mountbatten impressed on Monckton that Nehru had accepted that Mountbatten himself should undertake the negotiations for the three-subject accession.[103] Next day Monckton sent in a letter from the Nizam protesting against the Independence Bill's repudiation of his treaties and denial of Commonwealth membership unless he joined India or Pakistan.[104] On 11 July Mountbatten commended three-subject accession to a Hyderabad delegation that met with representatives of the Political and States Departments.[105] As Hyderabad was militarily defenceless, completely landlocked and surrounded by the Indian Dominion, H.M.G. would be unable to accept a commitment for its protection. The Nizam must accede to India to enjoy the benefits of Commonwealth membership.

The Government weathered the Commons' debate on 10 July without making an explicit statement on the international status of non-acceding states. Introducing the Bill, Attlee expressed the hope that in due course all states would find their appropriate place in one or other of the Dominions but accepted that until constitutions were framed there 'must necessarily be a less organic form of relationship between them and there must be a period before a comprehensive system can be worked out'. When paramountcy lapsed, the states would 'regain their independence', but he hoped that 'no irrevocable decision to stay out will be taken prematurely'. Monckton was pleased with the Opposition's response.[106] Leading for his party in Churchill's absence, Harold Macmillan referred to the states' right to join a Dominion or enjoy 'independent sovereign authority'. Both he and Sir John Anderson spoke of the need to ensure that no moral or physical 'pressure' should be brought to bear upon states while they were making their choice, and both believed that H.M.G. should enter into independent relations with states that requested them. On 12 July Mountbatten commended to Listowel the States Department suggestion that H.M.G. should announce that it was in the states' own interests to come to an arrangement with an appropriate Dominion over external relations.[107] He added that if he were successful at his meeting with the states' representatives on the 25th, then the question of international status would be 'resolved automatically', and that a prior parliamentary statement might queer his pitch. During the Lords' debate on 16 July, Listowel reaffirmed that on the lapse of paramountcy the states would be

> the masters of their own fate. They will then be entirely free to choose whether to associate with one or other of the Dominion Governments or to stand alone, and His Majesty's Government will not use the slightest pressure to influence their momentous and voluntary decision. . . . Whatever the future relationship between the new Dominions and the States may be, it will require prolonged consideration and discussion before the final adjustment can be made.

As prompted by Mountbatten, he said that it 'would be in the best interests of their own people, and of India as a whole', that the states should find their appropriate place 'within one or other of the new Dominions'. He went so far as to say: 'We do not, of course, propose to recognise any States as separate international entities.' However, questioned closely by Templewood, he conceded that to cover the contingency of a state failing to enter a Dominion, the question of international recognition would be 'left open to be considered on its merits when such a position arises'. Monckton was delighted by Templewood's 'masterly' leading of Listowel and believed that 'we have got something very valuable in the bag'.[108]

Notwithstanding Listowel's disclaimers, Mountbatten's speech of advice to the states' representatives on 25 July was minatory — 'the apogee of persuasion' in Menon's words.[109] He insisted that the three-subject accession would leave the states with internal autonomy and all the independence that they could, in reality, manage: '. . . these three subjects have got to be handled for you and for your convenience by a larger organisation.' Accession by 15 August was urgent in order to avert a chaotic void. He made it seem that Congress's generous offer of limited accession depended upon its immediate acceptance by all states. After 15 August non-acceding states would be isolated internationally and left to fend for themselves. He went further in letters to wavering princes.[110]

Listowel was alarmed at the tenor of Mountbatten's 'advice'. It was right to urge accession but 'we must . . . keep balance and not ourselves add to pressure which facts of the situation place in any case on States.'[111] He demurred at Mountbatten's intimation that H.M.G. would not continue relations with non-federating states and at his insistence upon accession by 15 August. Parliament had been told that the states might need more time. He did not see how they could be expected to accede by mid-August for even three subjects.[112] It would be better if the Dominions extended external protection to the states pending negotiations for accession. Such a course would be consistent with the Cabinet Memorandum and would relieve H.M.G. of the allegation of imposing pressure. When George Abell (Private Secretary to the Viceroy) put up a conciliatory draft response, Mountbatten minuted in red ink: 'I would like this redrafted to knock these arguments on the head' — after discussion with V. P. Menon.[113] On 4 August, Mountbatten cabled Menon's draft.[114] It explained that the princes could not afford to delay their accession until the Dominions made their constitutions, for after 15 August they would be faced with rebellions of their subjects. There was no question of pressure, merely of commending a good offer:

> I am doing my best while I have bargaining power in my capacity as Crown Representative to see that States get fair offer from Government of India and to induce them to accept it so that conflict which is inevitable if they do not accede should be avoided. . . . I am trying my very best to create an integrated India which while securing stability will ensure friendship with Great Britain. If I am allowed to play my hand without interference I have no doubt that I will succeed. If disintegration is to be avoided we have to act very quickly and should give every encouragement to States to come in and not to stand out.

Succeed he did, and within a few days Listowel cabled: 'We are full of admiration at your success in having overcome the hesitation of so many States about acceptance of the terms of accession offered by Patel.'[115] On the eve of Independence the repentant doubter added:

> I believe that your outstanding ability and fearless determination have saved India from unimaginable disaster and that your achievement will be remembered in time to come as one of the greatest feats of statesmanship in history.[116]

Attlee paid tribute to his 'amazing' skill 'in the successful achievement of a task of unexampled difficulty'.[117]

At 15 August only three of the 562 states were loth to join a Dominion: Junagadh, Kashmir and Hyderabad. Listowel felt 'some sympathy' for Hyderabad, for there were so many considerations in acceding, with a constitution not yet made, even for three subjects.[118] On 28 July, Monckton had told Mountbatten that the Nizam had decided against accession, which would precipitate a Muslim revolt. However, Mountbatten's speech of 25 July must have dimmed the prospect of his obtaining direct international relations with Britain. Monckton now felt 'the association of Hyderabad with the Indian Dominion [to be] inevitable in the interests of both', but it could not be rushed.[119] On 8 August the Nizam wrote to Mountbatten of his difficulty in aligning with India when his ties with Pakistan were numerous.[120] The Dominions might fail to agree on arrangements for defence and external affairs, hostilities might emerge between them, or India might leave the Commonwealth. He must wait and watch events for the moment. On the day of his historic advice to the princes, Mountbatten confided to Listowel his concern about India possibly deciding to leave the Commonwealth at some future time, and on the day that Monckton intimated that the Nizam would not accede, he raised the matter at a staff meeting.[121] Morris-Jones was to be asked to consider the possibility of India being accommodated in the Commonwealth permanently, but on a looser basis than Dominion status.[122] Attlee had already in June set up a committee on the question of future relations within the Commonwealth at large.[123] Both the committee and Morris-Jones concluded that India might remain in the Commonwealth even if a republican constitution were adopted. The likelihood might have steeled Mountbatten's resolve to reject the Nizam's offer on 8 August to enter into a treaty with India for defence, external affairs and communications. Hyderabad secured only a two-month extension of the three-subject accession offer.

To all intents and purposes Mountbatten had pursued a *de facto* policy of unification.

The Burden of History

The Cabinet Mission Memorandum's contemplated sequence of events was: the creation of an Interim Government and the opening of an interim period pending the transfer of power; the rapid establishment of sound administration and representative institutions in the states; the contraction of paramountcy as the states became self-supporting; negotiations between the princes, thus strengthened, and the successor government(s), either by the states entering a Constituent Assembly or otherwise; the making of constitutions; the transfer of power, the lapse of paramountcy, and the operation of standstill agreements until negotiations were complete; the definition of relations in federal terms or under 'particular political arrangements'. Existing relations between the Crown and the states would end at the transfer of power and no new relations were envisaged. Rather, the states would be either subordinated to the new nation(s) federally or by treaty. The failure of the Cabinet Mission scheme created a new situation. From 20 February until about 11 May, H.M.G. and sometimes Mountbatten contemplated the prospect of states becoming Dominions. Under the dual Dominions deal, Congress accepted an immediate partition that maximised the limits of British India by a process of self-determination (modified as necessary by a 'parapolitical' Boundary Award),[124] on condition that there should be no more Dominions. The Dominion constitutions could not now be available for scrutiny by the states prior to the transfer of power and lapse of paramountcy. Standstill agreements were struck, but the contraction of paramountcy was racing ahead of the intended emergence of representative institutions in the states. It was inevitable that it should, probably even under the more leisurely time-table of the Cabinet Mission Memorandum, and that the Crown would thus be returning powers to rulers lacking popular support. The Memorandum, and by implication the 3 June Plan, wishfully imagined reasonable negotiations between harmonious states and the successor government(s). Here was the rub. For the Congress 'nation' could, in reality, undermine or topple a prince by inciting his subjects to rebellion, and then (as the British had once done) intervene in the name of law and order. Ignoring such real prospects, H.M.G. observed constitutional proprieties in parliament, honestly convinced of its righteousness, while Mountbatten, aware of the tides of history, imposed the *de facto* or para-constitutional solution that the problem demanded.

Mountbatten, Nehru, Patel and V. P. Menon had found the solution to the problem of British India fragmentation in the dual Dominions deal, which blended elements of the 1935 Act and the Cabinet Mission scheme. They found the solution to the problem of the princes in the corollary of the deal, the scheme for three-subject accession, blended from similar elements. A negotiated settlement consonant with political realities emerged, maximising unity without the deployment of force (though three states achieved a brief 'independence', later to be destroyed by force). Mountbatten certainly used pressure not sanctioned by his instructions and repudiated in parliament. Certainly, too, the states lost the internal autonomy that Mountbatten, for the sake of tactics, assured them they would enjoy.[125] The alternative was the appearance after 15 August of a rash of unstable regimes, indefensible against external aggression and internally precarious. The situation would invite 'police actions' by the Dominions and, if it persisted long, foreign intervention. The alternative is illustrated by the problems caused by the residue of non-acceding states: Junagadh, Hyderabad and Kashmir.[126]

The residue may be held to reveal a weakness in Mountbatten's policy — say, the lack of a contingency plan, perhaps for accession by plebiscite after 15 August. But after the transfer of power, who was left to administer a scheme that one of the Dominions might find inimical to its interests? Mountbatten and H.M.G. had put their faith in the Commonwealth, operating through a common Governor-General, and in the development of a Joint Defence Council. It is as well that more was not expected of these supra-national agencies. The collapse of the common Governor-General scheme flowed from the fear of the smaller Dominion that the 'advice' of its larger neighbour would prevail in cases of conflict. The collapse of the Joint Defence Council resulted from its lack of military control after the transfer of power, a consequence of Jinnah's concern for immediate military independence. There persisted some hope that over time the geographical unity of the sub-continent would reassert itself. In June 1947 Morris-Jones was asked to evaluate the prospects for joint agencies.[127] His analysis was somewhat pessimistic but not despairing. In the air between Malta and Karachi, after securing the consent of King, Cabinet and Churchill to Mountbatten's remaining as Governor-General of India only, Ismay wrote a paper on problems already solved and those remaining:

> Then [he concluded] there is the North West Frontier of India. If India had grasped the elementary fact that . . . [it] is just as much their frontier as Pakistan's, I should be less disturbed. But as it is I doubt whether they will come to this way of thinking, except after bitter experience.[128]

It seems timely to recall such reflections in the wake of the invasion of Afghanistan in 1979.

In the end, of course, it was not the horrors in the Punjab, or India's police actions to capture the interset territories of Junagadh and Hyderabad, but the Kashmir problem that sundered Indo-Pakistan relations beyond early repair. The underlying logic of the dispute was rooted in the history of British imperialism in India. The plurality of princely autonomy and provincial democracy was responsible for the defeat of the all-India federal solution to the problem of unity in the 1930s. After Partition the violent consequences of political and cultural pluralism in Kashmir — a Hindu prince, with Muslim subjects, poised between India and Pakistan — blocked, at least for a generation, the possibility of a sub-continental defensive entente.[129]

NOTES

1. I have argued the relation between devolution by stages and division in *The Crisis of Indian Unity, 1917–40* (1974), *Churchill, Cripps and India, 1939–45* (1979) and 'The Problem of Freedom with Unity: London's India Policy, 1917–47', in D. A. Low (ed.), *Congress and the Raj* (1977), 375–403.
2. The arguments of this section appear in greater detail in 'Mountbatten, India, and the Commonwealth', *Journal of Commonwealth and Comparative Politics*, xix (1981), 6–43.
3. M. Gwyer and A. Appadorai, *Speeches and Documents on the Indian Constitution* (1957), 2 vols., II, 667–9.
4. Nehru to Gandhi, 24 February 1947, in Pyarelal, *Mahatma Gandhi, The Last Phase* (1958), II, 4–5.

5. C. P. Scott memo, 'Volunteer Organizations/Private Armies in India', 12 April 1947, in Mountbatten file 117. I am indebted to the Broadlands Trustees for permission to use Lord Mountbatten's Indian papers, and to the India Office Records for making their xerox copies available to me. The file numbers cited (MB) are those assigned temporarily to the copies by the I.O.R.
6. 'Rules of the All-India Muslim League National Guards', 1 October 1946, and E. J. Beveridge's Secret Minute, 8 November 1946, Home Dept. (Political), 28/4/46, Indian National Archives.
7. Patel to K. Dwarkadas, 4 March 1947, G. M. Nandurkar (ed.), *Sardar's Letters — Mostly Unkown*, II (1978), 209.
8. Ibid.
9. C.W.C. Resolution of 6–8 March 1947, Gwyer and Appadorai, op.cit., II, 669–70.
10. Mountbatten's own phrase in letter to Attlee, 11 February 1947, MB 109.
11. MB 191.
12. MB 191, 108.
13. Minutes of Governors' Conference, 15–16 April, L/P & J/10/79, India Office Library. For 'Plan Balkan', see Viceroy's Conference Paper No. 28, 14 April 1947, MB 151.
14. On the evening of 15 April, Sir Frank Mudie (Governor of Sind) suggested to Mountbatten the feasibility of a Pakistan that included only Sind and West Punjab. It would be no threat to Indian unity and might be seen as a large state that declined to join the Constituent Assembly. Mountbatten noted: 'This opens up a new vista.' On 12 April Patel suggested to him that a decision to partition Bengal and Punjab might cost Jinnah the support of Muslims in those provinces, and that if Jinnah could secure only Sind and West Punjab then the Muslim League might revolt against the idea of Pakistan. MB 192.
15. Patel to Mountbatten, 20 April 1947, in Durga Das (ed.), *Sardar Patel's Correspondence* (Ahmedabad, 1972), IV, 22–25.
16. A. Campbell-Johnson, *Mission with Mountbatten* (1951), 72.
17. In L/P & J/10/79.
18. Nehru to Mountbatten, 1 May 1947, MB 151.
19. For Nehru's plan see record of 8 May meeting, MB 196; for Gandhi's letter, Pyarelal, op.cit., II, 171–2; for Patel's statement, *Hindustan Times*, 10 May 1947.
20. See drafts of 1 and 10 May, L/P & J/10/79; Viceroy's Staff Meeting, 1 May, MB 201; Turnbull to Croft and Monteath, 7 May 1947, L/PO/428, I.O.L.
21. Ismay to Miéville, 12 May 1947, R/3/1/153, I.O.L.; Sec. of State to Viceroy, 12 May 1947, L/P & J/10/79.
22. Viceroy to Sec. of State, 13 May 1947, ibid.
23. India Committee meetings of 19, 20, and 28 May, ibid.
24. Nehru to K. P. S. Menon, 29 April 1947, in S. Gopal, *Jawaharlal Nehru*, I (1976), 343.
25. Menon to Patel, 10 May 1947, *Patel's Correspondence*, IV, 111–16.

26. Viceroy's Staff Meeting, 6 June 1947, MB 100.
27. An assessment of the literature on this subject appears in J. Manor, 'The Demise of the Princely Order', in R. Jeffrey (ed.), *People, Princes and Paramount Power* (Delhi 1978), 306–28.
28. Viceroy's Staff Meeting, 10 May 1947, MB 40.
29. Loc.cit.
30. Patel to Sudhir Ghosh, 8 May 1947, Sudhir Ghosh Collection, Nehru Memorial Library, New Delhi.
31. Enclosure by Menon to Patel, 10 May 1947, loc.cit.
32. Nicholas Mansergh and Penderel Moon (eds.), *Transfer of Power*, VII (1977), Doc. 262.
33. Sir Francis Wylie to Mountbatten, 12 August 1947, R/3/1/40, I.O.L. Corfield thought Wylie 'unsympathetic to the rulers'. Corfield, 'Some Thoughts on British Policy and the Indian States, 1935–47', in C. H. Philips and M. D. Wainwright (eds.), *The Partition of India* (1970), 527–34.
34. Penderel Moon (ed.), *Wavell: The Viceroy's Journal* (1973), 384.
35. Minutes of Residents' Conference, 16–17 December 1946, Political Dept. 113–P(S)47, N.A.I.
36. Loc.cit.
37. Attlee to Mountbatten, March 1947, in H. V. Hodson, *The Great Divide* (1969), 545–7.
38. Corfield's Secret Minute, 26 February 1947, Pol. 27 R(S) 1947, N.A.I.
39. Crown Rep. to Sec. of State, 27 February 1947, ibid.
40. Sec. of State to Crown Rep., 5 March 1947, ibid.
41. Ibid.
42. Corfield's draft, 31 March 1947, ibid.
43. Ibid.
44. Minutes of Residents' Conference, 8–9 April 1947, Pol. 1- R(S)47, N.A.I.
45. Loc.cit. Yet Corfield, who was present, later disclaimed any recollection of seeing Mountbatten's instructions (letter mentioned in T. Creagh Coen, *The Indian Political Service* (1971), 125).
46. Corfield, 'Some Thoughts', loc.cit., 531. Cf. Corfield, *The Princely India I Knew* (Madras, 1975), 152.
47. In L/P & J/10/79.
48. Patel to Ghosh, 8 May and 29 June 1947, Ghosh Coll.
49. Revise of 8 May 1947, L/P & J/10/79.
50. Note of Discussion on Retraction of Paramountcy on 9 May 1947, d. 12 May 1947, L/P & J/10/79.
51. Viceroy to Sec. of State, 13 May 1947, ibid.
52. In Viceroy to Sec. of State, 13 May 1947, ibid.
53. Sec. of State to Viceroy, 20 May 1947, ibid.
54. Listowel's note on 'Relations Between H.M.G. and the Indian States after the Transfer of Power', 24 May 1947, pursuant to India Cttee decision of 22 May, and enclosing 'Revised Draft Statement', ibid.
55. Changes to the states paragraph of the 'deal' (in Viceroy to Sec. of State, 13 May, loc.cit.) were suggested by Listowel (memo. of 17 May,

in L/P & J/10/79) to avoid 'impression of pressing the states to enter these Constituent Assemblies, at any rate at this stage'. For Corfield's comments see Viceroy to Sec. of State, 21 May, ibid.

56. Nehru to Mountbatten, 4 June 1947, MB 142.
57. Miscellaneous Meeting, 5 June 1947, MB 196.
58. Interview, 6 June 1947, MB 84.
59. Miscellaneous Meeting, 7 June 1947, MB 196.
60. Nehru to Mountbatten, 9 June 1947, R/3/1/136, I.O.L., and B. N. Pandey (ed.), *The Indian Nationalist Movement, 1885–1947, Select Documents* (1979), 241–2. Far more than the destruction of records was at issue (Cf. Manor, op.cit., 318).
61. Rajaji to Cripps, 8 June 1947, R/3/1/136.
62. Cripps to Rajaji, 23 June 1947, CAB 127/146, Public Record Office; Rajaji to Cripps, 2 July 1947 and reply, 8 July 1947, ibid.
63. Hodson, op.cit., 359.
64. Viceroy to Sec. of State, 9 June 1947, MB 142.
65. The issue was three subject accession (see below). See Corfield in 'Some Thoughts', 533, but he is more specific in *Princely India*, 159. The earlier date of Corfield's decision to depart rends the fabric of such appraisals as Paul Scott's (*Times Lit. Supp.*, 16 July 1976), but is not sufficient to vitiate Scott's judgment of Corfield as a man of firm opinion and principle.
66. MB 193.
67. MB 196. V. P. Menon gives a full account of the meeting (*Integration of the Indian States* (1956), 85–90). See also, Corfield, *Princely India*, 155–7, where (as Manor notes, op.cit., 327, n. 52) Nehru is said to have alleged 'malfeasance' (evil-doing, or official misconduct in public affairs). Yet W. H. J. Christie's Diary for 19 June 1947 (I.O.L. D718) records that Corfield told him that Nehru had said he 'should be impeached for misfeasance'. Corfield 'was not too pleased by H. E.'s apparent lack of support'.
68. 'Some Thoughts', 532; see also *Princely India*, 157.
69. Summary of conclusions of meeting in Political Adviser's Room, 28 June 1947, Pol. 18 PR/47, N.A.I.
70. Pol. Dept. to Residents, 14 June 1947, Pol. 46 R(S)47, Part I, N.A.I.
71. Consolidated statement of states' reactions, 15 July 1947, Pol. 46R(S) 47 Pt. II, N.A.I.
72. See R/3/1/138, I.O.L.
73. Monckton to J. C. P. Brunyate, [beginning of] June 1947, Templewood Coll., E240/81, I.O.L.
74. MB 193.
75. Ibid.
76. E. W. R. Lumby, 'British Policy Towards the Indian States, 1940–7', in Philips and Wainwright, op.cit., 95–103, p. 103.
77. Menon, *Integration*, 94–9; cf. Hodson, op.cit., 366–9.
78. E.g. in interview with Bhopal and Indore, 4 August 1947, MB 194.
79. Nehru to Ismay, 19 June 1947, MB 210, also in Pandey, op.cit., 243–4.
80. E.g. Gwalior and Jodhpur interviews of 12 and 14 July 1947, MB 194.

81. Aiyar to Resident for Madras States, 10 July 1947, Pol. 46R(S)47, II, N.A.I.
82. Note by Govt. of Junagadh, 20 July 1947, ibid.
83. Monckton of Templewood, 15 January 1947, Templewood Coll., loc.cit. (hereafter T.C.).
84. Templewood to Monckton, 16 January 1947, ibid. For Churchill and the 'sham' federation, see my *Churchill, Cripps and India* (1979), 1–4, 23n. For an analysis of Templewood's 1953 allegation of sabotage by Churchill and the Indian Government of his scheme, see my 'The Making of India's Paper Federation, 1927–35', Philips and Wainwright, op.cit., 54–78.
85. Monckton to Templewood, loc.cit. It seems that Monckton knew that Mountbatten was to become Viceroy three weeks before Wavell was told of his dismissal, and a month before he was told of his successor.
86. Attlee to Maj-Gen. Sir Leslie Hollis, 10 May 1947, MB 152.
87. Meeting of Chiefs of Staff Cttee, with Ismay and A. V. Alexander, 12 May 1947, ibid.
88. See L/P & S/12/1081, I.O.L.
89. Monckton to Templewood, 18 April 1947. Sudhir Ghosh believed that Roger was paid £10,000 for his efforts, and that on the Portuguese side Dr. Antonio Bastroff, and on the British side Sir William Barton (Resident of Hyderabad, 1925–30), were also involved. Ghosh to Patel, 26 August 1947, Ghosh Coll. But on Barton, see Menon, op.cit., 388–9.
90. T.C.
91. Monckton's Note of 29 April 1947, Monckton Papers, Bodleian Library.
92. MB 70.
93. Monckton to Brunyate, [beginning of] June 1947, T.C.
94. MB 70.
95. MB 193.
96. Monckton to Butler, 19 June 1947, T.C.; Listowel's memo. of 24 June 1947, 'Proposed Parliamentary Question about Policy towards the States', L/P & J/10/81, I.O.L.
97. Monckton to Templewood, Butler, Salisbury, Bracken and Strauss, 25 June 1947, T.C.
98. India Committee Meeting, 26 June 1947, L/PO/431, I.O.L.
99. Memo. of 28 June 1947, commenting on Monckton's 'Hyderabad Note', 27 June 1947; MB 70.
100. Patrick to Corfield, 5 July 1947, MB 143.
101. Menon to Patrick, 7 July 1947, ibid.
102. Sec. of State to Viceroy, 8 July 1947, R/3/1/138, I.O.L.
103. Interview, 8 July 1947, ibid.
104. Monckton to Miéville, 9 July 1947, and enclosure, n.d., MB 212.
105. MB 196.
106. H. Gordon (Monckton's personal assistant) to Templewood, 12 July 1947, T.C.
107. Crown Rep. to Sec. of State, 12 July 1947, MB 144.
108. Gordon to Templewood, 21 February 1947, T.C. For Listowel's

'anxious moments in the Lords', see his 'The Whitehall Dimension in the Transfer of Power', *Indo-British Review*, VII, 3 and 4, 22–31, p. 30.

109. Menon, op.cit., 108. For the speech, see Mountbatten, *Time Only to Look Forward: Speeches* (1949), 51–6.
110. E.g., to the Maharaj-Rana of Dholpur, 29 July 1947, in Corfield, *Princely India*, 183–5.
111. Sec. of State to Viceroy, 1 August 1947, MB 144.
112. Listowel to Mountbatten, 2 August 1947, MB 176.
113. Abell's draft of 2 August 1947, R/3/1/139, I.O.L.
114. Viceroy to Sec. of State, 4 August 1947, MB 144.
115. Sec. of State to Viceroy, 9 August 1947, MB 176.
116. Sec. of State to Viceroy, 14 August 1947, L/PO/18, I.O.L.
117. Attlee to Mountbatten, 14 August 1947, ibid.
118. Sec. of State to Viceroy, 9 August 1947, MB 176.
119. Monckton to Mountbatten, 28 July 1947, MB 70.
120. Nizam to Mountbatten, 8 August 1947, MB 73.
121. Mountbatten to Listowel, 25 July 1947, MB 176; Meeting of 28 July 1947, MB 203.
122. Morris-Jones's paper, 'Position of India and Pakistan within the Commonwealth', 5 August 1947, MB 213, discussed at Staff Meeting, 5 August 1947, MB 41. See also B. N. Rau to Abell, 1 August 1947, and Morris-Jones's 'Note on Right of Secession', 11 August 1947, R/3/1/152.
123. Meeting of Ministers, 9 June 1947, MS Eur D714/81, I.O.L.
124. H. R. Tinker's phrase to describe Sir Cyril Radcliffe's 'solution to the problem of the Sikhs' (in 'Pressure, Persuasion, Decision: Factors in the Partition of the Punjab, August 1947', *Journal of Asian Studies*, XXXVI, 4 [1977], 695–705, p. 696).
125. These allegations were the gravamen of Corfield's case against Mountbatten: 'Some Thoughts', 531–2; *Princely India*, 158–60; Creagh Coen, op.cit., 125.
126. See Menon, *Integration*, 124–50, 314–415.
127. Morris-Jones's 'Note on Joint Organizations', n.d., but seen by Miéville on 9 July 1947, MB 93.
128. Undated and unsigned typescript, 'India: 18 March 1947–18 July 1947', evidently by Ismay, in W. H. J. Christie Papers, D718/2, I.O.L.
129. This chapter was completed in March 1980. For another view, see W. H. Morris-Jones, 'The Transfer of Power, 1947: a View from the Sidelines', Kingsley Martin memorial lecture, 1981, *Modern Asian Studies*, 16, 1 (1982), 1–32.

'THE MODEL COLONY': REFLECTIONS ON THE TRANSFER OF POWER IN SRI LANKA

K. M. de Silva

In the preface to his book *The Constitution of Ceylon*, published in 1949, Sir Ivor Jennings promised that he would some day 'explain in print how much Ceylon owes to Mr. [D. S.] Senanayake and Sir Oliver Goonetileke'. 'But for them', he wrote, 'Ceylon would still be a colony.' Jennings was eminently qualified for such a task; he was a constitutional lawyer and political scientist of the first rank, and above all it was on him that both Senanayake and Goonetileke relied for expert advice in their negotiations with the Colonial Office on the transfer of power. But the book was never written. There were, on the other hand, three works by Sir Charles Jeffries, who was Permanent Under-Secretary at the Colonial Office when these negotiations came to a successful conclusion, between 1945 and 1947. Jeffries wrote one book on the general theme of *The Transfer of Power* (London, 1960) and two others specific to the problems of Sri Lanka: *Ceylon: the Path to Independence* (London, 1962) and a biography of Sir Oliver Goonetileke. Not that these three volumes were particularly well-documented, but given the fifty-year rule on the release of official records which was then in force, the reticence on some of the more crucial issues was only to be expected. The material in these books was as much as one could expect from an official of Jeffries' rank and of his day, and by those standards it was comprehensive enough. At any rate these books appear to have convinced Jennings that the one he had in mind had been made superflous. He died before the thirty-year rule for the opening of official records to public scrutiny had been introduced, letting loose a flood of documents that will keep historians and political scientists busy for decades reconstructing the events and background of the transfer of power with a wider range of material than Jeffries ever contemplated using in writing his books.

To return to Jennings and his preface, the point he sought to make was that the transfer of power in Sri Lanka was an enormously complicated problem with an unusually formidable set of constitutional hurdles to be cleared before Sri Lanka reached the goal set for her by her most influential politician of the day, D. S. Senanayake. To change the metaphor, the goal could only have been reached by some shrewd and deft diplomacy. It is in this process that the concept of

'Ceylon, the model colony' first gained currency.

The concept seems in retrospect to have been a clever public relations job which owed its effectiveness to an unusual convergence of interests between Senanayake and his advisers on the one hand and the Colonial Office officials — Jeffries for one — on the other. The theme was later taken up by some historians of the Commonwealth at a time when faith in and enthusiasm for that institution as a viable multinational organisation were still quite strong. This convergence of interests could scarcely have been anticipated or predicted by Senanayake and Goonetileke at the time when they began the final phase of the negotiations for the transfer of power to Sri Lanka. The concept of 'Ceylon, the model colony' owed much of its effectiveness to the fact that, despite its intrinsically dubious origins as an exercise in image-making, there was enough of a correspondence to reality to sustain a genuine belief in it, and more to the point, to justify its acceptance as an adequate basis for the making of policy.

Three distinct elements went into the making of this image: first, the strategy; secondly, the tactics in the pursuit of the self-imposed goal of Dominion status; and thirdly, the hard reality behind it all, the political maturity of a ruling élite, and of the people at large — the first electorate in Asia to enjoy the benefits of universal suffrage — to say nothing of the socio-economic advances made by the country since 1931. The crux of the problem was that: 'No colony had yet become a candidate for independence status that carried with it membership of the Commonwealth. Ceylon was the first. [. . .] Ceylon was the first of the colonial territories (leaving aside the old colonies of settlement which evolved into dominions in the nineteenth century) to achieve independence. . . .'[3] Thus the transfer of power to Ceylon, which might have seemed at first sight a relatively easy and simple affair, involved in fact many constitutional difficulties. Moreover, it carried implications for the Commonwealth comparable in many ways with those involved in the transfer of power to India.[4]

It is against this background that the 'model colony' concept was developed by Senanayake's advisers. In insisting that Dominion status should be the primary objective and that this could be attained in association with the British rather than in opposition to them, Senanayake stood against the prevailing current of opinion in the Ceylon National Congress that independence rather than Dominion status should be Sri Lanka's goal. The model he chose for emulation was not India but the old settlement colonies of the Empire whose development to Dominion status was one of constitutional advance by measured stages. The underlying assumption was that self-government would come through the legislature becoming progressively more representative and exercising wider controls over the executive until it approximated to a Dominion parliament.

In a sense his choice of political tactics was determined by the goal he had set himself. Besides, that goal was also affected by considerations which had a great deal to do with external factors. With the defeat of Japan, the principal fear of Senanayake and his associates was India; membership of the Commonwealth appeared, at this time, to hold out the great attraction of enabling the island 'to treat with its formidable mainland neighbour on the basis of near equality'.[5]

Since Ceylon was a colony under the Colonial Office, the constitutional problems involved in her transition to Dominion status were extremely complex. The traditional pattern of constitutional evolution to that status for new members drawn from the self-governing colonies of British settlement had been through the route of self-government. They had become members of the British Commonwealth because they had attained responsible government. They had first framed their own constitutions, called into being their own parliamentary systems and cabinet form of government. What Ceylon was seeking to do was to reverse the process, and the steps involved in the change-over from colonial to Dominion status were unprecedented.[6]

Under Senanayake's leadership, Ceylon was seeking membership of an exclusive club. The conventions, practices and precedents involved in the process were determined by the older members. The emphasis was all on reasoned argument and negotiations. Senanayake's tactics were tailored for this purpose. But it would be unfair to Senanayake to argue that this was all there was to the tactics he used. The fact is that his tactics and his strategy were affected by his political instincts and inclinations as well as by the political traditions of the mainstream of élite politics in Sri Lanka with its well-known proclivity for peaceful constitutional agitation. In his strong commitment to this, D. S. Senanayake was only following a pattern set by men like Arunachalam, H. J. C. Pereira, James Peiris and above all his own brother F. R. Senanayake. All of them were willing to accept political concessions, grudgingly granted by the British in response to their demands, on the basis that half a loaf was better than none — indeed they were sometimes content with a single slice. They were realists who saw nothing dishonourable in a pragmatic acceptance of constitutional reform in instalments. Most of them (all, in fact, save Arunachalam) could scarcely conceal their disapproval of the agitational tactics introduced by A. E. Goonesinha, the labour leader in the 1920s, in the process of politicising the urban workers in and around Colombo. In the final phase of the negotiations, Senanayake faced a more cohesive 'radical' political force, the Marxists, who by the mid-1930s had displaced Goonesinha in the leadership of the indigenous working-class movement (the working-class movement in the island was divided on ethnic lines between the Indian plantation workers — and other Indian workers in the urban areas — on the one hand, and the numerically much smaller segment, the indigenous working class). Like Goonesinha with his professed adherence to Gandhian tactics of agitation, the Marxists advocated and imitated the political techniques of the Left wing of the Indian National Congress. To all of them Senanayake was strongly opposed, just as much as he voiced his disapproval of the younger elements in the Ceylon National Congress, led by J. R. Jayawardene and Senanayake's son Dudley, who were seeking to build up links with the Indian National Congress.

His insensitivity to the grievances of the politically radicalised urban working class and white collar workers was such that he generally viewed them as a threat to the existing social order, and this strengthened his commitment to the peasantry between whom and the élite he saw if not an identity of interests at least a potentially harmonious working relationship. Thus the adherence to peaceful constitutional agitation was the instinctive response of a conservative politician who feared the potential for disruption and violence in mass agitation.

In his successful insistence on peaceful constitutional agitation he was seen — in later years by historians of the Commonwealth — as a statesman in the mould of the leaders of the old dominions. It was a role he relished and played with remarkable panache. His critics saw and condemned this as indestructible 'anglophilia'. He prefered to see these criticisms as an enormous compliment. All this was part of the process that contributed to making up the myth of the 'model colony'. A third very essential ingredient in the tactics adopted by Senanayake was strong support of the allied war effort. Not merely D. S. Senanayake, but every member of the Board of Ministers, and all sections of political opinion in the legislature except the Marxists[7] were united in this. This was in strong contrast to the leadership of the Indian National Congress. The result was that the principal British officials civil and military, who worked in association with Senanayake lent their support to him in extracting political concessions from Whitehall. Thus in 1943 Caldecott the Governor and Sir Geoffrey Layton the Commander-in-Chief[8] joined forces in persuading the war cabinet to make a more generous pronouncement on constitutional reform for the island than Whitehall had been inclined to make.[9] In 1944 Lord Louis Mountbatten as head of South-East Asia Command whose headquarters were in Kandy, supported Caldecott and Layton in a successful pressure to advance the date of appointment of the commission on constitutional reform which had been officially promised, in 1943, for after the termination of hostilities; the Commission was appointed in late 1944 well before the end of the war. Then again, the Soulbury Commission enthusiastically endorsed the principles of political reform set out in the Minister's Draft Constitution of 1944.[10] In a challenging final sentence of their report they expressed their belief (and hope) that their recommendations if adopted, would 'enable Ceylon to enjoy forthwith a full and ample means of self-government and in due course to assume the status of a Dominion, thereby bringing nearer the ultimate ideal of British statesmanship, the fusion of Empire and Commonwealth'. For all of them — Caldecott, Layton, Mountbatten, the Soulbury Commissioners, and Monck-Mason-Moore, Caldecott's successor as Governor — the record of war-time co-operation was a decisive factor in the backing they gave Sri Lanka's leaders in their campaigns for constitutional reform.

By 1946 the Labour government had accepted the recommendations of the Soulbury Commission as the basis of Ceylon's future constitutional status: full internal self-government, but with Whitehall control of defence and external affairs. The promise was held out that full responsible government would come after the new constitution had been worked successfully for some time. The period that Whitehall had in mind in 1945–6 was six years or more.[11] There were lingering doubts in the Colonial Office, no less than in the cabinet, about Sri Lanka's competence to handle the responsibilities of dominion status without such a period of further tutelage.

Indeed, in 1944, despite all the support he was to give Senanayake in his campaigns for constitutional reform, Caldecott went on record that the 'implications and obligations of Dominion status are either not understood or are being deliberately ignored by people who should know better'.[12] In 1945, Monck-Mason-Moore told Whitehall that he 'appreciated that His Majesty's Government may not be prepared to give Ceylon a blank cheque for self-government in six years time'.[13] Again, despite the reassuring tones of the British government's White Paper on Constitutional reform issued in 1945 and the hopes expressed there that 'in a comparatively short space of time' the goal of Dominion status would be reached, it was made clear that the 'actual length of time occupied by this evolutionary process must depend upon the experience gained under the constitution by the people of Ceylon.[14] Senanayake and the Board of Ministers would have been appalled if they had known that by 'a comparatively short space of time' the British Cabinet meant 'not less than six years', and that the British Prime Minister, Clement Attlee, held the view that even if Ceylon 'emerged successfully from the test', it could not be taken for granted that 'she would automatically attain full Dominion status'. This they did not know.

Within two years of this, however, Senanayake's objective was achieved. In early 1947 with general elections to the new Parliament scheduled for August-September 1947, Senanayake pressed Whitehall for a more precise statement of policy on its time-table for the island's attainment of Dominion Status. Arthur Creech-Jones was much more receptive than all his predecessors as Colonial Secretary had been to Senanayake's request. On 20 February 1947, the British Cabinet had made its historic policy statement on India's independence. With the partition of the Indian sub-continent into the states of India and Pakistan and the grant of independence to Burma, Ceylon's claims for equality of treatment with these former units of the British Raj could no longer be overlooked, especially in view of her record of war-time co-operation — a point which both Senanayake and Goonetileke emphasised in their negotiations with Whitehall.[15] Besides there was also a clearer understanding of the imperatives of the island's political situation, with Senanayake and the moderates facing a general election in which they confronted a serious challenge from Left-wing forces. The immediate grant of Dominion status was essential to ensure the success of Senanayake and the moderates in meeting this challenge. In recognition of this fact, the British government made the official announcement on 10 June 1947 that Ceylon would receive 'fully responsible status within the British Commonwealth of Nations'. Curiously enough the formula adopted for this purpose — an Order-in-Council and Agreements on Defence and External affairs — had been first mooted by Senanayake (on the advice, it would seem, of Sir Ivor Jennings) in August 1945 when he was in London for negotiations with the Colonial Office. The officials there had not shown much enthusiasm for it on that occasion, but in the changed circumstances of 1947 they adopted that line of action.[16]

Looking back on the events that led to the transfer of power to Sri Lanka, it is all too easy to see it as weariness on the part of the British, a divesting of responsibility after the decision to dismantle the Raj had been taken. It was far from clear, at that time, that colonial rule was soon to be over. Indeed the preoccupation of the Colonial Office at the end of the 1940s was to make colonial rule more effective, not to hasten its end. Thus the procedure adopted in the transfer of power to Sri Lanka was all of a piece with the general run of things.

So, by the beginning of 1948, Sri Lanka had become a Dominion. What had seemed so difficult for the British Cabinet even to contemplate in 1945 had happened within two years. It would seem today that events were moving so rapidly that no amount of statesmanship could have checked them for long. Yet this was not so obvious at that time either to Whitehall or to men like Senanayake. For them, despite the retreat from Empire in the Indian sub-continent and Burma, Britain still had an Asian empire and did not intend to quit Asia. She still had a vital role to play as an imperial power. Indeed she was still a world power, and the immediacy of the Commonwealth in support of its role — it was still 'Anglo-American imperialism' in the eyes of its critics and it was to take at least fifteen years before the 'Anglo' part of it was dropped! — was there in full measure during the first post-war decade. Hence the insistence on a defence agreement before the transfer of power to Ceylon:

> A basic requirement of Commonwealth strategy was the maintenance of communications in the Indian Ocean by sea and air. Ceylon occupied a commanding position as a base for defence communication, without which control over the Indian Ocean would be seriously weakened. It provided the only existing fleet base between Malta and Singapore.[17]

Ceylon was vital as a link in a chain of defence requirements, which included the Indian Ocean and the Southern dominions of the British Commonwealth. For Senanayake no less than for Whitehall, these defence agreements were part of a process of adjusting to the uncertainties of a new pattern in South Asia where India was an independent state. If the defence agreements with Sri Lanka were important to Whitehall because of Britain's interest in the Indian Ocean, especially for securing her links with Australia and New Zealand, for Sri lanka they served a different but no less important purpose. The Sri Lankan negotiators and their advisers believed that the agreements offered them security against possible threats from India to Sri Lanka's independence.

The manner in which power was transferred to Sri Lanka proved somewhat controversial, and the defence agreements were at the heart of the problem. It seemed to suggest a qualitative difference in the nature of the independence that was being conferred on Sri Lanka — in comparison with the cognate process in India, Pakistan and Burma — when no meaningful difference in status was either intended by Britain or accepted by Sri Lankan leaders in the Board of Ministers prior to independence, and later in the first Cabinet. Once Senanayake had set his sights on Dominion status and membership of the Commonwealth, the manner in which it was attained seemed less important than the fact of its attainment. But his most vocal critics on the Left of the Sri Lanka political spectrum, who had no faith either in Dominion status or in the Commonwealth, denied that the island was really independent and pointed to the defence agreements as evidence of this.

As for Whitehall, it sought to justify Sri Lanka's passage to self-government in 1948 on the basis that it was not merely a special case but an unusual one as well because of the strength of her civil society, the political maturity and sophistication of her leaders, and above all the fact that she had had adult suffrage for nearly two decades.

The emphasis at that time — it must be noted — was also on the characteristic British belief that there was something unique in each of her colonial dependencies. The uniqueness of India, for instance, was regarded as so self-evident that it offered no precedent for other colonies save possibly Ceylon. The constitutional future of that island could hardly be separated from the momentous decisions on India then being taken.

The general significance of her advance from Colonial to Dominion status was thought to be far-reaching. 'This is the first occasion in our history,' Lord Addison, the Lord Privy Seal and a former Colonial Secretary, said in introducing the second reading of the Ceylon Independence Bill in the House of Lords on 4 December 1947, 'upon which a colony, developing this system of self-government of its own accord, had deliberately sought to become a Dominion state in our Commonwealth, but we hope and expect it will not be the last.'[18] In 1960 Sir Charles Jeffries justified the decision to concede Sri Lanka's case for Dominion status because 'of its size, its economic strength, its advanced state of social organisation. Since 1931 it had in fact had a form of political constitution which placed the main responsibility for the conduct of its affairs on an elected State Council and on Ministers answerable to that [body].' Ceylon in brief, was a special case. He added that 'no other colony seemed to be in sight of fulfilling these conditions. If Ceylon was the forerunner, it had a long start.'[19]

Mansergh, the historian of the Commonwealth, had seen it in much the same terms:

> Ardent nationalists from other and less peaceful lands might allude in tones of condescension to Ceylon's fight for freedom but the gentlemanly pressure for independence exerted by its conservative nationalist leaders upon Whitehall made up in good sense what it lacked in political passion. As a result Ceylon acquired the status of a Dominion of the British Commonwealth without bitterness, by orderly constitutional advance which made the matter of its attainment a source of unfailing satisfaction to British constitutional historians and its status in the academic world that of the model Dominion.[20]

Ceylon, then, was at the head of the queue, but it was not expected that others would follow too soon along the path cleared by her statesmen. By the 1960s others had followed this path in Africa and Asia, no less than in the Carribbean. And as colony after colony reached independence, men like Jeffries and Duncan Hall saw the transfer of power in Sri Lanka as a historic event, and the 'model colony' concept was given a sharper and clearer meaning.[21] Thus Hall argued:

> Historically, Ceylon had almost as much right as India to be regarded as an original member of the Commonwealth. It was not only the first of the 'colonies' (the dependent areas administered by the Colonial Office) to achieve full membership of the Commonwealth. It was also the first to envi-

sage, to look forward to, and to prepare for that goal. And it pursued that goal steadily, without ambivalence, patiently and without violence.[22]

Jeffries was just as enthusiastic about Ceylon's special claims:

Ceylon provides the classic example of how with good sense and good will, two peoples can carry through the extremely difficult and delicate transition from a ruler-subject relationship to an equal partnership.

Ceylon has been the prototype and model for the new Commonwealth of the latter part of the twentieth century. In Ceylon the British learnt, by trial and error, the art of colonial administration; but they learnt, also, the wisdom of relinquishing control when it was no longer tolerable by a people willing and able to maintain itself as an independent state.[23]

As we reflect on this, we see that what was happening was that the responsibility for a particular set of events — the rapid progress in decolonisation in the 1960s — was being attributed to the initiatives and intentions of those in Whitehall who had participated in the late 1940s in the making of policy on Ceylon's future. The fact, however, is that there was nothing which amounted to a consistent application of a policy on decolonisation; instead there were *ad hoc* decisions taken to resolve each particular crisis as it arose. True enough, these thereafter provided a rough pattern of action for the future, applicable as a remedy whenever a colonial crisis arose which called for a re-arrangement of power, and this in turn evolved into something approximating to principles of reform. But when it was no longer thought possible to resist pressure for decolonisation, and indeed once that process was rapidly accelerated, notions of a desired set of principles simply disappeared.

By the mid-1950s, however, Sri Lanka's claim to the status of a model colony had been devalued. Not merely was Ghana now playing a similar role for Africa, but, more important still, Sri Lanka's politics were in a state of turmoil and the political assumptions that had gone into the making of the 'model colony' concept were being abandoned in rapid succession in the heady aftermath of the general election of 1956, which brought S. W. R. D. Bandaranaike to power. Sri Lanka in 1947–8 had been, in contrast to the Indian sub-continent and Burma, an oasis of stability, peace and order. The transfer of power has been smooth and peaceful, and one saw very little of the divisions and bitterness which were tearing at the recent independence of the other countries of South Asia which had once formed part of the Raj.

Within a few months of independence in 1948 one of the most intractable political issues in Sri Lanka — the problem of the indigenous Tamils, which had absorbed the energies of its politicians and the British themselves to an inordinate degree since the early 1920s — seemed on the way to amicable settlement. G. G.

Ponnambalam, who had led the Tamils in their political campaigns since his entry into the State Council in 1934, became a member of the Cabinet bringing with him into the government the bulk of the leadership and members of the Tamil Congress. In so doing he had helped convert D. S. Senanayake's government into what was very much a consensus of moderate political opinion in the country.

In retrospect it would seem that the rights of minorities did not receive adequate protection in the Soulbury Constitution — which, unlike India's constitution, lacked a bill of rights — but at the transfer of power the constitutional guarantees against legislation likely to discriminate against minorities (Section 29[2][b]) seemed sufficiently reassuring to them, largely because of the trust and confidence they reposed in D. S. Senanayake.

In the years after independence, one of the important pre-occupations of the government under D. S. Senanayake's leadership was the subordination of communal differences to the common goal of fostering democratic institutions and strengthening the foundations of nationhood. The primary aim was the establishment of a stable equilibrium of ethnic forces within a multi-ethnic policy. For many years it seemed as though these policies had succeeded, but beneath the surface powerful and insidious forces were at work. Ideals of reconciliation and harmony gave way before the stresses released by the divisive forces for language and religion. With this there was a tendency for the Sinhalese to equate their own ethnic nationalism with the wider one of a Sri Lanka nationalism and to assume that these were one and the same.

The 'model colony' concept had as its foundation another version of nationalism: a Ceylon or Sri Lankan nationalism, the special feature of which was an emphasis on the reconciliation of the competing interests of the island's various ethnic and religious groups. This would come about through the establishment of a stable equilibrium of political forces based on a softening of Sinhalese dominance. There would be recognition of the legitimate rights of the minorities, and an emphasis on secularism, i.e. a refusal to mix state power with religion, despite the acceptance — in a decidedly low profiled way — of the state's special responsibility for the fostering of Buddhism. (Its most influential advocate at the time of the transfer of power was D. S. Senanayake.) In 1948 this version of nationalism seemed a viable alternative to the competing ethnic nationalisms of the Sinhalese and Tamils, and held out the prospect of peace and stability in the vital phase of independence. The constitution devised for the transfer of power and the political structure at independence reflected this balance of forces. But the stability of this balance was only apparent not real, and was easily upset even though this did not seem likely in 1948.

This Sri Lanka or Ceylonese nationalism had a crucial flaw. It was basically élitist in conception, and it had little support outside the political establishment. It required Senanayake's enormous personal prestige and consummate statecraft to make it viable. With the elections of 1956 there began a purposeful attempt to demolish the balance of political forces, which Senanayake had tried hard to establish and sustain as the basis for the post-colonial Sri Lanka policy. What this amounted to was a rejection of the concept of a Sri Lanka nationalism, which Senanayake had striven to nurture, and to substitute for it a more democratic and populist form of nationalism. The latter was, at the same time, fundamentally divisive in its impact on the country. This shift was consistent with the essence of party politics in which, given a common basis of agreement, the numerically larger group could peacefully alter the power structure. The Sinhalese Buddhist majority, long dormant, began to assert its national dominance.

The basic instability of the balance of forces which went to form the essence of Senanayake's scheme of things in a 'model colony' sprang also from another source. There was no great emphasis on far-reaching changes in the economic structure inherited from the British. This economic structure had taken firm root in the period of British rule, and the process of introducing changes in it was more difficult than seemed likely, while any hope of dismantling it was outside the realm of political politics. Besides, the system itself was still viable, and its potential for expansion was, if not undiminishing, at least reasonably good. It was also true that the political leadership of the day was reluctant to make changes in an economic system with which its own interests were identified. The result was that in the economic structure, as in the political, there was an emphasis on maintaining the *status quo*.

It is ironical that in the period after 1956, just when the ideologues of the new Commonwealth were most effusive in their praises of Sri Lanka's role as the 'model colony', its essential features relative to the balance of forces in the island's politics had been successfully undermined and systematically rejected within the island.

NOTES

1. Sir Charles Jeffries, *O. E. G.: a biography of Sir Oliver Goonetileke* (London, 1969).
2. H. Duncan Hall, *Commonwealth: a history of the British Commonwealth of Nations* (London, 1971), 795.
3. Sir Charles Jeffries, *Ceylon: The Path to Independence* (London, 1962), preface.
4. Duncan Hall, op.cit., 795.
5. Mansergh, *Survey of British Commonwealth Affairs: Problems of Wartime*

Co-operation and Post-war change, 1939–1952 (Oxford University Press, 1958), 246.

6. This point is discussed in H. Duncan Hall, op.cit., 797.
7. The Lanka Sama Samaja Party was, since its foundation in 1935, the main Marxist party. It had two representatives in the State Council, and attracted some fellow-travellers as well. In 1940 the party split into two factions, the Trotskyists and the Stalinists. Of these the Stalinists co-operated in the war effort after the Soviet Union entered the conflict.
8. Layton was appointed Commander-in-Chief of the British forces in the Island on 5 March 1942. His authority was not restricted to the armed forces but extended to the civil government as well — he was authorised to use the Governor's reserve powers under the constitution to any extent he desired or thought fit.
9. For discussion of this see my article 'The Transfer of Power in Sri Lanka; a review of British perspectives', *Ceylon Journal of Historical and Social Studies*, IV (1 & 2), 8–19.
10. Ibid
11. See my article 'D. S. Senanayake and the Passage to Dominion Status, 1942–1947', *Sri Lanka Journal of Social Sciences*, III (2).
12. Colonial Office despatches series 54, vol. 980, file 55541, part I (hereafter CO 54/980, etc.) Caldecott's 'personal and most secret' letter of 23 December 1941 to Gent, a senior civil servant at the Colonial Office.
13. CO 54/986, file 55541/5, secret and personal telegram from Monck-Mason-Moore to Hall (Secretary of State for the Colonies), 17 October, 1945.
14. CO 54/986, file 55541, Minutes of Cabinet Meeting of 29 October 1945.
15. See my article 'The Transfer of Power in Sri Lanka — a review of British Perspectives', *CJHSS*, IV (1 & 2), 8–19. See also Sir Charles Jeffries, *The Transfer of Power* (London 1960), especially ch. 8, 'Ceylon Crosses the Line', 57–69; *Ceylon: the Path to Independence* (London, 1962) and *O. E. G. : a Biography of Sir Oliver Goonetileke* (London, 1969).
16. See my article 'D. S. Senanayake and the Passage to Dominion Status' op.cit.
17. H. Duncan Hall, op.cit, 802.
18. Addison's speech *House of Lords Debates* Vol. 152 Coll. 1204–6, cited in Mansergh, *Survey of British Commonwealth Affairs, Problems of Wartime Co-operation and Post-war Change, 1939–1952*. p. 246
19. Sir Charles Jeffries *The Transfer of Power*.
20. Mansergh *op.cit*. p. 246.
21. As early as 1945 Martin Wight in his book *The Development of The Legislative Council, 1606–1945* (London, 1946), p. 14, referred to Ceylon's role as the constitutional 'pioneer of the non-European dependencies' and the 'senior colony of the new empire'.
22. Hall *Commonwealth*. p. 795.
23. Sir Charles Jeffries. *Ceylon, The Path to Independence*, preface.

THE DYNAMICS OF POLITICAL INTEGRATION AND DISINTEGRATION[1]

James Manor

Some years ago, Myron Weiner set forth five definitions or types of political integration. First, there is *national integration*, 'the process of bringing together culturally and socially discrete groups into a single territorial unit and the establishment of a national identity'. This use of the term is generally applied to 'an ethnically plural society' and refers to the need for a 'sense of territorial nationality which overshadows — or eliminates — subordinate parochial loyalties'. This type of integration is closely related to a second, *territorial integration*. This refers to 'the problem of establishing national central authority over subordinate political units or regions'. It involves 'the subjective feelings which individuals belonging to different social groups or historically distinct political units have toward the nation'.

A third type of political integration he called *élite-mass integration*. This refers to 'the problem of linking government with the governed'. Between the élite and the mass, the apex and base of the political system, there are 'marked differences in aspirations and values'. These differences do not in themselves represent disintegration or a lack of integration 'so long as those who are governed accept the right of the governors to govern'. Integration between the élite and the mass 'occurs not when differences among the two disappear, but when a pattern of authority and consent is established'.

A fourth type is termed *value integration*, referring to 'the minimum value consensus necessary to maintain a social order'. This may entail 'ends values', values concerning appropriate collective goals. Or it may involve ideas concerning means, 'for the achievement of goals and for resolving conflicts'. In either case, the concern here is with 'desirable and undesirable conduct'. Finally, there is the matter of *integrative behavior* which involves 'the capacity of people in a society to organize for some common purposes'. In some societies, this capacity tends to be a near monopoly of the élite(s). In others, people throughout the population possess the will and ability to organise with others.[2] These then are the five types of political integration which Weiner identified. Taken together, they refer to that '*which holds a society or a political system together*'.[3]

This essay is divided into two parts, each of which is intended to serve a distinct purpose. The first offers a cautionary reminder to analysts of political integration and disintegration in South Asia of the daunting complexities which await them. It briefly examines ways in which integrative and disintegrative forces can impinge upon the political system and upon one another. It discusses the ambiguities and contradictions which can emerge from this process. The second part of the essay focuses mainly upon the broad theme of élite-mass integration and disintegration in India and, to a less extent, Pakistan and Sri Lanka since Independence. We concentrate primarily upon élite-mass integration partly because some other contributors are dealing with other forms of integration, but also because we believe that its importance is often underestimated. The discussion seeks to extend our understanding of the survival of open, parliamentary politics in India (as against its collapse in Pakistan) during the first two decades after 1947. It also deals with the threats to its survival which have arisen more recently, and analyses the recent restructuring of Sri Lanka's political institutions, which is intended to promote some forms of integration while thwarting or creating alternatives to others. We then discuss the impact which similar changes might have upon India's crisis of élite-mass integration. In the course of the discussion, we shall propose an amendment to Weiner's views of political integration.

No matter which definition(s) of political integration we use, we soon find ourselves in a thicket of complexities. It is impossible within our present scope to present anything approaching an exhaustive list of the forms in which the problem of political integration has manifested itself in South Asia, or of the ways in which the various forms of integration have made their impact upon the political process. The purpose of this section is to present several examples of the ambiguities and paradoxes that can arise.

Any comparison of the different nations of South Asia will soon collide with the problem of scale. When Hugh Tinker jokingly told this writer that Sri Lanka was 'only a third the size of Trichinopoly District', he was of course exaggerating. But a few Indian districts (though not Tiruchirapalli) *are* larger than Sri Lanka. India is more than forty times the size of Sri Lanka and eight times larger than Pakistan or Bangladesh. In discussions of political integration and disintegration — particularly in terms of élite and mass — India's regional arenas offer the most helpful comparison with her neighbours (although India as a whole can hardly be disregarded). But even comparisons among India's regions raise problems. Bihar, Maharashtra, Madhya Pradesh, West Bengal and Andhra Pradesh are all three to four times larger than Punjab (which is roughly the size of Sri Lanka). Add to that the cases of Uttar Pradesh (twice the size of Andhra and

West Bengal) and of Himachal Pradesh and Kashmir (one-third the size of Punjab) and we see how daunting the problem can be.

These differences in scale generate radical contrasts in the process of political integration. It is well known that identifications with linguistic and religious groups in Sri Lanka have impeded national integration. It is not our purpose here to enter the debate on whether these identifications are best seen as primordial or ethnic or whatever.[4] We wish simply to observe that in Sri Lanka the most compelling of what are sometimes called 'primordial' loyalties has at most times been not the identification with a person's caste but with his linguistic group. When Sinhalese use the word *jati* (meaning their own 'kind' or 'ilk'), they usually refer not to their sub-caste or endogamous group as in India but to the Sinhalese collectivity.[5] When this is expressed in English, as it often is, the word 'race' is routinely used to refer to the Sinhalese — even by leaders who know that the varied ethnic origins of the Lion 'race' make the use of the term absurd.[6] This tendency among the Sinhalese majority (72.0 per cent of the island's population) has naturally intensified suspicion and solidarity among the Ceylon Tamil (11.2 per cent) and Indian Tamil (9.3 per cent) minorities. These suspicions have at times reached such a pitch that the balkanization of the island has seemed a real, although not a strong, possibility.

When the balkanisation of post-Independence India is discussed, however, we find that so-called 'primordial' loyalties have on balance had the *opposite* effect. The question of scale is crucial here. If the threat of balkanization is to become serious in India, sentiment favoring separation from the Indian union must develop in one or more states. (If discontents develop within sub-divisions of states, they lead to demands for secession from the state, not from India.) For that to happen, great solidarity at the state level is required. But it is precisely this solidarity within the states that has never materialized. This is partly the result of sensible policies from New Delhi. By allowing the reorganization of state boundaries in 1956 so that they were roughly congruent to lines separating linguistic groups, India's leaders removed the main grievance which was available to would-be secessionists in the regions. By avoiding severe inequities in the distribution of resources among states ever since, they have helped to prevent serious discontent in the states.

But the actions of the authorities at the Centre have played a comparatively minor role in this process. Intense solidarity has not developed at the state level in India mainly because of political and social fragmentation within individual states. Perhaps the most potent cause of this fragmentation are the so-called 'primordial' loyalties. These may bind people to a religious group, a tribe, a clan, a *jati* (usually meaning, in India, an endogamous group), or a cluster of *jatis* under an occupational or 'caste' label (such as 'Jadhav' or 'Vokkaliga'). There is also more than a faint whiff of the 'primordial' about their identifications with groups of *jatis* under what we might call stratum-oriented labels such as the 'backward classes', particularly when we see how such labels are made known to people through the mediation of 'caste' leaders, rallies and *sanghas* and through rhetoric heavily laced with 'caste' references.[7] The fragmentation which these and other forces cause within the state-level political arenas in India prevents the kind of tight political integration at that level which might threaten national integration. So although the Indian union may not be so tightly integrated as some other federal systems, this is no cause for concern. It need not be so tightly integrated because of the rather loose integration within the arenas that form its constituent parts.

To return to our original point, the kind of 'primordial' loyalties which impede national integration in Sri Lanka ease the task of national integration in India by impeding integration and the development of solidarity at the state level in India. The role of 'primordial' loyalties varies according to the scale of the national arena.

If we look at one of these examples from a slightly different angle, a further set of complexities emerges. It is possible to argue — by using different definitions of political integration — that Sinhala Buddhist chauvinism in Sri Lanka has operated *simultaneously* as (*a*) a force for disintegration, (*b*) a force for integration and (*c*) an alternative to integration. Indeed, it is possible that the situation is even more complicated than that, but the picture is already sufficiently byzantine to illustrate the need for caution in discussions of political integration and disintegration.

It should already be clear how Sinhala Buddhist chauvinism operates as a force for disintegration. It generates suspicions among Tamils which in turn feed the Sinhalese suspicions that began the cycle. It undermines 'the process of bringing together culturally and socially discrete groups . . . and the establishment of a national identity', Weiner's description of national integration. Indeed, a prominent element in Sinhalese chauvinism is the equating of the 'nation' of Lanka with the Sinhalese 'race' or, very often, with the Buddhist faithful among the Sinhalese.[8] The poisonous bigotry that is generated makes it exceedingly difficult for Sinhalese and Tamils to work together for common purposes, and places severe difficulties in the way of integrative behavior.

But can this same chauvinism also be seen as a force for integration? If the promotion of integration between the rulers and the ruled, between the élite and the mass, means cultivating in the minds of the mass acceptance of the authority of the élite — then the answer is a qualified 'yes'. Clearly some of the ruled (principally the Tamils) will be alienated by national leaders' use of Sinhalese chauvinism. But most of the ruled, most members of the large Sinhalese majority, have usually responded warmly to its use by their leaders. This has solidified the position of Sinhalese leaders at the apex of their parties and the political system. And to this observer at least, it appears to have fostered mass acceptance of the party system and the parliamentary system among the Sinhalese, when these systems (particularly the former) had very few achievements to recommend them. This same chauvinism has also helped leaders to overcome divisions among Sinhalese: divisions between Kandyans and low-country Sinhalese, between rich and poor, between urban and rural dwellers, and most especially between 'castes' or clusters of 'castes'. The use of chauvinism by Sinhalese politicians helped them to establish and maintain 'a pattern of authority and consent' among most of the island's people, especially between 1955 and 1970. It has aided élite-mass integration.

And yet if we define élite-mass integration differently, it becomes possible to argue that Sinhalese chauvinism has also served as a substitute for and alternative to political integration. This leads us into a small comment upon Weiner's views on political integration. His discussion of integration in general and of élite-mass integration in particular is pitched more at the level of ideas and perceptions than at the level of interaction. (This is also true of the writing of those upon whom he draws in this essay.) In dealing with élite-mass integration, for example, he speaks of 'differences in aspirations and values' and 'a pattern of authority and consent'. Nowhere in his comments on the various forms of integration is a distinction drawn between integration at the level of ideas and integration at the level of interaction, but phrases such as these tend to emphasize the former over the latter. This complaint cannot be made about the rest of Weiner's work on India, but in this essay he says very little about interaction, about people and institutions (formal and informal) at different levels and in different sectors of the political system being knitted together by interactions and by reciprocal rights and duties expressed in action.

The distinction between ideas and interaction is important, as the Sri Lanka case illustrates. Sinhalese chauvinism has promoted élite-mass integration at the level of ideas by generating support among the majority for Sinhalese leaders and the political system. But leading politicians in Sri Lanka have failed miserably at providing people below the level of the small national political élite with opportunities for substantive participation in the power game. Power under all of Sri Lanka's governments has remained so highly centralized that the organizations of the two major parties have remained extremely flimsy. Leaders at the apex have refused to delegate authority and to distribute, rationally and routinely, substantial quantities of political spoils to lower echelons within their parties. As a result, they failed to forge strong transactional links with persons of ambition and influence from local power centres throughout the island. The national élite's parsimony with power is also apparent in the chronic weakness of intermediate and local councils in Sri Lanka.[9] If an integrating force is that which, in Weiner's words, '*holds a society and a political system together*',[10] then transactional bonds between people at different levels in the political system have done precious little integrating in Sri Lanka.

How has the national political élite maintained its dominance through more than three decades, eight general elections, an abortive coup and an abortive insurrection? The answer is far from simple. Part of the explanation has to do with the curious persistence of deference to the élite, and to certain individuals and families within it, a subject which must await discussion on another occasion. But in large measure, the élite and the political system have survived through the use by Prime Ministers of Sinhala Buddhist chauvinism as an alternative means of maintaining their authority in the eyes of the Sinhalese majority.[11] Élite-mass integration at the level of ideas can thus be used as a substitute for élite-mass integration at the level of action and transaction.

If different forces can play different and even contradictory roles at the same time, it is also true that the same force can play contradictory roles at different times. Consider one example which was much in the news in India during the late 1970s — promises of preferment in education and government employment for certain allegedly and often genuinely underprivileged social groups. The complications that can arise from such promises will be more clearly discernible if we take an example from some years ago. In 1956, territories which had previously been governed by five different administrative authorities were merged to form the enlarged state of Mysore, now called Karnataka. The cultivating groups, which enjoyed a dominant position in villages throughout most of the state by virtue of economic and numerical strength (although they were never more than a large minority in any district), belonged to the Lingayat sect. This sect also contained a large number of non-cultivating groups, including two smaller, highly urbanized and traditionally literate groups: the priestly Jangamas and the trading Banajigas. Relations between these urban groups on one hand and the cultivating groups on the other had not always been untroubled. Indeed, relations between the Banajigas and the formidable Sadar cultivating group had been marked by considerable hostility. At the unification of Karnataka in 1956, it was clearly in the interests of leading Lingayat politicians to find a means of bridging these divisions. If they could do so (and if they could arrive at an understanding with the other powerful landed group, the Vokkaligas), they could count on Lingayat ascendancy in Karnataka for many years to come. Lingayat unity was a particularly compelling notion to their most prominent leader, S. Nijalingappa. He came from the rather small Banajiga group, and if traditional divisions came to the fore, he had little hope of retaining the leadership.

One key element of Nijalingappa's campaign to build Lingayat solidarity was his promise to give Lingayats preferential treatment in allotting scholarships, places in schools and jobs in the public sector. This had an especially strong appeal among prosperous cultivating groups like the Sadars who had been unable to make the kind of gains in education and urban employment that they desired or that the traditionally literate Banajigas and Jangamas had made. In response to these promises, Sadars and other cultivators gave Nijalingappa and the Lingayat cause their firm support. Lingayats soon gained a pre-eminent position in Karnataka politics that looked wellnigh unassailable. The promises of preferment helped to bind together different Lingayat groups that might otherwise have been antagonists. And since Lingayats could control or influence less powerful groups by persuasion or intimidation, these promises also helped to knit together large numbers of people who might otherwise have remained unintegrated. The promises also helped to bind together Lingayats who had lived under different administrative authorities and had thus had little or no contact with one another on a political level (or, in many cases, on any other level). The promises of preferment were clearly an integrating force.

As the years after the Lingayat takeover in Karnataka passed, however, certain questions began to arise about the promises. They had initially been presented with a great fanfare and the implicit blessing of leading Lingayat *swamijis* who are deeply revered by members of the sect. This generated euphoria and soaring expectations. And yet by the late 1960s, it was becoming apparent that while there were enough places in schools to absorb ambitious Lingayat youths, there were not enough scholarships or rooms in hostels or places in élite professional schools to satisfy their inflated aspirations. Those students who obtained places in colleges and professional schools which were expanded and created to meet the demand found that these institutions tended to be run mainly for the profits that their Lingayat patrons could make from the parents of Lingayat students. In 1973, a very well-known Lingayat politician interrupted an inspirational lecture in English to this writer on the evils of bribery to negotiate in Kannada (a language he thought this writer could not understand) a bribe of Rs. 5,000 from a man who sought a place for his son in a medical school. This mixing of piety and graft, to which Lingayats were subjected quite routinely, rankled with many. Graduates of schools and colleges often found that their education was of little avail in finding employment in the urban literate sector. There were certainly not enough jobs in the public sector, and those that existed went to candidates with the best connections. As dissatisfaction grew, particularly among Lingayat cultivating groups, the old suspicions of the urban Banajigas and Jangamas were revived. Their children had done better in the race for advancement, partly because the urban, literate environment in which they were raised gave them a headstart but also because their families had close ties to men of influence. The merits of even the best Banajigas did not impress groups like the Sadars who smelled a conspiracy to defraud them. By 1972, widespread disaffection had developed under the surface of events among agrarian groups of decisive importance to the survival of Lingayat raj. When Devaraj Urs became Chief Minister in that year and mounted a cleverly planned but perfectly obvious assault on Lingayat power, it crumbled in a matter of weeks to the astonishment of most observers. It crumbled because the promises of preferment with which Nijalingappa had once united Lingayats had become a force for disintegration.

The Lingayats are not an exceptional case. Politicians in India have often used promises of preferment to unify and mobilize supporters. It has lately been particularly fashionable to do so among the 'backward classes' in various parts of India, particularly in the Hindi belt. And yet this is inevitably a two-edged sword which can gain temporary political advantage but which is sure to divide and disillusion constituents in the long term. Such promises are always made to populous groups who have been less than famously successful in the quest for education and public sector jobs. But financial and institutional constraints make it patently impossible to avoid failure in meeting the aspirations which are generated. A shrewd politician will see the need to prepare for the inevitable backlash by providing other advantages to his followers to mitigate their resentment. But few have had the insight to do so.[12]

Indeed, there is reason to believe that the case of the Lingayats rather understates the potential complexity of the problem. The promises to them came at a comparatively early stage in Karnataka's political development. Social groups less advanced than the Lingayats were as yet insufficiently politicized to react strongly against these promises. And the people to whom the promises were made were the most powerful groups, economically and politically, in the state. The only group more advanced than the Lingayats who could have seen the promises as a threat to dispossess them were the Brahmins. But they were economically weak and constituted less than 4 per cent of the state's population. Thus the Lingayats faced no serious resistance from those above and below them in the socio-economic order.

More recent cases in which politicians have used such promises to draw groups into political competition suggest that after 1970 or so, the process has become less simple. In Bihar in the late 1970s, for example, a government led by Karpoori Thakur came to power on the basis of support from the 'backward classes' — people from the middle and lower-middle strata of rural society. They faced opposition both from above and from below. The 'twice-born' castes who stood above them had gained a disproportionately large share of the political spoils since Independence. They had also enjoyed great success in education and jobs in government service, partly on merit and partly by political influence. They felt threatened by the new government, particularly by the promises of preferment for the 'backward classes' which were a central element in its program.

The people beneath the 'backward classes' in the traditional hierarchy, the scheduled castes, also felt anxious. They feared that their quotas of places in schools and government service might lose their significance if similar quotas were created for those less deprived than they. The Karpoori Thakur government might have overcome scheduled caste suspicions by making concessions to them and by creating social and economic programs to uplift them. If this had been done before the promises of 'backward class' preferment were loudly trumpeted, it might have prevented a split in what was potentially a solid majority coalition. But from the start, the government stressed preferment so heavily that it inflamed the political atmosphere. It was thus unable to consolidate and extend its social base, and within a few months it had collapsed.[13] Even the temporary advantages gained from the promises of preferment can be undercut if care is not taken to limit their disintegrative impact on potentially broader coalitions.

Further examples could be presented, but those already enumerated should suffice to show how fraught with complexity discussions of integration and disintegration are. What we take to be an integrative force can unexpectedly change shape. It can turn back upon itself, upon the politicians who seek to exploit it and upon political analysts who seek to understand it.

Difficulties such as these assail discussions of political integration and disintegration, even when the scope of analysis is quite limited. The problems are greater when the scope is extended. But if it is impossible to escape these complexities, it is also impossible to avoid the large, inexhaustible questions which a region like South Asia generates. The remarks which follow probe two such questions. First, how do we explain the survival — at least to the beginning of the 1980s — of the open, multi-party parliamentary system in India? What did India possess that was missing in Pakistan and many other new nations that abandoned the open, multi-party system? And second, what has happened in recent years in India to generate the anxieties which many observers — including this one writing in the immediate aftermath of the 1980 Lok Sabha election — feel about the survival of that open system? A discussion of patterns of élite-mass integration and disintegration can carry us some way toward answers to these questions.

In the comments that follow, the distinction between political integration at the level of ideas and integration at the level of interaction, mentioned in the previous section of this essay, will be important. A political system (or organization) which is well-integrated at the level of ideas is one in which 'a pattern of authority and consent is established',[14] in which those in the mass accept or at least acquiesce to the authority of the élite(s). In this discussion, the term 'consent' will not be interpreted so broadly as to allow it to refer to people who have acquiesced in élite authority under coercion. A Hobbesian definition of 'consent' would admit such persons to the category of consenters, but Weiner probably would not. He and other writers on this subject are silent on this point.

Élite-mass integration at the level of interaction can be accomplished by various types of political systems or organizations. Marxist parties operating through cadres have shown themselves capable of this in some places — although not in South Asia, with the possible exception of West Bengal after 1977. Élite-mass integration has tended to occur in South Asia by way of transactional links, ties based upon mutual interest, between the élite(s) at or near the apex of the system, and sub-élites at various levels between the apex and the base. Political patronage and the endorsement of a political party are passed down from higher to lower levels of the system in exchange for political support from those lower levels. Spoils can be channelled downward through formal institutions of state or informally through a party structure. But they must be distributed rationally, reliably and with reasonable regularity. For such a system to be well-integrated, people operating at or near the local level must be knitted into these partronage networks. Those so integrated must exist in reasonably large numbers and be present in most parts of the spatial arena in question. In South Asia, this kind of integration has only developed to any great extent in India.

It must be emphasised at the outset that by separating and contrasting two types of integration — one the product of ideas and the other the product of interactions — we are creating something of a false dichotomy. Both are inextricably bound up together. It is precisely for this reason that in his most famous essay, the man whom we honor in this volume spoke of political 'languages' and 'idioms'. He found the ambiguity of these words 'quite fitting'[15] because it blurred the distinction between perceptions and behavior. As he rightly believed, the two can never be wholly separated. In the present essay, we artificially overstate the distinction between ideas and interactions in order to make a point. The point is that ideas have received far too much emphasis and interactions too little in most explanations of what held the Indian political system together during the first two decades or so after independence. It is a question of emphasis, not of 'either-or'.

There is also the question of *which* ideas were more crucial in ensuring the survival of open, parliamentary politics in that period. It is often argued (sometimes by implication) that during the struggle for independence, people from a wide range of regional and social backgrounds in India were strongly influenced in their perceptions of politics by their adherence to Gandhian principles and by their experience of the democratic process both in the Indian National Congress and in the elected councils of the British Raj. The democratic, libertarian, permissive side of the split personality of the Raj — there was an authoritarian side to it too, of course — is seen to have fostered in and beyond the Indian middle classes a commitment to liberal ideals. The British willingness at most times to tolerate a reasonably free press, their commitment at most times to the due process of law, the creation of universities to convey a sophisticated understanding of the principles on which the metropolitan power conducted its public life, the admission of Indians into the bueaucratic, judicial and ultimately the representative institutions of the Raj — all of these things inculcated in a great many Indians liberal habits of mind. Because the people involved in this process came from diverse religious backgrounds, it is argued that many (though by no means an overwhelming majority) of these people acquired a rather secularized outlook.

These habits of mind are said to have developed not only among urban middle-class Indians, but to some extent among those rural élites — predominantly landed, cultivating groups — who played an increasingly prominent role in the national movement in most parts of India from the mid-1930s onward. These shared perceptions entailed a sense of belonging to a common Indian nation and a belief that regional loyalties were superseded by the link with the nation. In other words, they promoted national and territorial integration. They are also seen to have inspired integrative behavior and to have provided a good deal more than a 'minimum value consensus' among important élites on 'legal norms . . . the legitimacy of the constitutional framework and the procedures by which it should operate'.[16] These habits of mind are said to have linked people at different levels of the political system by providing a common sense of national identity and a common set of procedures on how the business of the Congress should be conducted. The national struggle was genuinely a mass movement only in limited areas of India and then only intermittently.[17] But these shared perceptions held by people at every level of the political system, including a great many at and near the local level, are seen as a major force in integrating élite and mass in India.

There is no denying that this view has considerable validity. But again, the important question is: how much emphasis should it receive in explanations of the survival of open, parliamentary politics in India between 1947 and 1967? Our view is that it has been overemphasized in two ways. First, ideas had less importance than interactions in holding the system together in this period. Second, while this set of ideas or habits of mind has some importance in integrating that system, another set which was closely bound up with the interactions in question had more importance.

It is generally acknowledged that after India gained Independence, many elements in the pre-Independence nationalist approach to politics declined in importance. The 'saintly idiom' declined mainly because the unique bearer of the idiom was murdered in 1948, but also because its relevance to a self-governing parliamentary system was limited.[18] Agitational politics declined sharply since it was inconsistent both with the new rules of politics and with the national consensus that the Congress Party claimed to represent. But what was more surprising and far more revealing was the crumbling of the other great pillar of the pre-Independence Congress, the constructive work program. There was no diminution after 1947 in the need for efforts for Harijan uplift, *khadi* and other cottage industries, village sanitation and so forth. But the level of effort declined markedly.

This appears to have happened for at least two reasons. First, the impression seems to have got about that the goals of the constructive work program could be better realized through the initiative of the state, now that Congress held power. This could be interpreted as a sign that Congressmen were becoming inspired with the ideals of socialism and the notion that the poor were now able to bend the resources of the state to their needs. But a closer look at the doings of politicians in at least one state — and the comparatively innocent, politically genteel state of Mysore at that — has left this observer feeling too jaded to accept this view. Politicians' interest in 'socialism' had less to do with an acceptance of the Laskian or Nehruvian vision of social democracy than with a desire to get their hands on new resources for the spoils game by extending the state sector. Corroboration for this view can be found in the paltry contribution which the state sector made either to Nehru's dream of greater social justice or to the goals of the constructive work program.

The second reason for the decline in constructive work was the decline of constructive workers. The people who had been the driving force behind campaigns for temperance, Harijan uplift and the like found that they, their skills and their idealism were not needed or wanted in the post-Independence Congress. They were displaced by people of a different type who had come into Congress during the last decade or so before, or soon after, Independence. These newcomers were people with influence in local power centers, usually with land and connections among relatives and fellow-castemen who also had land, lent money and could muster clout. They were drawn to Congress by the scent of spoils and Congress leaders at and below the state level took them in because they needed them to win elections. Most constructive workers, most genuine Gandhians would not or could not turn themselves into harvesters of votes which the new rules of politics demanded. Some could and did, but in the process made so many compromises with parochialism, bribery and the like that they ceased to be good Gandhians.[19]

Within a few years of coming to power, a once-great movement became a political machine — a machine headed by a man who found machines unedifying, but a machine nonetheless. In the transition, it jettisoned many patently irrelevant things inherited from the nationalist struggle such as its agitational techniques. But a lot of ideas which had considerable relevance to a free India were jettisoned as well by party workers operating below the rarefied atmosphere of the party high command. These included not only constructive work but the vision of radical agrarian reform which Nehru and others continued to affirm.

What then, at the level of ideas, were the main integrating forces in Indian politics over the first two decades or so after Independence? What ideas held the party — and, since the party was so pervasive, the political system — together? Liberal or democratic or socialist or Gandhian ideals provide part of the answer, but a rather minor part. The main integrating ideas were opportunism, self-aggrandizement, the impulse to enter into patron-client relationships and to forge deals via the mutual pursuit of the main chance. But these ideas possess less importance in themselves than they do as guides to interaction. And it is at the level of interaction that the integration of the Indian polity in the first two decades after Independence is best understood.

This is a useful place to ask again what India had between 1947 and the mid-1960s which was missing in Pakistan where open, parliamentary politics failed to survive. Perhaps most obviously, India had Nehru until 1964 while Pakistan lost Jinnah in 1948 and found no replacement. But even individuals of their stature are not of decisive importance in such massive historical processes. India had territorial unity which the old Pakistan lacked. This was a serious handicap for Pakistan, as time has shown. Important elements of India's élites were more secularized in their outlook than were the élites that created the Islamic state of Pakistan. But while these secular values bolstered open, parliamentary politics in India's plural society, it can be plausibly argued that Islam contributed to national integration in Pakistan and could thus have aided the development of parliamentary politics there.

What of liberal values? After the transfer of power, were the lawyers and judges of Karachi less committed to the rule and due process of law than their counterparts in Bombay or Bhuvaneswar? Were the journalists of Dacca less concerned with press freedom than those of Madras or Lucknow? Were Lahore's legislators less keen on representative institutions, were its academics less protective of their right of free enquiry than those of Bangalore or Calcutta? The answer may not be a flat 'no', but it is not far from it. It must be said, however, that liberal values did not penetrate so effectively beyond the urban professional élites to landed élites in Pakistan — most especially in old West Pakistan — as in India. There were two main reasons for this. First the socio-economic structure of West Pakistan provided infertile soil for such ideas. Land was distributed quite inequitably, and great power was concentrated in the hands of a super-élite which provided many of the urban liberals but which behaved very illiberally toward subordinate groups in rural areas. Secondly, old West Pakistan lacked a political organization which could act as the bearer of liberal ideas and could penetrate significantly among the rural population.

This brings us to our main point. The thing of decisive importance which India possessed and Pakistan lacked during the first two decades after independence was a ruling party with a formidable organization operating on the principle of representation at every level of political system as the main integrating force in the new polity. Neither Jinnah's Muslim League nor any subsequent party organization in Pakistan (or indeed Bangladesh) ever possessed the substance and penetration which were required if it was to assist substantially in élite-mass integration (or any other form of integration) in those polities. Had such an organization existed in Pakistan, the death of Jinnah and the territorial division might well have been weathered successfully.

In India during the years before Independence and particularly before council entry in 1937, ideas *had* played a crucial integrating role in the Congress. Gandhi did not just invite Congressmen to commit themselves to a canon of ideas. By requiring them to undergo certain rites of passage, most especially *satyagraha*, he forced persons from widely varied backgrounds to undergo shared adversity which caused a great number of them to form a shared commitment to the ideas that he preached,[20] a commitment which for a time at least was quite genuine. Those who shrank from the rigors of the rites of passage usually lost influence in the Congress, so that the organization was able to maintain discipline and adherence to these ideas.

But after the mid-1930s when the Congress began to seem the likely successor to the Raj and attracted opportunists, the importance of the Gandhian canon waned. By the mid-1950s in most regions of India, the Congress was firmly in the thrall of persons drawn from or dependent upon dominant landed groups. They naturally affirmed their commitment to 'democracy, socialism and secularism' and cheerfully passed legislation embodying Nehru's vision of social and economic reform in the Lok Sabha and the state assemblies. But in rural areas, they either acquiesced in the efforts of prosperous cultivating and money-lending groups and high and upper-middle castes to thwart the laws' implementation, or (more often) used their influence with civil servants to assist in the thwarting.

It would be an oversimplification to say that liberal habits of mind were swallowed by self-aggrandizement and horse-trading among powerful groups. In fact the two modes of perception and behavior existed alongside one another during most of the first two decades after Independence. Erstwhile liberals at and below the state level had to learn how to wheel and deal in order to survive politically. Seekers after loaves and fishes had to learn to exert leverage within the legislatures and the Congress in accordance with parliamentary procedure and the principles of representation and majority rule. Indeed, *within* the various committees of Congress and *within* the legislatures in that period, there was very little conflict between the liberal and transactional modes.

But in saying that we have not said enough. We only get at the essential logic of Indian politics in that period when we look *beyond* the legislatures and Congress committees to the roots of Congress power in rural areas. There we find powerful landed elements using their economic power, numerical strength, traditional prestige and brute force (or the threat of it) to guide the votes of weaker groups. Had liberal perceptions and procedures within the legislatures and party councils in that period come into conflict with the interests of the powerful agrarian groups which controlled Congress, they would probably have been swept aside. But little conflict arose because the legislatures and party councils rested upon a decidedly illiberal system of minority dominance in rural areas. If the political system is seen to consist only of the formal institutions of state and informal party institutions, then the liberal and transactional modes balanced one another in that period. But if the political system embraces all of the power relations in society — and this is the view that we prefer — then the main thing which held the Indian political system together up to the mid-1960s was transactional dealings among representatives of landed interests whose power was largely based upon wealth and coercive resources.[21] It is at the level of this sort of interaction that the integration of the system in that period is best understood. An analysis of the most crucial of those interactions should inspire dismay rather than euphoria in liberal observers.

Some people claim that this is all that there is to say about Indian politics, but they are mistaken. Things have changed since the mid-1960s. There are still plenty of places in India where the old cynicism about politics is warranted. But in many areas, a curious reversal has occurred. Liberal democratic values which for so long were stifled by dominant caste power have become a major force while transactional networks have been severely damaged.

Over the last fifteen years or so, the egalitarian assumptions which lie behind the open, parliamentary system have become widely (if imperfectly) known and accepted among most members of the weaker sections of Indian society. The first clear signs of this can be found in the results of the 1967 general election and in survey data from the late 1960s.[22] The popular response to Mrs Gandhi's radical slogans at the 1971 election provided further evidence. Election data from the 1970s and 1980, movements during the 1970s of people from the lower-middle stratum of Indian society and the success of a small number of state governments at building coalitions of the poor and slightly less poor[23] all reflect the change. Poor people in most areas now refuse to allow themselves to be dictated to on polling day. They are far more assertive and better organized than before 1965 and they tend to throw up their own leaders rather than having them appointed from above by politicians. In many places, where once they settled for promises or tokenism, they are prepared to reject any leader or government that does not deliver substantive political spoils. It has become possible in several regions to build governing coalitions upon the support of those who were once dominated by landed groups.[24] If these trends continue and if the open, parliamentary system survives, the day may not be far off when it becomes *necessary* for politicians to rely primarily on their support.

There is reason to fear for the survival of that system, however. The main reason for this is the serious decay that has occurred since the late 1960s in the organizations of every party in India except those of the left (and possibly the Jan Sangh). This is a more serious development for India than it would be for other parliamentary systems, since the central integrating institution of the system up to the late 1960s was the Congress Party. The decay in Congress was apparent in the ossification in the old transactional patronage system in the late 1960s as key operatives became aged or complacent and in such problems as bogus membership lists which left party leaders in considerable uncertainty about their support base.[25] Perhaps the most serious blow was the abandonment in the early 1970s by both wings of Congress — and every other center party including, latterly, Janata — of the principle of representation in selecting personnel for party committees.[26] It seriously impaired the ability of these parties to learn of or respond to grievances and pressures from important groups at various levels. The *coup de grace* was administered in the most important organization of the early 1970s, Mrs Gandhi's Congress, by the Prime Minister herself. Between 1971 and 1977, she attempted to wreck what remained of the old spoils machine. Her incompetence and that of her lieutenants as political managers prevented total devastation in some regions, but the overall result was near-ruination.

The relationship between the growing assertiveness of less prosperous groups and the decay in party organization is a subject which cries out for thorough research. Clearly each development influenced and reinforced the other. But pending further research, it seems an oversimplification to say simply that the emergence of poorer groups *caused* the collapse of the old transactional system or that the powerful landed groups abandoned the principle of representation to protect their interests from the rising poor. They might have wished to do so, but they were not consulted. Mrs Gandhi's efforts to wreck the old machine were made on behalf of urban industrialists and middle class folk. But she can hardly be seen as the agent of prosperous *rural* groups. She was too distrustful of them and too inept at creating alternatives to the party machine[27] to be an effective champion of their interests. She and the leaders of other center parties appear to have abandoned the principle of representation — and hence any hope of strong, transactionally-based organizations — mainly to gain a narrow personal advantage in the power game.[28]

To summarize, it is our view that the open, parliamentary system was held together during the first two decades after Indian independence mainly by a political machine based on transactional alliances which were developed around the distribution of spoils. The survival of the parliamentary system owed rather less to the strength of liberal values since it ultimately depended on the pleasure of powerful agrarian groups who controlled the rural poor by decidedly illiberal means. As India entered the 1980s, however, things had changed. Strong national party organizations no longer provided an integrative framework for the system, based upon transactional politics. And yet the values which form the basis for an open, parliamentary political system had gained very wide acceptance in India. A few shrewd, forceful leaders at the state level have even shown that it is possible to gain and retain power by building bases of support among poorer groups upon these shared values. But in the absence of a strong national party organization, India's leaders appear to feel threatened by the increasing assertiveness of the populace — hence Mrs Gandhi's reliance upon promises of law and order rather than the old reformist rhetoric during the campaign preceding the 1980 election and her aggressive police policies after taking power.

Formal institutions of state have absorbed some of the stress once borne by the dominant party organization in its days as India's central integrating institution. But it seems quite likely that the new national leadership will seek to alter this institutional structure and to centralize power within it in order to cope more effectively with élite-mass disintegration. It is here that the case of Sri Lanka deserves brief discussion, since that system has been restructured recently in response to the problems of a lack of integration and outright disintegration. The constitution of 1978 and subsequent legislation have not yet taken sufficiently clear shape in practice to warrant a definitive comment on their effect. But it is clear that they are intended to cope with three problems of integration.

The best known of these is the crisis of national integration which springs from deep distrust between Sinhalese and Tamils. The new constitution seeks to reassure the Tamils by granting them a range of fundamental rights which include freedom from discrimination on grounds of religion or language. Tamil is made a national language, with meaningful provision for its use in Tamil-majority areas, although Sinhala remains the only official language. A system of proportional representation for parliamentary elections and the use of second and third preference votes in balloting for the powerful executive President are intended to increase substantially the weight of Tamil votes.[29] Other provisions of the constitution are intended to reassure the Sinhalese, to prevent the kind of bigoted backlash which swept away several earlier attempts at reconciliation. Still more important is a new initiative to create regional councils which may end the secessionist movement among Tamils by giving them a considerable degree of autonomy in areas where they predominate. These councils are intended to knit Tamils more loosely into the system than before, since the old order — in trying to integrate them too tightly into a highly centralized, unitary state — was so constrictive that it alienated them and produced *dis* integration.

The second aim of Sri Lanka's new constitution is to prevent conflict between Left and Right from becoming a serious disintegrative force. (Left-Right political integration does not fit perfectly under any of Weiner's five headings; it is probably best characterized as a form of value integration, although in practice it has as much to do with expedient interactions as with shared perceptions and values.) The adoption of proportional representation for parliamentary elections and the transferable vote system for choosing the President will work to the advantage of moderate centrists. It will impel politicians away from extreme positions and will probably ensure that the island will be governed by Centre-Right or Centre-Left coalitions.

Finally the new structures are intended to cope with the problem of the lack of élite-mass integration in two somewhat contradictory ways. In our view this is the principal cleavage in Sri Lanka politics and has contributed very substantially to the persistence of the Sinhalese-Tamil cleavage. By creating regional councils and granting them a new cadre of district ministers and modest resources formerly controlled from the capital, the constitution-makers have de-centralized power. By creating an executive Presidency and arming it with enormous powers on the French model, they have also centralized power. But while the decentralization is somewhat limited, the centralization is very substantial. By decentralizing, they hope to give people in local-and intermediate-level arenas a chance to participate in some minimal way in substantive politics. For most people at those levels, this is their first chance to do so. They hope that this participation will reduce widespread suspicions and unrealistic expectations of the political system among influential people at those levels. At the same time, by concentrating great power in the President's hands, they seek to maintain the dominance which the small national political élite has enjoyed over the political system since Independence. The over-riding aim of the reforms, then, is to maintain the gap (in terms of meaningful interaction) between élite and mass which has always existed in Sri Lanka, except on polling day.[30] The modest opportunities for participation in the regions are mainly intended to bolster the existing pattern of authority and consent, at the level of ideas.

It is too early to say whether the restructuring of institutions in Sri Lanka will succeed in its aims of promoting and thwarting the various types of integration which it addresses. But despite serious doubts about its prospects,[31] it has far more promise than any schemes for restructuring which are likely to emerge in New Delhi. The changes in Sri Lanka have been shrewdly devised, either to neutralize hitherto disintegrative forces or to redirect them into constructive channels. If this restructuring fails, it will not be because of any lack of subtlety in its design. The changes which, at this writing, are being contemplated in India lack subtlety of purpose which is bound to entail a lack of subtlety in design. Their purpose is to centralize power at the apex of the Indian political system.[32]

And yet it is difficult to see how *any* centralizing plan can work in India unless the open, parliamentary system is abandoned. The massive size of the polity makes it far more difficult to anchor the political system in a powerful centralized executive than in Sri Lanka or France. India, unlike Sri Lanka, has a long history of compromise between central authority and regional, sub-regional and local power centers. Indeed, it can be forcefully argued that such compromises formed the central principle in the logic of politics under three 'successor corporate dynasties': Company, Crown and Congress (up to 1967 or so).[33] India's tradition of de-centralized government is embodied in highly developed institutions of state at many levels and in the expectations and participatory experiences of people at those levels — both of which are absent at intermediate and local levels in Sri Lanka. Sri Lanka's leaders are working to maintain a pre-existing pattern of dominance by the national political élite, while India's are seeking to create this anew. Even if the countries were of similar size and complexity, the task in Sri Lanka would be far easier. And if the incompetent (and occasionally mindless) management of the Indian emergency of the mid-1970s is any guide,[34] India's leaders lack the formidable manipulative skills which President Jayawardene and a very small number of his colleagues possess in abundance. However much centralization within the Indian polity is advertized as a solution to the crisis of disintegration between élite and mass, it seems destined only to make things worse.

NOTES

1. The author is grateful to the U.S. National Endowment for the Humanities, the U.K. Social Science Research Council, the British Academy and the Nuffield Foundation for grants in aid of research for this essay.
2. M. Weiner, 'Political Integration and Political Development', in J. L. Finkle and R. W. Gable (eds.), *Political Development and Social Change* (2nd. edn., New York, 1971), 643–54. Quotations are from pp. 643–5 and 650.
3. Weiner, 'Political Integration', op.cit., 645 (italics his).
4. There is a considerable literature on the subject. For a small sampling, see: C. Geertz, 'The Integrative Revolution: Primordial Sentiments and Civil Politics in New States', in C. Geertz (ed.), *Old Societies and New States* (New York, 1963), 105–57; P. Brass, *Language, Religion and Politics in North India*, (London, 1974); articles by Brass and F. Robinson in D. Taylor and M. Yapp (eds.), *Political Identity in South Asia* (London, 1979), 35–112; and C. Young, *The Politics of Cultural Pluralism* (Madison, 1976), especially ch. 2.
5. I am grateful to Gananath Obeyesekere for this information. See also, R. B. Inden and M. Marriott, 'Caste Systems', *Encyclopaedia Britannica, Macropaedia* (Chicago, 1974)3, 982–91.
6. Interview with one such leader, J. R. Jayawardene, Colombo, 11 September 1978.
7. There were clear instances of this in the late 1970s in, for example, Haryana, Uttar Pradesh, Bihar and Karnataka.

8. See for example, M. Roberts, 'Foundations of Sinhala and Tamil Nationalisms and Some Implications', *Ceylon Studies Seminar*, 1973.
9. Both themes are dealt with at much greater length in J. Manor, 'The Failure of Political Integration in Sri Lanka (Ceylon), *Journal of Commonwealth and Comparative Politics*, VIII, 1 (March, 1979), 21–46. Developments within the United National Party since J. R. Jayawardene took it over in 1973 and within the formal institutions of state since his electoral victory in 1977 present something of an exception to this pattern. But we leave discussion of this until the next section of this essay.
10. Weiner, 'Political Integration', op.cit., 645 (italics his).
11. This takes some rather elaborate explaining, which is impossible here given limits on space. It is set down more fully in J. Manor, 'The Failure of Political Integration. . .'
12. For further discussion of this problem, see J. Manor, 'Pragmatic Progressives in India's Regional Politics: The Case of Devaraj Urs' *Economic and Political Weekly*, annual number (February 1980).
13. I am grateful to Walter Hauser and Francine Frankel for information on Bihar. See also H. Blair, 'Rising Kulaks and Backward Classes in Bihar: Social Change in the Late 1970s', *Economic and Political Weekly*, 12 January 1980.
14. Weiner, 'Political Integration', op.cit., 650.
15. W. H. Morris-Jones, 'India's Political Idioms', in C. H. Philips (ed.), *Politics and Society in India* (London, 1963), 133–54.
16. Weiner, 'Political Integration', op.cit., 644.
17. See the studies in D. A. Low (ed.), *Congress and the Raj: Facets of the Indian Struggle* (London, 1977).
18. Morris-Jones, 'India's Political Idioms', op.cit.
19. These views are developed more fully, as applied to the case of Mysore, in J. Manor, 'The Lesser Leader amid Political Transformation', in W. H. Morris-Jones (ed.), *The Making of Politicians: Studies from Africa and Asia* (London, 1976), 140–55 and *Political Change in an Indian State: Mysore, 1917–1955* (New Delhi and Canberra, 1977), especially ch. 9 and conclusion.
20. I am grateful to Ravinder Kumar for these ideas, derived from conversation. See also R. Kumar, 'Class, Community or Nation? Gandhi's Quest for a Popular Consensus in India', *Modern Asian Studies*, iii, 4 (1969), 357–76.
21. It must be emphasised that, as Robert Dahl and others would argue there is not a necessary contradiction between transactional politics and liberal perceptions and procedures. But when those involved in the transactions come from élites that maintain ascendancy over the majority by such means, then a contradiction exists.
22. D. L. Sheth (ed.), *Citizens and Parties: Aspects of Competitive Politics in India* (New Delhi, 1975). This important volume deserves a wide readership.
23. For discussions of the most notable example of such a government, see J. Manor, 'Structural Change in Karnataka Politics', *Economic and Political Weekly* (29 October 1977), 1865–9, and 'Pragmatic Progressives in India's Regional Politics', op.cit.

24. These comments are based upon discussions with politicians, civil servants and political analysts in Delhi and five Indian states during December 1979 and January and February 1980. A detailed study emerging from this research will be published in due course.
25. See F. Frankel, *India's Political Economy, 1947–1977: the Gradual Revolution* (Princeton, 1978), especially pp. 444–6, 474–5, 481–3 and 518; and J. Manor, 'The Decay of Party Organisation in India', *The Round Table*, 272 (October, 1978).
26. I am grateful to Myron Weiner for stressing this point in conversation.
27. See J. Manor, 'Where Congress Survived: Five States in the Indian General Election of 1977', *Asian Survey* (August, 1978).
28. Despite Mrs Gandhi's huge electoral victory in 1980, the Congress is so highly centralized and so ineptly run that it possesses little substance. The few reliable political managers it contains seem unlikely to be given important tasks by a leader frightened of potential rivals.
29. For a fuller discussion, see J. Manor, 'A New Political Order for Sri Lanka', *The World Today* (September 1979), 377–86.
30. J. Manor, 'The Failure of Political Integration', op.cit.
31. J. Manor, 'A New Political Order', op.cit.
32. These comments are based on necessarily off-the-record interviews with politicians, academics and officials in New Delhi during January 1980. No one will be more pleased than the author if, in time, this discussion is rendered irrelevant by the abandonment of these schemes.
33. This view has been persuasively presented in conversation by R. E. Frykenberg. See also, for example, his ' "Company Circari" in the Carnatic, *c.* 1799–1859: The Inner Logic of Political Systems in India', in R. G. Fox (ed.), *Realm and Region in Traditional India* (New Delhi, 1977), 117–64.
34. J. Manor, 'Where Congress Survived', op.cit.

EAST-WEST CONFLICTS IN PAKISTAN: BENGALI REGIONALISM, 1974–1970

M. RASHIDUZZAMAN

'Regionalism can be defined simply as a strong sentiment of loyalty or attachment among the population of a geographical segment of a state to that particular territory.'[1] Following Clifford Geertz, it is mainly a primordial attachment 'especially troublesome in geographically heterogeneous areas'.[2]

The case of Pakistan deserves special attention because of her regional conflict. The conflict between the two wings of Pakistan involved linguistic and cultural differences, too, but the lack of geographical continuity proved a very important factor in the case of Bengali regionalism, which finally threatened the physical integrity of the state.

With her geographical abnormality, Pakistan had been described as a 'double country';[3] in the absence of a physical link between the two wings, she could hardly achieve the social mobilisation necessary for a common nationhood.[4] Communication between the two regions was always difficult and expensive for the common man and it eventually contributed to enormous difficulties for effective national integration. While inter-wing travel by air increased, it remained confined to businessmen, administrators, politicians and other members of the élites. A more dangerous effect of the geographical separation was the economic disparity between the two regions.[5]

Several important circumstances created regional economic disparity. First, the capital was located in West Pakistan, so that administrative energies and governmental expenditures tended to be concentrated in the West not East Pakistan. Secondly, there was a lack of entrepreneurial Bengali families in East Pakistan, since more major Muslim trading families settled in West Pakistan. Thirdly, Bengalis were not proportionately represented in the Army, and their inadequate representation in the bureaucracy led way to the charge that senior civil servants were not responsive to Bengali interests. Fourthly, most of the defence budget was spent within West Pakistan for the security of that region. And finally, some argued that the weather and enormous population growth of East Pakistan hindered Bengali development.

While the economic disparities continued to be the focal point of conflict between the two wings of Pakistan, the worst frustration came through the inadequate participation of the Bengali élites in the centralised political system built up by Ayub Khan. The Ayub regime publicly defended its centralisation for economic development as well as national integration. In the final analysis, the centralisation became counter-productive: it failed to achieve a parity of economic development between East and West Pakistan, and as a result the regional conflict was exacerbated. By supporting and creating a *de facto* unitary government dominated by non-Bengali military and bureaucracy, the Ayub regime was in fact denying effective participation by the Bengalis who constituted the majority of Pakistan's population. It also rejected the Bengali demand for maximum provincial autonomy as essentially disruptive. The policy of centralization and the lack of adequate participation of the Bengalis in the decision-making process of Pakistan was met with formidable opposition from East Pakistan. We shall identify here the leading factors of regionalism in East Pakistan and analyse how the lack of political participation for the Bengalis intensified regional conflict in Pakistan.

Leading Groups and Issues of Regionalism

Regionalism has been a dominant theme in Pakistan's politics for many years. As indicated in numerous writings, opposition politics in East Bengal had grown with the ventilation of regional grievances. The 1954 elections in the province had replaced the Muslim Leaguers with a new political élite, more committed than their predecessors to redressing the Bengali differences in the East. After 1954 the leading Bengali groups bargained strongly for greater autonomy for East Pakistan; and the conflict with the centre over this and related issues eventually led to the disintegration of Pakistan.

The Bengali counter-élite which emerged after the 1954 elections readily took up the cause of regional disparity and entered into negotiations with the centre. Table 1 explains the various political groups articulating the issues of regionalism. It appears that the regional demands articulated by various groups in East Pakistan gradually polarised and finally asked for complete independence.

Serious bargaining between the leaders of the two wings regarding the granting of greater regional autonomy and distribution of resources began when the second Constituent Assembly met in July 1955. The West Pakistani leaders made it clear that the future National Assembly would consist of an equal number of members from both the wings of Pakistan and that in the future political structure of the country there would be only two provinces, East Pakistan and West Pakistan. For their part, Bengali leaders made it clear that no constitution would be acceptable to them unless it fulfilled at least these terms.[6]

The Awami Leaguers were infuriated with the central cabinet for their modification of the provincial autonomy plan, known as the Murree Pact. As a result they opposed the Constitution Bill in the Pakistan Constituent Assembly in 1956. While debating the Constitution in January 1956, Abul Mansur Ahmed, a prominent Awami Leaguer, outlined the main Bengali grievances: first, the need for greater regional autonomy; secondly, the economic disparity growing out of geographical conditions; thirdly, cultural differences between the two regions; fourthly, negligence by the central government in redressing Bengali grievances; fifthly, inadequate representation of Bengalis in the government services; and finally, need for a three-subject (defence, foreign affairs and currency) central government giving a larger share to the provincial administration.[7]

Economic development in Pakistan's first decade had been characterised by unbalanced regional growth. Much of the respon-

Table 1
LEADING GROUPS AND ISSUES OF REGIONALISM IN EAST BENGAL

Period	*Leading Groups*	*Regional Issues*
1947–54 Muslim League dominant	Landlords, lawyers, students	Language, provincial autonomy, allocation of resources, higher jute prices for development by the central government
1954–1958 Changing coalition of regional parties	Lawyers, students, workers, Bengali businessmen	Economic disparities, grant facilities to Bengali businessmen and industrialists, maximum provincial autonomy, larger allocations of resources, parity of representation in the services.
1958–69 Centralised polity of Ayub Khan and frustration of regional élites	Lawyers, teachers, students, Bengali businessmen, workers, organised peasants	Economic disparities, Bengali language and culture, regional participation, full regional autonomy symbolised in the six-point demand, eleven-point demand of the students
1969–71 Mass-movement, election, aggregation crisis and disintegration of Pakistan	Students, workers, organised peasants, guerrillas, armed personnel, Bengali civil servants, teachers, lawyers, Bengali businessmen	Economic disparity, maximum autonomy, complete independence for East Bengal, Bangladesh movement

Source: Newspaper reports, political party pamphlets, etc.

sibility for regional disparities could also be laid at the door of the accidents of migration when Pakistan was originally established and to private enterprise, which was allowed to flourish in Pakistan under state patronage. The social bases of the two wings of the country were substantially different and contributed to the frustrating situation. While West Pakistan was reluctant to abolish the feudal interests which dominated politics, East Bengal had abolished the landed gentry in 1950 by doing away with the *Zamindari* system.[8] The Hindu moneylenders and business élite in East Bengal had migrated to India soon after Independence, leaving a vacuum in the area which was gradually filled by the two leading Muslim trading communities, the Khojas and Memons who had migrated from India. They were not 'sons of the soil' in Bengal, and their only interest was commercial: the 'exploitation' of such resources as jute, tea and other raw materials. On the other hand, the western wing started with an advantage. There had been no large-scale emigration of the business élite from there, and some of the trading families like the Saigols, Haroons and Chinotis began to utilise all the commercial opportunities of a new state. The Khojas, Memons and other Muslim business elements who migrated from India preferred to settle in Karachi which was closer to Bombay, their principal centre of business activities in British India. Even some of the prominent non-Bengali firms operating in the East Wing had their 'headquarters' in Karachi and other parts of West Pakistan. The location of the national capital at Karachi was of definite advantage to them, since official patronage was readily available there.

Bengali business interests in East Pakistan were slow to emerge. Only two significant types of local business were visible. First, numerous small traders and retailers developed in Dacca, Chittagong and Khulna, the principal cities of the province, and secondly, some local contractors who were also predominantly based in these areas demanded greater official patronage in the form of liberal import licenses, permits, shipping facilities, and so on.[9] It was obvious that Bengali traders and businessmen obtained some of the advantages provided by the new state as old trade links with Calcutta were severed and new patterns of trade and new economic activities developed within the province. Their frustrations arose when they learned that the lion's share of privileges and opportunities was being made available to the non-Bengali commercial community operating from Karachi. As the champion of regional autonomy, the Awami League appeared to be the principal ally of the emerging Bengali élite. When the Awami League was in office in Dacca and constituted the central government in 1956–8, the grievances of Bengali businessmen were brought forward for their redress.[10]

While group interests in East Bengal were demanding a larger share of Central government spending and official patronage, the economic disparities were becoming increasingly evident in the country's overall economic development. West Pakistan's economy grew at the rate of 3.6 per cent but East Pakistan's grew at only 1.7 per cent; the *per capita* rates were 1.2 and 0.6 per cent respectively.[11] Besides the benefits derived from private enterprise, which tended to accrue most to the West Wing, large-scale government spending located there also contributed to the economic gap between the two wings. Central government spending on defence was largely confined to West Pakistan as the military headquarters were situated there. Nor did East Bengal obtain any worthwhile advantage from expenditure on the central bureaucracy, since the federal capital was also located in the West Wing. The inter-regional mobility of labour and capital remained negligible. There was hardly any sizeable representation of Bengalis in the Army and the civil service, which only added to resentment.

Economic disparities attracted attention because they are quantifiable and because Bengal's economists are numerous, excellent and articulate.[12] As early as 1956, Bengali economists were arguing that because of her geographical nature, Pakistan was a two-economy state. They demanded that the economy of the two wings of Pakistan be regarded as completely separate and argued that separate economic planning was necessary for the development of the two regions. They further emphasised that there should be a restriction on resources being transferred from East to West Pakistan.[13] In 1956, while the Constituent Assembly was considering the future constitution of the country, students and teachers at Dacca University earnestly debated the questions of regional disparity. And under the influence of articulate economists, Bengali politicians also supported the two-economy policy, until it was rejected by the military regime of Ayub Khan in 1958.

The Frustrations of Non-Participation

The military take-over in Pakistan has been explained in various ways. According to President Iskander Mirza, martial law had been necessary because the constitution of 1956 had proved unworkable. Later he held that his purpose was to restore a pattern of democracy akin to the American presidential system. In his autobiography, President Ayub Khan described Mirza as the architect of the martial law regime, and the person who actually invited him to take over. It appears that very soon after General Ayub was called upon to take power, he decided to dislodge his patron. While the truth remains a matter of debate in the absence of authentic evidence, some explanations stress a regional interpretation of the emergence of military rule in Pakistan. For example, the former Chief Minister, Ataur Rahman Khan, alleged in his memoirs that the military *coup d'état* was the result of a 'conspiracy' against democratic institutions in Pakistan. According to this view, Iskander Mirza realised that there would be little chance for him to remain President if the 1959 elections were held, and this motivated him to abrogate the Constitution and declare martial law.[14] He is also reported to have believed that only martial law could prevent mounting regional demands from being realised after the elections scheduled for the early part of 1959.

By its very nature, the military regime was highly centralised and left little room for regional loyalties. Although the legislation for One Unit in West Pakistan was passed by the civilian regime before 1958, the actual implementation of it took place during the military regime headed by Ayub Khan.

From the point of view of politically activated elements in East Bengal, military rule was bound to be of little consequence, since Bengali representation in the armed forces was minimal.[15] Even more serious, during the martial law period from 1958 to 1962, was the fact that the Army took a hard line against politicians, particularly those who had been active in regional politics. It appears that the Awami Leaguers were the first target of arrests during the period of military rule. So also were the leftist National Awami Party (N.A.P.) leaders from East Pakistan who demanded maximum regional autonomy. Two leading spokesmen of regional autonomy, Sheikh Mujibur Rahman and Maulana Abdul Hamid Khan Bhasani, were detained in prison for 'security reasons'. The Governor of East Pakistan was removed and a retired Inspector General of Police (a Bengali) was appointed in his place by the new regime. In fact, he was the only Bengali Governor during the martial law period. Soon the idea of planning East Pakistan's development separately, promoted by the Awami League Cabinet in 1956–7, was completely rejected, and emphasis was laid on centralised planning. It was also obvious that the provincial administration had no separate existence under martial law except what was desired by the central authority. Although the day-to-day administration was largely in the hands of the civil servants in the provincial government, all major decisions were taken by non-Bengali military officers, and these were reported to be of a conflicting nature. Some of the top civil servants in East Bengal who were alleged to have been in favour with the former Awami League cabinet were 'screened out'.[16]

With few Bengalis in the new power élite of Pakistan, it was obvious that the East Wing participated little or not at all in the military regime of Pakistan. The political realities of Bengali regionalism could hardly be ignored by President Ayub whose military regime was overwhelmingly West Pakistani in complexion. He first consolidated his regime and then launched a twofold programme to legitimise his rule: Basic Democracies and development of the economy.[17] To deal with the discontent in the Eastern province, he made an unequivocal promise to hasten industrialisation, and the second Five-Year Plan was modified to meet certain demands of East Pakistan. In order to fill the political vacuum of the regime as a result of inadequate Bengali representation in the new military regime, President Ayub Khan adopted a pragmatic policy and introduced several measures to neutralise regional political forces. First, he publicly admitted that there was economic disparity between the two wings of the country and that it should be narrowed. Secondly, he decided to place Bengali officers in important administrative positions in East Pakistan. Thirdly, he agreed to appoint a Finance Commission to recommend a more equitable allocation of resources between the centre and provinces. And fourthly, he transferred some of the government-run development agencies like Water and Power Development Authority (W.A.P.D.A.) and Pakistan Industrial Development Corporation (P.I.D.C.) to East Pakistan.

Table 2
PER CAPITA G.D.P. IN EAST AND WEST PAKISTAN AT 1959–60 CONSTANT PRICES

	Per Capita G.D.P. East	*Per Capita G.D.P. West*	*West-East Disparity Ratio*	*Index of Disparity*
1959–60	269	355	1.32	100
1960–1	277	363	1.31	97
1961–2	286	376	1.31	97
1962–3	277	393	1.42	131
1963–4	299	408	1.36	113
1964–5	293	426	1.45	141
1965–6	295	427	1.45	141
1966–7	290	448	1.54	169
1967–8	307	468	1.52	163
1968–9	312	490	1.57	178
1969–70	314	504	1.61	191
growth over the decade	17%	42%		
growth in Third Plan period	7%	18%		

Index of Disparity: (Disparity ratio-1) × 100 expressed as index with base 1959–60.

Source: Planning Commission, Government of Pakistan, Report of the Panel of Economists on the Fourth Five-Year Plan, 1970–5, Islamabad, May 1970, p. 2.

The extent of regional disparity between the two wings can be illustrated with the help of the following tables. Table 2 shows in column 8 that the proportion of development expenditure devoted to the two wings changed markedly, with the proportionate share of East Pakistan rising while West Pakistan's share fell. Nevertheless, even in terms of the figures available for 1969–70 East Pakistan received only 36 per cent while West Pakistan received 64 per cent of the Federal budget, thus providing further evidence of the *per capita* disparity in Gross Domestic Productivity (G.D.P.). Two principal explanations could be offered for such a growing *per capita* disparity: East Pakistan received less federal grants for her development, while the foreign exchange earned from the export of jute was spent more in West Pakistan which contributed towards its increased gross productivity; secondly, East Pakistan was used as a 'captive market' for West Pakistan's products and she suffered from the lack of adequate investment and productivity.

The failure of the Ayub regime to achieve progress towards regional distributive justice was indeed a defeat for the centralised policy it created; in fact, it aggravated the regional conflict. All efforts were mobilised to establish a strong central bureaucratic power with only marginal participation of the regional political élites. The latter were allowed to operate, if at all, through the restricted electoral process and dwarfed legislatures.

Pakistan's indirect electoral system was faulted on two counts. First, it was alleged that it was under the influence of district officers who indeed were the controlling authority of Basic Democracies. These officers were blamed for influencing the electors in favour of the governing party. Secondly, the electoral college was accused of large-scale corrupt practices. It was widely known that the electors were bribed by the candidates and that votes were given to the highest bidder.

The Widening of the Cleavage

The frustration caused by the Ayub regime was inherent in its autocratic nature. In terms of the models of political change, the Ayub system could be described as a 'modernising autocracy'.[18] In spite of its various attempts at adjustments, the character of the regime remained fundamentally unitary and centralised. While the legitimacy of the system remained unacceptable to the major political components, the challenge and polarisation took place in several stages. The Ayub regime was itself parochial in character as its two principal sources of support — the army and the bureaucracy — predominantly represented one region — the West Wing. The regional cleavage at the

Table 3
REVENUE AND DEVELOPMENT EXPENDITURE IN EAST & WEST PAKISTAN

Period	*Revenue Expenditure*	*Development Plan Exp.* *Total*	*Public*	*Private*	*Outside Plan Exp.*	*Works Programme*	*Total Dev. Exp. (3 + 4 + 5)*	*Total Exp.*	*Dev. Exp. Regions as % of total for all Pakistan*
1.	2.		3.		4.	5.	6.	7.	8.
East Pakistan									%
1950/1–1954/5	171	100	70	30	—	—	100	271	20
1955/6–1959/60	254	270	197	73	—	—	270	524	26
1960/1–1964/5	434	925	625	300	—	45	970	1,404	32
1965/6–1969/70	648	1,656	1,106	550	—	—	1,656	2,141	36
West Pakistan					Indus Basin Works Programme				
1950/1–1954/5	720	400	200	200	—	—	400	1,129	80
1955/6–1959/60	898	757	464	293	—	—	757	1,655	74
1960/1–1964/5	1,284	1,840	770	1,070	211	20	2,071	3,355	68
1965/6–1969/70	2,223	2,610	1,010	1,600	360	—	2,970	5,195	64

Note: (*a*) Revenue Expenditure in East Pakistan is the expenditure of East Pakistan Government excluding debt service plus 15% Central Government expenditure, civil administration and 12% of its defence expenditure. The rest of the Central Government expenditure of the West Pakistan Government is shown as Revenue Expenditure in West Pakistan transfer payments of the Central Government, i.e. debt services, grant-in-aid to provinces, and expenditure on foreign affairs have been excluded.

(*b*) Public sector development expenditure of the Provincial Government plus that of the Central Government on projects located in the Province, mainly based on Planning Commission estimates. Private development expenditure as estimated by the Planning Commission.

Source: Planning Commission, Government of Pakistan, *Report* of the Panel of Economists on the Fourth Five Year Plan, 1970–5 (Islamabad, May 1970).

heart of the system proved to be its greatest handicap. Minor adjustments failed to correct this limitation and expand the support base. Regional grievances were mobilised in East Pakistan by the opposition in an effort to eliminate the unitary system. The regional cleavage was intensified as a culmination of the Bengali resistance to the centralised polity.

While Ayub Khan's pragmatic policy designed to reduce regional discontent became increasingly inadequate, the 1965 conflict with India produced a shattering effect. Two aspects of the eleven-day war were politically devastating. First, Ayub Khan suffered a severe loss of prestige, especially in West Pakistan, where political discontent came to the surface for the first time. Secondly, East Pakistan, being cut off from the rest of the country, was left virtually defenceless, and later stood in opposition to the Ayub regime.

Bengalis found that even more decisions than they had thought were made in Islamabad. During the war and for some weeks thereafter, virtually no steps could be taken by the bureaucracy as the affairs of government remained virtually unattended.

The effective articulation of Bengali grievances took place through the Awami League's Six-Point Demand, announced by its leader Sheikh Mujibur Rahman in early 1966.[19] It constituted the biggest challenge Ayub Khan's political system had faced. The salient features of the six-point programme could be summed up as follows:

1. The Constitution should provide for a federation of Pakistan in its true sense, on the basis of the Lahore Resolution of 1940, and for a parliamentary form of government with supremacy belonging to a legislature directly elected on the basis of universal adult franchise.
2. The federal government should deal with only two subjects, e.g. Defence and Foreign Affairs, and all other residuary subjects should rest in the federating states.
3. Two separate but freely convertible currencies for the two wings might be introduced, or, if that is not feasible, there should be one currency for the whole country, but effective constitutional provisions should be introduced to stop the flight of capital from East to West Pakistan. Furthermore a separate Banking Reserve should be established and separate fiscal and monetary policies should be adopted for East Pakistan.
4. The power of taxation and revenue collection should be vested in the federating units, and the federal centre should have no such power. However, the federation would be entitled to a share in the state taxes to meet its indispensable expenditures.
5. Two separate accounts were to be provided for foreign exchange earnings of the two wings: the foreign exchange requirements of the federal government should be met by the two wings equally or in a

ratio to be fixed; indigenous products should move free of duty between the two parts of the country, and the constitution should empower the federating units to establish trade links with foreign countries.

6. East Pakistan should have a separate militia or para-military force.

As a challenge to Ayub Khan's political system, the six-point demand had two major consequences. First, it precipitated a series of actions by the government against the Awami League and, secondly, it reactivated mass participation in the movements for the redress of regional grievances. The government's reactions to such a separatist demand could have been foreseen. Ayub Khan publicly denounced Sheikh Mujibur Rahman's demand as a proposal for separating the East Wing from the rest of the country. The strategy of the Ayub administration was to identify the autonomists in East Bengal as secessionists, out to destroy the national identity. At one time Ayub Khan went so far as to declare that more autonomy would mean the disintegration of the country.[20] Official policy continued to refuse to open the political system to wider participation. Instead of attempting to deal with the source of discontent, the government tried to attribute the six-point demand to the personal ambitions of Sheikh Mujibur Rahman. Its policy culminated in the arrests of prominent Awami Leaguers, including Sheikh Mujibur Rahman himself, and in the suppression of protests organised by his supporters in 1966. As events proved, the policy of repression failed to lessen the sense of regional grievance.

For the Awami League, the six-point demand proved effective in more than one way. Although the 1964 draft manifesto of the Awami League had called for full autonomy for the regions, the party had remained organisationally weak, after a long period of inaction. To the Awami League, the six-point demand provided a rallying symbol of mobilisation in East Pakistan. While other parties were caught up in the debate for the 'restoration of democracy', Sheikh Mujibur Rahman's Awami League found the articulation of regional grievances the most effective means of awakening popular support.

The Government failed to crush the autonomists through the usual punitive measures, but it pursued other means as well. After about a year of active public agitation on behalf of the six-point proposal launched in 1966, several Bengali civil servants and military officers were arrested on the charge that they had committed high treason. Eventually the so-called 'Agartala Conspiracy Case' was initiated against Sheikh Mujibur Rahman and others for an alleged conspiracy to separate the East Wing by violent means, in collusion with India. The conspiracy was alleged to have been planned in an Indian town call Agartala near the border between India and East Pakistan. Such a case appeared to have multiple purposes. It was certainly designed to reduce the public esteem in which Sheikh Mujibur Rahman was held. Sheikh Mujibur Rahman denied the charges and accused the Government of malicious designs against him as well as his party. Another objective of the Government was to gain legitimacy for further action against the proponents of greater autonomy.

Eventually the political impact of the Agartala case went against the centralised polity established by Ayub Khan. The trial, conducted by a special tribunal consisting of senior judges of the Supreme Court and High Courts of Pakistan, opened at the Dacca Cantonment in the autumn of 1968. Eleven of the accused turned approved witnesses on behalf of the Government (by whom they were pardoned) but the rest, including Sheikh Mujibur Rahman, denied the charges brought against them. The trial soon became the target of a mass movement opposing the Ayub regime and demanding greater autonomy for East Pakistan. Sheikh Mujibur Rahman emerged from having been the principal defendant in a treason trial to the status of a leader dominating the political scene. Accumulated feelings in East Bengal ran high against West Pakistan and the central administration of Ayub Khan. During the political unrest, the Army (mostly from West Pakistan) had been used to put down agitations and many people had been killed in the East.

Political concessions were now promised by Ayub Khan, but these did not succeed in satisfying the agitators. The Agartala Conspiracy Case was withdrawn and Sheikh Mujibur Rahman, along with other accused, was set free. He was the principal spokesman on behalf of East Pakistan at the Round Table Conference in March 1969, and it was now difficult for him to moderate his previous demands without risking his own political future. He maintained that the existing political system did not confer effective power on the East Wing and argued that the six-point demand was the only practical solution in view of the unique situation of the country with the two wings separated by 1,000 miles of Indian territory.[21] After agreeing at the conference table to introduce a parliamentary system with direct adult franchise, Ayub Khan was reported to have asked Sheikh Mujibur Rahman privately not to push his demands for regional autonomy until these two basic reforms had been passed in the National Assembly.[22] However, only a few days later, Sheikh Mujibur Rahman submitted draft constitutional amendments to the President which envisaged a federal system based on his original six-point demand.[23] It was also proposed that the draft bill be placed before the National Assembly. President Ayub Khan was concerned that Sheikh Mujibur Rahman's amendment might just be carried with the support of the Sindhi, Bengali and Pathan members of the National Assembly, or that the private bill would create a deadlock in the Assembly itself. Eventually Ayub Khan handed over power to the army stating that Sheikh Mujibur Rahman's amendments 'would liquidate the central government and the army'.[24]

Linguistic and Cultural Distinctiveness

When the demand for the recognition of Bengali as one of the state languages was conceded in the 1956 constitution, the language issue lost its salience, but during the Ayub decade it again figured significantly in different perspectives. No political account of regional awareness in East Bengal politics can be complete without a reference to the vernacular movement. Broadly, it had two main objectives. There was a growing demand that English be replaced by Bengali in all spheres of administration and education. It was in fact a pressure for greater opportunities for people educated in their own languages *vis-à-vis* the privileged few who had prospered on account of their proficiency in English. It was also a symbol of resistance against a non-Bengali élite. The central government was blamed for not introducing Bengali as the official language in an effort to perpetuate its domination over the East Wing. To the regionalists, the obvious strategy was to eliminate the influence of the non-Bengali bureaucracy by forcing the use of the Bengali language in administration.

Furthermore, the language demand took the shape of a regional and cultural movement. The Awami League activists, the East Pakistan Students' League and the Left-wing East Pakistan Student Union all stressed cultural separatism for East Bengal through their pressure for the official use of the Bengali language. One of these groups had been emphatic that the East and West Wings were bound to reflect separate cultures in view of their basic social differences. On some of the popular cultural issues the Government's decision became a source of conflict. One such major issue was the dispute over Tagore's songs and writings, which have a universal appeal among Bengalis and are popular among the intelligentsia of East Bengal. A serious public controversy arose when the Government banned Tagore's songs on the radio and television. While the songs remained officially banned following the Indo-Pakistan War in 1965, private cultural bodies continued to organise public recitals of them. Teachers in colleges and universities also raised their voices against the Government's action. Except for the pro-Government National Students' Front and the Islamic Students' Groups, all the anti-establishment student forces organised protests against the 'interference' of the authorities with the cultural life of East Bengal.

As a protest against the Government's policy, the student forces in the country became more aggressive in their cultural and linguistic demands. Students as well as private cultural organisations enthusiastically observed Rabindranath Tagore's birthday in Dacca and the outlying towns. Another significant day which emerged for celebration was the Bengali new year (*Pahela Baishakh*). All these activities were disapproved of by the Government, and Governor Abdul Monem Khan publicly denigrated them as un-Islamic practices encouraged by anti-Pakistan elements. To commemorate the language movement of February 1952, 21 February began to be celebrated more vigorously, from 1962, as *Shahid* Day (Day of the Martyr). The activists also demanded that the Bengali language be used in all commercial displays and signboards. There were reports of intimidation against those who refused to do so. Bengali student activities had their impact on the non-Bengali residents from India and West Pakistan. They began to learn and speak Bengali though they usually preferred to speak their own languages and lead a life distinct from the Bengali way of life and culture. Demands were also made that Bengali be used for the number-plates of motor vehicles. Protests were raised against English-medium private kindergarten and missionary schools; they were said to spread 'alien' culture.

This linguistic nationalism was also an expression of the interests of rural-based young men who were for the first time entering colleges and universities in larger numbers.[25] A steady decline of teaching in English had taken place at the school-level since 1947. Students coming from the villages remained weak in English and faced unequal competition in the universities and colleges with those who had studied in English-medium schools which were mostly situated in urban areas. Only a fraction of rural-based students fared well in university examinations conducted in English.

The Government proved relatively weak in moving against the various linguistic and cultural demands of the regionalists. The experience of 1952 indicated that mass movements in the province could easily be ignited by any move to suppress the linguistic aspirations of the Bengalis. Consequently the policies of the Government on questions of language and culture tended to be defensive. All Government patronage was withdrawn from activities considered to be an expression of cultural separatism. Through the Writers' Guild, the Bengali Academy and the Bengali Development Board, encouragement was provided to a group of local Bengali littérateurs who were willing to focus on the Muslim contributions to Bengali literature. One major demand of the students was probably met when February 21 was declared a holiday in all educational institutions. The government also passed an order for the use of Bengali on vehicle number-plates in East Bengal. All the universities of East Bengal agreed in principle to introduce Bengali as a medium of instruction by gradual stages. Students were permitted to write examinations in Bengali. In order to help with the introduction of Bengali as the medium of instruction, the Government approved a scheme of translating English textbooks into Bengali and Urdu.

Changing Slogans and Symbols

Gradually the slogans and symbols of politics underwent a significant change marking an increased radicalisation of Bengali demands. The abrogation of the 1962 constitution and the imposition of martial law by General Yahya Khan in March 1969 failed to alter the basic issues in the politics of Pakistan or the grievances of East Pakistan. For West Pakistan the rule of the Army was in effect the rule of their own men. From Dacca, however, things looked very different: martial law and military presidents all emanated from West Pakistan, and for practical purposes they came to be seen as manifestations of foreign rule. To dilute Bengali resentment against military rule, General Yahya Khan pledged that power would be transferred to the 'representatives of the people elected freely and impartially on the basis of adult franchise'. Consequently Bengali political élites began preparations to contest the elections scheduled for 1970 on the issue of maximum regional autonomy for East Pakistan.

A definite change in symbols and slogans was also visible in the wake of public agitation in East Pakistan. The Awami League activists introduced the slogan *Joi Bangla* (Victory to Bengal) during the anti-Ayub movements, and it continued to be the catchword of the party. There was hardly any such slogan as *Pakistan Zindabad* (Victory to Pakistan) among Bengali political activists. Public meetings became a platform for explaining the 'injustices' and 'exploitations' of the East by the West Wing. Writings on walls, handbills, and posters, circulated secretly as well as in public, were another means of political protest. There had been clashes between regional protagonists and nationalist elements among students.[26] Now the attention of regional activists was directed towards capturing the students' unions in the colleges and universities in East Pakistan.[27]

The unity of the students in East Bengal provided by the Students' Action Committee (S.A.C.) had also dwindled by the end of 1969. After a period of united action achieved through a joint proposal called the eleven-point programme during anti-Ayub agitations in 1969, the differences between the Left and Right became apparent. The pro-Awami League East Pakistan Students' League became the chief target of attack by the Left-wing East Pakistan Students' Union. One of the major allegations against the East Pakistan Students' League was that it had manipulated the eleven-point programme to push the

Awami League six-point demand for regional autonomy. The extreme radicals among the students argued that such reformist proposals were an inadequate response to the ferment of 'revolution' in the country.[28] The leftists viewed the Awami League six-point programme as a proposal to replace the non-Bengali bourgeois with their Bengali counterparts.[29] The Awami League's decision to contest the elections in 1970 further accentuated the differences. While the radicals remained indifferent, the leaders of the Awami League concentrated on a pre-election campaign so as to mobilise support.

While Awami League supporters launched an electoral campaign in January 1970, the militant pro-Chinese Leftists unleashed a campaign against the elections with the slogan 'Food before vote'.[30] In their anti-election drive, they directed their campaign against authority and against the orthodox Islamic groups; however, one Left-wing faction planned to go beyond with *Joi Bangla* slogans and demand secession for East Bengal.[31]

For all practical purposes, the strategy of the radicals was to work against the increasing popularity of maximum regional autonomy through the six-point programme advocated by the Awami League. They feared an electoral victory for the Right-wing nationalist Awami League which championed the cause of regional autonomy.[32] The radicals had suffered a loss of face for not supporting the Awami League six-point movement in 1966, a movement which became popular until the Government began to repress its supporters. They also realised that the Awami League would eventually develop into a secessionist movement if they failed in their six-point demand. Hence the young left radicals prepared to move one step ahead of the Awami League. They were confident that time was on their side. Even if the Awami League was able to gain power through a coalition with forces in the West Wing or through mobilizing on the basis or regional grievances, it would fail to solve the economic problem. That would inevitably force a confrontation between the Awami League and a populist movement in East Bengal.

Although the Awami League had agreed to the electoral formula promised by General Yahya Khan, there were elements within it who were not convinced of its viability for attaining the six-point demand for regional autonomy for East Pakistan. Their feelings surfaced when General Yahya Khan announced the Legal Framework Order (L.F.O.) on 30 March 1970. The Order declared that the future constitution of Pakistan must preserve five fundamental principles: an Islamic ideology, territorial integrity, free elections, the independence of the judiciary, a federal system ensuring autonomy to the provinces as well as adequate legislative, administrative and financial powers to the central Government, and full opportunities to the people of all regions for participation in national affairs.[33]

Both the Awami League and the leftist National Awami Party raised objections to the Legal Framework Order announced by General Yahya Khan. They pointed to the danger of accepting the Order as it would stand in the way of the six-point programme. The ultimate veto power of the President was seriously questioned. In a meeting of its Working Committee, the Awami League urged General Yahya Khan to make amendments to the Legal Framework Order (LFO) to 'bring it in conformity with fundamental democratic principles'.[34] Deliberations continued for two days. The younger section of the party favoured a strong line.[35] They questioned the justification of participating in an election to a National Assembly which would not be able to exercise its power as a sovereign body. A few days later, the Awami League student activists of Dacca University observed 'Demand Day' for the withdrawal of the President's Legal Framework Order.

Students in secondary schools in East Pakistan launched a movement in the autumn of 1970 demanding immediate withdrawal of a text book called *Pakistan: Desh o Krushti (Pakistan: Land and Culture)* from the reading lists. In Dacca, a number of protest meetings, processions and demonstrations were mounted by students before the office of the Director of Public Instruction and before Government House. The protest meetings served as a signal for a united struggle for the realisation of their demands. They further demanded that the Government should introduce a democratic, scientific and popular system of education.[36] On the face of it, this was a movement against a text book which the students found 'difficult and burdensome'. But the agitation against the book continued even when its reading requirements were considerably reduced. In reality it was a political move against 'indoctrination' on the concept of Pakistan.

A rift developed among the student activists when Sheikh Mujibur Rahman, along with other personalities in the party, decided to go ahead with their preparation for elections. Abdur Rab, the Vice-President of the Dacca University Students' Union, emerged as the leader of the dissident group. In one of his public speeches Rab was reported to have said that he wanted to see a 'new map' for East Bengal. This speech was interpreted as a shift in the East Pakistan Student League's demand for autonomy. By implication, it meant to some a separate state for East Bengal. Soon student activists began to challenge those who gave unqualified support to the Awami League decision to contest elections. Differences between these two factions of the East Pakistan Student League, which was in fact the student front of the Awami League, soon turned into physical clashes at the University.[37] It was clear that the slogans and symbols of Left-wing and Right-wing activists were changing. Regional demands were becoming increasingly extreme and were indications of an outright demand in 1971 for the secession of East Pakistan.

Conclusion

East-West conflicts in Pakistan from 1947 to 1970 provided evidence of a patron-client relationship among the political actors in the former East Pakistan. On an all-Pakistan basis, the Muslim Leaguers of Eastern Bengal were more often treated as the clients of national élites based primarily in Karachi and Islamabad. But as events proved, this pattern did not last for long as the Bengalis of the Muslim League were associated with the ruling party and found themselves discredited in East Pakistan. During the early years of Pakistan, opposition elements contributed signally by making the people of East Pakistan aware of the maladministration of the Muslim League cabinet. Later these oppositional forces challenged Ayub Khan's authoritarian political system. Finally, their entire weight was mounted in favour of the anti-Ayub movement in the early months of 1969. In the process regional grievances were articulated and intensified. The centre-province conflict that developed in Ayub Khan's political system so exacerbated the divisions between East and West Pakistan, becoming for the Bengalis the sole issue in politics. Regionalist forces gathered strength and momentum.

Bengali perceptions of persisting regional economic disparities contributed to a high level of frustration and sharpened a regional polarisation in politics. Demands for eliminating economic disparity were no longer voiced by one or two politicians or groups of intellectuals; they became a crucial issue for all parties in East Pakistan. In the end the demand for maximum regional autonomy advocated in the 1950's became in the 1970 election a minimum demand, even for the conservative party of East Pakistan.

NOTES

1. Mohammed A. Nawawi, 'Stagnation as a Basis of Regionalism: A Lesson from Indonesia', *Asian Survey*, IX, 12 (December 1969).
2. Clifford Geertz, 'The Integrative Revolution: Primordial Sentiments and Civil Politics in the New States', in Finkle and Gable, *Political Development and Social Change* (New York, 2nd edn), 658.
3. Richard Weeks, *Pakistan: Birth and Growth of a Muslim Nation* (Princeton); also quoted in Rounaq Jahan, *Pakistan: Failure in National Integration* (New York, 1972), 3.
4. For a recent study on the subject, see Rounaq Jahan, *Pakistan: Failure in National Integration*, op. cit.

5. For a detailed account on the subject see also Mohammad Anisur Rahman, *East and West Pakistan: A Problem in the Political Economy of Regional Planning* (Cambridge, Mass.: Center for International Affairs, 1968).
6. See also Rounaq Jahan, *Pakistan*, op. cit.,
7. Abul Mansur Ahmed, *Amar dekha*, etc. 293. Also the political commentaries of the Awami League daily newspaper, *Ittefaq*, July–August, 1955.
8. Abul Mansur Ahmed, *Amar dekha*, op. cit.
9. Constituent Assembly Debates, 16 & 17 January 1956; see also Abul Mansur Ahmed, *Amar dekha*, op. cit.
10. For a detailed account of Awami League rule in East Pakistan and its relations with the centre, see Ataur Rahman Khan, *Two Years of Ministership*.
11. Wahidul Huq, 'Development Policies and Regional Justice in Pakistan', unpublished paper, 1970.
12. W.H. Morris-Jones, 'Pakistan Post-Mortem and the Roots of Bangladesh', *Political Quarterly*, 43(2), April–June 1972.
13. A. Sadeque, *The Economic Emergence of Pakistan* (Dacca, East Bengal Government Press, 1956) and Rehman Sobhan, 'Imbalance in Economic Development in Pakistan', *Asian Survey*, 2, 1962.
14. For details see Abul Mansur Ahmed, *Amar dekka*; Ataur Rahman Khan, *Ujarati doi basar*; Kamruddin Ahmed, *Social History*; and Mujibur Rahman Khan, *Friends Not Foes* (Dacca, 1967). The last-named book was banned for criticising martial law.
15. Ataur Rahman Khan, *Ujarati doi basar*; see also *Pakistan Observer*, 27 June 1960, for his reply to the questionnaire circulated by the Constitution Commission of 1960 appointed by Ayub Khan to consider proposals of the future constitution of Pakistan.
16. Ataur Rahman Khan, *Ujarati doi basar*.
17. See also Rounaq Jahan, 'Ten Years of Ayub Khan', and Mujibur Rahman Khan, *Friends Not Foes*.
18. For this concept, see David E. Apter, *The Political Kingdom of Uganda* (Princeton University Press, 1967).
19. For details, see *Six-Point Formula: Our Right to Live* (Dacca, 1966); and the author's 'The Awami League in the Political Development of Pakistan', *Asian Survey*, July 1970.
20. *Pakistan Observer*, 30 November 1966. All the leading political speeches of Ayub Khan underlined this theme. For details, see also Mohammad Ayub Khan, *Speeches and Statements* (Karachi, Pakistan Publications), vols. I–IV.
21. *Address* of Sheikh Mujibur Rahman at the Round Table Conference (Dacca, 1969).
22. *The Times* (London), 9 April 1969.
23. A copy of the draft bill was made available to the author by Tajuddin Ahmed, Secretary, East Pakistan Awami League. See also *Pakistan Observer*, 26 March 1969.
24. *The Times* (London), 9 April 1969.
25. There is no accurate figure for the actual proportion of students who came

from rural backgrounds, but the following observation from an official report may provide a general indication: 'Students are now drawn from all strata of society, but quite a number of them come from families in which they are perhaps the first to reach institutions of higher learning. Their background, outlook and behavior patterns are very different from those of earlier generations who belonged, for the most part, to the upper and middle strata of society' (*Report of the Commission on Student Problems and Welfare*, Government of Pakistan, Ministry of Education, 1966, 177).

26. In one of the clashes in Dacca University in the autumn of 1969, one pro-Islamic student leader was killed.
27. There is no consolidated data about the students' election results but in most of the colleges, the Awami League Student Front E.P.S.L. captured the unions. Our information is based on newspaper reports and interviews with E.P.S.L. leaders.
28. *In the Context of January Movement* (a Bengali pamphlet circulated by the EPSU, Dacca, 1970).
29. See the author's 'The National Awami Party in Pakistan: Leftist Politics in Crisis', *Pacific Affairs*, Fall 1970, and Nurul Huq Choudhury, *Vote Barjan Kane (Why Discard Vote)*, op. cit.
30. For details see *A Programme for Independent, Democratic and Peaceful, Neutral and Progressive East Bengal* (a Bengali pamphlet, Dacca, n.d.).
31. Ibid.
32. For a detailed discussion of such an apprehension, see Nurul Huq Choudhury, *Why Discard Votes*.
33. See also President's Order, 3 November 1970. The order also stipulated that if the President refused to authenticate the constitution, the National Assembly would stand dissolved and that he would be the sole arbiter in interpreting the order.
34. *Pakistan Observer*, 12 April 1970.
35. Ibid. Also author's interviews with some of the former East Pakistan Students' League leaders.
36. *Pakistan Observer*, 2 September 1970.
37. *Purbadesh*, 19 September 1970; there were also reports of a split in East Pakistan Students' League following such differences.

CULTURAL POLICY, THE TEXTBOOK CONTROVERSY AND INDIAN IDENTITY

Lloyd I. Rudolph
Susanne Hoeber Rudolph

Nineteen seventy-seven was an extraordinary year. Democracy was restored and authoritarianism defeated. For the first time since independence, an opposition party, the Janata, displaced the Congress party at the center. India's party system seemed to be transformed from one-party dominance[1] to two-party competition.[2] However, Janata as a governing party failed to institutionalize these historical possibilities. While many elements contributed to the ultimate fragmentation of the party, the explicit ideological and policy grounds on which those struggles took place were secularism and 'dual membership', specifically, whether members of the Janata party could also belong to a doctrinaire Hindu nationalist organisation, the Rashtriya Sevak Sangh (R.S.S.). The effort to define and deal with secularism and communalism has been an important aspect of cultural policy from the beginning of the nationalist period. The inability of Janata to resolve the question of secularism satisfactorily highlights the importance of its cultural policy, the principal concern of this paper.

Locating Cultural Policy

The substantive or phenomenological policy universe encompasses economic, foreign and state policy, as well as cultural policy. Economic policy deals with how states attempt to manage or control in the short and long run the production and allocation of goods and services, the distribution of wealth and income and the level of employment and prices. Foreign policy deals with states' efforts to influence other states in ways that promote national interests, however defined. National integrity and security and national economic viability are among the principal concerns that states bring to the conduct of foreign policy. State policy deals with efforts by governments to define the rules for the conduct of politics. Its domain is procedure and legitimacy. In one fashion or another state policy addresses the problem of regulated conflict among domestic actors. Cultural policy encompasses efforts by states to articulate and define national identity and a public philosophy. It answers questions such as what does it mean to be an

Indian, how should Indians live, what should they value and how can they realise the things they value.

At the level of actual policy discourse and action, substantive policy types intersect and overlap. For example, cultural policy is likely to raise questions of procedures and rights and of resource allocation. Cultural policy can affect the viability or territorial integrity of states, as is attested by the partitions of India and, later, of Pakistan; the threat of Soviet-backed Afghan claims on behalf of Baluchi or Pathan irrendentism; or Hitler's claim to rule all Germans, particularly those in Austria and Czechoslovakia.

There are other ways to locate and characterize policy types. For example, Theodore Lowi has argued for the validity and explanatory power of four functional types of policy, distributive, re-distributive, regulatory and constitutive.[3] Respectively, they allocate resources to defined categories of political actors in ways that are not perceived to discriminate among them or to be at the expense of other categories; extract and allocate resources among categories in ways that benefit some at the expense of others; license and control those wishing to provide goods or services; and establish or enact rules for activities deemed public. Like phenomenological types each functional type is said to generate policy arenas with distinctive properties and dynamics.

A heuristic matrix that encompasses phenomenological and functional categories allows a variety of combinations. For example, cultural policy, by allocating values on a non-discriminatory or discriminatory basis to certain cultural categories, can be distributive or redistributive. Thus Hindus, who favor a ban on cow slaughter, may be able to impose the ban on Muslims, Christians or Untouchables who do not. Cultural policy can be regulatory, as when it licenses or de-licenses textbooks. It is pre-eminently constitutive, in that it can allocate first-class and second-class citizenship status on the basis of religion, e.g. when the state declares a particular religion official. In fact, constitutive policy is very like what we have identified as state policy.

We have said that cultural policy is about national identity and public philosophy. What do these terms suggest or refer to? National identity raises questions about what and who is Indian, about being Indian and un-Indian, questions that in turn raise more specific problems about the meaning and value of history, the past; what ought to be common or shared, the present; and goals and how to reach them, the future. Public philosophy raises questions about the political and social order. What are its principles and how should they be realized in practice? What are India's publicly shared values and how are they to be expressed in institutional arrangements?

India's national identity and public philosophy are inter-related.

They capture different facets of an effort to articulate a distinctive world view or civilization from the complex and diverse elements of a shared but disputed past, a common but contradictory present and an uncertain and only partially determined future. Cultural policy can be animated by civilizational concerns even though the civilization at issue is amorphous and disputed. In India, the meaning and application of history to contemporary issues are central features of political consciousness and political controversy.

India and the United States of America are professed secular states[4] with overwhelming Hindu and Christian majorities that lack confessional parties to translate their convictions into action.[5] Instead, Hindu and Christian values are articulated by organized movements such as the R.S.S. and the Moral Majority who seek to realize their religious values by determining policy choices through their influence in political parties such as the Jan Sangh and the Reagan Republicans. In the absence of confessional parties, politics and policy are animated by Hindu and Christian values applied to current policy issues such as, in India, teaching in state schools about Mughal ('Muslim') rule, preventing the slaughter of cows or imposing prohibition, or, in America, insuring the 'right to life' or teaching in public schools about 'creation'.[6] The commitment to formal secularism has not, in either the United States or India, eliminated the problem of the degree to which the values and practices of religious communities are recognized or the political balance among them.

Many Indians recognize the legitimacy of the 1950 Constitution, agree that secularism, socialism and democracy are desirable ideological goals, and celebrate the great founders of the Indian nation and state, Gandhi and Nehru. But the country has had difficulty agreeing on whether the Constitution makes Parliament or the Supreme Court the final arbiter of constitutional questions,[7] on the meaning, relative standing or relevance of the founders' teaching and example, or how to translate into practice the sometimes contradictory and in any case ambiguous meaning of the ideological terms that all major parties endorse. India is divided over the meaning of its public philosophy rather than over which public philosophy to follow.

So far we have been dealing at a general level with what the term cultural policy suggests. We turn now to the less abstract question of what cultural policy refers to, i.e. the more specific policy arenas and issues within them that taken together constitute a type of policy that can be distinguished as cultural. We include the following arenas: history, religion, language, minorities, education, the arts, and science and technology. Clear and impenetrable lines do not separate these sub-sets of cultural policy. Indeed, a number tend to be cumulative and reinforcing as in the case of the Urdu-speaking Muslim minority. Yet each has characteristics that distinguish it from the others.

In this paper we deal with only one item of Janata's cultural policy, the so-called textbook controversy. It is a chapter of the larger history of cultural policy that encompasses the nationalist era and the interventionist state of the post-Independence period. As we shall see, cultural officials in Mrs Gandhi's pre-1977 Government brought to the task a very different orientation from officials in Janata's 1977–9 Government.

Cultural policy in historical and political perspective

The Janata Government did not invent the idea of a national cultural policy. It constituted a critical problematic for Indian nationalists seeking a politically workable definition of Indian identity. Bipin Chandra, author of one of the textbooks involved in the controversy, argues that the vicissitudes of Indian nationalism fed communal history, i.e. history that celebrates or denigrates the identity of particular religious, cultural or ethnic communities. 'The teaching of Indian history has a great deal to do with the spread of communalism in the last 100 years. In fact, it would be no exaggeration to suggest that a communal historical approach has been, and is, the main ideology of communalism in India.'[8] This strongly stated view is supported by a variety of analyses and explanations: 'Communalism among the historians spread mainly because of its ability to serve as "vicarious" or "backdoor" nationalism. Communalism enabled them to feel nationalistic without opposing imperialism.'[9] For the most part, historians could not side with the rulers, yet they were not willing to risk opposing them either. Backdoor nationalism which took the form of regional or community history 'could satisfy their nationalist urge and yet not be looked askance at by the authorities who encouraged any and all approaches which would create division in Indian society.'[10]

There are many examples of Chandra's proposition, not only among nationalist historians but also among the creators of nationalism. Tilak's famous speech praising the Hindu general Shivaji's treacherous slaying of the Bijapur (Muslim) general Afzal Khan,[11] and Bankim Chandra Chatterjee's (Hindu) ascetics fighting Muslim rule from their forest ashram, the *Ananda Math*, provide obvious examples of Chandra's backdoor nationalism.[12] However, some backdoor nationalism was sufficiently transparent for the British authorities to be under no illusions about its meaning. Tilak's Afzal Khan speech figured in his treason trial.

Another element, according to Chandra, in the growth of communal history was the historical treatment of 'Hindus, Sikhs, and Muslims as distinct, separate socio-political entities'.[13] This treatment paralleled British official categories. ' "Islam" is made an active entity — almost given a personality. "Islam" conquers, "Islam" thinks, "Islam" decides, "Islam" benefits . . . The Maratha empire and states, Rajput states and chiefs, Jat chiefs, etc. are all lumped together as Hindu states, while the southern and northern states headed by Muslim rulers are described as Muslim states.'[14] Chandra's assertion agrees with other scholarship on the subject. 'The very idiom of British rule after 1857', writes Peter Hardy, 'encouraged the development of political consciousness by religious communities.'[15] One of the consequences of W. W. Hunter's official report on Indian Muslims was to endow them with a corporate character they had not had before. Hardy cites Lord Salisbury's typical formulation:

So far as I can judge the feeling of our *Mahomedan* subjects at the moment is eminently satisfactory . . . But all the Government officers whose special business it is to study and watch *Mahomedan* feeling in India are of the opinion . . .[16]

The tradition of communal history which Chandra describes is no monopoly of British or Hindu historians. Muslim anti-nationalists in the pre-Independence period and Muslim orthodoxy in contemporary India have shown considerable enthusiasm for Muslim communal history. One of India's most distinguished historians of Mughal history, Professor Irfan Habib, whose analysis of the economic causes of the decline of the Mughal empire provides a model for social historians in the current generation, was reminded by the President of the Students' Islamic Union of India:

We want that every teacher of the [Aligarh Muslim University] should be loyal to the Islamic Faith and Community. He must not do anything that should be detrimental [sic] to the interests of Islamic culture, community, and this University. Not only the present statement of Irfan Habib, but his attitude in the past as well, was always inimical to Islam and the community. . . .[17]

If the idea of a national cultural policy had its roots in the turmoil and controversy of the nationalist past, it also had a past among Janata's predecessors, the Congress party. For a time Nehru's *The Discovery of India* and *Letters from Prison* constituted a tacit statement of Congress' cultural policy, in part because those who might have objected were reluctant to challenge a prime minister who commanded wide political support. Indira Gandhi's accession to power marked the beginning of a more articulate and aggressive left secularism in institutional arrangements, ideological formulations and scholarship. When Janata came to power in March 1977, its government intervened in textbook certification and appointments to cultural bodies in the name of rectifying a decade of partisan patronage by Congress governments to left academia. Congress governments had founded, funded and favored the Jawaharlal Nehru University, staffed by nationally-recruited faculty and a student body with a reputation for progressive perspectives. Left Congress sympathizers, a memorandum to the prime minister alleged, had colonized independent government-funded research organizations such as the Indian Council of Social Science Research, the University Grants Commission, and the Indian Council of Historical Research. Nurul Hasan, a leading Marxist historian and former professor of history at Aligarh Muslim University, had been put in charge of the Education Ministry.

This Janata view did not credit important differences within the Congress. Lines of support and cleavage were by no means clear. Shifting ideological orientations and regime types divided Congress' supporters. Congress' left or progressive ideological orientation had been evident since the 1969 split when members of the Congress Forum for Socialist Action, especially Mohan Kumaramangalam, a former member of the Communist Party of India, became influential with Mrs Gandhi.[18] Congress-I began to shift in a more conservative and authoritarian direction after Kumaramangalam's death in May 1973. Yet left and right tendencies persisted side by side. Under the Emergency (1975–7) Sanjay Gandhi's influence on party and government became dominant, and the party moved toward a more conservative (anti-Communist) economic and ideological position. But because Sanjay Gandhi took little interest in cultural policy, the left intellectual establishment was able to maintain its influence through the Emergency. The Emergency, however, divided progressive historians into two broad groups, those committed to constitutional democracy and the insulation of scholarship from ideology and those who supported authoritarianism under the Emergency and thought scholarship benefitted from ideological commitment.

When the Janata party came to power in 1977 in a national reaction to the Emergency regime, the Desai-Jan Sangh section of the party concerned with cultural policy did not attend to these distinctions. It was confident that there was a discernible and homogeneous left Congress ideological position. A distinct view of the relationship between scholarship and ideology and its bearing on cultural policy can indeed be discerned in a volume published on the eve of the Emergency entitled *Towards a Cultural Policy*.[19] It contained papers and proceedings of a seminar held well before the Emergency, in June 1972, at the Indian Institute of Advanced Study, Simla. The volume's contents, in the words of the Institute's director and conference convenor, S. C. Dube, reflects the work of 'an interdisciplinary group of scholars, specialists working in diverse cultural fields, and practitioners of the arts.' They took stock of the cultural situation in the country, analytically examined the emerging trends, and 'endeavored to evolve the broad outlines of a cultural policy for India'.[20] The book was edited by a recognized scholar, the anthropologist Satish Saberwal, and contained substantive essays devoted to 'The Context' (five); 'Languages' (three); 'The Arts' (six); 'Science, Technology and the Mass Media' (four); and 'Education' (four). The quality and length of the papers varied greatly. Their orientations to the relationship between scholarship and ideology and its implications for cultural policy were by no means uniform.

The possibilities of a left cultural policy are apparent in the 'policy guidance' provided by the convenor, S. C. Dube, and chief guest and patron, the Education Minister, Nurul Hasan. Dube introduced his theme paper with the remark that

> at the suggestion of the Ministry of Education . . ., the . . . Institute . . . is holding a seminar in honour of Lenin. . . . The seminar is not designed to be merely an act of homage to Lenin or a routine academic exercise. It is intended to provide a springboard for a realistic appraisal of the cultural situation in India that may lead to the emergence of an outline of a cultural policy.[21]

Dube and Hasan faced the question of choosing the Marxian revolutionary and statesman, Lenin, as the inspiration for cultural policy in India in somewhat different ways. Dube found a Marxian way out of a potential dilemma:

> A seminar associated with Lenin's memory must . . . face the question — if values, symbols, and myths are merely the super-structure dependent upon and secondary to the basic structure of material relations, why then should we concentrate on this secondary domain? The answer lies in the acceptance of Marxian thought itself of the proposition that this super-structure has a measure of autonomy and under certain conditions can influence and transform the structure of material relations.[22]

Dube went on to reject past approaches as mythic, myopic, arbitrary and divisive. He asked, 'How can we redefine Indian-ness without glorification of segmental achievements of the past?'[23] The answer lies first in displacing self-appointed guardians of culture who are 'doomed to petrify' because 'they remain uninfluenced by the social and cultural milieu . . . [and] abjure social responsibility'.[24] Fudging the super-structure sub-structure causal relationship, Dube argues that fundamental alterations in the structure of society are 'inevitable'. Along with them a cultural transformation is also imperative. 'It . . . can be planned and guided. A cultural policy, thus, becomes necessary.'[25]

Unlike Dube, Nurul Hasan in his inaugural address did not credit the possibility of super-structural autonomy. The conference for him was a tribute to the memory of Lenin,

> the man who worked for and led a successful revolution in which power was

transferred from the hands of a small coterie of feudal lords and the nascent bourgeoisie. . . . This small class of rulers . . . was . . . highly 'cultured' . . . it produced great masterpieces of literature and art, but it was the culture of an oppressive class. . . . Lenin . . . emphasized the need to broad base culture, the need to harmonize the great cultural achievements of this small class with the urges and aspirations of the masses, and the need to pursue a policy whereby all the various sections of the Russian empire which had been subject to the tyranny of Russification could come into their own and develop their culture. He emphasized that culture cannot really grow and develop without adopting a scientific and humanistic attitude towards life.[26]

The Education Minister then applied his interpretation of Lenin's view of cultural policy to India. Indians must adopt a different attitude toward the past. Much of it

is totally out of harmony with the urges of the masses. Indian society in the past, like societies in every other part of the world, was a class society sharply divided between the masses and those who appropriate the fruits of their labor and evolved theories and philosophies. . . . The culture of the upper class was an injustice and supported an outlook which could only be sustained on the basis of obscurantism and revivalism.

Hasan then praised the resilience of India's traditional culture because of its capacity to assimilate new ideas. This eclecticism produced both irrationalism *and* a rejection of dogmatism. In the past the masses under the influence of undogmatic irrationalism

could simultaneously continue traditional modes of as well as adopt new modes of thought and value judgments. I am not pleading for the continuance of irrationalism but I am pleading for this quality of Indian culture.[27]

What is needed today according to Hasan is

a composite culture which is characteristic of India. . . . At the same time let us move forward and build a culture of the future. . . . based on modern science and technology and on the new relationships in society which all of us wish to bring about.

By the eighteenth century, according to Hasan, 'irrationality had lost its progressive role.' India in turn lost its resilience and declined. 'This decline came because we could not reject that irrationalism which had stood us so well in the earlier centuries. Modern society . . . cannot simultaneously be obscurantist and scientific. . . . We will have to choose between preserving class relationships in society and moving towards a society in which there will be no exploitation of man by man. . . .'[28]

It is possible to view these two ideological interpretations of history and its relation to cultural policy as expressing the dilemma faced by all responsible scholars, how to bring their sense of craftsmanship and historical or social scientific 'truth' into congruence with efforts to direct social change towards desirable goals — a dilemma of special poignancy for scholars to whom academic writing represents a form of praxis. From this point of view Dube and Hasan were simply trying to clarify their own stance as intellectuals and scholars. However, their remarks were not merely the personal clarification of private scholars. They assumed considerable political significance because Dube led India's leading centrally funded academic think-tank, and Hasan the education ministry. No official programs reflecting the policy guidance which they provided were adopted; but under the Emergency regime, when the Indian state pursued a corporatist strategy that patronized academic and intellectual associations that favored Congress-I party loyalists, their views influenced appointments and the kind of scholarship pursued by those concerned to please the powerful.

The Textbook Controversy

Leadership of the new Janata government in 1977 fell to Morarji Desai, an eighty-four year old self-proclaimed Gandhian. Desai's Hindu cultural revivalism, *noblesse oblige* high-caste attitudes and economic conservatism provided the political and ideological conditions for an evolving *rapport* between him and like-minded members of the Jan Sangh faction. His Hindu revivalism first became apparent in policy terms early in the Janata period when he sanctioned inquiries about certain textbooks enjoying government patronage. Other policy initiatives that appealed to an important section of the Jan Sangh appeared later. He was sympathetic to the Freedom of Religion Bill which, by creating penalties for conversion, alarmed Christians; supported a constitutional amendment that opened the way to ban cow slaughter throughout the country; and was committed to nationwide prohibition.

The textbook controversy can be best understood in the context of the internal politics of the newly-formed and fragile Janata party.[29] Prime Minister Morarji Desai's efforts to undermine his principal rival for party leadership, Charan Singh, head of the agrarian B.L.D. faction,[30] eventually complimented those of the Hindu-oriented Jan Sangh faction, which sought to increase its influence in the party to approximate its plurality of seats. Initially, the Jan Sangh established close working relations with the B.L.D. factions at the state level. When, later, it challenged B.L.D. leadership in four northern states, it jeopardized its national relationship with Charan Singh's faction and moved closer to Morarji Desai.[31]

Before launching this account of the textbook controversy, which depicts Janata in Hindu revivalist mode, we want to stress that its foreign, economic and state policies were very different in character. The Janata government proved to be more 'secular' and less ideologically anti-Communist than many of its critics anticipated it could be, given its R.S.S.-Jan Sangh component and its prime minister's Hindu values. It improved relations not only with the United States and China, which was expected, but also with Pakistan, which might have been problematic. It did so even while maintaining India's friendly relationship with the Soviet Union. Its employment-oriented development strategy featuring investment in agriculture and small-scale industry proved to be an imaginative if uncompleted effort to combine growth with redistribution based on expanded income generating employment opportunities. Many of these initiatives have been carried forward by the post-1980 Congress-I government. Perhaps its most memorable contribution was in the realm of state policy, the restoration of constitutional democracy.

Among the most controversial cultural initiatives during Janata rule was a private member bill introduced in Parliament in December 1978 by O. P. Tyagi, a leading member of the Jan Sangh faction of the Janata party. Euphemistically named the 'Freedom of Religion Bill', the proposed legislation made it a criminal offense to use 'force, fraud and inducement' to bring about religious conversions. Christians felt alarmed because the bill seemed to challenge their constitutionally-protected freedom to propagate their religion, and threatened because their philanthropic activities, such as hospitals and schools, could be regarded as 'inducements'. Although a private member bill, it was supported not only by much of the Jan Sangh faction and others but also had the tacit approval of the prime minister.[32]

Government introduced the Constitution (50th Amendment) Bill making cow protection a concurrent subject. Without such an amendment, the states would continue to exercise exclusive jurisdiction over this subject. Had the amendment passed, the center could have introduced legislation banning cow slaughter in all states. Such legislation would have affected particularly West Bengal and Kerala, the two states whose non-Janata governments were explicitly and unequivocally opposed to such a ban, in part because of their strong Communist parties, in part because of their large and influential Muslim and/or Christian populations. This effort aroused criticism and opposition in the Janata itself, and ultimately aborted.

Desai's efforts to impose prohibition on the country was more successful than his moves to stop conversions or end 'cow slaughter', although he was far from his objective of total prohibition within four years when his government fell after twenty-eight months in office. Public drinking in bars, clubs and restaurants was banned in most states and the number of dry days (no liquor sold in stores) per month substantially increased.

It was Desai's cultural policies, which appealed to the Jan Sangh faction but alarmed the Socialist faction, that triggered the conflict over secularism in the Janata party. While it is not clear that a concern for secularism exhausted Charan Singh's and Raj Narain's motives, it was the issue which they used to carry on the power struggle against Desai and, in time, to justify the successive splits that destroyed the party.

The textbook controversy began at the end of May 1977, less than three months after the Janata government assumed office, when V. Shanker, principal secretary to Prime Minister Morarji Desai, sent a note to the Education Minister, P. C. Chunder, saying that the Prime Minister's attention had been drawn to the contents of four books on Indian history.[33] Shanker endorsed the contents of a detailed anonymous memorandum to the Prime Minister which held that the contents of four textbooks were prejudicial to the study of Indian history; he informed Chunder that the Prime Minister thought the Education Ministry might consider withdrawing the books from circulation. The Prime Minister was particularly concerned because the books were used in schools. Shanker, it should be noted, had been secretary to the Iron Sardar, Nehru's rival for national leadership, Vallabhai Patel, the culturally conservative and authoritarian-inclined Deputy Prime Minister and Home and States Minister until his death in 1950. Shanker, like Desai, was in his eighties but had been brought out of retirement by the Prime Minister.

The books at issue were *Medieval India* (1967) by Romila Thapar, *Modern India* (1970) by Bipan Chandra, *Freedom Struggle* (1972) by Amales Tripathi, Barun De and Bipan Chandra, and *Communalism and the Writing of Indian History* (1969) by Romila Thapar, Harbans Mukhia and Bipan Chandra. In August 1977, during the height of the controversy, a fifth book, *Ancient India* by R. S. Sharma was published. Thapar, Chandra and Mukhia were — and are at the time of writing — professors in the Centre for Historical Studies, Jawaharlal Nehru University, New Delhi; Sharma is head of the Department of History, Delhi University, and was for some years director of the Indian Council for Historical Research (I.C.H.R.); Tripathi is Head of the Department of History, Calcutta University; and De is Director of the Institute for Social Sciences, Calcutta. They are influential and productive scholars from some of India's most serious intellectual institutions and departments. Within the broad parameters of close attention to economic determinants, their political views varied widely, from being pro- and anti- the authoritarian Emergency regime imposed by Mrs Gandhi in June 1975 to being pro- and anti- the two principal Communist parties, the C.P.I. and C.P.-M. They also varied with respect to methodology, especially to the weight attributed to ideal as against material factors in historical explanation, although they leaned to the latter.

Three of the books (Sharma, Thapar and Chandra) were published by the National Council for Educational Research and Training (N.C.E.R.T.) for use at the school level. The Chandra, Tripathi and De volume was published by the National Book Trust on the occasion of the twenty-fifth anniversary of Indian Independence. The Thapar, Mukhia and Chandra book was published by the progressive People's Publishing House after its three essays were read (in an abbreviated form) at a seminar organized by All-India Radio on 'The Role of the Broadcaster in the Present Communal Situation' in October 1968.

The most disputed feature in the textbook controversy was the interpretation of 'medieval' Indian history, which corresponds to the period in which Muslim rule prevailed in much of India. The focus of controversy was the textbook historians' attention to social and economic history, and their propensity to explain conflict among élites primarily in political rather than religious terms. This latter feature was the main target of the memorandum to the Prime Minister seeking to have the textbooks withdrawn. For example, Thapar's *Medieval India*, written in a language of discourse appropriate for Middle School students, was scolded for a lack of anti-Muslim and pro-Hindu enthusiasms. An examination of the book suggests the main fault was not a skewing of generally known facts, but an absence of the requisite fervor:

Memorandum: 'For example, Mahmud Ghazni's destroying of Hindu temples has been justified on the ground that he wanted to plunder them. His proud claim as breaker of idols has been almost ignored.'

Thapar, *Medieval India*: 'Mahmud attacked only the temple towns in Northern India. He had heard there was much gold and jewelry kept in the big temples in India, so he destroyed the temples and took away the gold and jewelry . . . He could claim, as he did, that he had obtained religious merit by destroying images' (p. 36).

Memorandum: 'In a very subtle manner Aurangzeb's religious intolerance which led to the revolts in many parts of the country has been defended . . . among the causes of the downfall of the Mughal empire, Aurangzeb's contribution, particularly his policy of religious intolerance, had not been listed at all.'

Thapar, *Medieval India*: 'To make matters worse, Aurangzeb was influenced by an orthodox Muslim group and he decided that he would rule in accordance with the laws of Islam. This was a policy different from that of his ancestors who were tolerant and liberal rulers. Besides, it was quite a wrong policy for a country such as India which has always had a mixture of all kinds of people and religions and where no type of orthodoxy could have worked. Aurangzeb did not understand the problems of India as well as Akbar had done. He became unpopular when he introduced *Jaziya* and when he destroyed temples. What he did not realize is that the job of a king is to rule efficiently and that religion should not be allowed to interfere with the government' (pp. 152–3).

The memorandum V. Shankar forwarded to the Prime Minister

also protested Bipin Chandra's critical treatment of the nationalist generation: 'The nationalists such as Tilak and Aurobindo Ghose have been held responsible for creating disunity between Hindus and Muslim.' The implication of this and other citations is that critical treatment of the communal views of some heroes of the nationalist movement is unacceptable in a government-sponsored publication. The memorandum concludes by complaining about Communist infiltration of the Indian National Congress and of cultural institutions under the control of Congress governments.

An element in the controversy, never explicitly confronted, was a struggle over how to write history — the problem of method and historiography. The disputants disagreed not only about what questions to ask and what theories and concepts to use in answering them, but also about the intimately related questions of where to look for evidence and what counts as evidence.[34] These differences reflected in part methodological differences among generations of historians. The reliance on texts for categories and evidence which characterized the older generation and scholarship through the 1940s has been gradually supplemented by an innovative social and economic history grounded in archeological remains and physical evidence and in a socio-economic framework of explanation. It has also been supplemented with a critical sociology-of-knowledge perspective on the texts themselves. But the approach of younger historians is resented by those for whom *Manusmriti* is a sacred text, not a Brahmanic rationalization of the dominance of the high (twice-born) castes within Hindu society.

Some of the disputed textbooks are not beyond criticism, although one of the problematic elements, the reductionist treatment of British imperialism in India, might not trouble the author of the memorandum. The Chandra, Tripathi, De *Freedom Struggle* offers a rather pronounced historical materialist interpretation. The motives for Britain's acts on the subcontinent are pictured as exclusively economic in character. Motives of an ideological kind that might expand the framework of explanation — evangelism, utilitarianism — are not attended to. The relationship of diverse and often contradictory British policies in India to the shifting fortunes of English parties plays no role. While British historians and policymakers are rightly castigated for a false homogenization of 'Hindus' and 'Muslims', for the authors of *Freedom Struggle* all Englishmen are the same, and so are all policies and ideologies of British parties. The consequences of imperialism are uniformly negative, the impoverishment of India. British industrial development grew on the 'economic underdevelopment and social and cultural backwardness of India'.[35]

The Indian National Congress, in its early phases, is pictured as uniformly in support of progressive and nationalist economic policies.

The complexities and anomalies created when early Congressmen nervously resisted as too radical the peasant-oriented policy of Congress friend Alan Octavian Hume, or when Punjab Congress lawyers opposed the progressive and pro-peasant Punjab Land Alienation Act launched by peasant-oriented British officials, do not figure in the account.[36]

Communalism also loses its complexity. Communalism was certainly in part a creation of British political ideology and strategy. The authors acknowledge it was also a result of the religious and local symbolism used by regional nationalist leaders in Mahrashtra, Bengal and Punjab to broaden the base of popular mobilizations. For the three authors, however, communalism remains mainly an imperial creation. They argue that Sir Saiyed Ahmed Khan, the pre-eminent leader of the 'modernist' Islamic revival in the late nineteenth century, became apprehensive about Congress nationalism because 'the British also pulled strings behind the scenes.' They reject as 'contrary to facts and unscientific and irrational'[37] Sir Saiyed's views and those of other Muslim leaders that the diversity of Indian society and Muslim corporate interest and identity are incompatible with a common Indian nationalism. Presumably, in the absence of British manipulation, science and reason applied to the evidence would have led Sir Saiyed to a Congress nationalist perspective. The textbook writers follow Jawaharlal Nehru in the belief that the religious dimension of the Pakistan demand is a mystification[38] created by Muslim landlords who 'were afraid that the increasingly radical agrarian program of the Congress would undermine their semi-feudal position.'[39] That 'modernist' Muslims were British loyalists and orthodox Muslims pro-Congress nationalists can not easily be accounted for by the authors' explanatory framework. In fact, all political mobilizations not based on class are suspect. Even Gandhi's campaigns on behalf of India's dispossessed communities did not qualify: 'A new trend away from mass movements was the revival of Gandhiji's old concern for gaining support from the Harijans, Scheduled Castes and Tribes.'[40] In brief, the interpretive consistency of *Freedom Struggle* is achieved at the expense of attention to causes and explanations more in accord with the complexity and indeterminacy of Indian history, a shortcoming no doubt but one that is hardly a reason for withdrawal.

The battle over the propriety of the Prime Minister's suggestion raged in the press and journals of opinion and in parliament throughout 1977 and into early 1978.[41] On 29 July 1977, it was discussed in the Rajya Sabha (upper house) of Parliament. The Education Minister, Dr P. C. Chunder, allowed that some British historians distorted Indian history but avoided direct comment on the impugned textbooks. Dr V. P. Dutt, professor at Delhi University, a progressive

China scholar and Congress-I member, warned that medieval history had been used by communal forces to divide the country and pleaded for history that promoted integration.Nurul Hasan, the Education Minister in the Gandhi Congress-I Emergency government and himself a former professor of medieval Indian history, took a more overtly Marxist position similar to that expressed in his remarks at the 1972 Simla seminar on cultural policy. In his opinion medieval Indian society, like all other medieval societies, was an exploitative one. The religious beliefs of rulers and ruled were irrelevant. Hindus and Muslims had developed common cultural traditions while retaining their own religions. It was the job of the N.C.E.R.T. to commission textbooks that would provide school children with wholesome history.

The practical consequences of the Prime Minister's suggestion became clear when R. S. Sharma's book *Ancient India*, published in 1977 at the height of the controversy, was withdrawn in July 1978 by the Central Board of Secondary Education from the syllabus of Class XI in the 1,100 Board-affiliated schools. The Board's chairman, R. P. Singhal, said at the time that there was no plan to withdraw Romila Thapar's *Medieval India* and that no decision had yet been taken on a third prescribed textbook, *Modern India* by Bipan Chandra. Although the books were not formally withdrawn, *de facto* their distribution was sharply reduced.[42] Minister of State for Education Renuka Devi Barkataki told the Lok Sabha on August 12, that the Board took the decision in consultation with the N.C.E.R.T. and the Ministry of Education. She said the book contains some 'controversial passages'. She also listed in her statement another thirty-one books, including fourteen history textbooks that an expert committee of N.C.E.R.T. on the basis of 'objective criteria' had recommended for withdrawal from school use. R. S. Sharma's book does not seem to have been considered in the light of the N.C.E.R.T. criteria as it does not figure in the list of thirty-one books screened by the committee.[43]

It would seem that the decision to de-license R. S. Sharma's book was taken independently and at the highest levels. This surmise was strengthened in October 1977 when government on the 14th denied him a passport and thus prevented him from leaving India at the head of an eight-person I.C.H.R. delegation to attend a conference in the Soviet Union on 'Ethnic Problems of the Early History of the Peoples of Central Asia in the Second Millenium B.C.',[44] i.e. the question of who were the Aryans? Sharma had already been relieved of his post as director of I.C.H.R.

The alternative establishment Janata had in mind was composed of historians broadly identified with the Bharatya Vidya Bhavan, a government-sponsored organization established in 1938 as a national institution to promote education, art and culture. Its eleven-volume

The History and Culture of the Indian People was edited by R. C. Majumdar,[45] an eminent historian, formerly professor at Dacca and Banaras and past president of the All India History Congress. Majumdar's historical writings in the 1950s with Kali Kinkar Datta deal with Mughal history in a manner reminiscent of the celebratory interpretations by Vincent Smith, doyen of the British Indian historians of the pre-First World War period. For Smith, Mughal rule had constituted one of the glorious eras of Indian history. By 1963, Majumdar had adopted a more Hindu nationalist position.[46] Muslims had become foreigners in the land. Interpreting Gandhi's 1919 alliance with Indian Muslims concerned about the Allied treatment of the *khalif* of defeated Turkey, he writes:

> If a hundred million of Muslims are more vitally interested in the fate of Turkey and other Muslim states outside India than they are in the fate of India, they can hardly be regarded as a unit of the Indian nation. By his own admission that the *Khilafat* issue was a vital one for Indian Muslims, Gandhi himself admitted in a way that they formed a separate nation: they were in India but not of India.[47]

Professor Majumdar's approach, which would limit Indian identity to those whose roots can be shown to be wholly indigenous, raises a host of complex problems. Among these are how to interpret the continuous inmigration of new peoples through the Khyber Pass, and the even more complex question of the origin of the peoples referred to as the Aryans. While the evidence is complex, it is difficult to imagine any credible historical reconstruction which would deny that Vedic civilization itself had elements that were 'foreign'. The search for 'the indigenous' may well be an infinite regress.[48]

Janata's effort to reconstitute the historical establishment began with an abortive effort by some members to promote the appointment as I.C.H.R. chairman of Kali Kinkar Datta, author of *Modern Indian History* and the *Advanced History of India* and sometime vice-chancellor of Magadh and Patna Universities. Intimations of his appointment were subjected to such severe professional criticism[49] that his name was withdrawn. In the meantime, the Janata Government reconstituted the Council with people considered more sympathetic to it. 'The powers of certain senior officials, known for their progressive outlook, were . . . reduced to bring them in line with government's thinking. And some, it is alleged, bent over backward to please Janata leaders.[50] By March 1980, just after Congress returned to power, the publication program of the I.C.H.R. had been 'virtually in cold storage for the past two years'.[51] The impasse featured the Janata Government's efforts to block translations into Indian languages of disfavored authors, including the textbook authors, and to transfer the 'Towards Freedom

Project' (a history of India's freedom struggle in ten volumes) to the Bharatya Vidya Bhavan, whose interpretation of history had been questioned by the earlier Council members on the ground it was 'obscurantist and communal'. The pre-Janata Council had refused to translate most of the books brought out by the Bhavan under the Majumdar-edited *History and Culture of the Indian People.*[52] The Janata Government not only pressed the Council to re-do its translations and publications program in ways more in line with the Bharatya Vidya Bhavan's historical perspective but also encouraged the creation and funded a rival organization, the Indian History and Culture Society, after the Indian History Congress strongly endorsed the textbook writers.[53]

In 1978, A. R. Kulkarni, a respected historian not directly involved in the textbook controversy, was appointed chairman of the I.C.H.R. In May 1981, at the end of Kulkarni's term and sixteen months after Congress returned to power, Niharranjan Ray, a respected cultural historian also less involved in the cultural battles, became chairman. Ray's initial act was to suspend the research grants of ten historians appointed under Janata auspices and order an inquiry into the manner in which they were funded.[54] Clearly, the question of maintaining an autonomous realm for quasi-government agencies charged with supporting culture has not yet been solved.

Implications of Cultural Policy for Politics and Indian Identity

We conclude by returning to the origins of the textbook controversy and some observations on its bearing on cultural policy. Prime Minister Morarji Desai was urged in a confidential memorandum not only to proscribe certain textbooks but also to appoint a committee to look into the infiltration by persons of 'Communist' persuasion of academic positions, research grants, publication subsidies, and teaching positions. His suggestion to the Education Minister that he consider withdrawing the textbooks from circulation in the schools was accompanied by a more general campaign against so-called Communist historians and social scientists. They were said to be entrenched in the I.C.H.R.; J.N.U.'s Centre for Historical Studies; the Institute for Social Studies, Calcutta; and even the U.G.C., the I.C.S.S.R. and the N.C.E.R.T. From these bastions they propounded a wrong and dangerous view of Indian history and culture and promoted the partisan and personal interests of those who thought as they did.

The response to the Janata cultural fundamentalist attack was to depict it as part of an effort to destroy some of India's finest institutions and most promising careers. Both sides became deeply suspicious of their opponents' motives and goals. In time, the secularism issue surfaced within Janata itself and contributed to its demise.

Janata's cultural policy has to be understood not only in terms of its prime minister's endorsement of policies and cultural interpretations that challenged and sought to displace Congress' secularist and progressive formulations, but also in terms of Janata's response to the historic opportunity its 1977 electoral victory created. Janata was driven by two contradictory impulses, the first statesmanly, the second partisan. Its statesmanly objectives included restoring the Constitution and reconstituting the party system in a two-party mode. Its partisan objective was to exploit the powers of incumbency in order to consolidate and expand its party advantage. After twenty-five years in the political wilderness, its loosely consolidated factions seized the opportunity to allocate patronage and resources to their respective minions. It tried to displace what were perceived to be Mrs Gandhi's beneficiaries and acolytes in cultural and academic posts.

While Janata made solid advances toward its first objective of restoring the Constitution, it proceeded to self-destruct in pursuit of the second. The intra- and inter-party struggle over power, spoils and ideology destroyed Janata's fragile credibility and unity. In the process, it also aborted national two-party competition.

The secularist issue within the party took the form of an attack on 'dual membership', i.e. simultaneously belonging to Janata and the R.S.S. The attack became credible and effective after two distinct but mutually reinforcing developments: a factional re-alignment that involved the erstwhile Jan Sangh shifting its support from the Charan Singh-led B.K.D. to the Morarji Desai-led Congress-O and Desai's tilt towards a cultural orientation and policy initiatives that were more Hindu communalist than Gandhian.

The textbook authors were in a poignant position. A number of them, as opponents or critics of Mrs Gandhi's authoritarian regime, had been supporters of persons now associated with Janata. At the same time, they were long-term beneficiaries of Congress policies and resources that supported their secular and/or progressive history. In Janata's eyes they seemed appropriate targets for a partisan re-allocation of cultural and academic posts and resources. Thus the motive and strength of the communalist attack was not wholly ideological. It also involved access to resources, organizations and career opportunities for 'outs' who had been in the political and academic wilderness for a generation or more.

The textbook controversy raised two complementary issues in making cultural policy: the role of partisan or personal interests in the allocation of scholarly resources and authority; and the political consequences of historical interpretations for Indian identity and public philosophy. Neither is easily resolved.

Could personal and partisan struggles over resources, prestige and scholarly standards be avoided if the central government abandoned the practice of selecting (i.e. officially certifying and/or producing) textbooks for use in the proportionately small but enormously influential centrally-controlled school sector? This raises a second question: what happens when textbooks are selected from private publishers by bureaucracies representing state education departments, or by boards of study? There is little evidence to suggest that they consistently prefer scholarly, engaging texts published by independent, established firms to shoddy or partisan ones. Economically and politically vulnerable mushroom firms spring from the soil of cozy patron-client relationships between local educational institutions and entrepreneurs. Given the well-documented limitations of India's myriad and often ephemeral private-sector publishing firms, it can be argued that commissioning and/or selection of texts by agencies of the central government provides the leadership and guidance needed to protect scholarly standards from the debilitating effects of an imperfect market.

However, if the central government is to encourage and protect scholarly standards, better means are required to insulate those responsible for selection from the consequences of the partisan political struggle and efforts at personal aggrandizement. Organizations such as the I.C.H.R., N.C.E.R.T., and National Book Trust are meant to be autonomous bodies capable of acting in terms of professional criteria. Their autonomy, however, is conditioned by the motives and expectations of those who offer and accept appointments on them. The textbook controversy and the related struggle over the leadership and policies of the I.C.H.R. make it clear that the problem of effective insulation has not yet been solved by present institutional arrangements.

The textbook controversy renewed a century-old effort to articulate a national identity and public philosophy for India. Partition followed by the Nehru consensus on the secular state left unanswered questions about India's minorities. Not least among them was how to interpret the role of Muslims in Indian history. Civic incorporation or alienation of 70 million people (11 per cent of the population) depends in considerable measure on historical interpretation. Interpretative differences go beyond positive and negative evaluations of Muslim conquest and rule and their alien or assimilated relationship to Indian culture. They reach the question whether the scholarly pursuit of historical knowledge can be compatible with the creation of a shared national identity and public philosophy. Nehru's secularism was based on a commitment to scientific humanism tinged with a progressive view of historical change.

Gandhi's secularism was based on a commitment to the brotherhood of religious communities in their respect for and pursuit of truth. The élites of the founding generation used but did not replenish the political and cultural capital Nehru's and Gandhi's leadership created.

While Congress secularism has served Muslims well, it has not faced up ideologically to the consequences of a persisting Muslim cultural identity for Indian national and public philosophy. Nehru and most of the textbook writers avoided the issue by interpreting Muslim interests in class terms and by claiming there was a scientific humanist and progressive culture and a secular state public philosophy to which Muslims could and should be assimilated. Gandhi's doctrine of pluralism based on brotherhood came closer ideologically to accommodating a distinct Muslim presence in the Indian nation and state but it has been abandoned by Congress and betrayed by the Janata communalist group. When the Janata cultural fundamentalists challenged the Nehru cultural settlement by raising the textbook controversy, they made apparent that many Hindus did not adhere to that settlement or its public philosophy of a secular state and equal citizenship for all religious minorities.

NOTES

1. For accounts of the dominant party system, see W. H. Morris-Jones, 'Dominance and Dissent,' *Government and Opposition*, 1, 4, August 1966, and 'The Indian Congress Party: a Dilemma of Dominance', *Modern Asian Studies*, 1, 2, 1967; Rajni Kothari, *Politics in India* (Boston; Little Brown & Co., 1970), ch. 5.
2. In the 1977 parliamentary election, Janata won 55 per cent of the seats with 43 per cent of the votes. In prior parliamentary elections, with exception of the fourth (in 1967), Congress had won two-thirds or more of the seats with 40 per cent or more of the votes. By 1980, Janata had fragmented. Its components' vote shares were as follows: Lok Dal (9.4 per cent), Janata (18.9 per cent), Congress-U (5.3 per cent).
3. For Lowi's initial formulation which does not include constitutive, see 'American Business, Public Policy, Case Studies, and Political Theory', *World Politics*, July 1964, 677–715.
4. For a discussion of Indian secularism, see Donald E. Smith, *India as a Secular State* (Princeton University Press, 1963).
5. See Lloyd I. Rudolph and Susanne Hoeber Rudolph, 'The Centrist Future of Indian Politics', *Asian Survey*, 20, 6, June 1980, for some consequences of a lack of confessional parties in India.
6. For a wide ranging account of the newly powerful biblical fundamentalist attack on 'secular humanism' and increasingly successful attempts to substitute literalist versions of biblical for scholarly and scientific knowl-

edge in educational and cultural institutions, see 'The Right's New Bogyman,' *Newsweek*, 6 July 1981, 48–50. See also 'Penthouse Interview: Reverend Jerry Falwell', *Penthouse*, March 1981; 'Evangelicals Debate Their Role in Battling Secularism', *New York Times*, 27 January 1981; 'Baptists in Attack on Moral Majority', *New York Times*, 26 March 1981; Senator Jesse Helms' and Congressman Henry J. Hyde's letter to the editor, *New York Times*, 12 April 1981; 'Conservatives' Social Agenda Is Refusing to Remain Hidden' and 'Banning a Textbook', both in *New York Times*, 31 May 1981.

7. See our 'Parliamentary Sovereignty *v.* Judicial Review, Struggle over Stateness in India', *Journal of Commonwealth and Comparative Politics*, November 1981.
8. 'Historians of Modern India and Communalism', in Romila Thapar, Bipan Chandra and Harbans Mukhia, *Communalism and the Writing of Indian History* (Delhi: People's Publishing House, 1969), 36.
9. Ibid., 44.
10. Ibid., 45.
11. See Stanley A. Wolpert, *Tilak and Gokhale: Revolution and Reform in the Making of Modern India* (Berkeley: University of California Press, 1962).
12. Bankim Chandra Chatterjee, *The Abbey of Bliss*, a translation of Bankim Chandra Chatterjee's *Anandamath* by Naresh Chandra Sen-Gupta (Calcutta: P. M. Neogi, 1906).
13. Bipin Chandra, 'Historians', 47.
14. Ibid., 47.
15. Peter Hardy, *The Muslims of British India* (Cambrdige University Press, 1972), 116. Also p. 129, where Hardy speaks of government 'endowing Muslims with a separate social as well as religious personality'.
16. Ibid., 118. Our emphasis. For alternative views which present Indian Islam as characterized by social, economic and doctrinal differences, see Hardy himself, 117–18, and Anil Seal, *The Emergence of Indian Nationalism*, (Cambridge University Press, 1971), 27, 300, 339.
17. Cited in Romila Thapar, 'Academic Freedom and the AMU Crisis', *The Radical Humanist*, April 1981.
18. For a telling account, see Francine Frankel, *India's Political Economy, 1947–1977; The Gradual Revolution* (Princeton University Press, 1978), 407 ff.
19. Satish Saberwal (ed.), *Towards a Cultural Policy* (Delhi, Vikas, 1975).
20. Ibid., v.
21. Ibid., 3.
22. Ibid., 4.
23. Ibid.
24. Ibid., 8.
25. Ibid.
26. Ibid., 13.
27. Ibid., 15.
28. Ibid., 16.
29. There is a long literature on the controversies of 1977–9. See, for example, L. K. Advani, *The People Betrayed* (New Delhi: Vision Books,

1978); A. B. Vajpayee, 'All Responsible for Janata Crisis', *Indian Express*, 2 August 1979; Janardan Thakur, *Indira Gandhi and her Power Game* (New Delhi: Vikas, 1979); Nana Deshmukh, *R. S. S.: Victim of Slander* (New Delhi: Vision Books, 1979); Banu Sengupta, *Last Days of the Morarji Raj*, (Calcutta: Ananda Publications, 1979).

30. Lloyd I. Rudolph and Susanne Hoeber Rudolph, 'Agrarianism in India and America,' *Emerging Sociology* (Meerut, U.P., India: vol. II, 1980); Susanne Hoeber Rudolph, 'Agrarianism and Rural Development' and Lloyd I. Rudolph, 'Agrarianism in Comparative Perspective', papers presented at a seminar on 'Dynamics of Rural Development', held at Mussoorie, India, 23–25 May 1980, sponsored by U.S. International Communication Agency, New Delhi, and published in *Proceedings* of the Seminar.

31. 'The Janata Party had been formed by six groups: the Organization Congress led by Morarji Desai, the Prime Minister; the Jan Sangh, led by Mr A. B. Vajpayee, the External Affairs Minister; the *Bharatiya Lok Dal* (BLD), led by Mr Charan Singh, the Home Minister; the Socialist Party, led by Mr George Fernandes, the Minister of Industries; the Congress for Democracy (CFD), led by Mr Jajivan Ram, the Defence Minister; and dissident Congressmen, led by Mr Mohan Dharia, the Minister of Commerce . . . *The Hindu* on June 24 (1977) gave the representation of these groups as follows: *Jan Sangh* 90; BLD 68; Organization Congress 55; Socialists 51; CFD 28; dissident Congressmen 6. Their numerical majority gave the two right wing groups — the Jan Sangh and the BLD — a dominant position, and the Chief Ministers who took office in Bihar, Haryana, Himachal Pradesh, Madhya Pradesh, Orissa, Rajasthan and Uttar Pradesh after the (state assembly) elections in June 1977 . . . were all drawn from these two groups.' *Keesing's Contemporary Archives*, 8 December 1978, 29343.

32. For comprehensive treatment of the bill, including similar acts in Madhya Pradesh, Orissa, and Arunachal Pradesh, and court decisions that upheld the validity of the state acts, see Jose Kananaikil, 'Social Change in Rural India: The Changing Self-Image of a Scheduled Caste', unpubl. Ph.D. dissertation, Department of Sociology, University of Chicago, Chicago, 1981. An interdenominational delegation of Christian leaders was given to understand by the prime minister on 7 April 1979 in Shillong, that the Freedom of Religion Bill would go through substantially unchanged. When the delegation asked him to arrange for its withdrawal, he responded, 'It will not be done.' Mimeo, no author, no date, *circa* Spring, 1979, followed by M. A. Z. Rolston, General Secretary, National Christian Council of India, 'A Report on the Situation of Christians in Arunachal', Nagpur, 8 January 1979. See also, Mathai Zachariah (ed.), *Freedom of Religion in India*, (Nagpur: National Christian Council of India, 1979), for a critical review of the private member bill, prior state acts and court decisions, and Richard W. Lariviere, 'The Indian Supreme Court and the Freedom of Religion', *Journal of Constitutional and Parliamentary Studies*, IX, 2, April–June 1975, for a review of earlier court decisions.

33. Copy of V. Shanker letter of 27.5.1977, No. P. 388/EM/76. The Prime Minister is reported as suggesting that 'suitable steps [be] taken to ensure that readers do not get wrong ideas about the various elements of our history and culture.'
34. For an effort by self-identified 'younger historians', (p. i) some of whom were progressive, to establish new concepts, explanatory frameworks, and techniques for identifying new forms of evidence and reinterpreting conventional forms, see *Problems of Historical Writing in India*, Proceedings of the Seminar held at the India International Centre, New Delhi, 21–25 January 1963. New Delhi, India International Centre, 1963.

    In their introduction S. Gopal and Romila Thapar identified the overall theme of the seminar as 'the emergence of new techniques and methods of interpretation' and gave as its purpose 'a probe to see what problems most required attention, both at the level of historical reconstruction in research *and at the level of teaching history* as a *discipline* of the Social Sciences and the Humanities' (our emphasis).
35. *Freedom Struggle*, 30–1.
36. For a discussion of Hume's peasant strategy and its negative reception among Congressmen and British officials, see John R. McLane, *Indian Nationalism and the Early Congress* (Princeton University Press, 1977), 114 ff. McLane elaborates a detailed picture of the formulation of Congress land policies in the latter part of the nineteenth century, including the Punjab Land Alienation Act. See chs. 6–8.
37. *Freedom Struggle*, 103.
38. *Discovery of India* (John Day and Co., 1946).
39. *Freedom Struggle*, 209.
40. Ibid., 186.
41. In addition to extensive coverage in English and Hindi dailies, *Mainstream* ran articles by prominent historians on 10, 24, and 31 December 1977 and 7 and 14 January, 4 February and 4 March 1978, as did *Seminar* in January and February 1978 (by S. Gopal and Ashish Nandy) and *Economic and Political Weekly*, XIII, 14, 17, 18, 19, 23, 29 and 37, April–September 1978. *Past and Present* (Oxford) carried a signed editorial in its November 1977 number. *The Hindu* carried commentary in its weekly supplement. See also Aligarh Historians Group, 'The R. S. S. Camp in the I.C.H.R.: its First Fruits', *Social Scientist*, 7, August–July 1978–9, 58 ff.
42. Interview with a high-ranking education official under the Janata and Congress-I governments.
43. For an account of the minister's statement and a list of the books recommended for withdrawal, see *Data India*, 21–27 August 1978, 533–4. 'Of the 31 books recommended to the States for withdrawal, 27 were considered unsuitable because their content or tenor militated against national integration or because they reflected vestiges of imperialist thinking on India. Four books were considered to have material which was not up to date or not of a high standard.'
44. For details and background of this event see Vijay C. P. Chaudhury's polemical account, partisan to the textbook writers, *Secularism Versus Communalism: an Anatomy of the National Debate on Five Controversial History*

Books (Patna: Navdhara Samiti, 1977), 69–79.

45. Bombay, Bharatiya Vidya Bhavan, various years.
46. R. C. Majumdar, H. C. Raychaudhuri, Kali Kinkar Datta, *An Advanced History of India* (London: Macmillan, 1953). Comparing the treatment of the *Khilafat* issue (p. 984) in *An Advanced History* with that in volume XI of *The History and Culture of the Indian People* (1969), 319, suggests the nature of Majumdar's shift. Vincent Smith's *Akbar the Great* (Delhi: S. Chand, 2nd edn, 3rd Indian reprint, 1966), is an influential work characteristic of British historiography of the medieval period.

    For a critique of such Akbar eulogies on the ground that they flow from a personalized view of history and that no medieval state could 'by its very nature, be secular', see Harbans Mukhia, 'Medieval Indian History and the Communal Approach', in Thapar *et al.*, *Communalism and the Writing of Indian History*, 23. 'The communal historian can also afford to shower praises on Akbar's liberalism, for having done that he would be free to condemn every other ruler with the charge of dogmatism' (p. 27).
47. *Struggle for Freedom*, vol. XI of *History and Culture of the Indian People*, at p. 319.
48. See Romila Thapar's discussion of the question in 'Communalism and the Writing of Ancient Indian History', in *Communalism and the Writing of Indian History*, 11. For an important new study of the archaeological, linguistic and textual evidence linking Harappan and Aryan peoples and cultures, see Malati Shendge, *The Civilized Demons: the Harappans in the Rgveda* (New Delhi: Abhinav Publications, 1977).
49. Chaudhury, *Secularism*, ch. II: 'Kali Kinkar Datta', 32–41, for a vituperative version of the criticism.
50. Hasan Suroor, 'Historians in Cold Storage', *Statesman*, 9 March 1980.
51. Ibid.
52. Ibid.
53. See Romila Thapar, 'Sources of Encroachment on Academic Freedom', *Radical Humanist*, 43, 11, February 1979.
54. *Statesman*, 19 and 23 April 1981.

THE SINHALESE-TAMIL RIFT IN SRI LANKA

C. R. de Silva

At the start of her existence as a newly-independent state in 1948, Sri Lanka (then known as Ceylon) seemed to be — in contrast to the sectarian violence that accompanied the birth of India, Pakistan or even Burma — to be relatively at peace. D. S. Senanayake, the first Prime Minister, was not only accepted as the leader of the majority Sinhalese community but seemed to have contrived a consociational arrangement with the middle-class leaders of most of the island's minority ethnic and religious groups. This was by no means a foregone conclusion, for in the 1930s G. G. Ponnambalam, the leader of the principal Ceylon Tamil political grouping, had gained the support of many minority leaders for a cry for weightage for the minorities in political representation. On the other hand organisations which campaigned for Sinhalese and Buddhist rights like the Sinhala Maha Sabha had also risen in the same period. However, Senanayake was able to attract the stalwarts of the Sinhala Maha Sabha to join the new United National Party (U.N.P.) he formed in 1946 and shortly after independence he persuaded G. G. Ponnambalam to join the Cabinet.[1] The country seemed on the way to achieving a political compromise in relation to its major ethnic and religious groups.

Thirty years later the situation had changed. Few Tamils remained in the two major political parties — the U.N.P. and the Sri Lanka Freedom Party (S.L.F.P.) — while the chief Tamil political organisation, the Tamil United Liberation Front (T.U.L.F.), campaigning for a separate state for the Tamils, obtained a very large measure of support from the Tamils of the northern and north-eastern parts of the country at the General Election of 1977. The changed picture indicates how the rift between the Sinhalese and the Tamils has widened in the three decades since independence. The main purpose of this essay is to examine and explain this development.

The Sinhalese comprise a group of people speaking an Aryan language also called Sinhala. The first Sinhalese migrants arrived in Sri Lanka some 2,500 years ago. Since then, they have inter-mixed not only with the aboriginal inhabitants of the island but also more substantially with later migrants from the Malabar and Coromandel coasts of South India. Nevertheless, they developed a distinct identity not only because of their language but because they were virtually all

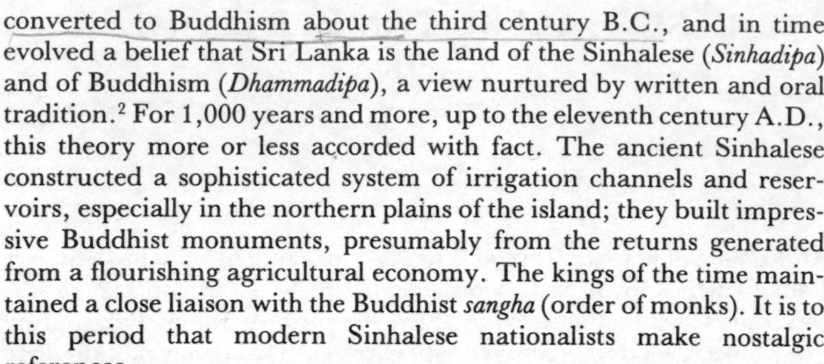

converted to Buddhism about the third century B.C., and in time evolved a belief that Sri Lanka is the land of the Sinhalese (*Sinhadipa*) and of Buddhism (*Dhammadipa*), a view nurtured by written and oral tradition.[2] For 1,000 years and more, up to the eleventh century A.D., this theory more or less accorded with fact. The ancient Sinhalese constructed a sophisticated system of irrigation channels and reservoirs, especially in the northern plains of the island; they built impressive Buddhist monuments, presumably from the returns generated from a flourishing agricultural economy. The kings of the time maintained a close liaison with the Buddhist *sangha* (order of monks). It is to this period that modern Sinhalese nationalists make nostalgic references.

It is possible that some Sri Lanka Tamils may have come to Sri Lanka as early as or even before the Sinhalese. The available evidence, however, suggests that substantial Tamil settlements were established only centuries after the Sinhalese arrived. In the first millenium following Sinhalese colonisation of the island, ethnic conflict was probably not a major factor. Indeed it has been suggested that a Sinhalese ethnic identity developed later than this period.[3] Sinhalese princes of the time fled to South India and returned with Dravidian mercenary troops to fight their rivals. The case of Duttagamini, a Sinhalese prince portrayed by the chronicles as a hero who fought Elara, a Tamil king, provides evidence that Elara had considerable Sinhalese support while Duttagamini had to contend for power with Sinhalese rivals.[4]

After the rise of powerful South Indian Hindu states from the fifth century A.D. onwards, the situation changed. These states invaded Sri Lanka from time to time, and the conflicts which resulted appear to have aroused an identity consciousness among Tamils and Sinhalese in the island. The Hindu Tamil population in the north gradually increased as a result of immigration from India, and eventually, when the Sinhalese kingdom on the northern plain collapsed in the thirteenth century, the Sinhalese moved southwards and an independent Tamil kingdom, largely based on the Jaffna peninsula, came into existence.

This independent Tamil kingdom lasted from the mid-thirteenth to the early seventeenth century, but conflicts between the Sinhalese and Tamils during this period were sporadic rather than continuous. This was partly because an extensive no-man's-land, comprising the largely abandoned centres of the old civilisation, separated the two ethnic kingdoms and partly because neither had the resources to extend its authority over the whole island for extended periods of time. However, there were other contributory factors such as a long tradition of mutual tolerance and co-operation. The Sinhalese kings occasionally married South Indian Tamil princesses, and Tamil officials were known to hold high positions in Sinhalese courts; also Tamil rulers of Jaffna are known to have assisted Sinhalese kings against their enemies. Buddhist temples gradually came to accommodate shrines to Hindu gods within their premises.[5]

The colonial impact generated by the Portuguese, the Dutch and eventually the British brought about many changes. In the first place, despite the Europeans' awareness of the cultural identity of the Ceylon Tamils, and despite their action in codifying the customary Tamil law, the administrative unification of the northern areas with the south tended to integrate Tamil areas into the governmental structure of a united Ceylon. The development of road and rail transport strengthened this effect. On the other hand, unlike in neighbouring India, local government institutions were slow to develop and often almost non-existent. Thus, at independence Ceylon's new rulers inherited a workable machinery for governing the whole country, while the minority ethnic and religious groups found no institutional framework within which to organise themselves, even in the areas where they were dominant.

However, colonial rule did not have an effect that was altogether unfavourable to the Tamils; indeed, in some ways it strengthened them *vis-à-vis* the Sinhalese. For instance, the successful resistance of the kingdom of Kandy in the central highlands up to 1815 led to the creation of a distinction between the Low-Country Sinhalese and the Kandyan Sinhalese. The former, because of their longer experience under the western powers, were better equipped to seize the new economic opportunities which arose in the highlands after a plantation economy came into being there in the nineteenth century. Low-country Sinhalese entrepreneurs moved up to the hill-country as traders, contractors, craftsmen and professional men; however, they encountered opposition from the Kandyan Sinhalese who remained attached to traditional values and who as a consequence found themselves outpaced in a period of rapid change. Although the tension between the two groups of the Sinhalese rarely came to the surface, and was often tempered by inter-élite marriage alliances, it enabled the Sri Lankan Tamil minority to lay claim to being one of the three major ethnic groups in the country.

These claims were strengthened by the importation by the British plantation-owners of indentured Tamil labour from India to work their plantations; the colonial administration also used these workers to undertake some of the ill-paid and unpleasant work in the urban sector. By 1931 the Indian Tamil immigrants outnumbered the Ceylon Tamils, and together the two Tamil groups comprised some 25 per cent of the country's population. However, the fact that the new immigrants settled far away from the regions where the Ceylon Tamils predominated, as well as the differences in social composition between the two Tamil Hindu groups, inhibited the formation of close links between them despite their cultural and linguistic affinities. On the other hand, the presence of a large number of Tamil immigrants in the plantation districts made the Kandyan Sinhalese feel themselves to be a minority in some of these areas. Feelings of hostility towards Tamils developed among the Kandyan Sinhalese.

The colonial period also saw the emergence of a stronger sense of ethnic identity among both Sinhalese and Tamils. The Sinhalese attitude was partly the result of prolonged resistance to Western domination. Both groups however were also influenced by religious revivalist movements which made their presence felt in the second half of the nineteenth century, and which were largely a reaction against the proselytising activities of Christian missionaries. The publication of newspapers in the Sinhalese and Tamil languages strengthened this tendency; later, the development of indigenous literature and drama instilled a sense of belonging to one's cultural heritage. In this respect the novelist N. V. Thirugnanasambanda Pillai (1886–1955) performed much the same role among the Tamil community as did the dramatist John de Silva (1857–1922) and the great Sinhalese journalist Piyadasa Sirisena (1875–1946) among the Sinhalese.[6]

Two more aspects of the colonial impact should be noted. First, by the twentieth century education in English had become the key factor for access to the lucrative professions and higher posts in government service. Because of numerous Christian mission schools teaching in the English medium in the Jaffna peninsula, the Sri Lankan Tamils

secured a lead in their knowledge of the English language. For example, in 1911, 4.9 per cent of Sri Lankan Tamil males were literate in English, as opposed to 3.5 per cent of the Low-country Sinhalese and 0.7 per cent of the Kandyan Sinhalese males. The growth of government schools in Sinhalese areas, especially after 1920, and the closing of the Malayan public service to (largely Tamil) applicants from Sri Lanka in 1922 increased competition for state employment in Sri Lanka, but even in 1946 the proportion of Tamils to Sinhalese in the élite Ceylon Civil Service was 1:2; the proportion in the Judicial Service was 2:3.[7]

Secondly, the process of constitutional development in the nineteenth and twentieth centuries had its impact on the élites among the Sinhalese and Tamils. The Legislative Council, as it evolved from 1833 to 1931, was not constructed in terms of racial proportions — in 1921, for instance, the Council consisted of twelve Sinhalese and ten non-Sinhalese. But this position was changed with the introduction of universal suffrage in 1931, for it seemed inevitable that the Sinhalese, with more than two-thirds of the population, would obtain about two-thirds of the seats in the Legislature; and in 1931, of the fifty elected seats in a House of sixty-one (eight were nominated by the Govenor and three were official members), thirty-eight were won by Sinhalese. As the time for the transfer of power drew close, apprehensions among the Tamils increased, and their leader G. G. Ponnambalam put forward a scheme under which the Sinhalese would obtain only half the seats in the legislature and half the ministries in any Cabinet, a proposal which the Sinhalese unanimously opposed.[8]

Thus evidence of Sinhala-Tamil differences were manifest well before and during the time of the transfer of power. Yet, unlike the rest of British South Asia, the country suffered no violence. The new state emerged in an atmosphere of comparative peace and harmony, to the extent that Sri Lanka came to be referred to as the 'model colony'. Current historical writing assigns much of the credit for the balanced approach to the 'moderate' Sinhalese leadership of D. B. Jayatilaka and D. S. Senanayake, both of whom saw Sri Lanka as a multi-ethnic nation.[9] The Sri Lankan Tamil leadership for their part, though hostile at first, responded gingerly with their formula of responsive co-operation. A consociational understanding became possible because of the similarities in class and educational backgrounds of the respective leaderships. Yet another factor was the lack of 'political integration' which is more evident in Sri Lanka than in India.[10] The national leadership is a westernised group and depends much on personal prestige and family connections for political advancement. Consequently, in the period before independence, there was no political organisation in Sri Lanka like the Indian National Congress which was constantly under pressure from the rank and file. However, the disadvantage of these patterns of behaviour was that the mass of electors, who were increasingly becoming politically awake as well as literate, were not drawn into the processes of decision-making. The adverse effects of this were to be felt in later years.[11]

The 'political compromise' arrived at by an over-arching inter-élite accommodation produced a measure of Sinhalese-Tamil co-operation. But for the reasons stated, the compromises, being based on the concept of a secular state where all religions would enjoy equal support, were of a fragile nature and therefore could not last. English was to be gradually replaced by Sinhala and Tamil as official languages; this would provide equal opportunities for Tamils and Sinhalese. All minority groups were protected from discrimination by section 29 (2) of the 1948 Constitution, which stipulated that no disability or advantage could be conferred on persons of any community or religion which was not conferred on persons of other communities or religions. Finally, provision was made for weightage in representation to the minorities in the electoral system. Twenty-five seats in the House of

Representatives were distributed among the nine provinces according to area — one for every 1,000 square miles. The northern and eastern Provinces, where the Sri Lankan Tamils are concentrated, obtained eight of these twenty-five seats. Out of the ninety-five seats for elected members in the House of Representatives, as it was constituted during 1948–60, 26.3 per cent were allotted according to area. The northern and eastern Provinces thus obtained 8.4 per cent of the total seats, even before population was considered. This advantage that the Sri Lanka Tamils had enjoyed gradually declined as the Legislature expanded with the growth of population, for there was another provision which stated that one seat should also be provided for every 75,000 persons. Thus by 1970 the Legislature had 151 elected members, and the proportion of seats allotted according to area (twenty-five out of 151) had fallen to 16.3 per cent, and the share of the northern and eastern Provinces (eight seats) to 5.3 per cent. Nevertheless, the 1948 Constitution provided an advantage (albeit a gradually declining one) to the Sri Lankan Tamils of the northern and eastern Provinces. The latter group constituted only 13 per cent of the population but secured some 32 per cent of the seats allocated on an area basis. It was also felt that the provision for six nominated members to represent special and unrepresented interests would further help the minority groups. These arrangements, which were the foundation of the 'political compromise' when taken together, mark a considerable divergence from the *Sihadipa* and *Dhammadipa* concepts.

However, an area of conflict developed between the two groups over the question of voting rights for Indian Tamil settlers in Sri Lanka. At independence there were three groups of Indians in Sri Lanka. The first consisted of Indian Moors and diverse other groups from all parts of India who were prominent in the island's export-import trade; they also acted as money-lenders. A more numerous group were the urban labourers — mostly Tamil — who competed with the Sinhalese people for unskilled employment. But the most vital and significant group were the Indian Tamil workers in the plantations. In 1946 they formed over half the Tamil population of the island. Sinhalese fears of Tamil dominance in the Kandyan Sinhalese hill-country areas led to the Ceylon State Council (Elections) Order-in-Council of 1931 which imposed (*a*) the requirement of a literacy or property and income qualification or (*b*) proof of five years' residence in the form of a certificate of permanent settlement, before any undomiciled British subject was granted the power to vote. These restrictions were not implemented in the expected way, partly because British officials were not quite sympathetic to Sinhalese aims. Registrations of Indian voters grew rapidly in the 1930s, and despite some decline due to stricter imposition of the regulations in the 1940s, seven Indian Tamils gained seats in the first House of Representatives in 1947.[13]

Senanayake and the U.N.P. were determined to restrict the size of the Indian electorate. They regarded the Indian Tamil estate workers as temporary residents in the island with no abiding interest; some of them, however, belonged to families who had lived in the country for three generations or longer. Their attitude was strengthened by the fact that Indian Tamils were the only minority members to vote against accepting the 1948 Constitution on which Senanayake had set his heart. It was further confirmed when the Indian Tamils apparently voted — *en masse* — for Left-wing politicians in the 1947 general election wherever members of their own ethnic group did not contest. There was also the feeling that a new state had the sovereign power to frame its own nationality laws.

Thus very early in the life of the new state three laws came into force: the Ceylon Citizenship Act of 1948, The Indian and Pakistani Residents (Citizenship) Act of 1949 and The Parliamentary Elections (Amendment) Act of 1949. All three taken together effectively removed the vast majority of Indian Tamils from the electoral registers.[14] The Indian Tamil citizenship issue did not at that time create a rift between the respective influential sections of the Sri Lankan Tamils and the Sinhalese. The Tamil Congress led by G. G. Ponnambalam continued to work as part of the government. Nevertheless, the legislation in question led to two significant developments. First, the disfranchisement of a substantial sector of the population while the Constitution enjoined the distribution of seats according to the number of persons resident in the area led to serious electoral distortions. The Sinhalese gained at the expense of the Indian Tamils; they now came to hold 80 per cent of the seats in the Legislature. This in turn upset one element of the delicate 'political compromise' worked out in the 1940s because weightage introduced in favour of minority groups was now turned into weightage favouring the majority group. It was now possible for one of the major Sinhalese political parties to ignore the Tamil minority and still win an absolute majority in Parliament. D. S. Senanayake himself therefore paved the way for the undermining of the settlement on which he placed great store.

There was a second important consequence of the citizenship laws of 1948–9. A section of the Tamil Congress broke away under the leadership of S. J. V. Chelvanayakam and formed the Ilankai Tamil Arasu Kadchi (in strict translation, the Ceylon Tamil State Party) or the Federal Party. The Federal Party provided an organisation for the nationalistic elements among the Tamils. At the inaugural meeting of the Party in 1949, Chelvanayakam declared: 'We have met together with the common aim of creating an organisation for the attainment of the freedom of the Tamil-speaking people of Ceylon', and the first party convention in 1951 declared: 'The Tamil-speaking people in Ceylon constitute a nation distinct from that of the Sinhalese by every fundamental test of nationhood.'[15] Although the Federal Party won only two seats in the 1952 elections, it provided an alternative to the Tamil Congress which worked in those early years in co-operation with the U.N.P. Government, an alternative to which the Ceylon Tamils increasingly turned when they perceived Sinhala governments as becoming openly discriminatory in their policies towards the Tamils.

The reluctance of an important section of the Sri Lanka Tamil leadership to espouse the cause of the Indian Tamils in 1948–9 had an important effect upon the degree to which the communities would co-operate in the subsequent period. The Indian Tamil estate population remained organised under their own ethnic leaders, who often saw little common ground as existing between them and the Ceylon Tamil leadership. The key to the platform of the Federal Party — autonomous rule for the Tamils of the north and east — did not have much relevance to the Indian Tamils, who were mostly concerned with rights of citizenship, minimum wages and improvement of basic education and health facilities in the plantations. Thus after the agitation against the citizenship laws in the plantations petered out in 1950–1, the Indian leaders switched from political agitation to union action to obtain improvements in the living standards of the estate workers.

In the early 1950s, the position of the Indian Tamils seemed weak. They had lost their right to vote, and although they were unionised, their lack of financial resources and their poor educational background prevented them from mounting an effective campaign against the Government of the day. They had still to rely, to some extent, on their traditional protector, the Government of India. Eventually, in 1964, an agreement between the Governments of Sri Lanka and India made provision that of the 975,000 stateless persons of Indian origin, some 525,000 were to be granted Sri Lanka citizenship and allowed to remain. A further agreement in 1974 provided that the remaining 150,000 and their descendants would be shared on an equal basis. This meant that the Sri Lanka Government agreed to accept approximately 46.2 per cent of the Indian Tamils who were resident in Sri Lanka at the time of Independence. The Sri Lanka Government granted citizenship rights to about 134,316 Indian workers in the period 1949–64, and up to December 1980 a further 150,000 persons received Sri Lankan citizenship, while 260,000 were repatriated to India.[16]

The grant of citizenship to a substantial number of Indian Tamils meant that it became increasingly difficult to ignore them on the political scene. Although a resurgence of anti-Tamil feeling among the Kandyan Sinhalese in the difficult days of 1974–5 led to harassment, eviction and occasionally even starvation and death of some groups of Indian Tamils, and although they were consistently discriminated against in the distribution of land under the land reform laws in the 1970s and violently attacked in many areas by the Sinhalese in August 1977, the Indian Tamil leadership has acted with great patience and moderation. This is partly because the Indian Tamils have always been conscious that they are a relatively recent immigrant group and live in an area where the Sinhalese are in a majority. It is also perhaps partly due to the relatively low economic status and poor educational background of a majority of this community. Whatever the cause, the result has been that the rift between the Sinhalese and Indian Tamils is on a different plane from that of the Sinhalese and the Sri Lankan Tamils, who are involved in periodic confrontations.

There are four issues which continue to fuel conflicts between Sinhalese and Sri Lankan Tamils. These are language and employment; regional autonomy; settlement of Sinhalese on lands claimed to be the traditional homelands of the Tamils, and access to higher education. These issues, which are often intertwined, are not rigidly separated in the discussion that follows.

The language issue sprang from the thrust of the nationalist movement itself. It seemed logical that with Independence the language of the colonial master should be replaced in government, administration and education by the languages of the local people. Agitation for the use of *swabhasha* (by which was meant Sinhalese *and* Tamil) as state languages began in the 1920s, and the issue was raised sporadically in the first State Council. The Marxists who joined the Legislature in 1936 gave a fillip to the movement, and on 24 May 1944 J. R. Jayewardene moved a resolution in the State Council to take steps to make 'Sinhalese the official language of Ceylon within a reasonable number of years'. At the request of several Tamil politicians, Jayewardene accepted the amendment to add 'and Tamil', and the resolution was carried. Thus at Independence all political groups were committed to gradually making Sinhalese and Tamil the official languages of the country in place of English. Even S. W. R. D. Bandaranaike (Prime Minister, 1956–9), who saw himself as the spokesman and advocate of the rights of the Sinhala Buddhists and led the Sinhala Maha Sabha (the Great Council of the Sinhalese), reaffirmed his commitment to the bilingual policy in 1951 when he left the U.N.P. to form the S.L.F.P.

The movement to make Sinhalese the *only* official language thus originated from outside the entrenched political élites. It had a number of Sinhalese school teachers and Buddhist monks among its strongest advocates. The arguments against the two-language formula came to be advanced with greater vigour in 1953–4. It was claimed that parity of status for Tamil was an insidious return to the 'fifty-fifty' formula in electoral representation that had been put forward by the Ceylon Tamil leader G. G. Ponnambalam, and that if it were accepted, all Sinhalese who aspired to government employment would have to learn Tamil. It was also argued that the Tamil language had a larger reading public and a more developed vocabulary. Fears were raised that with equal status the Tamil language spoken in a large part of South India would eventually swamp the less developed Sinhalese language.

The movement for Sinhalese was closely connected with that for state patronage of Buddhism. The preparation for the celebrations connected with *Buddha Jayanthi* (the 2500th anniversary of the passing away of the Buddha) scheduled for 1956 heightened Sinhalese-Buddhist sentiment. Some modification was made in the concept of the secular state when the Government officially funded and sponsored some of these activities, but that did little to counter the growing feeling among the Sinhalese that neither their language nor their religion had been given its due place. This resentment was aggravated by the westernised 'playboy' image of the Prime Minister Sir John Kotalawala (1953–6).

The Buddhist activists were now in search of a leader. They first approached Dudley Senanayake, Prime Minister from 1951–3 and now in semi-retirement; he declined. The leader of the Sri Lanka Freedom Party, S. W. R. D. Bandaranaike, was more receptive. Later in 1955, Kotalawala during a visit to the north promised to make constitutional provision for 'parity of status' for both Sinhala and Tamil as official languages. This provoked strong opposition from the Sinhalese areas; Bandaranaike's party opted for 'Sinhala only' in late 1955 and shortly afterwards entered into a coalition with a few smaller parties to form the Mahajana Eksath Peramuna (M.E.P.) The new formation campaigned on a radical nationalist platform. In February 1956, Kotalawala and the U.N.P. abandoned their policy of parity of status for the two languages to one of Sinhala only, and his government dissolved Parliament to seek a mandate for its new policy. With the major parties compaigning for Sinhalese as the sole official language, it was clear that whatever group won power, the old political compromise on language was over.

The language crisis was perhaps the pivotal factor that drove the two communities asunder in the post-Independence period. The sudden change of policy by the two major political parties was interpreted by a vast majority of Tamils as a betrayal by the Sinhalese leadership. Many years were to pass before a prominent Tamil politician would again agree to join a government formed by one of the two major parties, and even then the decision was based on the understanding that he was in such a government to ensure that it would implement the understanding that it had reached with the Tamil party to which he belonged.[17] Among the Sri Lankan Tamils the Tamil Congress, which had for long espoused a policy of responsive co-operation with the Sinhalese leadership, was discredited, and the more militant Federal Party swept the board in general elections from 1956 onwards.[18]

The Tamils, especially the Sri Lankan Tamils, were shaken when the M.E.P. after their victory in the 1956 elections secured the passage of an Official Language Act declaring that 'the Sinhala Language shall be the one official language of Sri Lanka'. Due to further Sinhalese pressure in the formative stages of the Act, all references to the Tamil language were dropped. The Tamils feared not merely that they would be eventually shut out of the lucrative professions and from employment in government service but that the very existence of the Tamil language and culture would be threatened. These fears were aggravated when a peaceful demonstration organised by Tamil parties against the Official Language Act was disrupted by a counter-demonstration of pro-Sinhala elements in Colombo and when rioting between Sinhalese and Tamils led to many deaths and casualties at a settlement scheme at Gal Oya in the eastern Province.

Leaders on both sides were disturbed at the growing tension and outbreaks of violence, and after negotiations between the Prime Minister, Bandaranaike, and the Federal Party leadership, the Bandaranaike-Chelvanayakam Pact was signed on 20 July 1957. Among the main points in the formula, Tamil was recognised 'as the language of a national minority', it would be a 'language of administration' in the northern and eastern Provinces without prejudice to Sinhala as the official language, and subordinate law-making powers would be devolved to regional councils. Such councils were to have powers relating to agriculture, education and the selection of colonists for state-sponsored colonisation schemes.

Pro-Sinhalese organisations protested against the Pact. They were joined by the U.N.P., which at this stage was campaigning on a strongly pro-Sinhalese platform in an effort to regain power. A campaign organised by the Tamil Federal Party against Sinhalese lettering on number-plates of motor vehicles in the Tamil-speaking areas of northern and eastern Ceylon produced repercussions in the Sinhalese areas. Bandaranaike in the end yielded to pressure and in April 1958 repudiated his pact with the Federal Party. Widespread rioting followed. A state of emergency was declared and power was vested in the Governor-General. It was some time before normality was restored. Consequently the gulf between the two communities grew wider. Bandaranaike made an attempt at reconciliation by having Parliament enact the Tamil Language (Special Provision) Act no. 28 of 1958, providing for the use of Tamil in the spheres of education, public examinations, official correspondence with the Tamil-speaking public, and for prescribed administrative purposes in the northern and eastern Provinces. These were not brought into effect for many years. Their acceptance, however, served as a basis for future rapprochements.[19]

The Tamil Federal Party in subsequent years attempted to obtain a settlement on similar lines. When the March 1960 general election brought in a minority U.N.P. Government, it offered its support on the basis of the 1957 pact. When the U.N.P. refused, the Federal Party extended its support to the S.L.F.P. to oust the Government. At the general election that followed in July 1960, the S.L.F.P. obtained a clear majority. The new Government failed to make any effort to solve the Tamil problem. On the other hand, the Prime Minister Mrs Sirima Bandaranaike insisted on the implementation of the Official Language Act on 1 January 1961 without promulgating any regulations whatever under the Tamil Language (Special Provisions) Act of 1958. The Language of the Courts Act no. 3 of 1961 meanwhile provided for the progressive replacement of English by Sinhalese in all courts of law. Public servants appointed after 1956 were required to obtain proficiency in Sinhalese if they were to retain their posts, and in the 1960s it was becoming increasingly clear that career openings for Tamils in the public service were becoming extremely limited. Agitation and civil disobedience campaigns launched by the Federal Party in 1961 failed to produce results after the Government declared a state of emergency.

The Federal Party thereafter turned to the U.N.P., which offered to settle the Tamil question on lines similar to the pact of 1957 in return for guaranteeing Tamil support at the general election of 1965. The new U.N.P. government led by Dudley Senanayake enacted regulations under the Tamil Language Act of 1958, despite opposition not only from the S.L.F.P. but even from the Trotskyist Lanka Sama Samaj Party and the Communist Party — parties which had been in favour of parity of status for Tamil up to 1964. Indeed, opposition to the Tamil language regulations was so vehement that in 1968 the Government abandoned its plan to have district councils, although these institutions were to be assigned limited functions and were to work under the direction and supervision of the Central Government.[20]

Meanwhile, the issue of colonisation schemes remained. All governments since Independence have made efforts to reduce Sri Lanka's dependence on rice imports. One means of doing this was to construct irrigation schemes or to restore ancient ones that were in disrepair in order to encourage population in the densely-populated Sinhalese areas to migrate to the north-central and eastern regions of the country, which had remained sparsely populated for centuries. Most of the settlers being Sinhalese, the Tamils feared that such colonisation schemes would be used by Sinhalese-dominated governments to convert Tamil-majority areas into Sinhalese-majority areas. In fact the proportion of Sinhalese in districts such as Amparai and Trincomalee has risen sharply since Independence due to the establishment of such new settlements. This was partly why the Federal Party induced S. W. R. D. Bandaranaike to make locally-elected regional councils responsible for selecting colonists. This move, however, was interpreted by the Sinhalese as an attempt to secure large tracts of sparsely populated land in the north and east solely for the use of Tamil colonists. In the event, settlement of both Sinhalese and Tamils occurred in the 'frontier' region, and tension in those areas was often higher than in Tamil Jaffna or in the Sinhalese south-west.

The defeat of the U.N.P. by the S.L.F.P.-led United Front Coalition in 1970 boded ill for the Tamils, especially since the coalition obtained a three-quarters majority in Parliament and proceeded to use it to introduce a new Constitution which, to the dismay of the Tamils, not only reiterated that Sinhalese would be the sole official language but specified that the regulations passed under the Tamil Language (Special Provisions) Act should be regarded as subordinate legislation. To make things worse, the new Constitution did not incorporate section 29 (3) of the 1948 Constitution which, despite its shortcomings, had come to be regarded as an instrument for the protection of the rights of minorities. The section on fundamental rights, which was inserted instead, was not an adequate substitute. To compound a situation of doubt and suspicion, the judiciary was declared subordinate to the legislature. And, finally, a clause was incorporated stating that 'Buddhism shall have the foremost place'. This clause was strongly resented by the Tamil leadership. By the end of June 1971, the Tamil Federal Party had decided to boycott the Constituent Assembly, and took up the position that the Republican Constitution of 1972 did not have the sanction of the Tamil people.[21]

It was around this time that the question of admissions to universities gave rise to a serious crisis. Up to 1969, admissions were based on the final examination at the Senior Secondary School Level (Grade XII). In 1970, however, the United Front Government, having reviewed the exceptionally good performance of Tamil students in the science disciplines, took up the position that it was difficult to compare the relative standards of Sinhalese-medium and Tamil-medium students. It was decided to set cut-off points to regulate the quota of the admissions from each ethnic group. In effect this meant that Tamil students had to obtain higher marks than their Sinhalese counterparts to enter the science-based faculties in the island's universities. Due to the protest that the scheme roused, the government changed its policy to one of 'standardising' marks in 1973. There were various schemes of standardisation and district quotas from 1974 onwards, but the ultimate result of all these schemes was progressively to restrict the admission of Sri Lankan Tamil students to the attractive medical and engineering faculties. Thus, for example, the percentage of Tamil students admitted to engineering courses fell from 48.3 per cent of the total in 1969 to 24.4 per cent in 1973, and to 14.2 per cent in 1975. This led to considerable frustration and disappointment among Tamil youth in Jaffna. They were among the various Tamil groups who put pressure on the Tamil leadership to opt for a separate Tamil state.[22]

By this time the Sri Lanka Tamil leadership had begun to despair. Their negotiations with the U.N.P. and the S.L.F.P. over almost twenty years had brought them few tangible results, and the United Front Government used the excuse of the insurrection of 1971, which had not affected the Tamil areas, to continue the island-wide state of emergency well after all danger to security had passed. Emergency powers were also used to suppress political opponents. At this very time, the Indian Tamil leadership was also alienated by the Government's policy of distributing estate lands only to citizens of the country, thus leaving some of the Indian estate workers without land or employment. In 1974, for the first time since Independence, the Sri Lanka Tamil leadership (both of the Federal Party and the Tamil Congress) coalesced with the Indian Tamil leadship (the Ceylon Workers' Congress led by S. Thondaman) to form the Tamil United Front. In 1975 this organisation openly espoused the cause of a separate state and renamed itself the Tamil United Liberation Front (T.U.L.F.). Although the leaders pledged themselves to a policy of non-violence, violence was not eschewed by the militant youth elements. Attacks on police personnel occurred from time to time and were attributed to a group of Tamil youth termed the 'Liberation Tigers of Tamil *Eelam*', *Eelam* being the name of the proposed Tamil state. Nevertheless, the Indian Tamil leader Thondaman was never really reconciled to the separatist solution, for that could have involved the mass transfer of the Indian population from the central highlands to the north and east. In the elections of 1977 he made an informal agreement with the U.N.P., to which he swung much of the Indian Tamil vote.

The victory of the U.N.P. now led by J. R. Jayewardene, marked the beginning of an effort to reconcile the two ethnic groups. However, very early on there was a serious setback to this process as a result of the riots of August 1977. At the time of writing, the origins of these riots remain obscure, but they were at least partly fuelled by Sinhalese frustration at repeated reports of successful armed attacks by 'Liberation Tigers' on police personnel; in part S.L.F.P. elements were suspected of having a hand in it. Inflammatory speeches by some Tamil politicians, who campaigned (and won a sweeping mandate in the north) on the platform of a separate state for the Tamils at the 1977 general election, also roused passions. Stories of attacks on Sinhalese in Jaffna, reminiscent of the rumours which sparked off the 1958 riots, swept the Sinhalese areas, and resulted in attacks on Tamil residents in the south. Retaliation on Sinhalese on the north-east coast followed. The death toll was over 100, and thousands were made homeless. For similar reasons there was a recrudescence of such violence in June and August 1981, but on this occasion it was members of the state's security forces and of the governing party who promoted and/or participated in the violence.

However, the new U.N.P. Government, was determined to continue as a government of national reconciliation. A second republican Constitution enacted in 1978 contained many measures designed to win back the Tamils. For example, although Sinhalese remained the official language, Tamil as well as Sinhalese were constitutionally recognised as national languages throughout the country. Secondly, all the rights accrued by the regulations promulgated in 1966 under the Tamil Language (Special Provision) Act of 1958 were incorporated into the Constitution so that the rights of Tamils to be educated, to correspond with government institutions, and to sit for public examinations in their own language became constitutionally guaranteed. The Constitution also protected the right of any individual to obtain Tamil translations of Sinhala public documents. All laws and official reports were required to be published in both national languages. Provision was made for the use of Tamil in courts of original jurisdiction in the north and east. The Constitution further removed the distinction between 'citizen by descent' and 'citizen by registration' (mostly Indian Tamils), which had been introduced by the citizenship laws of 1948–9. All citizens were now to be citizens of Sri Lanka. Finally, the fundamental freedoms enumerated in the 1978 Constitution were made justiciable, and most of them were extended to all persons legally resident in Sri Lanka up to year 1988.[23]

The Indian Tamil leader, Thondaman, thought these measures generous enough to justify his joining the Government as a minister, and thus became the first Indian Tamil minister in independent Sri Lanka. The rise in the prices for tea and rubber after 1976 enabled the Government to raise wages in the estate sector substantially enough to raise the standard of living of the average estate worker (generally Indian Tamil). Legislation in 1977 removed the restrictions imposed in 1938 on the participation of estate workers in local government bodies. However, the T.U.L.F. leadership remained unreconciled;

they maintain that the retention of the clause giving Buddhism 'the foremost place' reduces non-Buddhists to a secondary position, and point out that in the new Constitution there is no decentralisation of power. The U.N.P. Government attempted to meet some of their criticism with a Development Councils Act which provided for a fair measure of decentralisation.

The government further abolished the system of 'standardising' marks for admission to the universities, so that the proportion of Tamils admitted to science-based courses has risen. However there are still two areas where there has been no settlement. These relate to employment and land settlement. The Tamils claim that they are obtaining less than their due share in public employment. The Government's response is that the numbers are comparable to the percentage of Tamils who are citizens, but the Tamils argue that these are much less than what they obtained before 1956.[25] The new policy of an open economy provides greater opportunities for employment, which can reduce the load on the system. But what has assumed greater significance is the question of land settlement. The major development strategy of the U.N.P. is based on a multi-purpose river development project called the Mahaweli Development Scheme, which will open up extensive new areas for cultivation in north-central Sri Lanka. The Tamil leadership has remained sensitive to this issue, and the government has remained inflexible on its stance that all nationals whether Sinhalese or Tamils are entitled to benefit from such settlement schemes. The effect of this policy, however, has been the continuing conversion of the 'frontier' areas to Sinhalese-majority areas.

Thus the situation which prevails at the time of writing remains one of fragile peace. The T.U.L.F. leadership has so far refused to give up its campaign for a separate state. Militant youth in the Tamil north bent on armed struggle have received some encouragement from expatriate Tamils, and they are kept in check only by a strong armed force. On the other hand, fear of a break-away state is alive among the Sinhalese, and there is no guarantee that the violence of August 1977 and of June and August 1981, will not recur. The Indian Tamil situation, on the other hand, has eased considerably with Thondaman joining the cabinet in 1978.

The rift between the Sinhalese and the Tamils in Sri Lanka has given rise to considerable discussion. Several writers have directly or indirectly made suggestions concerning the factors that have led to the rift and the nature of the rift itself. For instance Donald E. Smith, in a somewhat academic analysis of the interaction of politics and religion in Sri Lanka, has argued that the Sinhalese Buddhist resurgence of the 1950s and '60s was a passing phase. He suggests somewhat optimistically that it was a period of religious mass politics which provided the transition from the 'secular élite politics', which characterised the colonial era and the period up to 1956, to a period of secular mass politics which began in the 1970s when people shared greater concern for economic and social issues. Smith admits that the end of the era of 'religious mass politics' could be partly due to the fact that the Sinhalese demands of the time — the enthronement of the Sinhalese language and of the Buddhist religion — were achieved.[26] What he does not take into account is that religious and ethnic differences are deep-rooted, and that anything that appears to threaten the language or religion of either ethnic group may well revive an age of 'religious [or ethnic] mass politics'.

Michael Roberts, on the other hand, seems to place great emphasis on historical factors. He has emphasised the role of the Sinhalese concepts of *Sihadipa* and *Dhammadipa* emphasising how these old ideas came to be fused with the Western concept of a nation-state during the colonial era.[27] He has pointed out that the Sinhalese use the same word for race and nationality. Thus, 'federal structures of government, other pluralist solutions, even decentralised administration (e.g. the district council schemes in the 1960s) were treated as beyond the pale and more consistently undermined. In short it has long been a form of ideological blindness suffocating and debilitating the body politic.'[28] Roberts' argument regarding the potency of tradition has received support from other writers,[29] and it is difficult to argue that perceptions inherited from history do not contribute to ethnic tensions. On the other hand it is equally difficult to maintain that the legacy of history cannot be altered. Since 1977 several steps, including constitutional provision for making Tamil a national language and the establishment of development councils, have been achieved with surprisingly little opposition among Sinhalese nationalists.

Efforts to under-play the factors of history and cultural tradition and to bring economic factors to the fore have been made by some radical writers. Marxist and other Left-wing writings on this subject are often inadequately researched; they are generally polemical or theoretical.[30] They emphasise that the conflict over the official language issue had more to do with economic advantages, especially for the Sinhalese who were educated in their mother-tongue. There is of course some validity in this argument, but proponents of this theory often tend to under-value the strength of ethnic and religious loyalties and to argue that ethnic conflict will disappear with the advent of a socialist state.

Another explanation for the factors which cause the rift was advanced by James Manor, who suggests that the failure of politicians on both sides to arrive at a political accommodation is due in part to the lack of political integration in Sri Lanka.[31] Political integration is defined as the establishment of a two-way connection between the élite and the mass. Manor has argued that the lack of a developed 'grass-roots' organisation has made it impossible for any governing party to mount a campaign to convince its followers of the need for accommodation. Thus every government was vulnerable to any small group of determined agitators whose activities could threaten to whittle away the Government's majority in the legislature through defections. This was a problem faced by S. W. R. D. Bandaranaike in 1957–8 and by Dudley Senanayake in 1966–7. Manor suggests that accommodation can come only if either the party organisation is revolutionised or the whole political structure is changed.

In conclusion, it might be stated that the factors which created and widened the Sinhalese-Tamil rift in the three decades since Independence were complex, and that any monocausal explanation would distort the picture. History and tradition resulting in inter-group suspicions have provided some barriers to accommodation. The slow growth of the economy worsened tensions among the groups seeking to share limited wealth and resources. The weakness of the political structure and of political organisations no doubt contributed to exacerbating the conflict; however, it is important to remember that the rift in recent times has occurred because of divergence on specific issues such as language and employment, colonisation, education and regional autonomy. These issues played a major role in widening the rift. It was also worth noting that these issues did not arise wholly from historical or economic or political factors. Emotion has often been as important as calculation. In the past few years, the economic situation has changed, and constitutional structures have been radically altered.[32] Whether the cultural and historical legacies and the outstanding issues could be settled seems to depend as much on political will and leadership on both sides as on other factors.[33]

NOTES

1. For details and background see K. M. de Silva (ed.) *University of Ceylon, History of Ceylon* (Colombo: University of Ceylon Press Board, 1972), 489–533.
2. L. S. Perera, 'The Pali Chronicle of Ceylon' in C. H. Phillips (ed.) *Historians of India, Pakistan and Ceylon*, (London: Oxford University Press, 1961), 29–43; Kitsiri Malalgoda, 'Millennialism in relation to Buddhism', *Comparative Studies in Society and History*, XII (4), Oct. 1970, 424–41; Michael Roberts, 'Variations on the Theme of Resistance Movements: the Kandyan Rebellion of 1817–18 and latter-day nationalisms in Ceylon', *Ceylon Studies Seminar* 1970–2 series no. 9, 17–23.
3. R. A. L. H. Gunawardena, 'The People of the Lion: The Sinhala

identity and ideology in history and historiography', *Sri Lanka Journal of the Humanities*, V (1 & 2), 1977, 1–36.

4. S. Paranavitana, 'The Triumph of Duttagamini' in S. Paranavitana (ed.), *University of Ceylon, History of Ceylon* vol. I, (Colombo: University of Ceylon Press Board, 1959–1960), 144–61; K. Indrapala, 'Dravidian Settlements in Ceylon and the beginnings of the Kingdom of Jaffna' (unpubl. Ph.D. thesis, University of London, 1966); *University of Ceylon, History of Ceylon*, op.cit. vol. I, part II, passim.
5. K. Indrapala (ed.), *The Collapse of the Rajarata Civilization in Ceylon and the Drift to the South West* (Peradeniya: Ceylon Studies Seminar, 1971).
6. *University of Ceylon, History of Ceylon*, vol. III, op.cit., passim; S. Arasaratnam, 'Nationalism in Sri Lanka and the Tamils', in Michael Roberts (ed.), *Collective Identities, Nationalisms and Protest in Modern Sri Lanka*, (Colombo: Marga Institute, 1979), 500–19.
7. Robert N. Kearney, *Communalism and Language in the Politics of Ceylon*, (Durham, N.C.: Duke University Press, 1967, 70).
8. K. M. de Silva, 'Nineteenth Century Origins of Nationalism in Ceylon'; A. J. Wilson, 'The Development of the Constitution'; and K. M. de Silva, 'The Reform and Nationalist Movements of the Twentieth Century', in *University of Ceylon, History of Ceylon*, op.cit., 249–61, 359–80 and 381–407.
9. K. M. de Silva, 'The History and Politics of the Transfer of Power', in *University of Ceylon, History of Ceylon*, op.cit., 489–533.
10. For a discussion on this point see J. Manor, 'The Failure of Political Integration in Sri Lanka (Ceylon)', *Journal of Commonwealth and Comparative Politics*, XVII (1), March 1979, 21–46.
11. Ibid. and K. M. de Silva, 'Discrimination in Sri Lanka', in W. A. Veenhoven (ed.), *Case Studies on Human Rights and Fundamental Freedoms: A World Survey* (The Hague: Martinus Nijhoff, 1976), vol. III, 80–2.
12. *Report of the Commission on Constitutional Reform* (London: H.M.S.O., 1945); A. Jeyaratnam Wilson, 'Minority Safeguards in the Ceylon Constitution', *Ceylon Journal of Historical and Social Studies*, I (1), Jan. 1958, 73–82.
13. The term 'Indian Tamils' has been used in this paper to denote Tamil immigrants who arrived in Sri Lanka in the nineteenth and twentieth centuries, irrespective of whether they have obtained citizenship rights.
14. S. U. Kodikara, *Indo-Ceylon Relations Since Independence* (Colombo: Ceylon Institute of World Affairs, 1965), 79ff.
15. Cited in Kearney, op.cit., 93–4.
16. Information obtained from the Department of Immigration and Emigration, Sri Lanka; see also, W. T. Jayasinghe, *Tamils in Ceylon* (Colombo: Ministry of Defence and Foreign Affairs, 1976), 11.
17. This was what occurred when M. Tiruchelvam joined the U.N.P. cabinet in 1965.
18. For a lucid account of the events and factors leading up to the language crisis of 1955–6 see W. Howard Wriggins, *Ceylon: Dilemmas of a New Nation* (Princeton University Press, 1960), 169–210, 228–58.
19. Ibid., 259–69; Kearney, op.cit., 82–7.

20. Kearney, op.cit., 128–36.
21. K. M. de Silva, 'The Constitution and Constitutional Reform since 1948', in K. M. de Silva (ed.) *Sri Lanka: a Survey* (London: C. Hurst, 1977), 312–29; *The Constitution of Sri Lanka 1972* (Colombo: Department of Government Printing, 1972).
22. C. R. de Silva, 'The Politics of University Admission: a review of some aspects of the admissions policy in Sri Lanka 1970–1978', *Sri Lanka Journal of the Social Sciences* I (2), 1978, 85–123.
23. C. R. de Silva, 'The Tamils and the Constitution of the Second Republic of Sri Lanka (1978)', *Sri Lanka Journal of the Social Sciences* III (1), 1980, 33–41; see also N. Tiruchelvam, 'The Making and Unmaking of Constitutions: Some reflections on the process', *Ceylon Journal of Historical and Social Studies*, new series, VII (2), June–Dec. 1977, 18–24.
24. *Development Councils Act No 35 of 1980* (Colombo, Department of Government Printing, 1980), Articles 17 & 18.
25. This estimate is based on the examination of lists of employees given in the *Parliamentary Debates* in 1978 and 1979 as replies to questions.
26. Donald E. Smith, 'The Dialectic of Religion and Politics in Sri Lanka', *Ceylon Journal of Historical and Social Studies*, new series, IV (1 & 2), Jan–Dec. 1974 111–18.
27. Michael Roberts, 'Ethnic Conflict in Sri Lanka and Sinhalese Perspectives: Barriers to Accommodation', *Modern Asian Studies*, XII (3), 1978, 353–76.
28. Michael Roberts (ed.), *Collective Identities*, op.cit., 22.
29. Gananath Obeysekera, 'The Vicissitudes of the Sinhala Buddhist Identity through Time and Change', in Roberts (ed.), *Collective Identities* 279–313, and K. N. O. Dharmadasa, 'The Sinhala-Buddhist Identity and the Nayakkar Dynasty in the Politics of the Kandyan Kingdom 1739–1815', in Roberts (ed.), op.cit., 99–128.
30. For instance see [The] *Tamil Minority Question and the Revolutionary Workers Party*, Moratuwa (1979) and debates in the *Lanka Guardian* (a fortnightly journal).
31. J. Manor, op.cit., 21–46.
32. A. Jeyaratnam Wilson, *The Gaullist System in Asia: the Constitution of Sri Lanka (1978)*, London: Macmillan, 1980; *Ceylon Studies Seminar Post-War Economic Development of Sri Lanka, 15–20 December 1980*, University of Peradeniya (mimeo).
33. I am grateful to Professors K. M. de Silva, and A. Jeyaratnam Wilson and Dr J. Manor for their advice and other assistance in the preparation of this article.

THE CONCEPTS OF POLITICS AND POWER IN INDIA'S IDEOLOGICAL TRADITION

Dennis Dalton

If political theory is affected, let political theorists worry; if theories of politics tumble, political life will go on as before. I believe this to be a mistaken and shortsighted view. [. . .]. What the political philosopher believes and teaches today will in some measure mould what politicians believe and do tomorrow.[1]

The purpose of this essay is to examine how most of modern India's major political theorists conceived of politics and power. The analysis will seek to demonstrate the conceptual consensus that exists among them in their interpretations not only of these two ideas, but of the conceptual clusters that they represent. These clusters, it will be argued, form the basis of modern India's ideological tradition, a cohesive school of thought that was initially defined by Swami Vivekananda, and in this century came to include a rich variety of theorists.[2]

Why a given civilization manages to produce and clarify an ideological tradition is uncertain, but when and where this does occur, it seems to be identified with two phenomena. First, in a social sense, the traditions emerge as responses to social crises which theorists perceive as fundamental challenges to established sets of values. Second, in an intellectual sense, the traditions have been clearly marked by the logical manner in which they form constellations or clusters of ideas, commonly centering on the key concepts of politics and power. The example of India's ideological tradition fits this pattern: it emerged in response to the crisis of values introduced by British imperialism in the nineteenth century, and it soon formed into a cohesive cluster of ideas.

Traditions of political thought have conceptualized politics and power in at least three distinct ways. First, there was the theory, best set forth by classical Greek thought, of politics as an all-embracing activity. The political community, Aristotle announced in the opening chapters of the *Politics*, is 'the most sovereign and inclusive association', 'the final and perfect association', in that it represents the natural, teleological fulfillment of all other communities, and the individual may therefore achieve his highest moral attainment, the realization of law and justice, only within the political order, for 'man is by nature an animal intended to live in a *polis*.'[3] This classical view of politics was revived in modern Europe by Rousseau and Hegel, and it remains the dominant stream of Western political theory today, primarily found in the ideology of nationalism. The classical conception of power was allied to its view of politics. For Plato, power must be employed in an enlightened way, by leaders with philosophical insight, but when it is employed wisely, there are no limits on its use.[4] For the formation of the ideal *polis*, then, the sovereignty and broad scope of politics is matched by a sweeping justification of power. In his resurrection of Plato, Rousseau argued that the legislator should apply power in a majestic manner to inaugurate that all-inclusive political order, the civil state.[5]

The second theory of politics and power has some antecedents in earlier Western traditions, but it is chiefly a modern European development that finds its best expression in the thought of John Locke and John Stuart Mill. This conceptualization sees society, not the state, as primary, and stresses the sanctity of the private rather than the political sphere of human conduct. This is the 'liberal tradition' of political philosophy that believes in 'the minimal character of the political order'.[6] It seeks to place 'absolute' or 'inviolable' limits on the political authority of the state and its sphere of legitimate action.[7] The corresponding view of power is that if it invades the private, personal realm in the name of politics, then both politics and power will be corrupted: 'Politics is a necessary and important part of human life but it is not the whole of it and it becomes diseased if it aspires to more than its share.'[8]

The third conception of politics and power is a logical extension of the second and a direct refutation of the first. This is the anarchist perception, systematized first by William Godwin, and then developed by a wide variety of thinkers in Europe, Russia, and America in the nineteenth century. It reasoned from Locke's premises about the primacy of society and the need for placing limitations on the power of the state so that the best community would be purged of the excesses of political authority. However, anarchism went beyond Locke and liberalism in its vision of a social order without government, and in its attack on the law. Henry Thoreau wrote:

> I heartily accept the motto, — 'That government is best which governs least;' and I should like to see it acted up to more rapidly and systematically. Carried out, it finally amounts to this, which also I believe, — 'That government is best which governs not at all;' and when men are prepared for it, that will be the kind of government which they will have. Government is at best but an expedient; but most governments are usually, and all governments are sometimes, inexpedient . . . Law never made men a whit more just; and by means of their respect for it, even the well-disposed are daily made the agents of injustice.[9]

For Thoreau, as for all anarchists, politics and power are everywhere suspect not merely because they may tend to 'become diseased'; rather, they are themselves the source of the worst social disease, authoritarianism, and so they threaten society, like a contagious virus.

Strong parallels exist between the Western anarchist and modern Indian conceptions of politics and power. These similarities begin with Vivekananda, who more than any other nineteenth-century Indian theorist, shaped and inspired his country's ideological tradition. In each area of thought that he touched, Vivekananda placed his indelible stamp, but nowhere more dominantly than in his teaching about the relation of nationalism to politics and power. In 1897, when he returned to India from four years in America and England, he discovered that 'the Nation had already accepted him as its Guru',[10] and he eagerly embraced the role. He began by making a series of conceptual distinctions that starkly separated the cultures of India and England. 'The backbone, the foundation, and the bedrock' of India's 'national life', he declared, was its spiritual genius. 'Let others talk of politics, of the glory of acquisition' or of 'the power and spread of commercialism'; these cannot inspire India. Look at 'the Western and other nations, which are now almost borne down, half-killed, and degraded by political ambitions' and the futility of that existence will be clear.[11] Anyone who knows India must understand that 'politics, power, and even intellect form a secondary consideration here. Religion, therefore, is the one consideration in India.'[12]

Vivekananda's indispensable role in the conceptualization of politics and power in modern India, was to establish with extraordinary precision the central assumptions and lines of argument. Just as later ideologists, from Gandhi to J. P. Narayan, would attack Western political institutions and practices, so Vivekananda, decades before them, characterized 'parliaments' as 'jokes'[13] and 'party politics' as degenerate 'fanaticism and sectarianism'.[14] Preoccupation with political power was part of a distinctly Western 'vanity', a reflection of the 'material tyranny' which tyrannized over both colonized and colonizer, a terrible evil, for 'by this power they can deluge the whole earth with blood.'[15]

One of the key premises in the Indian conceptualization of politics and power lay in its attitude toward law, and especially in the relationship of law to individual morality and social change. Here, again, Vivekananda's voice was early and decisive. 'The basis of all systems, social or political,' he argued, 'rests upon the goodness of men. No nation is great or good because Parliament enacts this or that, but because its men are great and good.' The aim is to promote a sound body of individual ethics, and this must not be a political task, for 'men cannot be made virtuous by an Act of Parliament. [. . .] And that is why religion is of deeper importance than politics, since it goes to the root, and deals with the essential of conduct.'[16] Too often, the state 'tries to compel all men through rigid laws and threats of punishment to follow that path with unconditional obedience,' but this is disastrous for it means that 'the destiny of mankind becomes no better than that of a machine.'[17] The political history of India records 'a thousand years of crushing tyranny of castes and kings and foreigners',[18] but the spiritual tradition of Hinduism calls for resistance to this legalized oppression. 'The very word Sannyasin means the divine outlaw'[19] and since 'it is freedom alone that is desirable . . . it is not law that we want but ability to break law. We want to be outlaws. If you are bound by laws, you will be a lump of clay.'[20] Vivekananda concludes, therefore, that 'our aim should be to allow the individual to move towards this freedom. More of goodness, less of artificial laws.'[21]

If the threat of India's contamination by political power came from the West, then the antidote is found in her own tradition, and especially in the idea of spiritual power. The Western notion of power was corrupted by an obsession with its 'material', 'external' forms, while the Indian theory of power understood the superiority of its spiritual, 'internal' aspects.[22] Vivekananda's extensive discussions of the Indian concept of spiritual power clearly anticipate Gandhi's development of the idea of 'soul-force'. Like Gandhi, Vivekananda found this approach to power a unique, special component of the Indian genius, far superior in potential to what Gandhi called the Western idea of 'brute force'.[23] 'What power is there in the hand or the sword?' Vivekananda asked. 'The power is all in the spirit.'[24]

> Political greatness or military power is never the mission of our race; it never was, and mark my words, it never will be. But there has been the other mission given to us, which is to conserve, to preserve, to accumulate, as it were, into a dynamo, all the spiritual energy of the race, and that concentrated energy is to pour forth in a deluge on the world.[25]

Finally, Vivekananda signalled a crucial and prophetic departure from his classical tradition, by arguing that this spiritual power inhered in the masses. 'All knowledge is in every soul' regardless of caste or class, 'the same power is in every man.' This means, first, that Hinduism really promotes a 'wonderful state of equality'[26] but, equally important for the future of the country, that 'the only hope of India is from the masses. The upper classes are physically and morally dead.'[27] To his disciples he repeatedly urged, 'You must have a hold on the masses,', 'We must reach the masses.'[28] If only the people could unite, that would mean 'infinite power . . . Therefore, to make a great future India, the whole secret lies in organization, accumulation of power, co-ordination of wills. [. . .] That is the secret of power in India.'[29]

Emphatically, it was a power that could be summoned forth not from the imposition of alien forms of government and law, but only from the cultivation of India's own inspired cultural and religious tradition.

In one sense, Vivekananda's ideas powerfully influenced not only the political theory but also the political practice of twentieth-century India, if one considers the application of his thought to the Indian nationalist movement for independence. His aggressive nationalism, that attacked Western culture as inferior and emphasized the need for establishing a mass base of action, with corresponding stress on social equality and reforms, all inspired the independence movement. Yet, in another sense, his conceptualization of politics and power suggested a marked divergence between main currents of Indian political theory and the practice of Indian politics after 1947. The divergence occurs between a theory that is essentially anarchist in orientation and a practice that after Independence sought to integrate the nation under a centralized system of government. It is rather extraordinary that throughout this century India has produced a rich body of political theory, yet not a single major theorist of centralized authority. All of India's leading political thinkers have followed Vivekananda's conceptualization of politics and power. The first to accept him was also the most systematic political philosopher of this century, Sri Aurobindo Ghose.[30]

Among Aurobindo's most influential tracts was *The Spirit and Form of Indian Polity*.[31] The ideas on politics and power set forth here follow closely those of Vivekananda. 'The master idea that has governed the life, culture, social ideals of the Indian people has been the seeking of man for his true spiritual self and the use of life.' In this quest, politics cannot perform a significant role, for it inevitably belongs to the 'imperfect', 'grosser' area of human conduct, and 'the effort at governing political action by ethics is usually a little more than a pretence.'[32] Throughout its political history, Indian polities have approached spiritual realization in only a very limited sense, but even at its worst

> Indian polity never arrived at that unwholesome substitution of the mechanical for the natural order of the life of the people which has been the disease of European civilisation now culminating in the monstrous artificial organisation of the bureaucratic and industrial State.[33]

This kind of State comes at an 'advanced stage of corruption of the Dharma marked by the necessity of the appearance of the legislator and the formal government of the whole of life by external or written law and code and rule:'[34] The ideal society, dictated by the spirit of Indian polity, is where

> there is no need of any political government or State or artificial construction

of society, because all then live freely according to the truth of their enlightened self and God-inhabited being and therefore spontaneously according to the inner divine Dharma.[35]

A much fuller statement of these ideas is given in Aurobindo's two major works of political philosophy, *The Human Cycle* and *The Ideal of Human Unity*. In the latter book, he vigorously attacks the idea and reality of the modern state. 'The State principle leads necessarily to uniformity, regulation, mechanisation; its inevitable end is socialism.'[36] Not only the socialist state, though, has deprived individuals of their freedom. The democratic state has failed too, and 'we see today the democratic system of government march steadily towards such an organised annihilation of individual liberty as could not have been dreamed of in the old aristocratic and monarchical systems.'[37] The central problem lies in the very principle of the state, which in its fascist, socialist, or democratic forms promotes not merely 'tyranny of the majority', but worse, 'tyranny of the whole, of the self-hynotised mass over its constituent groups and units',[38] usually orchestrated by a small élite of demagogic politicians. Aurobindo saw this in 'Fascist Italy and Soviet Russia' alike[39], and in those states like Britain and America which claim to enjoy representative government 'legislators and administrators do not really represent their electors. The power they represent is another, a formless and bodiless entity, which has taken the place of monarch and aristocracy, that impersonal group-being . . . the huge mechanism of the modern State.'[40]

In successive chapters entitled 'The Drive Towards Economic Centralisation' and 'The Drive Towards Legislative and Social Centralisation and Uniformity', Aurobindo condemns in the 'history of the growth of the State . . . the development of a central authority and of a growing uniformity in administration, legislation, social and economic life and culture.'[41] This is wrong because no centralized political authority can represent or promote the realization of individual interests. Diversity, not uniformity and over-centralisation, is the 'law of life'; while order is necessary, it must be understood that 'the truest order is that which is founded on the greatest possible liberty.'[42] A society that achieves this ideal will be 'perfectly spiritualised . . . as is dreamed of by the spiritual anarchist' in which 'each man will be not a law to himself, but *the* law, the divine law . [. . .] His life will be led by the law of his own divine nature.'[43] This vision, from the ideal of an anarchist society free of state authority, to the promise of spiritual freedom that transcends the artificial regulation of politics, power and law, comes from Vivekananda.

At the same time that Aurobindo was writing, in the first quarter of this century, two other intellectual giants emerged on the national scene, Rabindranath Tagore and Mohandas Gandhi. As in the cases of

Vivekananda and Aurobindo, their contributions to Indian life ranged far beyond their theories of politics and power, yet their controversy over these two ideas deserves to be regarded as an unusually rich component of India's ideological tradition. Their debate was perhaps so fruitful because they shared so many basic attitudes on politics and power.

Before Gandhi had formulated his own political ideology, Tagore published in 1904 an important essay entitled 'Society and State'. Tagore emulates Vivekananda's formulation, first in the sharp demarcation drawn between society and state, and second, by associating the former with Indian civilization, and the latter with the British.

> The vital strength in different civilizations is variously embodied. The heart of a country lies wherever the people's welfare is centered. A blow aimed at that point is fatal for the whole country. In England the overthrow of the State might mean peril for the nation — that is why politics there is such a serious affair. In our country there would be danger only when the social body, *samaj*, becomes crippled. [. . .] England relies on the State for everything, from the relief of the destitute to the religious education of the public; whereas our country depends on the people's sense of duty. Therefore, England has to exist by keeping the State alive while we exist by preserving our social consciousness. [. . .] The government in our country has no relationship with our society and no place in the social organization, so that whatever we may seek from it must be bought at the expense of a certain freedom.[44]

Five years later, in *Hind Swaraj* (1909), Gandhi accepted the basic distinctions made between society and state, India and the West, set forth by Vivekananda and Tagore. Indeed, if anything, he drew the dichotomies between the spiritual, moral fabric of Indian society, and the violent, politically corrupt nature of the European state even more dramatically than any of his predecessors. He reserved his harshest language for the English parliamentary system,[45] and described all Western political power as 'brute force'.[46] Ancient Indian society was idealized, where 'kings and swords were inferior to the sword of ethics', and people enjoyed an organic social existence in small villages independently of the abuses of political institutions.[47]

As Gandhi became increasingly involved in politics, he maintained his view of its corrupt nature in the West, and seemed often ambivalent about whether it might be practised rightly in India. At best it was an impure, threatening activity:

> If I seem to take part in politics, it is only because politics, encircle us today like the coil of a snake from which one cannot get out, no matter how much one tries. I wish therefore to wrestle with the snake.[48]

Later, Gandhi would conclude his *Autobiography* (1928) with his famous defense that he had been drawn into politics irresistibly in his pursuit of truth,[49] but the overriding tone in Gandhi's discussions of politics is of its subordinate, inferior status. Thus, shortly after his most successful political campaign, he could write:

> My work of social reform was in no way less or subordinate to political work. The fact is, when I saw that to a certain extent my social work would be impossible without the help of political work, I took to the latter and only to the extent that it helped the former. I must therefore confess that work of social reform or self-purification of this nature is a hundred times dearer to me than what is called purely political work.[50]

For both Gandhi and Tagore, *swaraj* meant more than mere political independence; it meant India's spiritual liberation through a fundamental change in each individual's moral perception. This could hardly be achieved through legislative reforms. Tagore's comment on this reflects as well his generally low view of the potential force of law:

> Our woes, we fondly imagine, can be ended by legislation and we can become full-fledged human beings when we obtain seats in the legislature. But a nation's progress is not achieved mechanically. It cannot be achieved until we are prepared to pay the price.[51]

Politics and law were inevitably 'mechanical', 'external' and 'artificial', and usually corrupt and degraded. The 'price' for both Tagore and Gandhi must be paid in self-sacrifice, for that alone could produce the internal self-purification required for *swaraj*.

In all these respects, Tagore and Gandhi were in profound agreement. Their differences came over the issue of power. Gandhi believed that 'power is of two kinds',[52] one based on physical force, the other rooted in *satya* and *ahimsa*, 'truth-force'. Tagore, conversely, argued in his classic letter to Gandhi of April 12, 1919, at the outset of the Mahatma's first national campaign in India:

> Power in all its forms is irrational, it is like the horse that drags the carriage blind-folded. [. . .] The danger inherent in all force grows stronger when it is likely to gain success, for then it becomes temptation.[53]

At the end of the letter, Tagore grew more concilatory by acknowledging Gandhi's struggle against an 'overwhelming material power' that 'scoffs at the power of the spirit', and the rightness of his attempt to 'purge [India's] present-day politics of its feebleness'.[54] Yet Tagore's suspicion of politics and power increased as Gandhi pursued his aim of independence, and at the height of Gandhi's non-co-operation campaign of 1921, Tagore launched a salvo entitled 'The Call of Truth', which is perhaps unparalleled in Indian political literature for its eloquence. In it he concedes that 'to make the country our own by means of our creative power is indeed a great call.'[55] But the use of this power must be purely moral and not political, for politics and truth will not mix. Gandhi's supreme difficulty in responding to this charge was that he had himself set truth as his highest goal, and had acknowledged that the practice of politics meant 'wrestling with the snake', that power can be deadly poisonous, and even the best of men may be bitten. He could only seek to justify his leadership with the assertion that 'my politics are not corrupt, they are inextricably bound up with truth'.[56] It is Tagore who gets the better of this debate; for Gandhi is arguing not only with Rabindranath, but against a tradition, and ultimately with a part of himself.

However, perhaps Gandhi's best response to Tagore came not within the context of this debate, but rather in another aspect of his conceptualization of politics and power. This came with his development of a theory of decentralization, which his ideological tradition lacked before him. The theory was based, in part, on one main theme in the tradition, an idea that had been set forth first by Vivekananda, and then expanded by Aurobindo and Tagore. This was the concept of 'unity in diversity', which Tagore called 'the inmost creed of India'.[57] Aurobindo had explained that human communities should be formed on 'one essential principle of nature — diversity in unity'[58] and we must seek to realize the free play of interests and ideas that necessarily permeate all human relationships. Vivekananda and Aurobindo insisted that this free exchange need not give way to conflict and competition, as so often happened in the West, but could be grounded in an enlightened sense of spiritual unity. For if individuals are allowed the freedom to express and pursue their interests, they will gradually discover their identity of interests, as part of a spiritual oneness, that transcends all sense of separateness.[59]

Gandhi believed that he had discovered the essence of this principle early in his career, in South Africa, when he succeeded in resolving a legal dispute by discovering a common interest. This, he said, 'taught me to appreciate the beauty of compromise. I saw in later life that this spirit was an essential part of Satyagraha.'[60] On the basis of this insight, he constructed a theory of human nature which stressed people's capacities for compromise and mutual aid if these are allowed to develop freely.

In agreement with others in his ideological tradition, as well as with Western anarchists like Kropotkin and Tolstoy, Gandhi argued that the state represented the greatest obstacle to our realization of both individual freedom and social harmony.

> The State represents violence in a concentrated form. The individual has a soul, but as the State is a soulless machine, it can never be weaned from violence to which it owes its very existence.[61]

In the ideal society, 'there is no political power because there is no State', but in striving toward that ideal we may decrease the scope of violence and political power, and increase the sphere of individual freedom and voluntary action, by decentralizing the State's authority. Gandhi says that he views 'with the greatest fear' the increasing centralization of power in most states because this 'does the greatest harm to mankind by destroying individuality which lies at the root of all progress.'[62] Therefore, 'if India is to evolve along non-violent lines, it will have to decentralize,' because 'centralization as a system is inconsistent with a non-violent structure of society.'[63] Gandhi does not delineate the precise functions that would be retained by the central government; the important point is that Gandhi advocated for independent India 'the maximum possible decentralization of the political and economic power and resources of the state . . .'[64] Equally important, this position places Gandhi squarely in line with the thought of Vivekananda, Aurobindo, and Tagore, who share with him suspicion of state authority and a firm desire for its decentralization based on their common attitudes towards politics and power.

Thus far in this analysis, the examination of modern India's ideological tradition has been drawn from examples in the pre-Independence period. From one perspective, the strong antipathy which Vivekananda, Aurobindo, Tagore, and Gandhi demonstrate toward state authority might be attributed to their historical situation, that their thought understandably developed in opposition to the British Raj, and the oppressive nature of that imperial authority. It is obvious from their '*East* vs. *West*' theory that this was the case. However, as we move now into theorists of independent India, and observe how they continue this ideological tradition, it can be seen that the presence of the British is not a necessary condition for this particular line of thought. Indeed, the tradition not only survives but flourishes in independent India, enjoying the support of the country's foremost theorists since 1947. The enduring spirit and content of this tradition in the last three decades may be attributed, first, to the strength of its development during the nationalist period; second, to the continuing presence of a centralized state authority; and third, to the high quality and independent spirit of those theorists who have perpetuated it.

As a theorist and activist during the 1940s, '50s and '60s, Vinoba Bhave ably articulated attitudes towards politics and power that were representative of his ideological tradition. Vinoba was the first to use the term 'total revolution', in the sense of a movement of change that must transform 'all aspects of life'.[65] The goal was nothing less than 'to mould a new man . . . to change human life and create a new world.' For Vinoba, the departure of the British had not brought Indian society any closer to the realization of *sarvodaya*, and the main obstacle remained the same: centralized government. '*Sarvodaya* does not mean good government or majority rule, it means freedom from government, it means decentralisation of power.'[6] Gandhi had correctly defined the value of *swaraj* as necessary for *sarvodaya. Swaraj* meant 'ruling your own self', which implies 'not to allow any outside power in the world to exercise control over oneself' and 'not to exercise power over any other. These two things together make *swaraj* — no submission and no exploitation.' Government, with all its supposed services and benefits, inevitably violates this value of *swaraj* because it demands obedience. 'That is why my voice is raised in opposition to good government. [. . .]' People know 'very well that bad government should not be allowed, and everywhere they protest against it. But what seems to me to be wrong is that we should allow ourselves to be governed at all, even by a good government.'[67]

Vinoba distinguishes three theories of government to clarify better his own. The first wants the eventual 'withering away' of the state, but sanctions the present use of maximum state power in order to achieve its goal. 'Those who accept this theory are totalitarians in the first stage and anarchists in the final stage.' The second theory argues that government has always existed and must remain. The best course is to organize it so that everyone will receive some benefit. The third, Vinoba's theory, shares with the first the ultimate goal of a 'stateless society', but refuses to accept its means of attaining it. 'On the contrary, we propose to proceed by decentralising administration and authority.' It may take a while to 'advance from good government to freedom from government', but it is urgently necessary to begin this movement to the 'final stage' where 'there would be no coercion but a purely moral authority.'[68] Vinoba argues further that those who advocate the second theory, e.g. those on the Indian Planning Commission, rely heavily on centralization of power, but this leads the Indian people in the wrong direction for 'centralised arrangements will never bring us nearer to a stateless society', but only foster an addiction to politics and power. The immediate aim of the *sarvodaya* movement, therefore, is that 'production, distribution, defense, education — everything should be localised. The centre should have the least possible authority. We shall thus achieve decentralisation through regional self-sufficiency. [. . .] We must therefore start at once to introduce decentralisation, and this will be the basis of all our planning.'[69]

At the center of Vinoba's conceptualization of politics and power lies his basic distinction between '*raj-niti*, the politics of power, and *lok-niti*, the ethics of democracy'.[70] Vinoba believes that 'the world is at present in the clutches of centralised [state] power',[71] and people must learn that there is another source of change at their disposal, that 'non-violence is a great power,' the 'power of the Self',[72] and this can be found through pursuit of *lok-niti*, which strives to use 'the potential powers of the citizen'.[73] *Raj-niti* is enamoured of the wrong kind of power, and in its lust for acquisition of it, there ensues 'constant struggle' among parties and politicians, elections marked by a 'ceaseless rivalry for power'. *Lok-niti* would abandon political parties and elections, arrive at decisions through consensus, and forge an identity of interests that would ensure continuing social harmony.[74] Vinoba calls the power of *lok-niti*, which, following Gandhi is necessarily nonviolent, a 'third force', distinguished from both violent coercion and 'the force of law'.[75] For Vinoba, like others in his tradition, the impersonal force of law must be inferior to the personal influence of dedicated social workers who 'maintain the purity of their own personal lives', and shape a *sarvodaya* society with a 'third force' that is legitimate not because it has legal sanction, but rather because it is 'uncontaminated by any lust for [political] power'.[76]

A striking aspect of Vinoba's ideal society is the emphasis which he places on consensus rather than conflict. He repeatedly states that people must transcend 'seats, castes, parties, groups or isms' and deplores the fact that India at present is 'fragmented by innumerable divisions of race, caste, color, religion, and political ideologies. We need social integration if *Swaraj* is to survive.'[77] This spirit of integration and consensus cannot be imposed by law or state power; it is attainable through the kind of voluntary effort exemplified by *sarvodaya* workers, who encourage a genuine transformation of values. 'Every individual has to learn to put the interests of the village before his own' and so foster an organic conception of society so integrated that 'if every limb were to function smoothly, the whole body would function properly.'[78] The aims of *lok-niti* can never be to 'produce conflict' but always to achieve social harmony because 'co-operation is an eternal principle of life.'[79] This argument for an organic society and social consensus runs consistently through the Indian ideological tradition. It parallels directly positions taken in the West by anarchists such as Kropotkin and Tolstoy. But because it is essentially an anarchist conception, attacking state authority and championing natural, spontaneous forces of social harmony, it is directly opposed to the kind of political consensus advocated by apologists of a centralized state such as Rousseau and Hegel. Like the Western anarchists, the Indian theorists connect their idea of a consensus with a vision of small communities, free from coercive political institutions, precisely because people are inherently capable of organizing themselves without a strong government. It is not surprising, then, that Vinoba uses Aurobindo's term, 'spiritual anarchism' to identify his political philosophy.[80]

Because Jayaprakash Narayan articulates the essential values of modern India's ideological tradition with exceptional clarity and directness, an exposition of his theory may be used as a summation of that tradition — not only with respect to its concepts of politics and power — but also of the entire cluster of ideas that it has developed. Jayaprakash ('J. P.') begins, like all anarchists,[81] with a theory of human nature as benign: capacities for destructive behavior obviously exist, but if motives of compassion and non-violence, creativity and co-operation, are cultivated and reinforced by society, then people can unquestionably realize the essential spirit of goodness that lies within them. With the proper example and education to encourage them, individuals will choose to follow 'good men' and 'noble efforts'.[82] This in turn will lead to the evolution of the kind of non-violent community that Gandhi first called *sarvodaya*.

Methods of change commonly used by political or military regimes cannot create a *sarvodaya* social order. The example of the Russian revolution and Soviet state demonstrates the bankruptcy of violence, which only tends to 'ensure the victory of the party that is more skilled in its use', establishing an 'iron grip on the people', undermining all attempts at democracy and the attainment of social justice or equality.[83] Parliamentary democracies, on the other hand, are ineffective in their reliance on legislation. As the case of India's political system shows, legislation for the redistribution of land has failed because there has not occurred a corresponding change in moral values to enforce it. 'Law cannot come into effect without public opinion' to enforce it; 'legislation without conversion [first] is a dead letter.'[84] Echoing attitudes toward law and social change that hark back to Vivekananda, J. P. writes:

> It is not institutions, not laws, not political systems, not constitutions which create good people. For that you require a widespread process of education understood in the widest sense of the word. Education does not mean academic education, but the improving of human beings through service, love, examples, preaching, reasoning and argument.[85]

J. P. consolidates many of the ideas in his tradition in his most important work, *Reconstruction of Indian Polity*. This book has been given close scrutiny by commentators in and outside of India,[86] and the analysis of it here will be confined to the respects that it serves to clarify or enlarge India's ideological tradition. J. P., like all the others of his tradition, is concerned with reconstituting his past, deriving enduring truths from the lessons of 'ancient Indian polity'. This was, as noted above, precisely the task that Aurobindo undertook, and J. P. borrows extensively and explicitly from Aurobindo's work, praising 'that extraordinary, intuitive sweep of his vision [which] has laid bare the true nature of the foundations of Indian polity'.[87] On the basis of

Aurobindo's work, J. P. contends that in ancient India the political order was 'founded on the system of the self-governing village community' which lasted with remarkable 'sufficiency and solidity' until it was 'recently steamrollered out of existence by the ruthless and lifeless machinery of the British bureaucratic system.'[88] Classical India had discovered the key 'principle of an organically self-determining communal life', and today it is only 'a question of an ancient country finding its lost soul again.'[89]

Gandhi had contended in *Hind Swaraj* that Britain had seduced India into selling its soul to the demonic spirit of modern civilization, which included the false charms of parliamentary government. J. P. extends this line of argument, observing that independent India institutionalized a form of government that lacks both traditional sources and theoretical support from any major Indian political theorist. J. P.'s condemnation of parliamentary democracy is as sweeping and categorical as any made by an anarchist, Eastern or Western. He draws from a variety of political commentators, European, American, and Indian, to indict the intrinsic defects of the parliamentary system. The electoral system pretends to represent the wishes of an informed public, but instead serves only to fragment the body politic, confusing voters who are cynically 'manipulated by powerful, centrally controlled parties, with the aid of high finance and diabolically clever methods and super media'. Consequently, only the 'forces and interests behind the parties and propaganda machines' are represented, while the masses are subjected to continuing exploitation, and the society becomes increasingly atomized. But perhaps the most serious fault of parliamentary democracy lies in its 'inherent tendency toward centralism'. Just as Gandhi had believed that 'centralisation as a system is inconsistent with a non-violent structure of society', so J. P. saw centralized authority as invariably fostering vast impersonal bureaucracies and huge interest groups that made 'organic integration' impossible. The main remedy for this is to scrap the parliamentary system, and replace it with a 'communitarian democracy' and decentralized political economy.[90]

In his conceptualization of this communitarian democracy, J. P. consistently recapitulates the central attitudes of his ideological tradition. He wants to avoid 'competitiveness' because it is necessarily exploitative, and achieve instead a 'co-operative and co-sharing', 'integrated' social order in which there would be a true 'harmonization of interests'. Only a 'deliberate and bold process of devolution and decentralization', shaping all aspects of social development, may attain this goal. It needs to be initiated by 'hundreds of thousands of voluntary workers' who understand that the basic task is one 'of moral regeneration to be brought about by example, service, sacrifice and love'.[91] Although J. P. is more specific about the structural organization of his decentralized system than any of his predecessors,[92] the ideology that underpins it goes straight back to Vivekananda.

Fundamental criticisms have been made of J. P.'s thought by many of those familiar with his work, and these have been best expressed by W. H. Morris-Jones. A main concern running through Morris-Jones' critique is that there are elements in J. P.'s thought, such as his insistence on 'systematic mass participation' and 'identification of rulers and ruled', that in some political theorists have tended to 'prepare the way for totalitarianism'. In the case of Rousseau:

> Satisfied with nothing less than each man retaining his 'freedom' by taking full part in the laying down of laws he is to obey, he ends by asserting that some men will obtain their 'freedom' by being coerced; ordinary language and ordinary people both suffer when such violence is done to them.[93]

It is fair to ask if there is any explicit evidence in J. P.'s writings that he has either defined freedom in a manner similar to Rousseau, or shown himself insensitive to the dangers of totalitarianism. The answer must be 'no' on both counts. J. P. consistently defines freedom in the traditional, Indian sense as *swaraj*, and claims that it was his own quest for freedom in this sense that drove him away from Marxism.[94] Moreover, his writings are alive with warnings against totalitarian government, and in his last eloquent yet tragic writing, *Prison Diary*, he inveighs throughout against his main foe, a Prime Minister who destroyed democracy, substituting for it a 'totalitarian system'.[95] Here he argues for liberty in the fullest sense, and especially for freedom of the press.[96].

Yet Morris-Jones believes that there is an inescapable and intrinsic danger to freedom and liberal democracy in J. P.'s ideal of mass participation:

> Men want many things from governments and they may want to be governed in certain ways, but they do not want to do the governing. The dogmatic democrat who insists that they shall do so is bound to become a tyrant — or pave the way for one.[97]

Then Morris-Jones returns to his theme of J. P.'s parallels with Rousseau by linking his critique of the ideas of freedom and mass participation in J. P.'s thought with his concept of consensus:

> Moreover, the stress on consensus seems to imply a peculiar view of the common good. It is thought of as something single and simple — discernible to men of insight and goodwill, attainable (as Rousseau again believed) through the silencing of particular or selfish interests.
>
> But is this really our experience? Is the position not rather that the common good is something towards which we can approximate only through a forth-

right expression of all relevant clashing interests and their reconciliation so far as is possible? The pretence that interests do not clash, that a common interest is somehow always present and only needs to be uncovered, is likely to yield a good that is far from common. And there is no community, however organic it may be, without different interests . . . Consensus is a fair name for what could be an ugly reality.[98]

At the outset of this paper, it was suggested that when J. P. and other Indians of his ideological tradition are compared with Western political theory, they are allied not with the school of thought that links Plato and Rousseau, but rather with Western anarchists, and that the Indian ideological tradition itself constitutes a significant body of anarchist thought. The central differences between the Plato-Rousseau school and the anarchists hinge on the concepts of politics and power. Rousseau, following Plato, envisaged his political leaders or 'law-givers', attaining an advanced stage of consciousness, and then ruling with 'sublime reason, which is beyond the understanding of the vulgar . . . in order to compel by divine authority those whom human prudence could not move'.[99] No anarchist, Eastern or Western, could ever justify such a conception of leadership. This is largely because for Plato and Rousseau the unique capacity of the state was to create and nurture a life of virtue. Outside the realm of politics, justice and morality could not exist, and the role of legitimate authority was sanctified. This is at the opposite pole from the anarchists' perception, for whom politics and power remained not only inherently suspect but also singularly incapable of producing the virtuous individual or society. If there is a 'politics' of *Lok-niti*, it represents a kind that Plato and Rousseau would certainly regard as anaemic or impotent; they would be even less satisfied with the Indian view of the necessary limitations on law as a force in shaping human behavior.

The emphasis which Plato and Rousseau place on the unique role of politics is decisive, and nowhere more than in their view of the individual. For Rousseau, each individual 'puts in common his person and all his powers under the supreme direction of the general will' and so each becomes 'an indivisible part of the whole'.[100] The 'civil state' is thus born, with 'natural liberty' replaced by 'civil liberty'. For all J. P.'s stress on mass participation and the organic community, there is no language anywhere in his writings or in any of the others in his tradition, that compares with Rousseau's description of the supremacy of the general will, the sovereignty of the civil state, or his contention that 'anything which breaks the unity of society is worthless.'[101] On the contrary, the writings of those in the Indian ideological tradition are replete with statements like Vivekananda's that 'any system which seeks to destroy individuality is in the long run disastrous'[102] or Gandhi's that 'no society can possibly be built on a denial of individual freedom.'[103] Within the context of this ideological tradition, then, there would seem to be no theoretical justification for the creation of the 'ugly reality' that Morris-Jones fears. That sort of sanction comes from other traditions of thought, alien neither to India nor to the West, which rationalize political dictatorship.

These are not the only critical concerns that W. H. Morris-Jones has expressed about J. P.'s thought and those theorists related to it. He levelled a major criticism at this whole line of thought first in an essay called 'India's Political Idioms', where the idiom or language in India of 'saintly politics' was described and examined:

> . . . saintly politics is important as a language of comment rather than of description or practical behaviour. [. . .] Its influence is rather on the standards habitually used by the people at large for judging the performance of politicians. In men's minds there is an ideal of disinterested selflessness by contrast with which almost all normal conduct can seem very shabby . . . it contributes powerfully to several very prevalent attitudes to be found in Indian political life: to a certain witholding of full approval from even the most popular leaders; to a stronger feeling of distrust of and disgust with persons and institutions of authority; finally, to profoundly violent and desperate moods of cynicism and frustration.[104]

Morris-Jones reinforced this criticism in his new preface to his essay on J. P. with the comment:

> . . . very many people in India who are far too sceptical to embrace J. P.'s full doctrines nevertheless continue to adopt his norms, so that although they do not follow him in striving towards Utopia they use his utopian vision to look upon the functioning reality of everyday Indian politics with scorn and despair. The paradoxical consequence of the idealist is furtherance of cynicism.[105]

He concludes that it may be more constructive for a political theorist to advocate 'instead more modest versions of democracy and emphasising some of the neglected virtues of the system, imperfect but capable of improvement, which we have with us. . .'[106] This is an especially important criticism because it returns us to the view expressed in the opening quotation of this article from Morris-Jones concerning the purpose and impact of political theory. Since the dawn of political philosophy, its purpose has been to project a 'transcending form of vision' which meant 'thinking about the political society in its corrected fullness, not as it is but as it might be'. This essential character of vision served a function for human behavior. 'Precisely because political theory pictured society in an exaggerated, "unreal" way, it was a necessary complement to action. Precisely because action involved intervention into existing affairs, it sorely needed a perspective of tantalizing possibilities.'[107]

The Indian theorists examined here were above all visionaries in that they persistently posed the great Socratic question, 'Which course of life is best?' In their responses, they envisioned human nature gifted with such a panoramic range of capacities that a community based on mutual aid and non-violence truly offered 'a perspective of tantalizing possibilities'.

It is surely debatable whether their vision is the right one, especially if it encourages cynicism, frustration and despair. Yet it is not debatable that India needs a vision, for since Independence the nation has been strong on power politics but weak on those ideals that Mohandas Gandhi showed could inspire and mobilize the masses. Visions are sometimes difficult to conceive; and even then they are easily lost. India has been markedly unable to produce many in this century outside of those conceived by the theorists examined here. Instead, the nation has been integrated not only *sans* vision, but against a prevailing anarchist ideology that has persistently called for decentralization of political power. It remains to be seen how long this unusually wide gap between political practice and theory can prevail, and whether 'what the political philosopher believes and teaches today will in some measure mould what politicians believe and do tomorrow'.

NOTES

1. W. H. Morris-Jones, *Politics Mainly Indian* (Bombay: Orient Longman, 1978), 9.
2. The terms 'ideological tradition' and 'school of thought' in this context are used to suggest a number of political and social thinkers from India in the last one hundred years. These men may appear quite dissimilar in terms of their styles of thought, but they exhibit a clear consensus in their common commitment to ideas about human nature and the good society, the nature of authority and the relationship of the individual to the state, the values of freedom and equality, emphasis on consensus rather than conflict, co-operation rather than competition as social ideals, and on a method of change that relies on moral example and suasion rather than violent revolution or legislative reform. The concepts of politics and power are used here to focus the analysis on their agreement. These theorists include: Swami Vivekananda, Aurobindo Ghose, Rabindranath Tagore, M. K. Gandhi, Vinoba Bhave and Jayaprakash Narayan among those examined in this article; but also included in the school are M. N. Roy and Deendayal Upadhyaya. For analysis of the last two, see the author's 'Gandhi and Roy: the Interaction of Ideologies in India' in S. N. Ray (ed.), *Gandhi India and the World* (Melbourne: Hawthorn Press, 1970), 156–70; and 'Unity in Diversity', in Upadhyaya Memorial Lecture Series, September 1980.
3. *The Politics of Aristotle*, transl. by Ernest Barker (London: Oxford

University Press, 1958), pp. 1, 4–5.

4. *The Republic of Plato*, transl. by F. M. Cornford (London: Oxford University Press, 1958). The creation of the Republic, which is 'difficult but not impossible' (p. 208), can occur only when there will be 'power in the hands of men who are rich, not in gold, but in . . . a good and wise life' (p. 235). These are the Guardians, who will have complete command of political power.
5. Rousseau, *Political Writings*, transl. and ed. by F. Watkins (London: Nelson Philosophical Texts, 1953), *Social Contract*, I, ch. VIII, 19–20.
6. Sheldon Wolin, *Politics and Vision* (London: George Allen and Unwin, 1961), 308.
7. Isaiah Berlin, *Four Essays on Liberty* (London: Oxford University Press, 1969), 165–6.
8. W. H. Morris-Jones, op. cit., 26. See also 25, 27–44.
9. Henry David Thoreau, 'Civil Disobedience' in *Walden and Civil Disobedience* (New York: Norton and Norton, 1966), 224–5.
10. *The Life of Swami Vivekananda* by his Eastern and Western Disciples (Calcutta: Advaita Ashrama, 1960), 452.
11. Swami Vivekananda, *Complete Works*, III (Calcutta: Advaita Ashrama, 1960), 148
12. Ibid., 204.
13. Ibid., 158.
14. Ibid., VI, 8.
15. Ibid., III, 158.
16. Ibid., V, 200.
17. Ibid., IV, 435.
18. Ibid., III, 244.
19. Ibid., V, 193.
20. Ibid., 289.
21. Ibid., VI, 100.
22. Ibid., II, 65.
23. M. K. Gandhi, *Collected Works*, X (Delhi: Publications Division, Government of India, 1963), 42–7.
24. Vivekananda, *Works*, II, 21.
25. Ibid., III, 108–9.
26. Ibid., I, 426.
27. Ibid., V, 105.
28. Ibid., V, 36, 114.
29. Ibid., III, 299.
30. Sri Aurobindo has been rightly called 'the real intellectual heir of Vivekananda'. In Romain Rolland, *Prophets of the New India*, transl. by E. F. Malcolm-Smith (London: Cassell, 1930), 499.
31. Sri Aurobindo, *The Spirit and Form of Indian Polity* (Pondicherry: Sri Aurobindo Ashram, 1966).
32. Ibid., 20–1.
33. Ibid., 28.
34. Ibid., 31.
35. Ibid., 30.

36. Sri Aurobindo, *The Ideal of Human Unity* in *The Human Cycle The Ideal of Human Unity (and) War and Self-Determination* (Pondicherry: Sri Aurobindo Ashram, 1962), 673.
37. Ibid., 677.
38. Ibid., 678.
39. Ibid.
40. Ibid., 679.
41. Ibid., 615.
42. Ibid., 685.
43. Sri Aurobindo, *The Human Cycle* in Ibid., 347.
44. Rabindranath Tagore, 'Society and State' in *Towards Universal Man* (London: Asia Publishing House, 1961), 51–2.
45. M. K. Gandhi, op. cit., 16.
46. Ibid., compare Gandhi's use of 'brute force' in ch. XVI, 42–7, with his conceptualization of 'soul-force or truth force' in ch. XVII, 47–53, and his identification of 'brute force' as a weapon of the extremists (50). It is clear that the extremists have been infected by British methods.
47. Ibid., pp. 31–8.
48. M. K. Gandhi, 'Neither a Saint nor a Politician' in *Works*, XVII, 406.
49. Ibid., XXXIX, 401.
50. Ibid., XLVII, 246.
51. R. Tagore, op. cit., 172.
52. M. K. Gandhi, *Works*, XXV, 563.
53. R. Tagore in *Truth Called Them Differently*, ed. by R. K. Prabhu and R. Kelekar (Ahmedabad: Navajivan Pub. House, 1961), 14.
54. Ibid., 16.
55. Tagore, *Towards Universal Man*, 260.
56. Gandhi as quoted in D. G. Tendulkar, *Mahatma*. 8 vols. (Delhi: Government of India Publications Division, 1961), 3, 113.
57. Tagore, *Towards Universal Man*, 65.
58. Aurobindo, *Ideal of Human Unity*, op. cit., 560.
59. Vivekananda, *Works*, II, 153; V, 278, 536.
60. Gandhi, *Works*, XXXIX, 122.
61. Ibid., LIX, 318.
62. Ibid., 319.
63. M. K. Gandhi, *Harijan*, 18 January 1942, 5.
64. J. Bandyopadhyaya, *Social and Political Thought of Gandhi* (Bombay: Allied Publishers, 1969), 89.
65. Vinoba Bhave, *Revolutionary Sarvodaya* (Bombay: Bharatiya Vidya Bhavan, 1964), 1.
66. Vinoba Bhave, *Democratic Values* (Kashi: Sarva Seva Sangh Prakashan, 1962), 3.
67. Ibid., 12–13.
68. Ibid., 29.
69. Ibid., 30.
70. Ibid., xi.
71. Ibid., 117.
72. Vinoba, *Revolutonary Sarvodaya*, 49–50.

73. Vinoba, *Democratic Values*, xi.
74. Ibid., 86–8.
75. Ibid., 212–13.
76. Ibid., 223.
77. Suresh Ram, *Vinoba and His Mission* (Rajghat, Kashi: Akhil Bharat Sarva Seva Sangh, 1962), 208.
78. Vinoba, *Revolutionary Sarvodaya*, 45.
79. Vinoba Bhave, *Swaraj Sastra* (Rajghat, Varanasi: Sarva Seva Sangh Prakhashan, 1963), 63.
80. Vinoba, quoted in *The Social and Political Philosophy of Sarvodaya After Gandhiji*, by Vishwanath Tandon (Rajghat, Varanasi: Sarva Seva Sangh Prakashan, 1965), 124.
81. James Joll, *The Anarchists* (London: Eyre and Spottiswoode, 1964): 'The fundamental idea that man is by nature good and that it is institutions that corrupt him remains the basis of all anarchist thought' (30). Joll is one of the few analysts of anarchist thought who includes recognition and comment on Indian anarchism. See his brief mention of Gandhi, Vinoba, and J. P. (pp. 277–8).
82. Jayaprakash Narayan, *A Picture of Sarvodaya Social Order* (Tanjore: Sarvodaya Pracharalaya, 1961), 6. J. P. says: 'Man is essentially good and not bad.'
83. Ibid., 4–5.
84. Ibid., 9.
85. Ibid., 151.
86. See, for example, W. H. Morris-Jones, 'The Unhappy Utopia — J. P. in Wonderland', in *Politics Mainly Indian*, 97–106. This critique of J. P.'s *Reconstruction* first appeared in *Economic Weekly*, 25 June 1960, and prompted an exchange between William Carpenter and Morris-Jones, published in *The Economic Weekly Annual*, 4 February 1961.
87. Jayaprakash Narayan, *A Plea for Reconstruction of Indian Polity* (Rajghat, Kashi: Akhil Bharat Sarva Seva Sangh, 1959), 22.
88. Ibid., 22.
89. Ibid., 26.
90. Ibid., 66–8.
91. Ibid., 107.
92. J. P.'s ideas on the organization of his polity, often referred to as *panchayati raj*, are contained in the best collection of his writings, *Socialism, Sarvodaya and Democracy*, edited by Bimla Prasad (London: Asia Publishing House, 1964), especially the essay 'Swaraj for the People', 239–74.
93. W. H. Morris-Jones, *Politics Mainly Indian*, 102.
94. J. P. Narayan, *Picture of Sarvodaya Social Order*, 112.
95. J. P. Narayan, *Prison Diary* ed. by A. B. Shah (Seattle: University of Washington Press, 1977), 1.
96. Ibid., 105–6.
97. W. H. Morris-Jones, *Politics Mainly Indian*, 103.
98. Ibid., 105.
99. Rousseau, *Political Writings*, 44–5.

100. Ibid., 16.
101. Ibid., 148.
102. Vivekananda, *Works*, VI, 82.
103. M. K. Gandhi, 'Plain Thinking and High Living' in *Harijan*, 1 February 1942, 27. See also Vinoba Bhave, *Democratic Values*, 116: 'Every person must enjoy the fullest liberty for the propagation of his ideas.'
104. W. H. Morris-Jones, 'India's Political Idioms' in *Politics and Society in India*, ed. by C. H. Philips (London: George Allen and Unwin, 1963), pp. 140–41. This analysis is placed in a larger context in W. J. Morris-Jones, *The Government and Politics of India*, 3rd rev. edn (London: Hutchinson University Library, 1971), 59–61.
105. W. H. Morris-Jones, *Politics Mainly Indian*, 97.
106. Ibid.
107. Sheldon Wolin, *Politics and Vision*, 20–1.

PAKISTAN: UNITY OR FURTHER DIVISIONS?

Ataur Rahman

Ever since the creation of Pakistan in 1947, the ineluctable dilemma facing the nation has been to create a viable national identity out of diverse regional and linguistic loyalties. Ironically, in the last thirty-three years Pakistan failed to resolve the dilemma. With the disintegration of Pakistan in 1971 and the emergence of Bangladesh as an independent state marking the triumph of ethnic-linguistic nationalism, a phase in Pakistan's history ended. Dismembered Pakistan appeared to reinforce in itself the bonds of national unity in Pakistan with its overwhelming Islamic orientation, apparent economic cohesiveness and low saliency of Indian fear.[1] Credibility was added to this view by the performance of the Bhutto regime after the severe crisis and dislocations of 1971. The return to party competition, the adoption of a constitution with a federal structure, and the substantive economic recovery promoted by the Bhutto regime seemed to give the new Pakistani nation a momentum and a sense of purpose.[2]

However, contrary to expectations, Pakistan, after the initial years, began to spawn debilitating centrifugal forces. Regional ethnic groups provoked largely by a sense of economic deprivation, political isolation and intractable externalisation of internal problems were the obvious symptoms. Then followed the third military coup led by General Zia ul-Haq in July 1977. Immediately before the coup there were unprecedented mass protests accompanied by civil unrest against the Bhutto regime. Events in neighbouring Afghanistan worsened matters. Pakistan entered a new phase, perhaps the most dangerous in its history. These calamitous difficulties were by no means to be of short duration. They could cause the polarisation of Pakistani society along ethnic, religious and ideological lines; the country's unity, security and integrity seem to be threatened by the prospect of further territorial division.

How do we then explain Pakistan's present crisis of unity? What are the most potent disintegrative forces that have led to such profound scepticism concerning its future? Is the nation's capacity for survival at stake? If not, what forces and strata of Pakistani society perceive their future linked to a continuation of Pakistan in its present form? Answers to these questions are complex and hazardous because of the elusive character of Pakistan's politics. However, they must be examined to ascertain what lies in store for Pakistan in the future.

Pakistan, to begin with, was a fragile state carved out of Muslim-majority provinces in British India. With no solid nationalist basis, it proved to be an uneasy amalgam of distinct cultural, linguistic and ethnic groups. In the aftermath of Partition, the most ominous challenges to Pakistan's attempts at national integration came from separatist or irredentist forces operating along ethnic and cultural lines. In order to understand the present crisis of national unity in Pakistan, the 'interlocking tangle' of irredentist issues left by history and accentuated by state policies over the past years needs to be examined.

A legacy of bitterness

In the euphoric early days of independence, the political leaders of Pakistan did not give serious thought to the potency of regional and linguistic forces. They stressed the bonds of Islamic unity and pointed out that Islam recognised no regional or linguistic loyalties. The major constitutional conflicts that took place in Pakistan, however, arose largely over the question of representation to be accorded to major regional groups in the central legislature of Pakistan.[3] In fact, the demand for autonomy expressed itself in a demand for recognising ethnic regions in Pakistan. The demands were more forceful and strident than those emphasising Islamic order or the unity of the democratic system. Regional conflict therefore raised its head at the very moment of the creation of the new state.[4] It has gained momentum since the 1955 One-Unit Scheme and has left a profound legacy of bitterness among the Punjabis, Sindhis, Pashtuns and Baluchis who constitute the more important elements in Pakistan's ethnic mosaics.

The unification of West Pakistan into One Unit in 1955, mainly by the dominant Punjabi group, was resented by all other regional groups. The 'combination of force and cunning' used by the Punjabi group, particularly by members of the Constituent Assembly and by top civil-military bureaucrats, to eliminate opposition and impose integration created serious misgivings and suspicions among three other regional and ethnically distinct minority groups. While in Sind and the North-West Frontier Province, the opposition to One Unit was deep and widespread, it was the Baluchis who put up stiffer resistance to what they regarded as Punjabi domination. Some Baluchi tribes, particularly in the Kalat division, revolted against the Government, and for six months 15,000 soldiers of the Pakistani army battled against the rebels in the mountains of Baluchistan.[5] Pakistan's ethnic minority groups, particularly the Baluchis and Pashtuns, perceive the Punjabi élite as being domineering and never willing to concede equality. Such a perception has been more seriously reinforced by the Bangladesh episode.

Post-1971 regional and ethnic cleavages

After the separation of Bangladesh, Pakistan's new geographical entity appeared to provide a viable entity for achieving national consolidation. There were nevertheless potential threats to the new country's unity. To justify the legitimacy of post-1971 Pakistan, 'an important first task' undertaken by the Bhutto regime was the territorial and administrative consolidation of the state. A 'carrot and stick' policy was adopted by Bhutto in dealing with the Provinces. The restoration of Provinces to pre-1955 (One-Unit) status and the appointment of popular leaders such as Ghaus Baksh Bizenjo and Arbab Sikander as Governors of Baluchistan and N.W.F.P. respectively were important overtures made by the Bhutto Government.

In addition, Bhutto adopted several policies to ensure effective administration and to end feudalism. First, the northern territories of Pakistan (Chitral, Dir, Swat, Amb) had their 'special status through the introduction of various Ordinances and benefits' eroded — a process of integration that would lead to 'regularisation' and uniformity of administrative practices throughout the country. In such vein, Bhutto also abolished the Frontier Crimes Regulation and the *Jirga* system (of tribal elders), and replaced these with the jurisdiction of the High Court and Supreme Court. Secondly, 'to draw together the sprawling country' into a tighter communication and economic network, the Bhutto Government began constructing new roads, setting up schools and hospitals in the border lands of the N.W.F.P. and Baluchistan. To this end, generous development funds were distributed by the Bhutto regime.[6] At the same time, Bhutto began to use the state power to quell civil disorders and internal violence perceiving these as threats to the integrity of the state. The High Treason Act of 1973 and the Private Military Organisation (the Abolition, Prohibition and Prevention of Anti-national Activities) Ordinance were adopted for this purpose.

Bhutto's 'forward policy', however, aroused sharp resistance from Baluchistan and the N.W.F.P. The Baluch and Pashtun tribesmen suspected Bhutto's administrative and socio-economic measures as being deliberate arrangements intended to consolidate the day-to-day administrative control by the Central Government. Their resentment was exacerbated by their apprehension that Bhutto's measures for effective governance of the frontier regions would end the lucrative contraband trade they conducted between Afghanistan and Pakistan. In particular, the Marris and Mengal tribes who had been up in arms during the Ayub regime began to put up resistance to Bhutto's policies.

To make matters worse, early in 1973 when the elected state government in Baluchistan resisted the political and economic incursions of the Central Government, Bhutto dismissed the popular governor of Baluchistan, Ghaus Baksh Bizenjo, ousted the state cabinet, imprisoned the major leaders including the president of the National Awami Party, Khair Baksh Marri, on charges of sedition, imposed central rule and sent 70,000 troops to the Province.[7] An essentially political problem was thus turned into a military problem. The chain of events beginning in 1973 led Baluchistan to the verge of a civil war. To compound matters, the situation in the N.W.F.P. was also aggravated. The Governor of the Province resigned in protest against the Central Government's heavy-handed actions against the autonomy of the provinces.

Baluchistan: the separatist creed of a neglected province

Occupying nearly 40 per cent of Pakistan's land area, Baluchistan has a population of about 3 million. In spite of its vast area, abundant gas reserves, rich mineral wealth, luscious fruit and numerous sheep, the Province has remained underdeveloped. It is far behind the other Provinces in agriculture, industry and the infrastructure for development. The people are weighed down by a primitive tribal system. They suffer a sense of economic deprivation and political isolation. Since the British withdrawal from the sub-continent, the trans-national Baluch tribesmen who live in the inaccessible mountains and desert country of Western Pakistan tend to be in frequent conflict with the Central authority against the latter's 'calculated disregard of their ethnic and cultural identities'. In fact, Baluchistan like the North-West Frontier Province was reluctant to join Pakistan in 1947. The Khan of Kalat, one of the rulers of Baluchistan, refused to join Pakistan and declared his territory's independence.[8] Pakistan had to use military force to take over Kalat Division in 1948. Since then, Baluchistan has gone through repeated political upheavals, culminating in the most severe insurgency which lasted four years (1973–7) during the Bhutto regime.

In spite of the vast expanse of the region, Baluchistan under British rule was a Chief Commissioner's province even as late as 1935. Since it was a backward and neglected province of Pakistan, a major Baluch grievance was that outside interests dominated by the Punjabis reaped the benefits of their vast untapped natural resources but never cared for the improvement of the region's administrative structure or its economic development. The endless presence of the Army, the imposition of *ad hoc* administrative arrangements giving rise to endemic bureaucratic corruption, and development expenditure that was counter-productive led Baluchis to develop a hostile view of the Central

Government. The Baluchis resent the fact that while lack of industrialisation in the province forces them to migrate to industrial cities for jobs, the Punjabi farmers from outside the region are being increasingly settled in the arable areas of Baluchistan.[9] The Baluchis also resent the level of federal development expenditure on Baluchistan which they think is disproportionately low in relation to other Provinces in the country.[10] Moreover, most of the spending by the Central Government during the Bhutto years was either for military purposes or for the extraction of resources which would benefit outsiders.

Performance of the Zia-ul-Haq regime

The present military regime has tried to defuse the tensions in Baluchistan, so strong during the Bhutto regime. In March 1978, General Zia ul-Haq declared a general amnesty for persons who left their homes during the insurgency of 1973–7; he released Baluch political leaders like Bizenjo and Khair Baksh Marri and the N.A.P. leader, Wali Khan.[11] 'The intention' — as Zia ul-Haq pointed out — 'is to open a new chapter by letting by-gones be by-gones in the larger interests of the country, so that national unity is ensured through mutual understanding and love, and in the true Islamic spirit.'[12] The 'normalisation' efforts of General Zia's regime in Baluchistan included financial assistance to those who lost their lives and suffered injuries during 1973–7; the rehabilitation of people adversely affected by the insurgency, particularly students and government servants who abandoned their education or careers; and acceleration of development projects under federal government allocations.[13] The present regime claims that about 97 per cent of the tribesmen who had left their homes have returned.[14] Some moderate Baluch leaders think that an era of reconciliation might dawn in Baluchistan as the present regime has, for the first time in this sensitive province, sought direct contact with the Baluchs.

The moderates, particularly the older generation of Baluch leaders[15] mostly identified with the N.A.P., emphasised the need for negotiations and conferences with the present regime. Zia ul-Haq also made an overture by including Mr Mohyuddin Baluch in the federal Cabinet as Minister for Communications.[16] However, militant Baluch leaders like Khair Baksh Marri, whose tribe played an important role in the 1973–7 insurgency, and Baluch youth and intelligentsia insist that Baluch support to the present regime should be withheld until Zia ul-Haq withdraws the Pakistan Army, pays substantial compensation to the victims of alleged military atrocities and grants provincial autonomy in all spheres except defence, foreign affairs and currency.

While Zia ul-Haq promised to meet some of the demands as part of his 'normalisation' efforts, he has shown no signs of wanting to compromise on the key issue of provincial autonomy.

However, it is difficult to predict what success the present regime will have in checking the centrifugal force of Baluch regionalism in the foreseeable future without a meaningful political formula being devised to end the present impasse. The Marxist revolution in Afghanistan in 1978 and the Soviet invasion that followed have already had their impact on the political situation in Baluchistan. General Zia ul-Haq referred to the situation as 'critical'[17] because of the possibility of external forces in league with internal subversive elements posing a threat to Pakistan's national unity and solidarity. The convulsions in Kabul reinforced the stand of the militant Baluch elements. Even moderates like Khair Baksh Marri, the hereditary chieftain of the 113,000-strong Marri tribe[18] and the President of the outlawed N.A.P., who espoused a mild socialism and an ambiguously defined autonomy for the tribal areas have taken an increasingly militant posture in recent years.

The traditional Baluch leadership seems to be losing ground to the militant and Leftist groups who are more organised and more clearly aligned with the Soviet Union. The militant Baluch organisations like the Baluchi Peoples Liberation Front (B.P.L.F.) and the Mir Hazar Group have joined forces with a pro-Soviet group called the Popular Front for Armed Resistance.[19] These militant groups have become bolder than ever and are building guerrilla organisations[20] with the hope that hereafter neighbouring Afghanistan will support their demand for an independent 'Greater Baluchistan' comprising territory now within Pakistan and Iran. The suppression of normal political life and the prospect of a long period of military rule in Pakistan presents future dangers for the political integration of the Baluchs into Pakistan's body politic. Baluch youth and student leaders, particularly, see no future for them in Pakistan. However, romanticism rather than hard thinking underlies their attitudes.[21]

The Baluch insurgents in Pakistan are, however, faced with a number of problems. Baluchistan's population is heterogeneous. While Baluchs constitute about half of the population, the other half is made up of several other ethnic groups, particularly Pashtuns, Brahuis, Sindhis and Punjabis. The Pashtuns, for example, dominate the Quetta division and constitute almost 40 per cent of the Baluch population. The Pashtuns of Baluchistan have usually kept themselves free of involvement in the struggle of the Baluchs against the central authority.[22] Even the Baluchs are divided into many tribes and classes. The Soviet invasion of Afghanistan has further worsened the problem of ethnic and tribal diversity, and there seems to be a growing polarisation within the Baluch ranks. The political parties in Baluchistan, which are mostly regionalist and ethnocentric, have become more factionalised and polarised. The continuing arrival of Afghan refugees in the aftermath of the Soviet invasion — all of whom are Pashtuns — has inflamed smouldering Pashtun–Baluch tensions.[23] Thus the problems posed by ethnic and tribal diversity as well as the mutual suspicions and antagonisms between the rival groups limit the efforts of militant and Leftist insurgents to develop a province-wide organisational network and to create a united 'national' front against the central government.

Problems of Pashtun Separatism

Spanning many ecological zones, Pashtuns are the largest and most cohesive tribal group in Pakistan's ethnic mosaic. The demand for the creation of a separate state called 'Pashtunistan' (or Pakhtunistan) to include all Pashtu-speaking areas in the North-West Frontier Province, parts of Baluchistan and Afghanistan dates from the creation of Pakistan. In fact, Khan Abdul Gaffar Khan and his Red Shirts did not support the Muslim League plan to create Pakistan, but worked closely with Jawaharlal Nehru to preserve an undivided India[24] or to create a separate state — 'Pakhtunistan'. However, when Pakistan became inevitable, Gaffar Khan joined the new state. Pakistan's leader, M. A. Jinnah, gave Gaffar Khan an assurance that his Government would not interfere in any way in the traditional independence of tribal areas. The Pashtuns nevertheless were interfered with and have ever since been suffering from an identity crisis. The irredentist aspirations of Pashtuns are inspired by language, race (being Afghans by origin) and memories of history. In economic terms, the advocates of Pakhtunistan point out that they have oil and mineral prospects, as well as fertile agricultural areas and vast wealth in timber.

To add to the Pashtun sense of belonging to a separate 'nationality', Afghanistan began playing a direct manipulative role in the 'Pakhtunistan' issue. It is very clear from the record that the 'Pakhtunistan' issue had become a major Afghan concern whenever the Government of Pakistan sought to alter the *status quo* of the tribal 'no-man's-land' along the Durand line which left 7 million Pashtuns on the Pakistani side and 5 million on the Afghan side. Kabul never accepted the *de jure* boundary, which they considered an imperial legacy in flagrant violation of the ethnic and cultural identities of the Pashtun people. In protest, Afghanistan voted against the admission of Pakistan into the United Nations in 1948. The decision to merge all four provinces of the former West Pakistan into a single Unit in 1955, thus extinguishing the identity of the N.W.F.P. and Baluchistan, led to strong protests from Kabul culminating in the severance of diplomatic relations. (Turkey later mediated in their repair). It was at this juncture that the Soviet leaders, Nikolai Bulganin and Nikita Khrushchev, declared that they sympathised with Afghanistan's policy on the Pashtunistan issue, and since then Afghanistan has always received sympathy and support from the Soviet Union in its efforts to foment troubles in the Pashtun and Baluch areas. A number of Soviet scholars considered Pakistan as a collection of separate 'nationalities' and argued that 'the dismemberment of India along religious lines has not solved the national problem in the areas constituting Pakistan.'[25]

The 'forward policy' of Pakistan pursued under the Bhutto regime since the beginning of 1973 revived the demand for 'Pakhtunistan'. Bhutto's adoption of various measures for the effective control of Pashtun areas created suspicions among several independent tribes over whom neither Kabul nor Islamabad could ever exercise effective control. Moreover, the way in which Bhutto had been playing off the tribal leaders against one another created resentments among them. Khan Abdul Wali Khan, the most popular Pakhtun leader, characterised Bhutto's politics as a deliberate seeking of confrontation and interpreting every legitimate regional discontent as an act of treason of crisis proportions.[26] The National Awami Party of Wali Khan, the leading champion of provincial autonomy, was eliminated by Bhutto through a legal order in early 1975. The arrest of Wali Khan and other N.A.P. leaders by Bhutto on charges of treason, culminating in a prolonged trial, led to strong resentment in the N.W.F.P.

It may be said to the credit of General Zia ul-Haq that by abolishing the Hyderabad tribunal and releasing political leaders like Wali Khan,[27] he reduced the tensions in the Frontier. As a response to this gesture, Wali Khan, the principal leader of Pakistan's Pashtuns, tried to negotiate an arrangement with General Zia for holding nationwide elections leading to civilian governments in Islamabad and in the four Provinces of Pakistan. Wali Khan also made it clear that he had no intention of disturbing the quantum of provincial autonomy available under the 1973 constitution. But this autonomy, he insisted, should be implemented in both letter and spirit: it would require the equal representation of all the Provinces in the Senate and more financial and administrative powers to the Provinces. However, the negotiations broke down. General Zia embarked on a new course, appointing some Muslim League elements and technocrats from the N.W.F.P. as federal ministers.[28]

Like Baluchistan, the Pashtun areas are undergoing a gradual polarisation between moderates and hard-liners.[29] The moderates want a political settlement based on greater autonomy within the existing Pakistani political structure. Increased economic links between Pashtun areas and the rest of Pakistan, better representation of Pashtuns in the Army and bureaucracy and greater economic inducements are some of the positive factors working for the gradual integration of moderate Pashtuns in the Pakistani body politic. Yet some of the powerful independent tribes — the Afridis, Mohamands, Mahsuds and Wazirs, who showed considerable support for the Pashtunistan cause in the past — do not want to jeopardise the benefits they derive from the profitable smuggling operations made possible by their control of key sectors of the borders. Moreover, their attitudes to the present secularised national Communist government in Kabul is ambivalent[30] because their tribal political culture is dominated at once by ethnic loyalty and by religious fear: hence, while these tribes are attracted by the strong Pashtun cast of the new regime, they are also afraid of the godless Communism in Kabul destroying their Islamic traditions. There seems to be a revival of the Islamic spirit among the Pashtuns, with the fundamentalist Islamic parties more active than ever before in propagating Islamic values among the tribes. With the continuing arrival of Afghan refugees, mostly Pashtuns inspired with the spirit of *Zihad* (religious war) against Communist forces, the hard-liners linked to Kabul's new regime are increasingly losing ground.

The pro-Moscow groups who were better organized in the Pashtun areas seem at the time of writing to be divided. Unlike Baluchistan, Pashtun separatism could be better managed in the future if Zia ul-Haq could pursue his policies imaginatively.

Merits of 'Islamisation' and Prospects of Democracy

Soon after Zia ul-Haq assumed power in July 1977, he proclaimed the beginning of an Islamic era in Pakistan. He repeatedly told his audiences that the Islamic transformation of Pakistan occupied the highest position in his scale of priorities. Justifying the postponement of elections scheduled to be held in November 1979, General Zia said that his Government would only hold elections after he was convinced that the future elected Government would safeguard national integrity and enforce the Islamic system. 'He was of the opinion that in Pakistan sovereignty did not belong to the people nor had the country come into being for providing "*Roti, kapra our makaan*" [food, clothing and shelter — a popular P.P.P. election slogan]. Here sovereignty belongs to Allah and we are all His servants.'[31] General Zia dubbed as a 'poisonous virus' the propaganda that Pakistan had been established to fulfil the material needs of the people. Zia stressed that Pakistan would be an Islamic and ideological state.[32]

The revival of fundamentalist Islam in Pakistan by Zia ul-Haq following the coup of 1977 created suspicions among many people. Islam, which underlay Pakistan's nationhood, suffered radical distortions with its involvement in practical power politics in the aftermath of Pakistan. Islam was often used as a political rite performed to grant periodical legitimation for those who were in power or aspiring to power. It was also identified as a conservative force to suppress domestic dissent or to whip up public sentiment against India. In the process, Islam lost much of its meaning and significance for the majority of political leaders. The modernised version of Islam propagated by President Ayub was aimed at strengthening the state apparatus to perpetuate an unjust and inequitable socio-economic order in Pakistan. The five and a half years of Bhutto's rule witnessed a quixotic use of Islam. Bhutto's espousal of 'Islamic Socialism' was aimed at using Islam to pacify the religious people of Pakistan and to escape his opponents' charge that he was 'anti-Islamic'. In the fateful elections of 1977, the two major parties — the P.P.P. and the P.N.A. stressed their past and future services to Islam.

It was, therefore, not surprising that many people should have become suspicious when Zia ul-Haq announced his scheme of an Islamic Order in Pakistan. It was seen by some as a 'mammoth effort to legitimise and sell extended military rule to an increasingly sceptical public'.[33] Some interpreted it as a setback to Pakistan's political development[34] and a reassertion of the traditional role of Islam in the eccentric person of General Zia ul-Haq. The General's most compelling reason, however, was his desire to defuse the bitter political conflict generated during the Bhutto years; also to move the political debate in Pakistan on to a different plane. The policies pursued by Bhutto during his tenure had polarised Pakistan into combating groups, classes and regions. His increasingly socialist rhetoric and secularisation of politics through his brand of socialism ('*Roti, kapra our makaan*') accentuated class conflict in Pakistan.

Although this conflict was refreshing to radicals, it was alarming to landowning, business and religious interests. It was only to be expected, therefore, that the P.N.A., which drew its support largely from landlords, industrialists and small- and medium-scale merchant-traders,[35] spearheaded the massive movement against the Bhutto regime. The struggle of the P.N.A. to remove Bhutto stemmed from the suspicions that behind his political façade there lurked deep designs to introduce socialism and secularism which would strike at the very roots of Pakistan.[36] However, the P.N.A. was aware of the fact that they could not dislodge Bhutto by their movement unless the Army were to move in to overthrow his regime. The P.N.A. was not averse to such an eventuality; rather, it adopted the strategy of supplanting the P.P.P. with the military, whose attitudes and perceptions seemed more in tune with the dominant Islamic parties of the P.N.A. Thus, when the moral and political authority of Bhutto was seriously undermined by the P.N.A. movement, General Zia ul-Haq intervened, not only because the Bhutto regime had become ineffective but because there was also the general apprehension that, given a fresh mandate, Bhutto would pursue policies distasteful to the Army as an institution and to the ideology of Islam.

Measures for 'Islamisation' and national unity

For the first time in Pakistan's history, Zia ul-Haq introduced some 'fundamental and far-reaching measures' for the avowed purpose of Islamising Pakistani society. He inducted *Shariat* Benches in the Supreme Court and all High Courts to decide and determine the application of *Shariat* Laws, and prescribed punishment of crimes in accordance with these laws. Simultaneously with legal measures, Zia announced steps that would be taken towards an Islamic economy. Tax measures were introduced, and Zia himself declared that the enforcement of Islamic taxes would eliminate hunger and reduce the gap between rich and poor. He promised to abolish interest on capital in all fiscal transcations. He published a draft Ordinance proposing a compulsory 2.5 per cent levy (*Zakat*) deducted at source on all bank saving accounts, stocks and shares, life insurance policies, and so on. The same rate of tax was to apply, but on a self-assessed basis, on loans receivable by all individuals — thus excluding financial institutions, mineral producers, and industrial and commercial undertakings. A 5 per cent tax (*Ushar*) was imposed on all agricultural produce above 948 kilograms of wheat or the equivalent value. These two proposed taxes, *Zakat* and *Ushar*, were expected to yield around US$300 million annually, to be distributed by the Government according to Islamic principles.

The regime's bold attempt to utilise Islamic principles to govern the social and religious complexities of Pakistani society was hailed by its supporters in the Government as well as by the leaders of the six right-wing parties constituting the Pakistan National Alliance. The moderate political parties like Tehrik-e-Istiqlal, headed by Air Marshal Asgar Khan, thought that if the Government did not at the same time eradicate corruption and economic deprivation, the Islamism enforced would not be accepted. Some other parties like the National Democratic Party (N.D.P.) evasively remarked, 'It is the implementation of measures that has to be watched'. There is little doubt that by harping increasingly on the value of Islam as the ultimate bond of unity of the Pakistani nation, Zia ul-Haq was able to achieve a modest success. His commitment to an Islamic order gave his regime an aura of legitimacy, at least for a transitional period, which hitherto had not been possible for any military regime in Pakistan. It led the anti-Bhutto forces to support the regime. The hardcore organisation of the anti-Bhutto movement came from Islamic parties whose cohesion and strength lay in organisational units and cells like religious schools, mosques and commercial associations and federations. The sustaining force of the anti-Bhutto movement was from the commercial and landowning interests and urban merchants and shopkeepers.[37] The alignment of the military regime with these forces, and a growing convergence of interests and forces in favour of the regime, cutting across regional divisions, may be an important factor in promoting national integration in the future.

The regime, however, has yet to pacify and win over the supporters of the P.P.P. by its promise of an Islamic order. It was apparent that Bhutto, with political astuteness and by pursuing certain policies, had mobilised considerable support among the tenants, sharecroppers, industrial workers and common people. By exempting all landowners who owned up to 25 acres of irrigated land and 50 acres of non-irrigated land from payment of land revenue, he had won the support of millions of cultivators.[38] Similarly, Bhutto encouraged industrial labour groups in urban cities to keep escalating their demand for wages and bonuses regardless of labour productivity. His government had also devised a system of wage-price packages. In addition, prices of commodities like wheat were subsidised. In fact 60 per cent of the government's subsidies were devoted to keeping down prices[39] of commodities of industrial labour. Thus, Bhutto had created a vast constituency of support by his agricultural and industrial policies.[40] This explained why Zia ul-Haq, simultaneously with his Islamic measures, launched an assault on the malpractices and corruption of Bhutto and his P.P.P. in the hope of undermining their credibility and integrity.[41]

Uncertainties in the restoration of the democratic system

Although Zia ul-Haq committed the nation to an Islamic Order, he showed no genuine desire to restore democratic government in Pakistan. The repeated postponement of elections on the plea of maintaining the internal stability and territorial integrity of Pakistan indicated that he was not likely to hold elections and restore civilian rule until such time as he was reasonably confident that elections would bring a regime different from the one he had overthrown. In a speech in October 1980, he ruled out general elections as a risk to national unity and solidarity. He declared: 'As long as I am at the helm of affairs and there is with me the overwhelming force of Islam-loving people, we will not let the country go into the hands of anti-Islam and secular elements.'[42] Zia also announced his decision to expand his federal Cabinet and to create a Federal Advisory Council (*Majlis-i-Shoora*) comprising 250 to 300 members drawn from ten selected professions who, if they are not elected representatives of people, are otherwise 'true Pakistanis and Momins'.

Zia ul-Haq seemed to display aversion to politics on many occasions. At one press conference he observed: 'My own view is that the less political activity we have, the better would it be.'[43] The ban on political activity under Martial Law Order I of 1977 continues in Pakistan. Also, the military regime seems to believe in the atomisation of political forces in Pakistan. The composition of the federal Cabinet indicates[44] that Zia picked up some old-guard Muslim League leaders, representatives from the law, industry, commerce and the bureaucracy; most of these people are technically competent, but their choice seems to discount or underrate political variables. Zia ul-Haq has, furthermore, drawn many top military officers into the civil administration.

At the time of writing, however, the threat to the regime from the country's political parties appears to be much weaker. Opposition parties are by no means united. The P.N.A. is divided, not only on ideological matters but also over fundamental economic questions. The fundamentalist Islamic parties as well as the Muslim League are sympathetic to the rhetoric and values which the regime propagates and upholds. But the Pakistan People's Party which could pose a tangible threat to the regime, is highly demoralised, its prominent members having been prosecuted[45] or neutralised, and the party having lost much of its mass appeal. With its characteristic ruthless efficiency, the military has so far been able to put down any attempt to stir up major political trouble for the regime.

Despite the apparent success of the present regime in subduing its opponents and filling up political space by Islamic slogans, the question remains as to whether it could survive for long if political participation is inhibited indefinitely. Can military rule be a permanent feature in Pakistan's political system? Or will the regime be susceptible to coups and counter-coups which could lead to chaos, confusion and disorder? With the prospect of a return to democratic rule being bleak, these questions will haunt Pakistan for the foreseeable future unless the Islamic order brings solid benefits to the people and ensures their involvement in any proposed political mechanisms.

The economic and social dynamics of national unity

The economic situation and social dynamics inherited by the military regime in Pakistan were the culmination of a process that started right at the beginning of the Bhutto regime. The success of Zulfikar Ali Bhutto in the 1970 elections in Pakistan was to a great extent attributable to the economic and social programmes of his party, the P.P.P. Bhutto's brand of socialism had immense appeal to the groups and classes alienated and exploited during the Ayub regime. Massive support for his party came from east of the Indus river along the Grand Trunk road where lay the areas of industrial development and agricultural prosperity.[46]

Bhutto's 'recipe' for socialism included nationalisation of banks, insurance, heavy industry, energy sources and abolition of feudalism 'in accordance with the established principles of socialism'. As a socialist, one writer pointed out, 'it is to Bhutto's abiding credit that he launched a political party with a socialist manifesto, thereby bringing to the fore urgent economic and social issues that are directly relevant to teeming millions, and successfully detaching religion from politics.'[47] Gradually, however, it became apparent that through his strategy of promoting socialism, Bhutto was, in fact, amassing personal power. His policies led to accentuation of conflict among various groups, classes and regions — tenants *vs.* landlords, industrialists *vs.* labour, the private *vs.* the public sectors, landless labourers *vs.* the emerging capitalist farmers. The contradictions in Bhutto's economic and social policies resulted in feeble agricultural growth, industrial stagnation, rampant inflation and heavy foreign indebtedness in Pakistan. The political turmoil of 1977 further aggravated the economic situation.

Immediately on assuming office, the military regime of Zia ul-Haq had to face severe economic difficulties and social tensions — a legacy from the Bhutto regime and the political turmoil of 1977. For example, *per capita* income in Pakistan actually declined by 2 per cent during 1977. While economic growth during the five-year period 1972–7 was 4.9 per cent per annum, the commodity-producing sector — i.e. agriculture and industry — grew only at rates of 2 and 4 per cent per annum respectively, giving an average of 2.6 per cent, which was lower than the rate of population growth.[48] The external debt of Pakistan which was $3.1 billion in 1971 stood at $6.3 billion in June 1977.[49] The acute inflation due to the expenditure policies of the Bhutto regime had little regard to real resource availability. These furthermore retarded the growth of savings, distorted allocation of resources, caused serious hardships to the poorer sections of society and damaged the country's balance of payments.[50]

The foremost economic problem that Zia ul-Haq's government had to tackle immediately after it assumed office was that of Pakistan's agricultural production, a problem which necessitated a high level of food imports and which affected exports. The military regime attributed the setback to a great extent to the land reforms of 1972 and the manner of their implementation. Landholdings in excess of the ceiling were nationalised without compensation. This fact together with the threat of further reforms seriously affected investment in land and agriculture. A major disturbance in the agrarian sector of the economy was also created by the nationalisation of small agro-based industries for simple processing of agricultural produce in the rural areas or in the neighbouring towns. It led to a complete paralysis in investment activity since it was no longer possible for anyone to determine what limits the government had in mind in regard to its nationalisation programme.

Zia ul-Haq's regime in its first three years of power made major changes in government policies in the industrial sector. It argued that the thoughtless nationalisation in 1972 of the basic and key industries had disruptive effects on the economy. Hence there has been a reversal of earlier policies of extensive nationalisation, tight restrictions on the private sector and a rapid expansion of the public sector with a view to promoting industrial investment and growth. All agrarian processing units and some of the nationalised industries have been denationalised, and safeguards have been provided to private industry against further arbitrary government acquisitions. Tax holidays, excise and import duty concessions, earlier access to imported raw materials, concessionary credit and direct cash rebates have been granted to encourage private investment and exports. A basic redirection of Pakistan's industrial development strategy has taken place since 1977.

The Zia regime has also claimed that it has checked the country's high rate of inflation. The monetary expansion during the five-year period, 1972–7, was of the order of 131 per cent as against real growth of the G.N.P. by 26 per cent. Such a large disparity between the growth rate and monetary expansion led to serious inflationary pressures, which were reflected both in a sharp rise in the price level[51] and in sizeable balance of payments deficits. While Pakistan's balance of payments deficit on current account was only $100.8 million in 1972–3 it had jumped by 1976–7 to $901 million. The balance of payments gap for 1980–1 was estimated at $600 to $800 million although export earnings recorded a 40 per cent increase in 1979.

The aggregate success of the economy during the first three years of the military regime justified, to an extent, the regime's claim of an economic resurgence in the country. The Government has claimed an annual growth rate of G.D.P. at 6.4 per cent and of G.N.P. at 7.4 per cent[52] — an all-time record in Pakistan's economic history. An important contribution in this field has been made by labour migration to oil-rich Muslim countries.[53] However, it is hard to say whether the regime could maintain the upward surge of the economy without a substantial flow of aid from abroad. Net long-term official external inflows have declined sharply in the late 1970s, from about $570.0 million in 1976–7 to an estimated $300.0 million in 1979–80 in current dollars. While aid commitments to Pakistan have stagnated, the country's debt service obligations have risen. Unless the adverse trend in aid flows is reversed, payment difficulties could compel Pakistan to adopt import restrictions and inward-looking policies. Already expansion of the Government's development programmes has been limited, and in spite of its incentives, uncertainties have kept investors away from the industrial sector. The country's basic industry — textiles — remains in bad shape despite massive subsidies and various other forms of support. Although the rate of inflation has been brought down as claimed by the Government, it is hard to stabilise it, given the amount of deficit spending for increased subsidies.

Scepticism over the capability of the Zia regime to check escalating inequalities and to formulate appropriate policies for equitable distribution of resources is widespread. Few effective economic measures have hitherto been taken to alter the patterns of social and economic inequality and to reverse the trend towards mass impoverishment. The regime's emphasis is more on economic efficiency and growth than on distributive policies. In fact, after the imposition of Martial Law, thousands of tenants were forcibly evicted from lands in various districts.[54] There are frequent reports of workers being laid off in various factories.[55] To check the demand for bonuses and higher wages, there were severe retrenchments in the denationalised rice-husking, cotton-ginning and flour mills.

The stubborn persistence of regional economic disparities in Pakistan is another major problem faced by Zia ul-Haq's regime. In fact, a major share of responsibility for the exacerbation of politically volatile linguistic and cultural differences in the various regions of Pakistan can be attributed to the skewed regional distribution of resources perpetuated by successive regimes. After assuming power, Zia ul-Haq gave an assurance that he would give priority to the development of the backward regions of Pakistan, and the Fifth Five-Year Plan launched by the regime maintained that 'infrastructural links with the developed centres will be provided to promote inter-regional flows and national integration.'[56] However, effective and co-ordinated development of disaffected areas has yet to be undertaken. No separate allocations of federal development funds for the provinces are made in the Plan. Instead, it envisaged that the bulk of expenditure for the provinces would be in the form of projects to be accommodated in federal programmes.

However, the regime has taken some positive measures to pacify the grievances of economically underdeveloped regions in Pakistan. The

Government's decisions to start work on the long-delayed Chasmai irrigation system in the N.W.F.P. and to allocate Rs. 172 million for the completion of the works of the University of Baluchistan and Bolan Medical College indicate concern to help correct regional imbalances. However, it is difficult, as Zia remarked[57] in reference to the increasing trend of federal allocation of development expenditure to Baluchistan, to 'make up for the lapses of thirty years in one day'.

External fears and national unity

Pakistan's internal difficulties are heightened by external fears, particularly of neighbouring countries, and have raised to prominence a concern in the priorities of its foreign policy. Throughout the 1960s, Pakistan's major fear and principal preoccupation was the threat of India to its national integrity. The year 1971 was a great watershed for the state structure of the sub-continent in many ways. With the emergence of Bangladesh as an independent state, Pakistan's obsession with India was reduced; she looked increasingly towards the West[58] in search of friends, but also found an adversary in Afghanistan: from 1973, Afghanistan replaced India more and more as the major perceived threat to Pakistan's national integrity, as the main focus of dissent in Pakistan shifted from the former East Pakistan to Baluchistan and the N.W.F.P.

Although, from the Pakistani viewpoint, the Afghan threat was regarded as more manageable than that from India, the situation changed dramatically with the emergence of a Marxist government in Kabul. The Soviet invasion of Afghanistan further intensified the security concerns of Pakistan because Afghanistan is strategically well placed to assist secessionist and pro-Soviet Left-wing forces within Pakistan. Pakistan has a border with Afghanistan that is 1,000 miles long. The Durand Line which 'formalised' the long border was never accorded recognition by Afghanistan's rulers, and support for secessionist forces within Baluchistan and the N.W.F.P. has always been a traditional policy of Afghan governments. While the degree and scope of support has varied, commitment to the cause of the Pashtuns and Baluchis has never wavered. When Mohammad Daud came to power in 1973, he emphasised his country's support for Pashtun and Baluchi secessionists in Pakistan. In the next three years, Pakistan blamed Afghanistan for many violent disturbances and accused her of training as many as 15,000 Pashtun and Baluchi guerrillas to start a 'people's war' against Pakistan.[59] However, Daud agreed in 1976 to respect Pakistan's territorial integrity and to seek a peaceful resolution of their difficulties.[60] Some argued that Daud's reconciliation with Pakistan in 1976 contributed to his loss of support from pro-Soviet Left-wingers.[61]

After the Percham-Khalq coalition's ascent to power with Nur Mohammad Taraki (who came from a Pashtun tribe) as President, the probability of Afghan-Soviet support for secessionist elements in Baluchistan and N.W.F.P. increased, and Babrak Karmal, in his first speech as President of Afghanistan, vowed to respect the 'legitimate aspirations' of the Baluch and Pashtuns.

Pakistan therefore fears that Afghanistan, aided by the Soviet Union, will supply arms and financial assistance to Pakistan's troubled provinces of Baluchistan and the N.W.F.P. Although at the time of writing Afghanistan continues to face serious internal difficulties, in the long run the Afghans supported by the Soviets could, by large-scale intervention in Pakistan, help to create an independent state in the N.W.F.P. and Baluchistan.

Yet another serious perceived threat to Pakistan's territorial integrity comes from India: Pakistan fears that India might also join Afghan-Soviet ventures to dismember her territory; Pakistan's suspicions about India's motives can be explained by several factors. First, for historical and psychological reasons, India has still not reconciled herself to Pakistan's existence as a sovereign state; in India's strategic thinking, Pakistan is a potential adversary. Secondly, Pakistan's capacity to continue a confrontationist policy towards India continues to occupy the mind of India's policy-makers. Thirdly, India is often regarded as the lynch-pin of Soviet policy in South Asia. In the aftermath of the Soviet invasion of Afghanistan, India, which was initially in favour of the withdrawal of 'foreign forces' from Afghanistan, has now yielded to Soviet pressures and confined itself to issuing occasional statements. Therefore, the further disintegration of Pakistan and the creation of several small states on India's western front could lead to a complete Indo-Soviet hegemony over the sub-continent.

Despite these calculations, it is doubtful whether India would seek to promote the disintegration of Pakistan because India's own tenuous national integrity could be threatened. The dismemberment of Pakistan will have adverse effects on India's precarious federal structure. The awareness of a separate identity on the part of different regional-linguistic groups in the Indian Union is already becoming dangerously manifest.[62] India, will, therefore, prefer to maintain the *status quo* in the sub-continent in terms of its own interests; moreover, by attempting to dismember Pakistan, she also risks endangering her present good relations with Muslim states, particularly Saudi Arabia, Iraq, Iran and the Gulf states which supply most of India's oil requirements and employ a large number of Indian nationals. In addition, India would incur the displeasure of the United States, and the 'normalisation' of relations with China would be seriously jeopardized.

Pakistan for her part seeks to secure herself with assistance from the People's Republic of China and the United States. China, which has had very good relations with Pakistan over the last two decades, is concerned with Pakistan's security and would in all probability not tolerate any further extension of Soviet influence along the Sino-Pakistan border. China has already condemned the Soviet invasion of Afghanistan in the strongest terms, and there is evidence that she is aware of Moscow's efforts to change the situation in Baluchistan.

Pakistan's unity is clearly in the interests of the United States. From 1954 till the mid-1960s, Pakistan was regarded as the 'most allied ally' of the United States in Asia. However, the Indo-Pakistan war of 1965 made Pakistan realise that she could not depend on her American ally. In 1971, the U.S.-Pakistan relationship seemed to revive but this was more a U.S. effort. During the Bhutto regime, the United States did not want to be too involved in Pakistan's internal problems because of Bhutto's critical attitude towards her policies.[63] At the same time, American leaders were conscious of their country's long-standing ties with Pakistan, and did not want to see her disintegration. There has been concern too for the 'security, territorial integrity and independence' of Pakistan.[64]

The United States therefore continues to figure prominently in Pakistan's foreign policy, especially because the United States could provide security as well as economic assistance. There were some disagreements between the two countries during the Carter Administration: the United States imposed a *de facto* embargo on the supply of heavy weapons to Pakistan because of her insistence on acquiring a nuclear reprocessing plant from France. The controversy ended with France deciding not to export the plutonium separating facility.[65]

The Zia regime in Pakistan is more favourably disposed towards the United States than Bhutto. In the aftermath of the Soviet invasion of Afghanistan, the Carter Administration showed greater concern for Pakistan's security. Pakistan wished that the United States should carefully examine the entire context of the country's security needs and recognise the threats from its neighbours, and for this reason she sought substantial aid from the United States. But the 'aid package'[66] offered was eventually turned down as 'peanuts'. Although Washington showed a willingness to take appropriate measures against possible Soviet-sponsored intrusion into Pakistan, the United States is obliged to take note of possible hostile reactions from India. The U.S.-Pakistan relationship is therefore in uneasy balance, but fear of the Soviet Union leaves Pakistan with no alternative but to maintain her ties with Washington and Peking.

Conclusion

The future of Pakistan is in doubt. Threats to the unity of the nation arise from the social structure and from the external environment. Post-1971 Pakistan has witnessed a resurgence of regional and ethnic identities. Latent or arrested secessionist sentiments among the Baluchis and Pashtuns have surfaced sharply. Although many Third World countries must fashion viable nation-states from diversified ethno-linguistic social structures, Pakistan's situation is especially unusual and in many ways unique. It is unusual because Pakistan's tribal minorities constitute only 17 per cent of the population but have occupied 57 per cent of its land area. It is unique in that successive regimes, instead of accommodating ethnic and regional forces with policy and political concessions, have exacerbated these through neglect and the 'back-wash effects' of development.

The need for striking a balance between central and regional aspirations is imperative at the crucial point which Pakistan's history has now reached. While the present regime of Zia Ul-Haq realises the importance of a dialogue with the leaders of the aggrieved regions, it has yet to respond imaginatively and substantively to their demands for autonomy and redress of economic grievances. Islamic ideology, particularly at this juncture, may provide an over-arching force for unity, but this cannot be at the expense of neglecting the aspirations of the aggrieved provinces. Pakistan's leadership must realise that they inherited a federal society and that Islamic unity could be congruent with federal diversity. Unless the ruling élites in Pakistan come to grips with this fact, they will not be able to check the drift towards the 'Balkanisation' of their country.

The other most serious task is the need to alter the country's patterns of social inequality built up over several years. The nurturing of politico-commercial classes and landed groups by successive regimes have led to an enormous concentration of economic resources in an oligarchy. The resultant misery has not been alleviated. Neither Ayub's 'decade of development' nor Bhutto's era of so-called socialism reversed the trend towards mass impoverishment. In fact inequality has increased and state policies to reverse the pattern have yet to be effectively implemented. The plight of urban wage-earners, whose numbers have stagnated in recent years, has worsened with inflation. The rural pattern is similar. The fall in real value of commercialised crops has brought about a growing decline in peasant wellbeing. Although prices of major commercial crops are subsidised and fixed by the state, the villagers and peasants are at the mercy of middlemen.

During the last three years, Pakistan's economy experienced a modest growth. However, inflation continues to be out of control and is fuelled by huge government deficits. The most immediate economic pressures arise from the debt issue. A short-term solution of Pakistan's debt problem is not possible. Far-reaching measures are needed to improve production and productive capacity in agriculture and industry.

The social and economic challenges facing Pakistan have an enormous political dimension. When Zia ul-Haq took power, he passionately felt that secularism and corrupting materialism should be resisted and Islamic values restored to ensure national unity. Nevertheless his Islamic Order faces problems. He must produce an economic and political record that can offer indisputable evidence of progress. However, it is also true that no regime, of whatever ideological pre-dispositions, has been able to alter the country's debt-ridden inflation-torn and stagnated economy in the short run.

The authoritarian nature of government and concentration of power have left the state prone to policy miscalculations. The country's political structures are at odds. Technocrats and civil-military bureaucrats are increasingly entrusted with positions of trust and authority in planning and policies relating to social transformation. Although the regime at present faces no major threat from opposition parties, which are riven by personal, ethnic and ideological divisions, a broad support base for the military regime of Zia ul-Haq is yet to be consolidated. Although the support of fundamentalist Islamic parties is the most valuable asset that the regime enjoys outside the military, there is the possibility that it may face increasing opposition from secular and democratic forces in the foreseeable future. Only improved economic performance, alleviation of the deepening social crisis through fundamental Islamic reforms and the creation of some kind of participatory structures for channelling political grievances can halt the descent to disintegration and economic collapse.

The major threat to the regime is from internal violence along regional-ethnic identities triggered by outside powers. Pakistan's complex regional impasse is made more intractable by its internationalisation. Pakistan fears that the Soviet occupation of Afghanistan may encourage the Baluchis and Pashtuns. Indeed the Baluchis, who have long yearned for autonomy, might welcome a Soviet-inspired Afghan invading force that would promise to honour the 'legitimate aspirations' of the Baluch and Pashtun peoples, as the Afghan President Babrak Karmal vowed to do. It is the fear of Soviet-backed Afghan support for separatism in Pakistan that has heightened Pakistan's concerns and uneasiness about developments in Afghanistan. Pakistan is groping desperately to find a viable alternative which will ensure unity and integrity. But the choices are so limited and the difficulties so immense that to succeed in the struggle to preserve unity and to emerge from its economic morass will require exceptional dedication and consummate skill on the part of Pakistani leadership.

NOTES

1. Mohammad Ayoob, 'India and Pakistan: Prospects for Detente', *Pacific Community*, 8 (1), October 1976, 149–69.
2. Robert La Porte, Jr., 'Pakistan in 1972: Picking Up the Pieces', *Asian Survey*, 13 (1973), 195.
3. Khalid B. Sayeed, *The Political System of Pakistan* (Lahore: Oxford University Press, 1966), 67.
4. Sayeed, op. cit., 66.
5. *National Assembly Debates of Pakistan* (Karachi: Manager of Publications, 1962), I, 5, 166–8.
6. Elliot Tepper, 'The New Pakistan: Problems and Prospects,' *Pacific Affairs* 47 (Spring 1974), 57.
7. Selig Harrison, 'The Nightmare in Baluchistan', *Foreign Policy* (Autumn 1979), 138.
8. Ibid, 143.
9. Ibid, 145.
10. *Government of Pakistan, Pakistan Economic Survey, 1979–80* (The Manager: Printing Corporation of Pakistan Press, Islamabad), indicates lowest expenditures for Baluchistan. The Government says that the population density of Baluchistan is the lowest, i.e. only seven per square mile in an area of 134,054 square miles.
11. Referring to the treason charges levelled by the Bhutto regime against the Baluch and Pathan leaders, Zia pointed out: 'The intelligence reports that are received by me in my capacity as Chief of Army Staff, made me realise that the case was politically motivated to a large extent.' Gen. Mohammad Zia-ul-Haq, Chief of Army Staff and Martial Law Administrator, Press Conference, Rawalpindi, 1 January 1978 (Islamabad: Ministry of Informations and Broadcasting, 1978), 21.
12. Ibid, 22.
13. The present government allocated Rs. 709 million to the industrial sector, Rs. 764 million for mineral development, Rs. 1,847 million for transport and Rs. 551 million for cement plants, equipment and manufacturing plant under the Fifth Five-Year Plan; Planning Commission, Govt. of Pakistan, *The Fifth Five-Year Plan 1978–83* (June 1978).
14. *The Pakistan Times*, 25 October 1980.
15. Harrison, ibid., 151.
16. Mohyuddin Baluch is the son of the late Mir Ahmed Yar Khan of Kalat, Governor of Baluchistan from January 1974 till July 1977. He has a diploma in Business Administration from London, and was political Secretary to the Governor of Baluchistan.
17. *Dawn*, 27, October 1980.

18. Harrison, ibid., 148.
19. *Year book of International Communist Affairs* (Stanford, California: Hoover Institution Press, 1977), 359.
20. Harrison, ibid, 150.
21. Salamat Ali, 'Baluchistan: an Upheaval is Forecast', *Far Eastern Economic Review*, 19 October 1979, p. 41.
22. Mohammed Ayoob, 'Pakhtunistan: a Ghost Resurrected,' *Economic and Political Weekly* (Bombay), 8, 38 (29 September 1973), 1757–9.
23. Salamat Ali, ibid, 42.
24. Sayeed, op. cit., 186.
25. Yu. V. Gankovsky, *The Peoples of Pakistan* (Moscow: Nauka Publishing House, 1971), 217.
26. Khalid B. Sayeed, 'How Radical is the Pakistan People's Party?', *Pacific Affairs* (Spring 1975), 57.
27. Bhutto made serious propaganda against Wali Khan and his father Khan Abdul Gaffar Khan, the 'famed Frontier Gandhi', and accused them of being in league with either India or Afghanistan and sometimes with both.
28. The present federal cabinet is composed of ten members including the President. Sharifuddin Pirjada and Mahmoud A. Haroon are two old Muslim Leaguers. Pirjada was General Secretary of the Muslim League (N.W.F.P.) in 1945 and served in two cabinets in the former West Pakistan. Haroon was a member of the All-India Muslim League Council from 1942 and later of the All-Pakistan Muslim League.
29. Harrison, op.cit., 152.
30. Ibid., p. 153.
31. Nisar Osmani, 'Polls only when Enforcement of Islamic System Assured', *Dawn*, 24 September 1979, 1.
32. President General Mohammad Zia ul-Haq, 'The President on Pakistan's Ideological Basis', address at the inauguration of the Shariat Faculty of the Quaid-i-Azam University, Islamabad, 8 October 1979, Ministry of Informations and Broadcasting, Government of Pakistan.
33. Mohammad Ayub, 'Two Faces of Political Islam: Iran and Pakistan Compared', *Asian Survey*, 19 (June 1979), 539.
34. Ayoob, 'Pakistan Comes Full Circle', *India Quarterly*, 34, I (1979), 18.
35. Pakistan Study Group, Analysis of P.N.A. Class Structure and Movement (photocopy).
36. Khalid B. Sayeed, 'Mass Urban Protests as Indicators of Political Change in Pakistan,' *Journal of Commonwealth and Comparative Politics*, 27 (July 1979), 126.
37. Ibid., 129.
38. Pakistan Census of Agriculture 1972 (Lahore: Ministry of Food and Agriculture, 1975), 1.
39. Sayeed, 'Mass Urban Protests', 127.
40. The Zia ul-Haq Government complains that increased salaries were paid to industrial workers with more and more paper money, and their raised expectations were temporarily satisfied. The benefits like social security and participation in profits were extended to industrial labour during the Bhutto regime.

41. The Martial Law regime had instituted six cases against Mr. Bhutto and his more prominent party members. These related to election-rigging, evasion of taxes, misuse of government funds, violation of foreign exchange regulations etc. The unpopularity of the P.P.P. because of bribery and corruption was admitted by the Prime Minister's special Secretary. See *White Paper on the Conduct of the General Elections in March, 1977* (Rawalpindi: Government of Pakistan, July 1978), Annex 63, A 203–4.
42. *Dawn*, 26 October 1980, 12.
43. General Mohammad Zia-ul-Haq, press conference, op.cit., 25.
44. In 1981 the Federal Cabinet consisted of political figures like Mohammad Ali Khan of Hoti, Mahmoud A. Haroon, Mohyuddin Baluch; civil servants like Ghulam Ishaq Khan and Aga Shahi; and military officers like, Lt.-Gen. Ghulam Hasan Khan and Rear Admiral Mohammad Fazil Janjua.
45. The Martial Law authority under Martial Law Order No. 31 prosecuted a large number of members of the P.P.P. About 104 politicians were cleared; some are still under prosecution and are being summoned by the Martial Law authority.
46. Sayeed, 'How Radical is the Pakistan People's Party?', 55.
47. Khurshid Hyder, 'Pakistan Under Bhutto', *Current History*, 63 (November 1972), 202.
48. *Pakistan Economic Survey*; Also reported in *Pakistan Affairs*, 16 September 1977.
49. *Economic Resurgence in Pakistan* (Islamabad: Pakistan Publications), 7.
50. Ibid., 16.
51. Pakistan's index of wholesale prices has recorded increases of 4.7 per cent in 1971–2, 15.8 per cent in 1972–3, 32.8 per cent in 1973–74, 23.7 per cent in 1974–5, 8.6 per cent in 1975–6, 11.3 per cent in 1976–77, 5.2 per cent in 1977–8 and 10 per cent in 1979–80. *Economic Resurgence*, op.cit., 19.
52. *Pakistan Economic Survey*, op.cit.
53. The main support for Pakistan's balance of payments has been provided by substantial remittances of Pakistani workers in the oil-rich Middle Eastern Countries. These remittances are now running at around $1,700 million per annum; *Economic Resurgence*, 7.
54. From the office of the Land Commissioner, Sahiwal, Forcibly Ejected Tenants in Sahiwal District up to 30 November 1977.
55. This is being reported particularly after the denationalisation of medium and small-scale agro-processing units in major cities.
56. Pakistan Planning Commission, *The Fifth Year Plan* (1978–83) (Karachi: Manager of Publications), June 1978.
57. General Mohammad Zia ul-Haq, op.cit., p. 29.
58. Zulfikar Ali Bhutto, 'Pakistan Builds Anew', *Foreign Afairs*, 51 (April 1973), 545.
59. *Pakistan Times*, 25 August 1975.
60. Ibid., 24 August 1976.
61. Hannah Negaran, 'The Afghan Coup of April 1978: Revolution and International Security', *Orbis*, (Spring 1979).

62. In the North-Eastern region of India, it appears that the Assamese have developed a militant nationalism the strident gyrations of which are sending reverberations through the national politics in India.
63. Norman D. Palmer, 'The United States and South Asia', *Current History*, 76 (April 1979), 148.
64. The Kissinger visit of August 1976 was an occasion for the renewal of American concern. See *Pakistan Times*, 9 August 1976.
65. The effective withdrawal of France's agreement to supply Pakistan with a nuclear processing plant led to stronger criticisms of the United States by Pakistan. See Palmer, ibid, p. 149.
66. The 'aid package' was worth $400 million over a period of two years to bolster Pakistan's defence. *Time*, 28 January 1980, 27.

PLURALISM, REGIONALISM, AND DECENTRALIZING TENDENCIES IN CONTEMPORARY INDIAN POLITICS*

Paul R. Brass

Opinions on the nature of the balance between the center and the states in India's federal system have varied considerably over time since Independence. They have also varied at particular points in time depending upon the institutions and processes the observer is examining. Moreover, there have also been problems in how to interpret types of evidence in terms of whether or not they reflect tendencies towards centralization, decentralization, or disintegration. Unfortunately, though the subject is one that attracts persistent interest, political scientists have not responded substantially to Marcus Franda's call a decade ago to begin to collect data on center-state relations in India and to examine the decision-making processes of such critical institutions in those relations as the Planning Commission and the Finance Commissions.[1] Consequently, differing opinions on the nature of center-state relations remain opinions, based on limited evidence or on an examination only of particular institutions or processes in the Indian federal system. Still lacking is an overall view of the Indian federal system that encompasses all relevant aspects, institutions, and processes and that is grounded solidly in evidence. It goes without saying that it is hardly possible to arrive at definitive conclusions about the general direction of center-state relations in India until such an overall view is constructed.

Consider, for example, the difference between Morris-Jones' description of center-state relations in India in 1964 as a form of co-operative federalism that he characterized as 'bargaining federalism'[2] and a description published in 1977 by Haqqi and Sharma that characterizes center-state relations in India as a system of 'centralized federalism'.[3] The term 'bargaining federalism', Morris-Jones argued, described 'the character of Indian federalism throughout'. It referred to a pattern of center-state relations in which 'neither centre nor states can impose decisions on the other' and in which 'hard competitive bargaining' takes place in such institutions as the Planning Commission, the Finance Commission, and the Zonal Councils.[4] In these institutions, bargaining occurs between the center and the states and among the several states for the allocation of resources and patronage and for the solution of such divisive problems as the rights of linguistic minorities in the linguistically reorganized states. In contrast to this description, Haqqi and Sharma argue that, with the exception of the brief period between 1967 and 1971 when different parties ruled at the center and in many of the Indian states, the Indian 'constitutional form' has been 'centralized federalism'. Moreover, they argue that the long-term tendency has been towards increasing centralization of power, manifested particularly in concentration of authority at the center as power has shifted upward in the Congress party organization and in concentration of authority in the executive as power has moved laterally at the center from the Congress party organization to the central government. Although Haqqi and Sharma argue that the Indian federal system has always been highly centralized, they are arguing also that it is becoming even more so.

Looked at from the point of view of the states, the issue is usually phrased as one of the relative autonomy of the states in relation to the center. In 1968, Weiner argued that state autonomy was considerable and that it was safe from central encroachment. He remarked that 'it is most unlikely that the center will be able to take power away from the states. Indeed the trend has been just the reverse: the states have tended to become politically more autonomous and to accept central advice reluctantly.'[5] Eleven years later, Dua, in an article on 'Presidential Rule in India', commented that the 'increasing use' of President's Rule over the past twenty-five years had reduced the autonomy of the states 'to a farce'.[6] Unlike Haqqi and Sharma, however, who take the view that the system always has been centralized, Dua argues that the change in center-state relations has been accompanied by a change in the character of Indian democracy as well that amounts to 'a fundamental transformation of the system' such that it is 'useless' to 'search for continuity in political styles and traditions' between thc pre-and post-1969 periods.[7]

Differences concerning the nature of the Indian federal system often arise out of differences in the institutions examined. Scholars who look primarily at the Planning Commission and the Finance Commission or at the use of President's Rule (P.R.) have tended to argue that state autonomy has declined and central control over the states has increased. Those who look at the Congress organization have been more divided, some seeing a highly centralized organization, some seeing a highly decentralized one, others seeing changes from time to time in the structure and decision-making processes of the Congress from centralization to decentralization. Those who look at state party systems or at language policy tend to see regionalism and state autonomy predominant in center-state relations.

It is, of course, hardly surprising, in a federal system of India's size and diversity, that there should be contrary tendencies over time and among different institutions and policy areas. Problems of interpretation, however, become more serious when observers look at the same institution at the same point in time and reach different conclusions or feel incapable of deciding what are the implications of the evidence. For example, Venkatarangaiya and Shiviah argue that 'the Congress as a party has been a highly centralized organization' in which 'state units have had little freedom to take decisions on their own.'[8] Bombwall, in contrast, argues that the centralization of the Congress was a temporary and fortuitous phenomenon, a mere 'legacy from pre-independence days' and that the Congress High Command after Independence rapidly became 'a shaky colossus whose writ ran in state capitals in inverse ratio to the cohesion and stability of the state party units, the degree of rapport between the organizational and governmental wings of the party and the strength of the state-level leadership.'[9]

Since, as I have already suggested, most of the evidence is lacking that is required to come to an overall assessment of the character of the Indian federal system, it will not be possible in this brief paper to do more than offer another opinion based on fragmentary evidence about the long-term tendencies in center-state relations and about the dynamic character of the system. I do attempt, however, to present a coherent point of view concerning the overall character of the system and to offer some new evidence as well as suggest ways of reinterpreting the existing evidence in support of that point of view. The general argument of the paper is as follows. Insofar as long-term tendencies or underlying persistent patterns can be discerned across institutions and policy areas in India, the directions or the underlying patterns are towards pluralism, regionalism, and decentralization.[10] These tendencies run counter to the efforts of particular groups, such as the Hindi speech community, to impose their will over other groups; to the attempts by Mrs Gandhi to nationalize the electoral process; and to the persistent efforts of Mrs Gandhi to centralize political power and decision-making. The tendencies towards pluralism are, however, clearer than those towards regionalism and decentralization, which are qualified by a high degree of interdependence of the center on the states and the states on the center. Moreover, there is also a fundamental tension in the system which arises because the constitutional structure has many strong unitary features and because there are historical tendencies in India, shared by several leaders and parties, toward aggregation and consolidation of power. In recent years, the aggregative and consolidating tendencies have been set in motion most clearly by Mrs Gandhi. However, it is my contention that the process of consolidating power in India is inherently tenuous and that power begins to disintegrate immediately at the maximal point of concentration. At that point, regional political forces and decentralizing tendencies inevitably reassert themselves unless the national leadership chooses to attempt a more definitive consolidation by bringing into play the full range of unitary powers provided in the Constitution of India. However, it is also my contention that such an effort is doomed to failure in the long run[11] and that pluralist, regionalist, and decentralizing tendencies inevitably will reassert themselves against any centralizing, authoritarian regime. Evidence in support of the general argument will be provided below with respect to language policy, transfer of resources from the center to the states, patterns and trends in party support and inter-party relations, and the use of President's Rule.[12]

Pluralism and Indian language policy

For the first two decades after Independence, the most salient, divisive, and persistent set of issues centered around the various language problems of India, including especially the controversies over the linguistic reorganization of states, over the official language of India, and over the status of Urdu and other minority languages within the several states. In the minds of many observers and participants, these issues seemed to threaten the very basis of Indian unity and even to pose the prospect of a 'balkanization' or disintegration of India into a number of separate linguistic nations. For some time, the bench-mark study that presented the issue of the unity of India and the possibility of its disintegration most starkly was Selig Harrison's *India: the Most Dangerous Decades*.[13] Harrison saw the threats to Indian unity arising both from conflicts between the central government and regions asserting their separate cultural identities and from interregional conflicts, particularly between the Hindi-speaking region of north India and the non-Hindi-speaking regions of the country. He argued that, although Hindi-speakers constituted a large enough group in relation to all others 'to assert a dominant position', they were 'not quite large enough to achieve it.'[14] His prediction proved accurate as the Hindi movement failed in the 1960s to impose Hindi upon the rest of the country as the sole official language of India. During the past decade, moreover, several studies of various aspects of India's language problems have been published that have arrived at a consensus that the major linguistic issues have been resolved in a manner that preserves the cultural integrity of the major linguistic groups in India and the unity of India, though leaving still unresolved several matters pertaining to the rights of linguistic minorities and the status of migrants in the linguistically reorganized states.[15]

That the resolution of the major linguistic conflicts has been a pluralistic one can hardly be doubted. It is reflected both in official policy and its implementation and in the actual use of the major languages of India for various functional purposes. Insofar as the official language issue is concerned, the government of India has settled upon what amounts to an indefinite policy of bilingualism, with English and Hindi being alternative official languages at the center and alternative link languages for communication between the center and the states. Although the ideal of transforming Hindi into the sole official language of the country exists in the Official Language Act, 1963 and in the hearts of many Hindi-speakers and although plans have been partly implemented for increasing the use of Hindi by the central government, it has been made clear time and time again that the use of Hindi will not be imposed on non-Hindi speakers for official purposes in India. Moreover, progress in implementing the increased use of Hindi by central government departments has been slow. Rules for implementing the Official Language Act were not even framed until 1976 and the state of Tamil Nadu has been excluded from their purview.[16] In fact, one recent observer has argued that English continues to be dominant in practice as the official language of the Government of India, as the link language of the country, and as the medium of higher education.[17] The continued pre-eminence of English is a mark of India's pluralism, for it distributes the burdens of learning the principal language of official communication at the central and intergovernmental levels equally between Hindi-speakers and non-Hindi-speakers.

Insofar as bilingualism has been modified in practice in relation to the non-Hindi-speaking states, it has been modified in the direction of even greater pluralism. For example, all languages listed in the Eighth Schedule of the Constitution of India are acceptable media of examination for entry into the Indian Administration Service for the Essay and General Knowledge papers. In fact, however, English continues to be the overwhelmingly preferred language of applicants for both papers. In 1974, the latest year for which figures are available, 82 per cent of the essay examinations and 91 per cent of the general knowledge papers were written in English. The figures for Hindi were 14 per cent and 6 per cent for the two papers, respectively, and for all other Indian languages were 4 and 2 per cent, respectively, for the two examinations. On this most politically sensitive aspect of official language policy, therefore, it is clear that the policy of the government is a multilingual pluralism in which English remains dominant. English is even more dominant in the results of the examinations, for less than 5 per cent of the successful candidates choose a medium other than English.[18]

At the state level, in the linguistically reorganized states, the regional languages are becoming increasingly dominant as the official administrative languages, as the media of education in the schools, and as the languages of communication in the printed media. Even in the linguistically reorganized states, however, there remain significant pluralistic aspects of language policy and usage. English continues to be an important medium of higher education and of élite communication in the printed media, especially in the major metropolitan cities of the country. Various constitutional and other safeguards are supposed to be implemented in the states for the use of minority languages as media of education in the primary schools, for some official purposes, and for recruitment to the state services. However, the development of policies and procedures for the implementation of these safeguards is a recurring issue in center-state relations.

In fact, the major linguistic and ethnic problems of India today concern the status of minority languages, religions, and ethnic groups within the linguistically reorganized states. The status of Urdu continues to be a controversial issue in several of the Hindi-speaking states. Problems persist in implementing the established safeguards for other linguistic minorities in the states as well. Conflict between migrant and non-migrant populations has emerged as an increasingly important problem in some states, notably Assam.

In relation to the internal linguistic and ethnic conflicts of the states, the central government has usually played the role of protector of the rights of the minority populations. In fact, as I have argued elsewhere, the central government has consistently pursued policies of pluralism in relation to the rights of linguistic and religious minorities in India in the face of the assimilationist and discriminatory policies of several states in relation to their minorities.[19] Although the role of the central government is indispensable to the preservation of minority rights in India, one has only to read the annual reports of the Commissioner of Linguistic Minorities to appreciate how much the implementation even of agreed safeguards depends upon the voluntary co-operation of the state governments. The central government has never been able to impose upon recalcitrant states specific procedures and mechanisms to ensure that minorities receive instruction in schools through the medium of their mother tongue or that they are not barred from entry into state employment because of lack of proficiency in the regional language.[20]

Finally, India's pluralism in relation to language policy is evident also in the failure of Hindi to gain ground as the principal link language of the country. Hindi has been virtually excluded as a language of education in Tamil Nadu and is hardly used as a medium of printed communication anywhere outside the Hindi-speaking states. In fact, in the country as a whole, English newspapers continue to keep ahead of or close to Hindi in number and in circulation. The bulk of the

Table 1
CONCENTRATION OF NEWSPAPERS BY LANGUAGE
(*x 1,000*)

	1976		*1970*		*1960*	
Language	*No.*	*%*	*No.*	*%*	*No.*	*%*
English	2,765	20.76	2,247	20.36	1,647	20.52
Hindi	3,289	24.69	2,694	24.41	1,532	19.09
Urdu	975	7.32	898	8.14	680	8.47
Regional languages	4,755	35.70	3,974	36.01	2,718	33.86
Others	1,536	11.53	1,223	11.08	1,449	18.05
Total	13,320	100.00	11,036	100.00	8,026	99.99

Source: Compiled from Government of India, Ministry of Information and Broadcasting, *Press in India, 1977*, I (Delhi: Controller of Publications, 1978), 30–1; *Press in India, 1971*, I (Delhi: Manager of Publications, 1971), 19; *Annual Report of the Registrar of Newspapers for India, 1961*, I (Delhi: Manager of Publications, 1961), 19.

Table 2
CIRCULATION OF NEWSPAPERS BY LANGUAGE
(*x 1,000*)

	1976		*1970*		*1960*	
Language	*No.*	*%*	*No.*	*%*	*No.*	*%*
English	7,828	22.97	7,173	24.48	4,147	22.76
Hindi	7,738	22.71	5,852	19.97	3,583	19.67
Urdu	1,493	4.38	1,455	4.97	1,055	5.79
Regional languages	15,693	46.05	13,639	46.54	8,297	45.54
Others	1,323	3.88	1,184	4.04	1,137	6.24
Total	34,075	99.99	29,303	100.00	18,219	100.00

Source: As for table 1: *Press in India, 1977*, I, 34–5; *Press in India, 1971*, I, 44; *Annual Report of the Registrar of Newspapers for India, 1961*, I, 43

literate newspaper-reading public, however, reads newspapers in the predominant regional language of their province (tables 1 and 2).

From the point of view of Indian language policy and usage, therefore, there are several evident pluralistic features. The official language problem has been resolved in a partly bilingual, partly multilingual manner. English, rather than Hindi, continues to be the principal link language of the country. The regional languages are dominant in each of the states. Pluralism is qualified in practice at the state level by the discriminatory policies of some state governments towards their linguistic minorities. Effective protection of the rights of linguistic minorities by the central government cannot be implemented without the co-operation of the state governments. Here, cultural pluralism is countered by the relative autonomy of the states in practice in relation to the central government in educational and language policy and in recruitment to state services.

The increasing role of the states in employment and expenditure

In 1956, V. O. Key, in his book on *American State Politics*, dissented from the popular view that the American states had declined in political importance as a consequence of the increased role of the federal government under the New Deal. He argued to the contrary that 'state governments were expanding their staffs, enlarging the scope of their activities, [and] spending more and more money.'[21] It was not, however, their own money they were spending, but moneys raised by the federal government and then distributed to the states through federal grants. Insofar as the states raised money through taxes, they did not spend it, but distributed their tax proceeds to local governments. Thus, the states had been converted 'into governments that spend money they do not raise and raise money they do not spend.'[22] Yet, in this curious manner, the states had become more pivotal in the American political system in the previous two decades.

If we apply V. O. Key's standards to the position of the states in the Indian federal system, we would have to conclude that the importance of the states has increased vastly since Independence for their administrative staffs have expanded enormously, the scope of their activities also has enlarged dramatically, and they have been spending 'more and more money'. Not only have they been spending more, but they have been spending both 'money that they do not raise' and money that they do raise. Moreover, the control of the central government over state expenditures has decreased.

Consider first the size of the administrative staffs of the state governments in comparison with other units of government and the private sector in India. At the end of 1977, the state governments employed 5.2 million persons compared to 3.1 million employed by the central government, 2.0 million by local government, and 6.2 million in large-scale industry. State and local employment constituted 50 per cent of the total public employment in India. Moreover, state government employment was the largest growth sector among these employing agencies between 1961 and 1977. In that period, the number of state government employees increased by 71 per cent, local bodies employees by 61 per cent, central government employees by 42 per cent, and large scale industry workers by 23 per cent.[23]

There has also been an enormous increase in the development expenditures of the state governments, which grew from Rs. 1,702 to Rs. 9,155 crores between 1967–8 to 1977–8, i.e. by 450 per cent. The tax and non-tax revenues of the states also increased considerably between 1967–8 and 1977–8 by over 4 times in the case of tax revenue (from Rs 1,065 to 4,384 crores) and by nearly 5 times in the case of non-tax revenue (from Rs 399 to 1,969 crores). Although between 40 to 50 per cent of state revenues come from transfers of revenue from the central government, the states collect between 50 to 60 per cent of their revenues themselves.[24]

Nevertheless, it is a fact that the increase in state revenues has not kept pace with the increases in state expenditures and that the deficit has had to be made up by resource transfers from the central government to the states.[25] The constantly increasing needs of the states for resource transfers from the center has contributed in recent years to the developing controversy over the present status of center-state relations. Critics of the state governments argue that the states have been financially irresponsible, that they have used too many of their resources for nonproductive purposes, and that they have failed to mobilize enough resources of their own, particularly from the agricultural sector. Consequently, it is argued, revenues raised by the center that could be used by the central government to create new productive assets for the nation are being squandered in filling budgetary deficits created by the fiscal mismanagement of state governments. Supporters of increased state autonomy and other critics of the central government argue, in contrast, that the constitution explicitly provides for transfers of many taxes collected by the center, that the center controls many of the most elastic sources of revenue, and that it is properly up to the states to decide how these resources should be expended.

Whatever the merits of the argument on both sides, which is not the subject of this paper, there is no doubt that the proportion of central resources transferred to the states has increased substantially since Independence. For example, the percentage of the gross revenue receipts of the central government transferred to the states increased from 14.4 per cent under the award of the First Finance Commission (1952–7) to 22:1 per cent under the award of the Sixth Finance Commission (1974–9).[26] However, the proportion of resources transferred in relation to both the total expenditures of the states and union territories and the total expenditures of the central government have not increased dramatically. Both the states and the central governments are raising new resources and spending more and more, but the states have not become significantly more dependent on the center for resource transfers than they were in the 1950s with smaller expenditures. The proportion of resources transferred to the total expenditures of the state governments increased from 36 per cent in the First Five-Year Plan (1951–6) to 42 per cent in the Fourth Plan (1969–74), but declined somewhat in the Annual Plans thereafter from

1974 to 1979 to less than 40 per cent (see table 3). Similarly, the proportion of resources transferred to the total expenditures of the central government has remained since the 1950s in a narrow range between 30 and 35 per cent.

Neither the total amount nor the proportion of resources transferred from the center to the states indicates anything concerning whether control over and use of the resources transferred has been associated with a trend toward centralization and state dependence on the center or decentralization and increased state autonomy. In order to approach that issue, it is necessary to consider to what extent the Finance Commission, as a central agency, and the central government have been able to achieve their declared goals through the mechanism of resource transfers or whether the states or some group of powerful states have had their way in contradistinction to central policy goals. A related issue concerns control and use of central resources as an instrument of patronage. The relevant question in this regard is whether or not the central government has used the mechanism of resource transfers to reward states which have provided strong political support to the party in power and to punish those that have supported or been controlled by opposition parties.

Table 3
TRANSFER OF RESOURCES FROM THE CENTER TO THE STATES AND UNION TERRITORIES, 1951–52 to 1977–78
(Rs crores)

	(1) Net resources transferred	*(2)* Total expenditures of states and territories	*(3)* Column (1) as % of column (2)	*(4)* Total expenditures of central government	Column (1) as % of column (4)
1951–6	1,205	3,351	35.96	3,757	32.07
1956–61	2,449	5,845	41.90	7,824	31.30
1961–6	4,651	10,719	43.39	15,254	30.49
1966–9	4,074	9,912	41.10	13,685	29.77
1969–74	11,584	27,556	42.04	32,997	35.13
1974–8	15,410	40,487	38.06	49,643	31.04

Source: Calculated from figures provided in R. K. Sinha, *Fiscal Federalism in India* (New Delhi: South Asia Publishers, 1980), 60–1, citing *Basic Statistics Relating to the Indian Economy*, 1: All India, October 1978, Centre for Monitoring Indian Economy, Bombay.

With regard to the first issue, it has been the repeatedly declared policy of the several Finance Commissions to use the mechanism of resource transfers as a device for inter-state equalization or, in other words, 'as a means of redressing regional imbalances.'[27] Such a policy means that the central government engages in redistributive transfers 'to help the poorer areas of the country' by transferring 'resources from relatively better off states to the poorer ones.'[28] In fact, however, such redistributive transfers have been resisted effectively, for the most part, by the better-off states in the controversies that have surrounded the deliberations of the successive Finance Commissions. In fact, the more advanced states have tended to receive a higher per capita tax devolution than the less advanced states,[29] with the result that 'tax devolution' may have 'accentuated the disparities' among the states.[30] Other observers concur with this view. Venu, for example, has argued that, despite the weightage for backwardness in various Finance Commission formulas, 'the general redistributive results have been regressive.'[31]

Similar controversies have surrounded the deliberations of the Planning Commission which also has repeatedly declared one of its major goals to be balanced regional development in allocating central assistance to the states. However, the equalizing impact of the Planning Commission's distribution of central resources also has been very limited.[32] The prevailing method used by the Planning Commission until the current Five Year Plan was the so-called Gadgil Formula, which provided for only 10 per cent of 'central assistance to the states' in the plans to be distributed according to 'backwardness'.[33] The allocation of central assistance to the states under the plan adopted by the Janata government, however, gave greater weight to backwardness. The backward states of U.P., Bihar, Orissa, and Madhya Pradesh gained more central assistance, as did Tamil Nadu and West Bengal, whereas the more advanced states of Maharashtra, Punjab, Haryana, and Gujarat, along with Andhra and Rajasthan, received less proportionately than in the past.[34]

The fact that most of the backward states that gained under the Janata plan were also the principal states that supported Janata opens up the question whether or not there has been a general pattern of association between the distribution of central assistance and political support for the ruling party. In fact, however, there is no strong evidence for such an association. There is no strong association, for example, between the ranking of states in terms of per capita resource transfers during the periods of the Fifth and Sixth Finance Commissions[35] — whose recommendations were made during Mrs Gandhi's tenure at the center in 1969 for the period 1969 to 1974 and in 1973 for the period 1974 to 1979 — and support for or opposition to the Congress in this period. The only assertion for which there is consistent support in the record of the distribution of central assistance in the plans and of resource transfers by the Finance Commissions is that the major Hindi-speaking states of U.P., Bihar, and Madhya Pradesh, which have for long been areas of disaffection from the Congress and provided the principal bases of support for the Janata opposition, also consistently received less per capita support than most other states until the Janata regime, despite the fact that they always have ranked among the most backward states in the country. Therefore, it is possible that the failure of the center under Congress dominance to pursue more rigorously a policy of redistributive transfers had an underlying political basis.

Overall, however, it cannot be said that the central government has adopted either a clear or persistent policy of inter-state equalization or of rewarding friendly states and punishing recalcitrant ones. The Planning Commission and the Finance Commission have been arenas in which inter-state disputes over the allocation of resources have been resolved by the use of formulas that have not significantly redistributed resources in any particular direction. Consequently, there is not much support in the methods used to transfer central resources to the states for the view that there has been a significant increase in the willingness of the center to exercise stronger centralized authority over the manner of their distribution.

Nor has the central government had much success in persuading the states to increase their own sources of revenue through additional taxes, particularly on the agricultural sector. It has been pointed out that, although agriculture contributes 45 per cent of India's G.N.P., the agricultural sector 'contributes less than 1 per cent of the G.N.P.' in taxes.[36] The reason for this situation is that the state governments have been reluctant to tax the rural groups upon whom their support is based or even to secure 'reasonable returns on investments in irrigation and power projects',[37] which benefit directly those same groups. In fact, although the land revenue still comprises the major direct tax on rural landholders, it constitutes a steadily decreasing proportion of the total tax revenue of the states.[38]

Despite the fact that the central government has been unable to persuade the states to mobilize additional resources from the agricultural sector, the deliberations of the Seventh Finance Commission, which occurred during the Janata regime and in the context of increased pressure from the states for revision of previous patterns of resource transfers, resulted in major changes in favor of the states. The share of the states in central taxes, excise duties, and statutory grants was increased significantly, leading to an estimated overall devolution of resources from the Finance Commission award in the Sixth Five Year Plan of Rs 23,063 crores, up from Rs 11,168 crores in the previous plan.[39] Consequently, under the Janata regime, there was a noticeable shift in direction both towards increased devolution of resources to the states by the Finance Commission and towards increasing the share of the backward north Indian states in resources transferred by the Planning Commission.

These shifts in resource distribution also have been accompanied by a decline of central control over the way the states spend the resources transferred. It is well known that the Planning Commission in Nehru's time had considerably more power and authority than it does today and that the role of the states in plan formulation was 'quite limited'.[40] It is not clear that the role of the states in plan formulation has increased for most states have never developed adequate planning agencies comparable to the central Planning Commission.[41] It is clear, however, that the control of the Planning Commission and of the central ministries over state expenditure of central plan assistance has been reduced.[42] For a time, 'the number of centrally sponsored schemes' went down from 147 in 1966 to 90 in 1968 and to fifty two in the Fourth Five Year Plan[43] and the expenditures for such schemes also went down accordingly. During the past decade, however, the funding for various new centrally-sponsored programs, such as the Drought Prone Areas Program, the Small Farmers Development Agency, and the Marginal Farmers and Agricultural Laborers program, has risen dramatically. However, despite the increase in central funding for such centrally-sponsored programs, the distribution of funding to the states for them has been made increasingly on the basis of formulas that limit severely the discretion of the Planning Commission and prevent the old pattern of 'secret negotiations between the Planning Commission and individual states'.[44]

Moreover, there has been a long-term shift in the sources of funds transferred from the center to the states to the Finance Commission rather than the Planning Commission and away from discretionary loans and grants. The trends are brought out in table 4, which shows that the proportion of total resources transferred by the Finance Commission went up from less than one-third in the 1950s and 1960s to 48 per cent in the 1974–8 period and to an estimated 42 per cent in the Janata period (1978–80). In contrast, the proportion of total resources transferred by the Planning Commission decreased from 61 per cent in the period 1951–6 and somewhat less than 50 per cent during the next decade to below one-third in the period from 1966 to 1974 and back up again to 37 and 44 per cent, respectively, in the two most recent periods. The most dramatic shifts have taken place in the category of 'other transfers', mostly discretionary loans and grants, which showed a huge jump in the 1950s and 1960s, but were cut back again very substantially in the 1970s. The significance of these trends is that they represent a tendency for more transfers to be made through the Finance Commission, which has exercised the least discretionary

Table 4
TRANSFER OF RESOURCES FROM THE CENTER TO THE STATES BY THE FINANCE COMMISSION, THE PLANNING COMMISSION, AND THE CENTRAL GOVERNMENT
(*Rs crores*)

	Finance Commission		*Planning Commission*		*Other transfers*		*Total*	
	Amount	*%*	*Amount*	*%*	*Amount*	*%*	*Amount*	*%*
1951–6	447	31	880	61	104	7	1,431	99
1956–61	918	32	1,344	47	606	21	2,868	100
1961–6	1,590	28	2,738	49	1,272	23	5,600	100
1966–9	1,782	25	1,917	27	3,415	48	7,114	100
1969–74	5,316	36	4,230	28	5,307	36	14,853	100
1974–8	8,395	48	6,533	37	2,695	15	17,623	100
1978–80	6,358	42	6,672	44	2,171	14	15,201	100
Total	24,806	38	24,314	38	15,570	24	64,690	100

Sources: India, *Report of the Finance Commission, 1973*, 6, and *Reserve Bank of India Bulletin*, September-October, 1979, 568. The figures for total transfers in the last column of this table do not agree with the figures in Column 1 of table 3. I cannot account for the differences. I have found it virtually impossible to find two sources that provide identical figures on central and state finances in India.

power and has operated with formulas that do not involve major redistributive transfers or politically motivated transfers. At the same time, as already indicated, central control over the resources transferred by the Planning Commission has declined. Overall, therefore, while the center still has the potential ability to channel considerable financial resources in a discretionary manner, the long-term trend has been away from transfers of that sort to more automatic, formula-based transfers and to decreasing control over the use of the transfers awarded to the states.

On all these matters of resource transfers and central control of state expenditures, the Congress government of Mrs Gandhi holds different views from its predecessor. Mrs Gandhi continues to favor rapid industrialization, including growth of capital-intensive industries, which requires centralized planning and central control over resources. She does not support the massive shift of resources to agriculture favored by some elements in the previous Janata government and by the Lok Dal. On the contrary, she and her advisers have always favored additional resource mobilization by the states from the agricultural sector. She clearly does not favor the demands for increased financial autonomy proposed by states such as West Bengal and Tamil Nadu. After her return to power in 1980, the Sixth Five-Year Plan draft prepared by the Janata government was revised in favor of capital-intensive programs and away from the previous emphasis on welfare programs for the benefit of the poor. The role of the Planning Commission in revising the plan was considerably reduced. Formulation of the new draft was carried out by the central government, largely in secret, with the Planning Commission taking the view that its role was simply to allocate funds made available by the Union Finance Ministry 'as Central plan assistance under established arrangements',[45] but it was not clear to what extent this new procedure involved the exercise of increased discretion by the central government in allocating resources among the states or continued adherence to relatively impartial formula-based transfers of resources. There is not much doubt, however, that Mrs Gandhi on these issues, as in her political behavior, favors centralization and central control over resource allocation, distribution and expenditure. However, for the Congress to attempt to restore the power of the center over revenues and expenditures and the planning process that existed during Nehru's days would be to struggle against a secular trend toward and a widely shared demand for decentralization and increased state autonomy.

The persistence of regionalism and the absence of a national party system

The Congress. The Congress organization clearly has been the leading political institution in post-Independence India. There are now several Congress organizations in India: the governing Congress (I) of Mrs Gandhi, the all-India Congress (U), which became the fourth largest opposition party in the country in terms of the popular vote in the 1980 elections, and several single-state Congress parties, of which the Kerala Congress has persisted the longest. It is, nevertheless, a central fact of post-Independence Indian political history that there has always been one predominant Congress organization in the country, which has always been either in power or has been the largest opposition party in Parliament and which has also always had broader support in most states of the Indian Union than any other party, even though it has never won a clear majority of the popular votes in the country.

It is now fairly well agreed among most observers of contemporary Indian politics that the Congress organization has disintegrated in the districts in large parts of the country, especially in the north.[46] The party's popular vote total in the country also has declined somewhat in the era of Mrs Gandhi's dominance from its level in the Nehru era. In the first three post-Independence elections, the Congress popular vote share in the country as a whole ranged between 45.00 and 47.78 per cent, whereas the range in the 1967, 1971, and 1980 elections has been from 40.73 to 43.68 per cent. In the 1977 elections, the only one lost by the Congress, the party's vote share was reduced to 34.5 per cent.

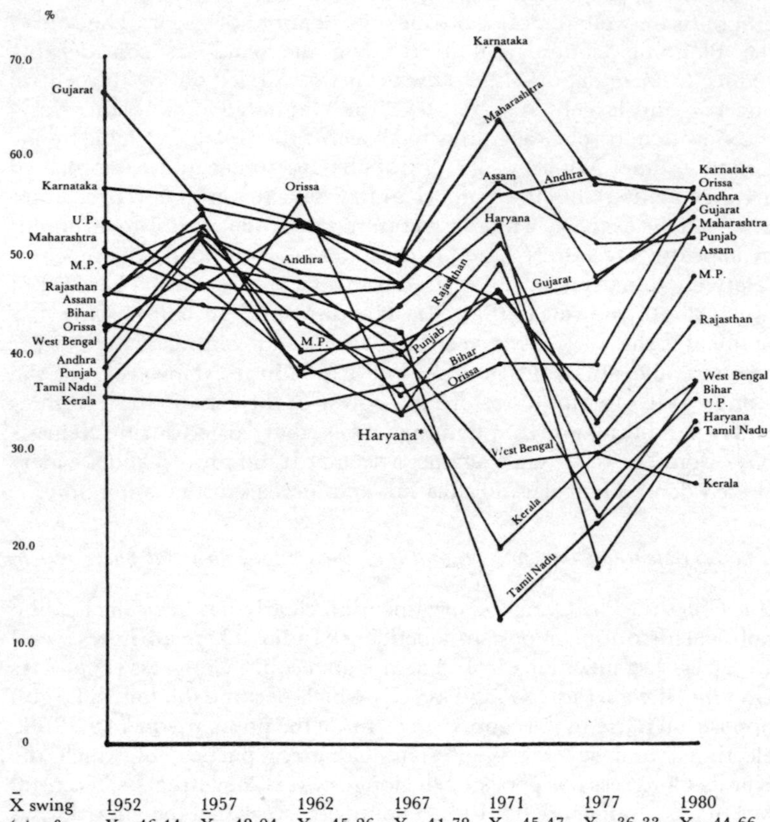

	1952	1957	1962	1967	1971	1977	1980
$\bar{X}$ swing (plus & minus)	$\bar{X}$ = 46.14 s = 8.63	$\bar{X}$ = 48.04 s = 5.76	$\bar{X}$ = 45.26 s = 6.57	$\bar{X}$ = 41.78 s = 5.80	$\bar{X}$ = 45.47 s = 15.21	$\bar{X}$ = 36.33 s = 12.70	$\bar{X}$ = 44.66 s = 10.57

$\bar{X}$ swing (ignoring plus & minus):

+ 2.20	− 2.97	− 3.46	+ 3.50	− 9.03	+ 8.54
6.13	6.11	5.14	11.72	12.22	9.13

* No figures available for Hariyana before 1980

Figure 1
VOTE FOR THE INDIAN NATIONAL CONGRESS FOR PARLIAMENT, 1952–1980

The relative stability of the Congress vote in the country as a whole masks some very dramatic changes and fluctuations that have occurred in the states that bear on the question of nationalization versus regionalism. Figure 1, which graphs the percentage of the parliamentary vote polled by the Congress in the fifteen major states in each of the seven elections, brings out one of those changes, namely the sharply increased dispersion of the vote for the Congress in the states in the last three elections compared to the first four.[47] The dispersion was greatest in the 1971 elections which, for the first time, delinked the parliamentary from the state assembly elections. Instead of having the hoped-for nationalizing effect, however, delinking initially had a strongly regionalizing effect. In fact, delinking was not complete in 1971 because simultaneous legislative assembly elections were held in Orissa, Tamil Nadu, and West Bengal. Although, by delinking, Mrs Gandhi hoped to free herself from dependence on the state Congress organizations and from locally powerful Congress leaders for success in the parliamentary elections, the Congress (I) became dependent in some states upon adjustments and alliances with other parties, which involved not contesting a large number of seats in states such as Kerala (delinked in 1971) and Tamil Nadu ('linked' in 1971). The very severe decline of the Congress vote in those states and in West Bengal was counterbalanced by the very sharp increases in the Congress vote shares in Andhra, Maharashtra and Assam. Paradoxically, the high vote in the former two states of Andhra and Maharashtra had much to do with the fact that the Congress organization still remained strong in those states and still under the control of locally powerful leaders.

Although the dispersion of the vote has been less in the last two elections of 1977 and 1980 than in 1971, it has been considerably above that in the first three elections, which is evident both from the graph and from a comparison of the standard deviations from the mean Congress vote by state in each of those elections. Moreover, the size of the mean swing away from and back to the Congress in these last two elections was much greater, in fact two to three times greater, than in any previous election The relatively low mean swing in the Congress vote from 1967 to 1971 masks the high volatility of the vote, for the fact that there was so much dispersion of the vote on both sides of the mean has led to an artificial evening-out of the mean swing to a relatively low +3.50. However, if the mean swing is calculated ignoring plus and minus signs, it comes to a much larger 11.72. On the other hand, it should also be noted that the swing of the Congress vote in the states from 1977 to 1980 was much more uniform than in any election since that of 1967. In fact, the swings in elections held since Mrs Gandhi first became Prime Minister have been fairly uniform in the sense that no less than two-thirds of the states have gone in one direction from one election to another with the vote for the Congress having gone down in ten of fifteen states in 1967, up in eleven in 1971, down in ten in 1977, and up in twelve in 1980. The big difference since Mrs Gandhi came to power and particularly since the delinking of parliamentary and state assembly elections has been the increased dispersion of the total vote in each state and the increased size of the mean swing.

Delinking, nevertheless, clearly has had the intended effect of separating voting patterns in national parliamentary and state legislative assembly elections. The closeness of the linkage before 1971 is apparent from figure 2, which plots the vote for the Congress for parliament against its vote in the legislative assembly elections in 1967, the last year in which linked elections were held in all states. In contrast to the famous 'coat-tails' effect in the United States, which normally means dependence of the votes for state candidates on the popularity of presidential candidates, the dependence in the Indian states in the linked elections was of parliamentary candidates upon the legislative assembly candidates. Figure 3 illustrates how delinking has led to considerable differences between the Congress vote for parliament and its vote in the nearest legislative assembly elections. Although the results in many states have not been substantially different as between the parliamentary and legislative assembly results, the clusterings around the dividing line on the graphs for the delinked elections clearly have been much less than that for 1967.

In effect then, the disintegration of the Congress organization, the delinking of the parliamentary from the state elections, and the focusing of the elections as a contest for or against Mrs Gandhi's leadership of the country have had contradictory effects with respect to nationalization and regionalization. The parliamentary elections have been freed from their dependence upon local bosses, with the result that, even when legislative assembly elections are scheduled closely after the parliamentary elections, the state and national results in many states are quite different. Moreover, most of the states tend to move in the same direction in the parliamentary contests. However, at the same time, regional differences in support for the Congress have become greater than before and the Congress has become dependent for electoral success in several states upon alliances with other parties.

The non-Congress Parties. With the exception of the 1977 elections, no single non-Congress party has ever polled even as much as half the Congress vote in the country as a whole. The results of the 1977 elections, in which the Janata polled 41.32 per cent of the vote nationally, nearly seven percentage points ahead of the Congress, and in which the two leading parties, Janata and Congress, together polled nearly 85 per cent of the vote, led at least one observer to speculate about the prospects of an 'emergent two-party system.'[48] However, nothing in the electoral or party political history of India suggests that such a development is likely in the foreseeable future. The more

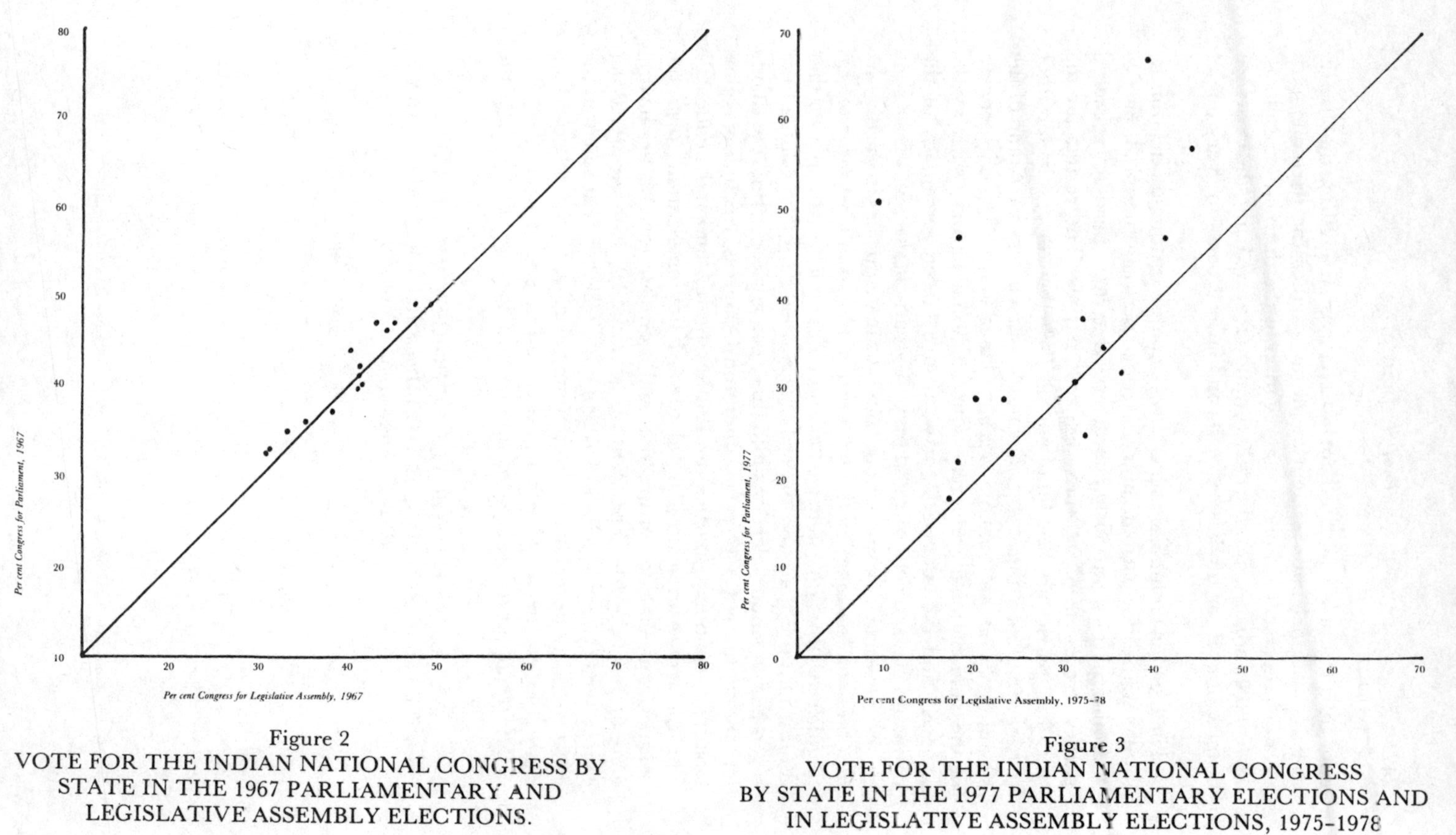

Figure 2
VOTE FOR THE INDIAN NATIONAL CONGRESS BY STATE IN THE 1967 PARLIAMENTARY AND LEGISLATIVE ASSEMBLY ELECTIONS.

Figure 3
VOTE FOR THE INDIAN NATIONAL CONGRESS BY STATE IN THE 1977 PARLIAMENTARY ELECTIONS AND IN LEGISLATIVE ASSEMBLY ELECTIONS, 1975–1978

relevant question is whether there has ever existed anything that can be called a national party system at all or whether the parliamentary elections represent simply an aggregation of the distinctive results in each of the Indian states, the only common feature being the existence of the Congress as the largest or second largest party in every one of them.

The Election Commission has always made a distinction in publishing the figures for parliamentary elections between 'national' parties and other parties, variously characterized as state parties, registered parties, 'recognized' or 'unrecognized' parties. The results for the 'national' parties are listed individually, whereas the results for other parties are often lumped together in the official reports. Some of the separately listed 'national' parties have failed to win even one per cent of the vote nationally whereas some regional parties, such as the D.M.K. and the Akali Dal, have won a larger percentage of the national vote, but concentrated only in a particular state.

Leaving aside for a moment the obvious inadequacies in the distinction between 'national' and other parties, it does at least serve to distinguish strictly single-state parties and independents from parties that contest in more than one state. Table 5 breaks up the results of the seven parliamentary elections into three categories — the vote shares for the dominant Congress, the non-Congress (including other Congress) 'national' parties, and 'other parties and independents'. The table does indicate a trend toward 'nationalization' over the decades, with the vote for the 'national' non-Congress parties having gone up from the 20–30 per cent range in the 1950s to the 30–40 per cent range between 1962 and 1971 to the 40–50 per cent range in the last two elections, with a corresponding decline in the relative vote shares of the category of 'other parties and independents'.

The trend, however, is partly illusory and does not at all indicate the

Table 5
VOTE SHARES FOR THE CONGRESS, 'NATIONAL' OPPOSITION PARTIES, AND OTHERS IN PARLIAMENTARY ELECTIONS, 1952–1980

	Congress	*'National' opposition*	*Other parties & independents*	*Total*
1952	45.00	29.57	25.43	100.00
1957	47.78	25.26	26.96	100.00
1962	44.72	37.85	17.43	100.00
1967	40.73	37.90	21.37	100.00
1971	43.62	34.23	22.15	100.00
1977	34.50	50.17	15.33	100.00
1980	42.68	42.39	14.93	100.00

Source: Official and, for 1980, provisional reports of the Election Commission of India.

existence in any meaningful sense of a national party system, for the following reasons. First, the number of 'national' non-Congress parties has been large and their existence unstable. Twenty-two parties have received such recognition as 'national' parties in the seven parliamentary elections.[49] However, beyond the Congress and the Communist parties, none of the other 'national' parties have persisted through time. Moreover, the second-place party has changed in every election since 1952, when the Socialist Party came in second with 10.6 per cent of the vote. The second-place parties in subsequent elections and their percentage of the total popular vote were as follows: 1957, P.S.P. (10.41); 1962, C.P.I. (9.94); 1967, Jan Sangh (9.41); 1971, Congress (O) (10.42); 1977, Congress (34.52); 1980, Janata (18.93). It is also important to note that, in any single parliamentary election, the second-place party is likely to be different in different states. For example, in 1980, in the fifteen major states, Janata was the second-place party in seven, the Lok Dal in three, the C.P.M. in two, the Akali Dal in one, and the AIADMK in one. In state legislative assembly elections, this kind of diversity is always even greater than in the parliamentary contests.

Secondly, many of the so-called national parties did not have a genuine national spread at all. For example, in 1980, in addition to the Congress, there were five 'national' parties, of which only the Janata and the I.N.C. (U), with 5.29 per cent of the vote share, had a fairly even spread in most states in the country. As for the other three, however, the Janata (S) or Lok Dal of Charan Singh polled 82.77 per cent of its 9.42 per cent national vote share in the five states of Rajasthan, Haryana, U.P., Bihar, and Orissa. The C.P.M. polled 67.45 per cent of its national vote share (6.16 per cent) in West Bengal alone and 80 per cent in the two states of Kerala and West Bengal. The distribution of the vote for most of the 'national' parties in all other elections is similarly skewed. In effect, therefore, most of the 'national' parties are regional parties or parties that have representation in two or more states, but not in all or most states in the country.[50]

A third reason for considering the trends in table 5 to be spurious is the fact that the fragmentation of the national vote for political parties has been very high and relatively constant over the seven elections. Rae's index of electoral fragmentation[51] for the seven elections gives the following figures: 1952, .78; 1957, .75; 1962, .77; 1967, .80; 1971, .79; 1977, .71; 1980, .76. These figures are what one might expect from a 'system' which, to the extent that it exists at all, could be characterized only as an unstable, fragmented multi-party system in which one party has always emerged dominant only because of the fact that the electoral system is based upon the single-member plurality district in which the candidate with the largest number of votes wins.

'Deviant' State Party Systems. The most important reason for doubting the existence in India of anything that can be called a national party system is the fact that all the Indian states have distinctive party systems. Although the Congress has strength in all states and is the strongest party in most, the configuration of the party system varies considerably from state to state. Some states have had multiparty systems in which the Congress has been dominant, others have had dualistic systems in which there have been two leading political parties, some have had multiparty systems with several strong parties, and still others have had fragmented multiparty systems with no strongly institutionalized parties. In some states, the parliamentary elections, even with delinking, are predominantly projections onto the national scene of distinctive regional patterns of competition and control or they

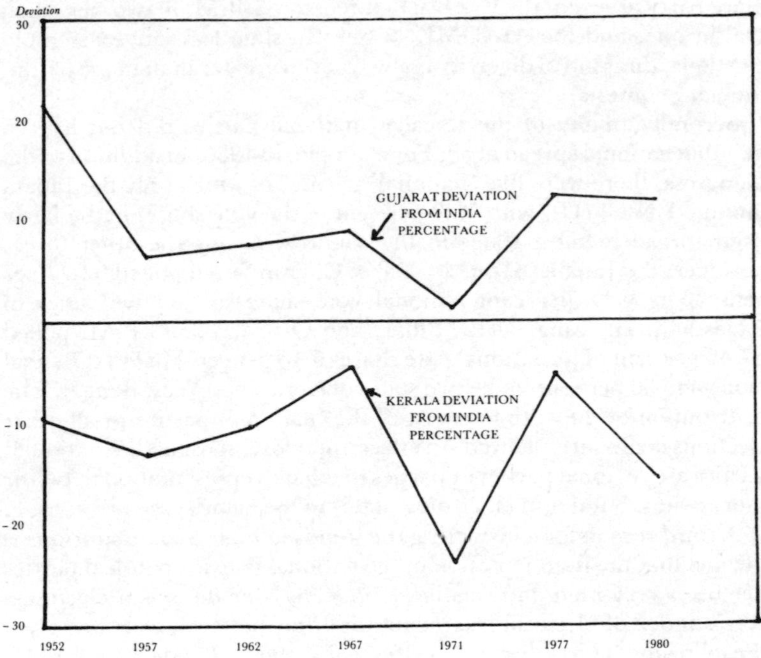

Figure 4
PERSISTENCE OF REGIONALISM: DEVIATION OF CONGRESS PERCENTAGES OF TOTAL PARLIAMENTARY VOTE IN GUJARAT AND KERALA FROM CONGRESS PERCENTAGES OF TOTAL NATIONAL VOTE, 1952-1980

involve primarily alliances and adjustments between national and regional parties.

Moreover, despite the tendency since delinking for most of the states to move in the same direction for or against the Congress in parliamentary elections, strong regional tendencies persist even in relation to the Congress vote. Figure 4 compares the deviation of the Congress vote from the nationwide Congress percentage in all elections from 1952 to 1980 in Gujarat and Kerala. These two states were at opposite ends of the continuum of support for and opposition to the Congress in 1952. In that year, the Congress polled 66 per cent of the vote in the Gujarat districts of the old Bombay province, but only 35 per cent in the present-day Kerala districts, a difference of 31 percentage points. Figure 4 shows that regional tendencies have persisted in both states, which have remained far from each other in voting patterns and often far from the mean vote for the Congress in the country.[52] Most important, although at times both states have moved towards conformity with national patterns, particularly in the period between 1957 and 1967 for Kerala and between 1957 and 1971 in Gujarat, the trajectory for both states overall has been highly individual and has moved away from the national norms.

Even those states which have generally been close to the national norm in relation to the vote for the Congress have differed considerably in one or more other respects. For example, the distinctiveness of the Punjab party system has centered around the entrenchment of the Akali Dal as the major rival of the Congress and the persistent inability of other non-Congress parties to acquire broad bases of support in the state as a whole. In this state, support for the Congress has not deviated markedly from national trends, but support for national non-Congress parties has been relatively weak.

Tamil Nadu has deviated even more strongly from national trends than Punjab, for here the Congress itself has been markedly weak except during the period of its dominance by Kamaraj Nadar. In four elections — 1952, 1971, 1977 and 1980 — the Congress vote deviated markedly and negatively from the mean Congress vote in the country as a whole. Moreover, except in 1971, when the Congress (O) led by Kamaraj polled a large share of the vote, the vote for the non-Congress 'national' parties has also deviated markedly and negatively from their mean vote in the country as a whole. The principal non-Congress parties in this state, of course, have been the D.M.K. and the A.D.M.K. The effect of Mrs Gandhi's involvement in Tamil Nadu politics and her destruction of a strong Congress organization there has been to solidify the regional aspects of state politics. In 1971, Mrs Gandhi pronounced the death knell of the Congress in Tamil Nadu by forming an alliance with the D.M.K. in which the Congress was given nine seats for Parliament in exchange for giving the D.M.K. a free hand in the rest of the Parliamentary seats and in the state assembly elections. In contrast to the Punjab, where the main dynamic has been between the Congress and the Akali Dal, the principal dynamic in Tamil Nadu since 1971 has been provided by the competition between the DMK and the ADMK. In this competition, the Congress has had to ally with one side or the other in order to win representation to Parliament.

It would be possible to take up each of the remaining Indian states one-by-one and demonstrate significant regional differences in each. Moreover, the regional differences would be magnified even further if one were to examine the party systems in relation to the state legislative assemblies rather than Parliament. However, enough evidence has been provided to assert confidently that the nationalizing tendencies induced by Mrs Gandhi's delinking of parliamentary and legislative assembly elections and by her controversial policies have not succeeded in eroding significantly the distinctiveness of regional political patterns in India nor in establishing a truly national party system.

President's rule and the cycle of consolidation and disintegration of central power

The increasing use and abuse of the emergency provisions in the constitution of India providing for the establishment of President's Rule (P.R.) in the Indian states has been cited frequently as an unequivocal demonstration of tendencies toward centralization in the Indian political system. In fact, however, a close examination of the history of the use of P.R. in post-Independence India and of the reasons for its use suggests another interpretation. The point of view that will be suggested below is that, although PR does represent an extraordinary device, not available in most other federal systems, by which the central government takes over governmental functions in the Indian states and by which it can intervene in state politics, the frequent use of P.R. is more appropriately to be seen as a failure of the government of India to exercise effective central control over state affairs than as an index of centralization.

Consider first the basic facts concerning the frequency, the duration in particular states, and the trends over time in the use of P.R. Counting only impositions of P.R. in the states and not the Union Territories, P.R. was used sixty-one times between 1951 and the end of 1980. It has been used for as short a period as eighteen days (in U.P. in 1970) and for as long as 712 days (in Kerala between 1965 and 1967). The average duration between 1951 and 1976 was 237 days, which means that most impositions of P.R. have been extended beyond the

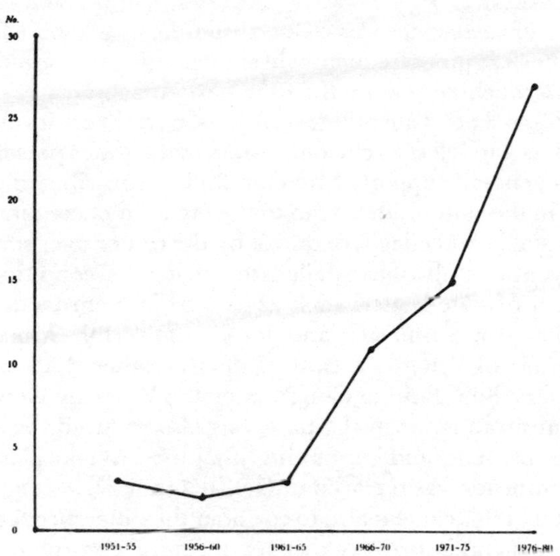

Figure 5
INCREASING NUMBER OF INCIDENTS OF IMPOSITION OF PRESIDENT'S RULE BY THE CENTRAL GOVERNMENT ON THE INDIAN STATES (EXCLUDING UNION TERRITORIES), 1951–1980

initial six-months' period. Several states have undergone P.R. five or six times since Independence and one, Kerala, has been under P.R. for a total duration, at different times, of over four years. Since 1967, there has never been a time when no state has been under P.R. Moreover, the average annual frequency of use of P.R. has gone up with each prime minister.[53] The frequency of use of P.R. has gone up steadily since 1960 and dramatically since 1966, when Mrs Gandhi became Prime Minister (see figure 5).

Although it is reasonable to conclude from the increased frequency of use of P.R. that there has been, as a consequence of it, a 'reduction in the degree of state autonomy',[54] this reduction has not meant effective central control over state politics or effective centralization of power. In fact, it is arguable that effective central control has declined. When the Congress was dominant in most of the country and when Nehru's leadership was unchallenged, central control over and intervention in state politics took place more frequently, though not exclusively, through the Congress organization rather than through the use of P.R. It is no doubt true that there were many states which remained under the political dominance of powerful state leaders in the Nehru era, in which central intervention was not necessary, and that the number of such states was reduced significantly after Mrs Gandhi began to interfere more frequently in state politics and began to use the government machinery more than the party machinery to control the states. Through her frequent interventions in state politics and because of her tendency to select as chief ministers of the states persons without strong independent support, Mrs Gandhi has contributed to political instability in the states rather than to the creation of conditions for the exercise of stable and effective control by the center over state politics. Her interventions also have failed to create the conditions for the development of state leaders such as existed in Nehru's day, at once loyal to the prime minister and locally powerful. Moreover, the increasing use of P.R. as a control device rather than the Central Parliamentary Board of the Congress or the Working Committee or respected arbitrators, as in the past, has also reduced the amount of 'discussion, consent, and bargaining' that used to take place before a state chief minister was replaced in Nehru's time.[55]

It is useful in this context also to consider the differences between the most dramatic and impressive display of central control over the provinces exercised during the Nehru era without resort to P.R. under the Kamaraj Plan of 1963, under which all the Congress chief ministers in all the states of India submitted their resignations at the request of Pandit Nehru and several were replaced, on the one hand, and Mrs Gandhi's replacements of chief ministers, on the other hand. The exercise of central control under the Kamaraj Plan involved extensive consultations with powerful regional leaders. It was an effort to consolidate power in the Congress by building a national coalition, which remained relatively stable through two successions, after the deaths of Nehru and Shastri. Mrs Gandhi, in contrast, has often imposed her will, replacing Congress chief ministers when she has considered it desirable, but there is no coalition of forces nor any organization to make such changes persist should anything happen to her. Instead, she has relied at the national level on cliques of political advisers, on senior bureaucrats, and on her sons to create an illusion of power through money and fear.

A final point to note with regard to the increased frequency of use of P.R. in the most recent period, 1976–80, is that it has been inflated by the simultaneous impositions of P.R. in nine states by the Janata Government to force state assembly elections in 1977 and in ten states in 1980 by Mrs Gandhi's government for the same purpose. Such use of the PR provisions of the constitution clearly was no part of the intention of the framers. It also reflects the recent attempts to nationalize the state assembly elections, turning them into aspects of the continuing struggle for power at the center and making the outcome of the struggle for power in the states subsidiary to and dependent upon the former.[56]

The use of P.R. in this way as a device to force state legislative assembly elections seems again, on the face of it, to confirm the centralizing and nationalizing tendencies in Indian politics. Yet, even here, the implications are not so clear, for there is an interdependence of the center on the states and the states on the center. If power in the states depends upon the outcome at the center, it remains the case, as always, that power at the center depends upon control over the states. Moreover, that control continues to be ever insecure and precarious. In fact, it is more insecure and precarious than it was in the Nehru era because of the decay of the Congress organization[57] and because of the increased importance of non-Congress parties in several states, particularly West Bengal and Tamil Nadu, in addition to Kerala, where non-Congress parties often held power even in the 1950s and 1960s. The center must use PR increasingly as an instrument of control both because the Congress monopoly of power in most of the states has been broken and because, even when the Congress captures control at both the center and in nearly all the states, its hold on power is tenuous since it is not based on organizational strength in the states and districts. The same holds true for the non-Congress parties who, when in power at the center, must confront their own internal lack of unity, their absence of grass-roots organization, and the fact that the Congress has never been ousted from power in all or nearly all the states.

The insecurity and precariousness of central control over state politics, whether the Congress or non-Congress parties are in power at the center are easily demonstrated by examining the types of situations that have led to the imposition of PR. Dua, in his excellent work on *Presidential Rule in India*, has examined all the cases of the use of P.R. in India as 'crisis episodes' that reveal the true nature of center-state relations and what he calls the 'pathology of federalism'. He argues persuasively that P.R. has been used and abused as an instrument of central control and of Congress control over state politics and as a method of removing 'undesirable' state leaders and that its frequent misuse in this way has fundamentally transformed center-state relations.[58] He demonstrates convincingly that P.R. has been used repeatedly for both partisan and personal reasons, by Nehru and Shastri to solve intraparty disputes and to weaken opposition parties, by Mrs Gandhi as 'an instrument to liquidate dissent of any kind', and by both the Janata Government and Mrs Gandhi to precipitate state legislative assembly elections. Dua also points out that Mrs Gandhi surpassed all other prime ministers of India in her abuse of P.R. by using it to resolve crises in state politics deliberately created by her.[59] Specifically, both Dua and Maheshwari Prasad have shown that P.R. has been imposed primarily in situations of cabinet instability in the states, but not always or even usually in a clearly impartial manner. Rather P.R. has been imposed in such situations in 'some cases' when 'it was not strictly necessary' and, 'in a large number of instances the return of popular government was postponed more for political reasons that administrative ones'.[60] In other cases, even stable governments were dismissed on grounds that there were mass public protests against it or, in one of the clearest cases of misuse of the power of declaring PR, on grounds of corruption and that the state government 'held out "veiled threats" of secession' in Tamil Nadu in 1976.[61]

It is clear therefore, that the use of P.R. has become a regular, normal feature of politics in India, rather than the exception, and that it is used at the most critical moments in state politics, namely, during ministerial crises. It is also used for the purpose of influencing the future course of politics in a state in such a way as to benefit the ruling party or parties at the center. The increased frequency of its use represents less an increase in centralizing tendencies than a shift in the instruments of central intervention and the arenas of center-state relations. The principal instrument of central intervention has become the central government and administration rather than the Congress organization. The arenas of center-state relations have also shifted from the Congress organization to the state legislatures and the electoral process.

In the 1960s, when the Congress monopolized power in both the center and the states, the principal path to power in the states was through the Congress organization by mobilizing support in the districts. In the late 1960s and 1970s, as the Congress lost its monopoly of power and as the Congress organization itself disintegrated, the principal path to power became the electoral process and the legislature itself. In a sense, therefore, central control over provincial politics has declined while the political contest has become more nationalized.[62] In the Nehru era, a Congress faction leader who wanted to capture control over a state government began by forming alliances in and gaining control over a majority in the State Parliamentary Board to ensure that a majority of the party tickets in the next election would go to candidates from his faction and allied factions. The next stage of the process occurred in the electoral arena where the main electoral contests were between rival factions in the Congress rather than between the Congress and opposition parties. A further stage occurred in the legislature after the election when it would be determined which factional coalition controlled a majority in the Congress Legislature Party. The process could be stopped or accelerated at any stage through central intervention, which occurred frequently. However, the process was self-contained in each state and involved only district, state, and central Congress actors, but did not overlap into other states. Finally, at all stages in the process, the locality (district) and the state were the focal points because power was built up from the localities to the state level. The Congress leadership represented a power that could always intervene and stop the process, but not change its character.

In the late 1960s and 1970s, the stakes and the stages in the process and the importance of particular arenas all changed. First, after the death of Nehru, the stakes expanded to include control of the prime ministership and the central government. For a while, this change meant only the addition of a fifth and sixth step in the struggle for power, namely, the aggregation of factional coalitions to the central level and a contest for control over the national Congress organization followed by a determination of the balance of forces in the Parliament. However, after the split in the Congress in 1969 followed by Mrs Gandhi's systematic elimination of most independent sources of power in the Congress and the consequent disintegration of the Congress organization, most of the main parties in Indian politics became shadow organizations dependent for their success and persistence upon the popularity of their leaders and their abilities to build electoral coalitions based upon broad social forces that cut across district lines and even state boundaries.

In the post-1969 process of struggle for power, the first stage occurs in the electoral arena as rival leaders in control of political parties, rather than factions, contest elections for control of the Parliament. Because the parliamentary elections have been held separately from the legislative assembly elections since 1971, success in these elections depends much less than in the past on powerful local leaders who control vote banks and much more on control over large blocs of voters — minorities, particularly Muslims, low castes and the poor, particular caste categories, and the middle peasantry especially. The second stage in the process, the selection of the Prime Minister, is similar to the situation that existed under Nehru if the Congress wins the election. If the Congress is successful, Mrs Gandhi automatically becomes the Prime Minister. If an opposition coalition is successful, the selection is made through consultation among top leaders of the party. Parliament plays no effective role in the process,[63] nor do the chief ministers of states as in the selection of Lal Bahadur Shastri. The third stage in the process is the precipitation of state legislative assembly elections in those states where parties are in power different from the victorious party at the center. At this stage, P.R. may be used either state-by-state or in a large number of states. The purpose of forcing elections, it is important to note, is not only to control the states — and not really mainly to control the states — but to consolidate power at the center by ensuring that elections to the Rajya

Sabha and for President of the country, for which the state legislative assemblies constitute the electoral colleges, result in an upper house controlled by the ruling party and a President who can be counted upon to carry out its will. The fourth stage, assuming the victory in the states of the party or coalition that controls the center, is the selection of the chief ministers of the states who are either chosen by the prime minister or are known allies of a powerful coalition leader at the center. The fifth stage is the disintegration of power in the states. If the Congress is in power in the states, the legislative party disintegrates into competing factions struggling to retain or replace the chief minister. If non-Congress coalitions are in power at the center and in the states, the various constituent parties and groups maneuver in the state legislature for the same purpose. During this stage, the central leadership will become involved in the struggles at the state level that focus on the office of chief minister, sometimes intervening to halt conflict, at other times to replace a chief minister. Ultimately, however, such *ad hoc* interventions cannot sustain stable governments in the states. As power disintegrates further in the states, and in an increasing number of them, there remain then two options before the leadership of the ruling group at the center: either move to prevent further disintegration by imposing Emergency rule and by using P.R. ruthlessly to remove any opposition in the states or permit the process of disintegration to continue until it causes the break-up of the ruling party or coalition at the center, when the process begins again.

Now, there are three principal differences between the processes outlined above in the Nehru era and in the 1970s that relate to the issue of centralization. The first is the disintegration of the Congress organization, which has had the following consequences: the considerable decline in importance of a non-governmental mechanism of central intervention in state politics, of powerful state party bosses with bases of power independent of the center, and of the district as a critical political arena in which struggles for power at higher levels are fought and from which power is aggregated to the state level.[64] The second difference is the enlargement of the political arena to include inter-party competition in the electoral process as a critical factor, which in turn has involved some nationalization of politics or at least the transcendence of district and state boundaries in electoral contests, and the turning of parliamentary elections into contests between alternative prime ministers somewhat like the British pattern. However, nationalization is not the same as centralization. The third difference is the increased interdependence of the center and the states in the outcome of political struggles for power. The last point is the most significant one, for it summarizes the basic change in the politics of center-state relations between the Nehru era and the present period. The center is not stronger than it was under Nehru. It is weaker. The central leaders are more dependent than ever on the outcomes of the struggles for power in the states, which is why they try ever harder to control state politics. The paradox is that the states too are weaker in relation to the center.

The explanation for the paradox is as follows. The center is stronger politically *in relation to the states* under Mrs Gandhi than it was under Nehru, but its strength is illusory. Mrs Gandhi and her inner circle of advisers at the center exercise more direct control more frequently over the selection and dismissal of chief ministers than was the case under Nehru, with the notable exception of the Kamaraj Plan. The selection of Congress candidates to contest legislative assembly elections also has come under greater control by the party center. However, the state chief ministers selected or approved by the center are often politically weak in their states. Factionalism persists in the state legislature Congress parties, with the struggle focusing on persuading the center of the incompetence and corruption of the incumbent chief minister as much as or more than on building an alternative coalition in the state party organization and in the legislature party. At the same time, the central leaders must remain concerned about the struggles for power in the states because their own power is more dependent upon the outcomes than in Nehru's time. The center cannot afford to permit state politics to follow their own course because there are fewer leaders left in the states with independent bases of power who can be counted upon to maintain control over their legislature parties and to organize successful electoral campaigns. The immediate consequence of relaxation of central control in many states at any point in time would be fragmentation of the Congress legislature party. Tenure of power in most states continues to be precarious, more dependent than in Nehru's time upon both central intervention and increasingly uncertain electoral outcomes. Paradoxically, therefore, although the center appears stronger in relation to the states than in Nehru's time, it is weaker and less effective in aggregating *and* maintaining a stable base of power, by conventional electoral and parliamentary methods, in the country as a whole than before.[65] Moreover, despite its greater willingness and capacity to replace chief ministers and select candidates for both parliamentary and legislative assembly elections, the center is no more effective, and may even be less effective, than in the past in ensuring that central policies and directives are implemented at the state level, particularly in the states farthest from Delhi and north India.[66]

The massive parliamentary majorities achieved by the Congress in 1971, the Janata in 1977, and the Congress again in 1980, like the great majorities achieved by the Awami League in Bangladesh, are facades that indicate not the power of the competing parties and certainly not the emergence of a two-party system, but the disintegration of party organizations with stable regional bases of support, the decline of the significance of district and state boundaries as self-contained political segments and the corresponding rise in the importance of waves of sentiment that affect large blocs of voters, and the increasing importance of a politics based on the appeals of popular leaders and mass movements. It is a politics of unstable interdependence between the center and the states. It is this underlying instability that impels a strong and impatient leader, such as Mrs Gandhi, to attempt to stop the process at the point of consolidation and not permit the disintegrative process to begin a new cycle.

It is also clear why the prospect of a presidential system might appeal to Mrs Gandhi and even to some opposition leaders. For, the principal advantage of a presidential system in this regard is that it would provide a fixed period of time during which power, so laboriously consolidated in Indian politics, could be maintained and exercised both at the center and, if a gubernatorial pattern were set up, in the states as well. However, the adoption of both the American presidential and gubernatorial systems would most likely foster state autonomy by protecting the states from perpetual intervention by the center and is not likely, therefore, to be acceptable either to Mrs Gandhi or to non-Congress leaders who favor a strong center. A presidential system with governors appointed by the center would, of course, move India quite in the opposite direction. It is likely that Mrs Gandhi and some opposition leaders as well would be more comfortable with the French type of presidential system with a strong executive and a weaker parliament and judiciary than the American, but the French system provides no model for a federal polity.

Insofar as the current Indian context is concerned, however, the frequent use of P.R. by the center is a consequence of the requirements necessary for aggregating power at the center in a highly regionalized federal parliamentary system, in which the aggregative and integrative capacities of the dominant political parties have declined. It does not, however, necessarily represent a trend toward the reduction of provincial autonomy. If there is a pathological element in the frequent use of P.R. in India, it is less a 'pathology of federalism' than a pathology of constitutional procedure that arises from the fact that no consistent conventions have been developed to enable the public to judge when P.R. is being used properly or improperly. Although the frequent use of P.R. threatens both the parliamentary system and state autonomy, it at least keeps state politics in the forefront. The greater danger, however, arises from the prospect that Mrs Gandhi or some other leader may attempt once again to stop the inevitable cycle of consolidation-disintegration at the peak point by making full use of both the emergency and P.R. provisions of the constitution to impose an authoritarian regime.

Conclusion: centralization, decentralization, or disintegration in India's Federal System

Although I have argued that the predominant tendencies in the development of India's federal system have been towards pluralism, regionalism, decentralization, and interdependence, there also exist strong forces in favor of centralization. At present, even more than in the past, the strongest force for centralization in the country is the Congress, led by Mrs Gandhi. Many of Mrs Gandhi's most decisive political actions have been taken with a view toward decreasing the power and independence of state politicians and the salience of issues specific to the states while centralizing authority and power in the Congress organization at the national level and in the central government in her own hands and those of her closest advisors and while emphasizing national issues. The specific measures that Mrs Gandhi has taken in the past fifteen years to centralize power and authority in her own hands and to nationalize political issues are well known and have been discussed above. They include the political destruction of the state political bosses, the consequent disintegration of the Congress organization in the districts, and the selection by her and her closest advisors of chief ministers in the states who lack independent bases of power and who can, therefore, be counted upon to follow the directions of the central government. They include also the delinking of parliamentary and state legislative assembly elections and the emphasis in parliamentary elections on programs, appeals, and issues that are national in scope.

For example, Mrs Gandhi has attempted, with some success, to build a national following among categories and groups of voters whose needs are not adequately satisfied by the state governments or who have identifications that cross state boundaries. Clearly included in such groups are the Muslims and other minorities, the Scheduled Castes, the tribal peoples, the poor and the landless, and the north Indian Brahman castes. The Brahman castes are tied to Mrs Gandhi and the Congress for a combination of emotional and practical reasons, including caste solidarity with Mrs Gandhi in an organization that is Brahman-dominated in many areas and opposition to the aspirations of non-élite castes who threaten Brahman preponderance in élite educational, administrative, and political positions. It should be noted that the main threats to the continued importance of Brahmans in public life come not from the Scheduled Castes but from other élite castes and from the 'backward' or middle castes. Measures that have been taken in the past or promised in the future to promote the interests of minorities and disadvantaged groups include strengthening the Minorities Commission, grants of money, plots of land, and other facilities and benefits to Scheduled Castes, identification with the Scheduled Castes and landless laborers who have been victimized by the landowning castes, promises to recognize Urdu as a second official language in states where Urdu-speaking Muslims are in a large minority, the establishment of the Small Farmers Development Agency and the Marginal Farmers and Agricultural Labourers Agency, and the nationalization of the banks and the establishment of regional and district banks explicitly designed to provide credit to the small and marginal farmers left out of local systems of power, patronage, and credit. It is noteworthy also that the Congress *Manifesto* for the 1980 elections specifically stressed that 'the planning process' would 'once again' be used 'to reorganise the national economy' and that the state governments would be persuaded to implement national, uniform policies on 'subjects included in the "State List" under the Constitution'.[67]

Despite her attempts to transcend regional issues and forces, however, they remain dominant in Indian society, in the economy, and in electoral politics. Every state in India has a distinctive group of landowning castes who continue to control the countryside. Where the Congress has lost support among such groups, as in north India, it is weak and vulnerable electorally. Such groups remain available to be organized by state-level politicians and regional parties. The interests of these groups also are best served by state governments and district institutions that they can control, by programs designed to satisfy local agricultural needs, and by taxation and price policies that favor the farmers. Linguistic and cultural differences also continue to provide strong support for regional political parties, persistent pressures for cultural pluralism, and demands for regional autonomy in states such as Tamil Nadu, Punjab, and West Bengal. West Bengal and Kerala also have maintained persistently distinctive leftist political traditions that serve to differentiate those states politically from other states and from national political patterns. However, it is not only these four states that are different. In fact, all states are politically distinctive in a more than superficial way on one measure or another.

Moreover, all the states have a common interest in relation to the center in extracting as many resources as possible for their own financial and developmental needs and goals. Had the center followed a consistent policy of either promoting the interests of the advanced or most 'progressive' states or alternatively had it pursued consistently a policy of inter-state equalization with significant redistributive effects, it might have divided the states into supporters and opponents of a strong center with discretionary powers in resource transfers. However, the pursuit of either of these alternative strategies would divide the country and threaten its unity. Since the center cannot or will not follow either strategy consistently and rigorously, the optimal strategy for all the states is simply to demand an increasing share of revenues collected by the center. The main differences among the states are in how strongly they wish to push for such increased shares and in whether or not they prefer to control the entire tax collection process themselves. Clearly, only the better-off states with greater resources than the rest can sensibly prefer the latter strategy. Most of the states, however, can be satisfied indefinitely by tax and resource distribution policies that give them access to a substantial share of centrally collected resources while not requiring them to tax politically sensitive sectors, particularly the prosperous peasantry.

The great dilemma for a centralizing leader or party in India is that stable power at the center can be built up only through control over the states and districts of the country. That kind of power, however, is inherently regional and local in character. Control over the states by the Congress in the Nehru days made it possible for the national leadership to pursue its fancy and attempt through capital-intensive industrialization policies to transform India into a major power with a modern industrial economy. However, in the process, most of the state governments, whose primary political constituencies were the landowning peasantry, became largely patronage-oriented rather than policy-oriented. They were also frequently castigated for failing to implement cherished policies of the national leadership, such as land reform, or for failing to mobilize resources from the agricultural sector to pay for the large-scale industrialization of the country in which they often had little interest.

However, as it became clear in the late 1960s that the Nehru industrialization policy was faltering and that it was failing to solve problems of poverty and employment and to promote equality, that inflation was becoming a major concern in the cities, and that agriculture was being neglected and when Nehru himself passed from the scene, the hold of the Congress over the country, particularly in the north, began to weaken. When the prospect of a Green Revolution also began to materialize, pressures for policies more oriented to the needs of agriculture also began to develop. Since agricultural resource requirements are highly variable and regional and local in nature and since rural power structures are also, by definition, local and regional, the pressure for a shift in economic policy orientations towards agriculture is also pressure in the direction of decentralization of both the economy and politics.

Thus, there is a logic in both the political economy of India and in center-state relations that explains Mrs Gandhi's methods of consolidating power, the social bases of her support and that of opposition forces, and the reasons for her defeat and subsequent return to power. The logic is as follows. Since the states could not be controlled by her when Mrs Gandhi first came to power and since the agricultural constituency is not a national one, Mrs Gandhi broke the power of the state bosses and sought a national constituency to free her to pursue the old policies of her father. However, since the landowning communities remain the principal political and economic forces in the countryside, Mrs Gandhi and the Congress everywhere have had to maintain some support among some of the landed castes as well as the poor and disadvantaged groups in order to win power in the country. Moreover, the destruction of the power of the state bosses has produced less a stable centralization of power than its fragmentation. The stability of few of the states can be counted upon. Consequently, it is ever more necessary for the center to intervene in the state legislatures for the sake of its own power at the center. The decline of the Congress party organization also, of course, has meant its decline as an effective electoral machine. Success in national elections increasingly depends not upon the ability of the party organization to build and maintain alliances and get its supporters to the polls, but on the ability of Mrs Gandhi to form alliances with leaders with influence over widespread voting blocs and on her personal ability to appeal to categories of voters.

Thus, the logic of India's political economy and center-state relations leads to contradictions in the Congress' support base and in Mrs Gandhi's methods of centralizing power. Mrs Gandhi seeks a national constituency, but she cannot free herself from the need for support from the regionally powerful rural landowning castes. She seeks to centralize power, but she continues to be dependent on control over the states, whose instability, which she has herself 'helped to create',[68] must be always watched for fear that the Congress will lose power in the legislature through defection or through an unfavorable electoral outcome.

At the same time, the opposition of the bulk of the middle peasantry, particularly in the north, to Mrs Gandhi and the Congress, provides a persistent base of support for opposition parties. Other bases of support for opposition parties also continue to come from the regionally dominant language, ethnic, and religious communities. Since both types of support are inherently regional and local in character, any opposition to Mrs Gandhi and the Congress at the national level will be an unstable coalition of parties and leaders with largely regional followings. It was such a coalition, whose central core was the north Indian middle peasantry and regional caste groups, supplemented by defections from Mrs Gandhi's support bases amongst the minorities and the poor, that defeated the Congress in 1977. However, that coalition, by its very diversity and lack of any genuine common interests beyond opposition to Mrs Gandhi, was difficult to put together, inherently unstable, and began to fall apart as soon as it was formed. When the coalition split and, at the same time, Mrs Gandhi rebuilt her coalition of minorities and the poor, supplemented by some of the landowning groups, her victory at the national level was assured.

The conclusion is inescapable, therefore, that centralization and consolidation of power in India's federal parliamentary system are bound to be ephemeral unless either authoritarian measures are taken to prevent the inevitable movement of the cycle towards disintegration and fragmentation of power or unless the institutional form of the system is changed to a presidential type. Both options hold great potential dangers for the future stability and integrity of India. The first option, already attempted once, would most likely culminate a second time, if pursued more single-mindedly, in a more violent way. The consequences of exercising the second option are more problematic, especially since there are several possible forms that a presidential pattern itself may take. The adoption of a presidential form that freed the center from dependence on state politics would probably enhance the stability of both. A presidential system of the French pattern, adopted with a view toward centralizing power and control over resources by the center, would probably be resisted strongly in those states with the most distinctive and 'deviant' political traditions, with the most divergent cultural traditions, and with the greatest internal resources, and might therefore ultimately also prove unworkable. Thus, there is no 'solution' to the conflicting drives towards centralization and decentralization in the Indian polity, only alternatives that might moderate or intensify their destabilizing effects. Centralization and authoritarian rule promise ultimately a violent breakdown. Maintaining the present system requires a willingness on the part of state and central political leaders with conflicting goals to tolerate the continuance of the laborious and frustrating cycle of consolidation-disintegration. Adoption of a presidential system of the American type might free the system from the uncertainties and instabilities associated with that cycle, but, if American history is any guide, it will not eliminate the struggles between centralizers and decentralizers which, like party competition itself, must be recognized as a persisting element in any healthy and viable federal republican system of government.[69]

NOTES

*I am indebted to Myron Weiner, James Manor, and John Wood for their careful, detailed criticisms and suggestions for revision of the first draft of this paper. Many of their suggestions have been incorporated into the final draft. I want to thank also Sri Ganesan, Secretary, Election Commission of India, for providing me with provisional figures for the results of the 1980 parliamentary elections. I am solely responsible for all opinions expressed and any errors of fact that remain.

1. Marcus F. Franda, 'Federalising India: Attitudes, Capacities and Constraints,' *South Asian Review*, III, 3 (April 1970), 199–213.
2. W. H. Morris-Jones, *The Government and Politics of India*, 3rd ed. (London: Hutchinson University Library, 1971), 150–6.
3. S. A. H. Haqqi and A. P. Sharma, 'Centre-State Relations: a Study of Structural and Processual Determinants', in K. A. Bombwall (ed.), *National Power and State Autonomy* (Meerut: Meenakshi Prakasan, 1977), 42–7.
4. Morris-Jones, *Government and Politics of India*, 152.
5. Myron Weiner, 'Political Development in the Indian States', in Myron Weiner (ed.), *State Politics in India* (Princeton University Press, 1968), 58.
6. Bhagwan D. Dua, 'Presidential Rule in India: a Study in Crisis Politics', *Asian Survey*, XIX, 6 (June 1979), 626.
7. B. D. Dua, *Presidential Rule in India, 1950–1974: a Study in Crisis Politics* (New Delhi: S. Chand, 1979), 396.
8. M. Venkatarangaiya and M. Shiviah, 'The Working of Indian Federalism', in Bombwall, *National Power and State Autonomy*, 63.
9. K. R. Bombwall, 'National Power and State Autonomy: A Note on the Socio-Political Dynamics of Indian Federalism', in ibid., 211.
10. By pluralism, I mean a system that contains a multiplicity of social, cultural, economic, and political groups and that does not permit the imposition of the ideas, values, culture, or language of a single group to be imposed upon the others. By regionalism, in the political sense, I mean patterns of politics in the states that are best explained primarily in terms of conflicts and issues that arise within the states rather than in the national political arena and that deviate in easily discernible ways, such as in political party formations and voting patterns, from national trends. By decentralization, I refer to a process in which economic resources are controlled and spent locally, however they are collected, in which the important decisions affecting economic and political life in a federal system are made by political leaders at the state level, in which power is built from the bottom up, and in which power at the federal or central level depends upon the support of state political forces rather than the reverse. The argument of this paper is not that India is a full-fledged pluralist, regionalist, and decentralized system but that tendencies and forces moving the country towards pluralism, regionalism, and decentralization are inherently stronger than those favoring homogeneity, nationalization, and centralization.
11. Cf. Rajni Kothari, who argued in 'Delivering the Goods', *Seminar*, 242

(October 1979), 12–17, that the Indian political system was in crisis, but that 'no centralized solution can work in solving the basic crisis in the system.'

12. The policy and institutional areas selected for discussion in this paper were chosen partly on the basis of my own expertise, partly on the consideration of availability of information, and partly because of their evident importance for center-state relations. Obviously, many other institutions and policy areas might have been selected, perhaps with different results. For example, in a personal communication, Myron Weiner has suggested that centralizing tendencies are more evident in 'the policy services and [in] the use of paramilitary institutions' and that particular ministries such as Home have 'more control' than earlier. A complete account of the current balance in and future prospects for center-state relations clearly would have to cover such areas, in addition to those discussed below.
13. Selig S. Harrison, *India: The Most Dangerous Decades* (Princeton University Press, 1960).
14. Ibid., 305.
15. See esp. Paul R. Brass, *Language, Religion, and Politics in North India* (New York: Cambridge University Press, 1974), Jyotirindra Das Gupta, *Language Conflict and National Development: Group Politics and National Language Policy in India* (Berkeley: University of California Press, 1970), and T. N. Madan, 'Linguistic Diversity and National Unity? Dimensions of a Debate', reprint from *Reflections on Economic Development and Social Change: Essays in Honour of Professor V. K. R. V. Rao*, 393–410 (no other publication details).
16. Sudhakar Dwivedi, 'Official Language Policy of the Union', in Government of India, Ministry of Home Affairs, Department of Official Language, *All India Official Languages Conference Souvenir* (New Delhi, 1978), 11–12 and 21.
17. A. P. Kamat, 'Ethno-Linguistic Issues in Indian Federal Context', *Economic and Political Weekly*, XV, 24 & 25 (14–21 June 1980), 1063.
18. Government of India, Union Public Service Commission, *Civil Services Examination: Report of the Committee on Recruitment Policy and Selection Methods* (New Delhi: Government of India Press, 1976), 19–21.
19. Brass, *Language, Religion, and Politics*.
20. See, for example, Government of India, Ministry of Home Affairs, *The Sixteenth Report of the Commissioner for Linguistic Minorities in India* (for the period July 1973–June 1974) (Delhi: Controller of Publications, 1976), 143 ff.
21. V. O. Key, Jr., *American State Politics: An Introduction* (New York: Knopf, 1956), 7.
22. Ibid., 8.
23. Government of India, Ministry of Planning, Department of Statistics, Central Statistical Organisation, *Monthly Abstract of Statistics, December, 1978*, XXI, 12, 3.
24. S. Venu, *The Finance Commissions of India* (Madras: Institute for Financial Management and Research, 1978), 104–5.
25. B. S. Grewal, *Centre-State Financial Relations in India* (Patiala: Punjabi

University, 1975), 85–6.

26. Birla Institute of Scientific Research, *Centre-State Financial Relations in India* (New Delhi: Abhinav, 1979), 127.
27. Government of India, *Report of the Finance Commission*, 1973 (Delhi: Controller of Publications, 1973), 8.
28. Birla Institute, *Centre-State Financial Relations*, 21.
29. Grewal, *Centre-State Financial Relations*, 104–8.
30. Ibid., pp. 129–30.
31. Venu, *The Finance Commissions*, 119.
32. Grewal, *Centre-State Financial Relations*, 55–61 and H. K. Paranjpe, 'Centre-State Relations in Planning', in S. N. Jain, *et al.*, *The Union and the States* (Delhi: National, 1972), 218.
33. Government of India, Planning Commission, *Draft Five Year Plan, 1978–83* (Delhi: Controller of Publications, 1978), 110.
34. *Asian Recorder*, 1979, 14816.
35. Venu, *The Finance Commissions*, 76–7.
36. Ibid., 110–11.
37. India, *Report of the Finance Commission*, 1973, 7.
38. V. K. Subramaniam, *The Indian Financial System* (New Delhi: Abhinav, 1979), 163.
39. S. Venu, *The Seventh Finance Commission's Report: A Critique* (Madras: Institute for Financial Management and Research, 1979), 14.
40. Birla Institute, *Centre-State Financial Relations*, 5.
41. Paranjpe, 'Centre-State Relations in Planning', 212.
42. Ibid., 216 and 234–5 and Grewal, *Centre-State Financial Relations*, 61.
43. Paranjpe, 'Centre-State Relations in Planning', 222 and 235.
44. R. K. Sinha, *Fiscal Federalism in India* (Madras: South Asian Publishers, 1980), 91.
45. B. M., 'Arithmetic is All', *Economic and Political Weekly*, XV, 52 (27 December 1980), 2169.
46. See esp. James Manor, 'Indira and After: The Decay of Party Organisation in India', *Round Table*, 272 (October 1978), 315–24.
47. It may help to interpret the significance of the increased dispersion of the Congress vote by comparing it with similar figures for the United States. In the United States, it is generally agreed that nationalizing tendencies have been at work since the end of the Second World War that have resulted in an increasingly even spread of the vote for president and increasing competitiveness in the fifty states in contrast to pre-Second World War patterns when sectionalism was greater. In pre-Second World War elections, some states would be carried by a presidential candidate by large margins while others would be lost by similarly large margins. The standard deviation for the votes by state for the successful presidential candidate between 1896 and 1944 ranged between a high of 17.5 in the former year to a low of 12.3 in the latter year. From 1948 to 1976 in contrast, the range has been between 5.8 in 1960 and 10.3 in 1964. Thus, the dispersion of the Congress vote in India since 1971 has been more in conformity with pre-World War II patterns of presidential voting, whereas the pre-1971 standard deviations were similar to post-

World War II American patterns. See Frank J. Sorauf, *Party Politics in America*, 4th edn (Boston: Little, Brown, 1972), 53.

48. Myron Weiner, *India at the Polls: The Parliamentary Elections of 1977* (Washington, D.C.: American Enterprise Institute, 1978), 97.
49. The parties are: Bharatiya Jan Sangh, Bharatiya Lok Dal, Bolshevik Party, Communist Party of India, Communist Party of India (Marxist), Forward Bloc (M), Forward Bloc (R), Hindu Mahasabha, Indian National Congress, Indian National Congress (0), Indian National Congress (U), Janata, Janata (S), Kisan Mazdur Praja Party, Krishikar-Lok Party, Praja Socialist Party, Ram Rajya Parishad, Republican Party of India, Revolutionary Communist Party, Samyukta Socialist Party, Socialist Party, and Swatantra.
50. The discussion in the above paragraph is based upon the statistical spread of the vote for the so-called 'national' non-Congress parties. There is, of course, a deeper question that requires a different kind of analysis, namely, whether or not the 'national' parties that exist in more than one state share much beyond a common name and a national executive committee. It can be argued that the Congress itself is a 'national' party only in limited respects. James Manor has remarked that 'the Congress organizations' in states he analyzed during the 1977 elections — Maharashtra, Gujarat, Karnataka, Andhra Pradesh, and Kerala — 'could be regarded primarily as regional parties alongside the regional parties ruling in Tamil Nadu, Kashmir, and West Bengal.' See his 'Where Congress Survived: Five States in the Indian General Election of 1977', *Asian Survey*, XVIII, 8 (August 1978), 803. Manor's argument is based partly on differences in the support bases of the Congress in these states and partly on the limited effectiveness of the central leadership in controlling the Congress governments and Congress organizations in them even during the Emergency.
51. The index is constructed on a scale of 0–1, with values closest to 1 representing the greatest fragmentation. See Douglas Rae, *The Political Consequences of Electoral Laws* (New Haven: Yale University Press, 1967), 53–8.
52. Compare the figure in Key, *American State Politics*, 27, which uses the states of Vermont and Florida to show an opposite trend of 'erosion of sectionalism' in the United States between 1896 and 1952.
53. The facts and figures in this paragraph come from Dua, 'Presidential Rule in India'; Shriram Maheshwari, *President's Rule in India* (Columbia, Mo.: South Asia Books, 1977), 166 ff.; and the *Asian Recorder*.
54. Dua, 'Presidential Rule in India', 614.
55. I owe this point to a personal communication from Myron Weiner.
56. Although the state assembly elections have been 'nationalized' in the sense that their timing has now come to depend upon the outcome of the Lok Sabha elections and struggles for power at the center, the actual results in the several states do not in fact show as close a correlation with the nearest Lok Sabha election as when the elections at the two levels were linked, as indicated in the text above.
57. See Manor, 'Indira and After', and James Manor, 'Party Decay and Political Crisis in India,' *The Washington Quarterly* (Summer 1981), 27–9.

Manor argues in the latter article that Mrs Gandhi's efforts to centralize power in her own hands have not only hastened 'the demise of the Congress machine' (p. 27), but have 'increased rather than reduced the disparities between national and lower levels' and have deprived 'the national level of reliable information from below' (p. 32). Another factor, therefore, in the decreased effective control by the center over state politics is lack of information about what is actually happening in the regions and localities and about the strength and reliability of local leaders and groups.

58. Dua, *Presidential Rule in India*, v, 1, 4, 21–2.
59. Dua, op. cit., pp. 612, 615–19, 622–6.
60. Maheshwari, *President's Rule*, 173.
61. Ibid., 174.
62 See also Manor, 'Where Congress Survived', 800, where he argues that Mrs Gandhi's 'centralizing efforts did not produce tighter integration of the national organization of the Congress.'
63. Parliament played no role in the selection process under Nehru either, as James Manor points out in a personal communication. In fact, the only occasion on which Parliament played a role at this stage was during the second selection of Mrs Gandhi in her contest with Morarji Desai after the 1967 elections. Cultivation of support in Parliament was also critical for the maintenance of Mrs Gandhi in power from 1967 to 1971 and in the defeat of Morarji Desai and the selection of Charan Singh in 1979. However, the second stage referred to in the text concerns the period just after an election.
64. I believe control of district political and economic resources remains very important, but the old Congress system which involved constant struggle among groups at the state level for control over a majority of districts, which then provided the victors with the chance to take power at the state level in the party and in the government, is gone, at least in the north Indian states.
65. In a personal communication, Myron Weiner has suggested that the central cabinet also is a weaker institution than it was under Nehru and that central co-ordination of programs is less effective than formerly.
66. Manor, 'Where Congress Survived', 802.
67. Indian National Congress (I), *Election Manifesto, 1980* (New Delhi: All India Congress Committee (I), 1979).
68. I owe this formulation to a personal communication from Myron Weiner.
69. It is not being suggested here that Mrs Gandhi would be inclined to approve the adoption of an American type of presidential system. If anything, it is more likely that, given a choice between the American and French types, she would prefer the latter. However, my points in this paragraph do not relate to the personal preferences of contemporary leaders but only to the possible consequences of the adoption of different types of systems.

THE FUTURE OF BANGLADESH

Talukder Maniruzzaman

It is easy to predict a dismal future for Bangladesh. A mere enumeration of its demographic characteristics suggests a bleak prospect for this new state: occupying only 55,598 square miles, it has a population of over 84 million, the world's eighth largest. With 1,511 people per square mile and 2,297 per arable square mile,[1] it is also the world's most densely populated country. Already the country is as crowded as the United States of America would be if that continental country contained all the people on earth. Yet, while the population growth rate of the United States remains close to zero, the population of Bangladesh continues to grow at a rate of about 3 per cent a year. At this rate, it will double in twenty-three years, its density rising to some 3,000 people per square mile.

About 80 per cent of the people of Bangladesh are illiterate. Nearly 75 per cent of them live below the poverty line, with annual *per capita* income at around U.S.$90. Agriculture produces nearly 54 per cent of the gross domestic product (G.D.P.) while providing 77 per cent of the jobs. But because primitive methods prevail in agriculture, yield per acre is very low,[2] although Bangladesh has among the world's finest soils. The annual shortage of foodgrains runs between 1.8 and 2.3 million tons. Organised industry contributed only 10.4 per cent to the G.D.P. and employs only 1.8 per cent of the total labour force. With almost no mineral resources, Bangladesh depends mainly on the export of jute and jute goods for its foreign earnings, and both face sharp competition from Indian jute and synthetic fibres. The annual trade deficit runs to about US$500 million, which must be supplied by foreign aid. Bangladesh also depends on outside sources for almost 75 per cent of its development funds.

Back during the Liberation War in 1971 many outsiders doubted that Bangladesh could become economically viable. Robert Dorfman of Harvard said that 'from an economic point of view East Pakistan is simply a mistake.'[3] Professor Kenneth Galbraith called Bangladesh an 'international basket case',[4] and many others called it a 'permanent disaster'. This line of reasoning could lead to but one conclusion: namely, that Bangladesh must collapse under the weight of its intractable economic problems, failing to survive as an independent sovereign state.

While Bangladesh faces formidable economic and political problems, they are not beyond solution. South Korea at the start, for example, had even less resources than Bangladesh. Nevertheless, South Korea has made extraordinary progress in social and economic fields since the 1950s,[5] and hence Bangladesh need not be written off because of its unfavourable demographic and economic situation.

In fact, Bangladesh started with certain advantages which many of the new nations acutely lack. First, culturally and linguistically, Bangladesh is the most homogeneous of the states of South Asia. India, Pakistan and Sri Lanka are all culturally diverse, and have respectively thirteen, four and two language groups.[6] Almost the whole population of Bangladesh speak a single common language — Bengali. Secondly, Bangladesh inherited a social structure without any sharp economic cleavage. With the partition of the former united Bengal in 1947, East Bengal's landlords, most of whom were Hindus, migrated to Calcutta where they already had homes. Thus Bangladesh (then East Pakistan) was able easily to rid itself of feudalism by the early 1950s. Bangladesh also dispensed with its capitalist class. West Pakistan's non-Bengali capitalists who had set up industries in Bangladesh abandoned their enterprises, fleeing to Pakistan just before Bangladesh emerged in 1971. Bangladesh could therefore start its social engineering without being hindered by powerful vested interests.

The political problems of Third World countries stem largely from one fact. These countries achieved statehood before they had become integrated nations. The 'identity crisis' is a recurring theme in the current literature on developing nations. Thus the third important advantage with which Bangladesh began was the strong sense of nationalism that Bangladeshis had developed by the time the new state was founded.

Indeed, one of the assertions of this essay is that the one strong element that ensures the survival of Bangladesh as a consolidated entity is the congruence between Bangladesh nationalism and the Bangladesh state. As with nationalisms in most countries, Bangladesh nationalism developed in its own unique way, and the social evolution of the nationalist movement in Bangladesh will determine how social and economic cleavages in this state can be resolved. Evolving Bangladesh nationalism conditioned Bangladeshis to particular patterns of political behavior and political attitudes. These behaviour patterns and orientations will persist and continue to affect the politics of Bangladesh at least in the foreseeable future. A discussion of the growth and scope of Bangladesh nationalism is, therefore, called for.

National identity of Bangladesh:[7] historical manifestations

To be sure, Bangladeshis as a linguistic group differ from others in the sub-continent. They, however, share a common language and have territorial propinquity with the people of the Indian state of West Bengal. The question of Bangladesh nationalism thus boils down to how fundamental the differences between Bangladeshis and West Bengalis are. Will geographical contiguity and linguistic similarity between Bangladesh and West Bengal erode the force of Bangladesh nationalism? Can an over-arching Bengali nationalism emerge, embracing Bangladesh and West Bengal? The 'syndrome of unique historical factors' clearly suggests a negative answer.

From the beginning of their recorded history in the early sixth century A.D., the peoples of the two areas roughly corresponding to Bangladesh and West Bengal maintained separate identities even when sharing common rulers and a common name. For nearly six centuries the two areas took different names — Bangladesh areas being usually called *Vanga* and the West Bengal region *Gauda*. Culturally, the two ancient Bengals differed fundamentally. The *Gauda* came early under Aryan colonisation and Aryan culture; but the Aryan influence could hardly penetrate the Mongoloid, Buddhist inhabitants of *Vanga*.[0] Politically, the *Vangas* valued independence, resisted foreign invasion and showed evidence of extreme individualism. The *Gaudas*, on the other hand, easily succumbed to foreign invasion and provided the least resistance to imperial powers; they lacked any markedly individualistic orientation.[9]

Beginning in 1204, the two Bengals continued to diverge for more than 500 years because of Muslim rule. Always fearful of being swamped by 'the Aryans and half-caste Aryans', the people of East Bengal rediscovered their own identity through their mass conversion to Islam.[10] This swift change of religion of the people of '*Bangala*'[11] helped to perpetuate differences between the two Bengals. In accepting Islam, however, the Bangalis kept their basic political character. The resistance of the *Bara Bhuiyan* (Twelve Landlords)[12] to Mughal supremacy offered one of many examples of '*Bangali*' nationalism. The people of East Bengal also rebelled against British rule. Serious peasant revolts took place in various parts of East Bengal in the late eighteenth and nineteenth centuries.[13] The West Bengal people, on the other hand, had for long accepted British rule without much demur.

The British government recognised, for the first time, the separate identities of East and West Bengal when Lord Curzon, for administrative as well as political reasons, partitioned Bengal in 1905[14] roughly along the historically evolved line of demarcation between *Vanga* and *Gauda*. Although this partition was voided in 1911 on pressure from the caste Hindus of Calcutta, East Bengal leaders like A. K. Fazlul Huq, Khwaja Nazimuddin, H. S. Suhrawardy and their kind, taking advantage of constitutional political practices introduced under British rule in the first half of the twentieth century ensured that East Bengal

Muslims would obtain their due. Indeed, these three leaders successfully established Muslim-dominated governments in Calcutta, enacted legislation and adopted other measures to promote the interests of the East Bengal Muslims, all at the expense of the vested interests of the Bengal caste Hindus.[15] Fearing continued domination by East Bengal's Muslim majority, the caste Hindus forced Bengal's partition in 1947.[16] Again, division took place roughly along the historically demarcated line — *Vanga-Gauda.*

The growth of Bangladesh nationalism

During the 1940s the Muslims of Bengal formed alliances with Muslims of other Indian provinces with two main purposes in view. First, they feared that on the eve of Independence the British might, under caste Hindu pressure, sacrifice Muslim interests as they had done in 1912 when they ended the partition of Bengal effected in 1905. Secondly, they felt that neither in organization nor resources could they match on their own the caste Hindus and their powerfull ally, the All-India National Congress. As a result Bengal's Muslims failed to win for themselves an independent state in Bengal. And the consequences of joining the newly-created state of Pakistan proved disastrous. The power-structure that evolved in Pakistan left the East Bengalis far removed from the seats of power, where decisions were made. Their ancient pursuit of freedom proved illusory since they failed to become masters of their own destiny.

But West Pakistan's ruling élite with its own colonial ways soon rekindled its defiance and propensity to resist alien rule. The people of East Bengal quickly reasserted their distinct national identity. In rapid succession came the language movement, the 1954 elections, the anti-Ayub movement of 1962, the Six-Point movement of 1966, the mass upheaval of 1969, and the 1970 elections.[18] Finally came the People's Liberation War of 1971.[19] In that war, Bangladesh made supreme sacrifices in blood and gold. About 1,500,000 people died, and property worth millions of Taka was destroyed.[20] Yet Bangladesh nationalism in its highest form was realised. The war created a nation of gallant people who had won independence in the teeth of a brutal Pakistani army. That historical struggle could be the strongest force to ensure Bangladesh's continuation as a separate sovereign state. The revolution created heroes, myths, and visions of a golden Bengal. Pride in that struggle could sustain the nation as it tries to realise that vision.[21]

Peripheral problems in Bangladesh nationhood

Bangladesh has its integration problems one of which is communal tension. Distrust pervades relations between Muslims, the vast majority of the population, and Hindus, the nation's largest minority.[22] This distrust could be a dysfunctional role in the nation-building process. Even though Hindu-Muslim riots have not recurred since Bangladesh's founding, caste Hindus who constitute around half the Hindu population are all suspect in the eyes of most Muslims. Muslims feel that caste Hindus are more loyal to India than to Bangladesh. This age-old conflict between Bengali Hindus and Muslims is not likely to die out quickly. To some extent the antagonisms are mitigated by the slow but constant migration of Hindus to India. According to the 1951 Census, they constituted 22.0 per cent of the population;[23] the 1961 Census showed 18.4,[24] but by 1974 the percentage was down to 13.73.[25] Many caste Hindus are elderly; having already sent their younger relatives to India, they stay in Bangladesh only to sell off their remaining properties. With their departure the number will decline sharply.

There is yet another factor which might relieve the communal problem. Muslims get along better with Scheduled Caste Hindus. The two groups often joined forces during British rule to fight caste Hindu 'domination' in Bengal; and these political ties still persist. Accordingly, as the caste Hindus continue to leave or die off, Hindu-Muslim relations are likely to improve.

The armed dissent by some of the tribal people in the peripheral district of Chittagong Hill Tracts seems at the present to be more disruptive of the state fabric than the subtle psychological dissonance between the Muslim and Hindus. Numbering only about 389,010 (0.5 per cent of the total Bangladesh population), this tribal people inhabits a hilly, sylvan territory covering about 9 per cent of the total area of Bangladesh.[26] The British governed these tribal people under special rules and administrative arrangements codified in the Hill Tracts Regulation of 1900.

After the emergence of Bangladesh, the Government of Sheikh Mujibur Rahman (Sheikh Mujib) abolished the Hill Tracts Regulation and extended the legal system of the deltaic region to the Hill Tracts District. Antagonised by this action, the tribal people organised against the Dacca Government. As a first step, they formed the Pahari Sanghati Party (Party for the Solidarity of the Hills people); next they formed a military front named the Santi Bahini (Peace Corps).[27] Mostly educated and young, the Santi Bahini members procured arms from Indian Mizo and Naga rebels and from Burmese Communist groups. They are now engaged in an all-out guerrilla war against

Bangladesh security forces in the area. Of the political forces in Bangladesh, only a faction of the East Bengal Sarbohara Party, one of Bangladesh's many Communist groups, has lent total support to Santi Bahini.

For its part, the Government of President Ziaur Rahman (Zia) rejected the Santi Bahini demand for a separate state. However, it tried to win over the Hill Tracts people by accelerating the process of economic development in their areas and by reserving seats for tribal students in universities and other educational institutions. At the same time the Government of Zia expanded and modernised the three cantonments which Sheikh Mujib had established in the area and reinforced the Army and police fighting the Santi Bahini guerrillas. The Government also encouraged the people of the overcrowded centre of Bangladesh to move in to the Hill Tracts areas, granting them both land and agricultural inputs. Already over 100,000 people from the plains have settled in the region. There were further plans to settle an additional 500,000 people so that they could act as a countervailing force against the tribal people.

But Santi Bahini insurgence has an international dimension. Out to destabilise regimes they disapprove of in Bangladesh, the Chinese and Indian Governments have on occasion lent support to the tribal rebels. If the Bangladesh Government succeeds in preventing foreign powers from meddling in the turmoil, the tribal insurrection could be contained. Only a small portion of the tribal people are involved in insurrectionary activity and of the Santi Bahini about 80 per cent come from one tribe, the Chakmas. Most members of the other twelve major tribes are loyal to Bangladesh. The terrain no doubt favours guerrilla war. But without far greater support from the tribal peoples, the Santi Bahini will be unable to counter Bangladesh armed pressure.

Economic disparity between Northwestern and Eastern Bangladesh

A major factor in East Pakistan's drive for greater autonomy and then for secession was the growing economic disadvantage it suffered at the hands of West Pakistan. Yet now in Bangladesh much the same kind of disparity is developing between its Northwestern Division (Rajshahi and Khulna, with 44 per cent of the total population) and the Eastern Division (Dacca and Chittagong, containing 56 per cent of the people). Since infrastructural growth in the former East Pakistan had to begin in Dacca, its provincial capital, and in Chittagong, its major port, any industry that developed centred around these two urban areas. The Northwest remained comparatively underdeveloped. By 1969, 75 per cent of East Pakistan's registered factories were located in the Eastern region, with 80 per cent or more of its industrial production coming from the same region.[28]

After Independence, the people of Northwest Bangladesh gradually became conscious of this disparity as well as of their under-representation in the private sector and in governmental and semi-governmental institutions. A Committee for the Removal of Disparity between the Northern and Eastern Regions recommended an end to these inequities.[29]

Nevertheless, the lopsided development continues as a result of the development strategy governments have pursued since Sheikh Mujib's overthrow in August 1975. Discarding Mujibist socialist pretensions and following the Pakistan model of development during the Ayub Khan phase, the Zia Government adopted the policy of development through state-sponsored capitalists. Sheikh Mujib placed a ceiling of Taka 30 million on private investment. Zia raised this ceiling to Taka 100 million, while also providing added incentives. Once the National Economic Council (N.E.C.) headed by Zia approved their projects, entrepreneurs went to government-established financial institutions like Bangladesh Shilpa Bank (Bangladesh Industrial Bank) and Bangladesh Shilpa Rin Sangstha (Bangladesh Industrial Credit Corporation) for 60 to 70 per cent of their investment outlays.[30] Nor were these easy loans the only incentive. Entrepreneurs obtained tax holidays for new industries, foreign exchange at subsidised rates, reduced import duty on capital machinery, and more. To attract foreign investment, the Government guaranteed non-nationalisation, tax holidays and permission to remit net profits to investors.

It is nevertheless true that the Government also offered incentives for establishing industries in less developed areas. These included a nine-year tax holiday as against seven years in developed areas, a 25 per cent rebate on import duty on capital machinery as against 20 per cent in advanced regions, electric power at cheaper rates, a 75 per cent discount of service charges by financial institutions, and so on.[31] The Government also established special development boards to speed development in backward areas.

But these efforts to arrest uneven growth are unlikely to succeed. Such incentives can scarcely match what Eastern Bangladesh offers: nearness to the seat of government, an existing industrial base, better communications and a better transport system. The regional breakdown of loans sanctioned by Bangladesh Shilpa Bank (B.S.B.) and Bangladesh Shilpa Rin Sangstha (B.S.R.S.) is enough to indicate the superior appeal of Eastern Bangladesh to investors. From 1972/3 to 1977/8, B.S.B. sanctioned loans totalling 1,027.91 million Taka. Of these, only 194.65 million Taka (18.93 per cent) went to industrial projects in the Northwest as against 833.26 million Taka (81.07 per cent) to those in Eastern Bangladesh.[32] Similarly, of the 1115.13

million Taka which B.S.R.S. loaned out from 1974 to 1978, only 459.26 million Taka went to Northwestern projects. Those in Eastern Bangladesh got the rest.[33]

Does this mean that Bangladesh will repeat the history of Pakistan? Will this uneven development foster regional hostilities threatening a unified Bangladesh? This is unlikely. Bangladesh's unity is protected in a number of ways. One is geographical contiguity, and another is the unlikelihood of Eastern Bangladesh permanently dominating Northwestern Bangladesh.[34] Besides, there are linguistic and cultural identities, a common history of many centuries, inter-regional mobility of labour, and the multiplier effects of one region's economic development on the other. These conditions could act to keep any latent regional hostility under control. For that matter, a resulting low-tension level of conflict between Northwestern and Eastern Bangladesh might even prove functional. It could encourage the two regions to enter into a healthy competition to outperform each other.

Social revolution: the wave of the future?

Although Bangladesh does not have big landowning and industrial classes, inequalities and cleavages nevertheless exist. At the horizontal level there is the cleavage between urban and rural areas, and at the vertical level between economic classes. The nature of these cleavages and the probability that they could sharpen political competition in the future are problems that need examination.

Bangladesh is predominantly rural. About 91 per cent of its people live in rural areas, and 77 per cent of them depend on agriculture. Since land is the chief means of production in rural areas, inequalities stem primarily from skewed distribution of landownership. Table 1 shows the distribution of landownership other than homestead land in rural Bangladesh.

Because of Bangladesh's huge farming population, farm properties are typically small. But as Table 1 shows ownership is also highly concentrated. The middle and large farmers constitute less than 15 per cent of the people but own almost 51 per cent of the land. Table 1 also shows that the small farmers who form about 15 per cent of the rural population own 24 per cent of land. In Bangladesh, holdings of 2.5 acres each are usually regarded as economically viable units. Thus, as Table 1 also shows, more than 29 per cent of rural people own holdings which are not economically viable. Since a holding of less than ½ acre is much smaller than a viable holding, 13.82 per cent of the rural population, owning holdings of below 0.50 acre each, are virtually landless. This last group of people can thus be categorised as landless along with the 27.10 per cent landless people who own no land other than home-

Table 1
SIZE DISTRIBUTION OF LAND OWNED OTHER THAN HOMESTEAD LAND IN RURAL BANGLADESH

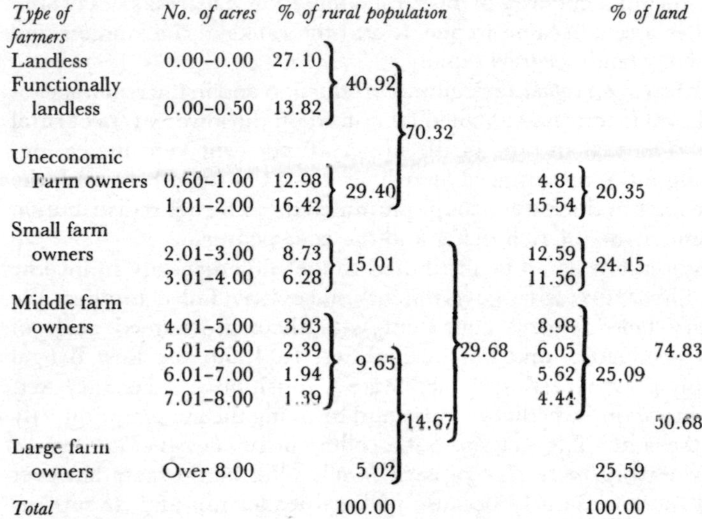

Type of farmers	*No. of acres*	*% of rural population*				*% of land*		
Landless	0.00–0.00	27.10	40.92	70.32				
Functionally landless	0.00–0.50	13.82						
Uneconomic Farm owners	0.60–1.00	12.98	29.40			4.81	20.35	
	1.01–2.00	16.42				15.54		
Small farm owners	2.01–3.00	8.73	15.01		29.68	12.59	24.15	74.83
	3.01–4.00	6.28				11.56		
Middle farm owners	4.01–5.00	3.93	9.65	14.67		8.98	25.09	50.68
	5.01–6.00	2.39				6.05		
	6.01–7.00	1.94				5.62		
	7.01–8.00	1.39				4.44		
Large farm owners	Over 8.00		5.02				25.59	
Total			100.00				100.00	

Source: Derived from Table DII ('Size Distribution of Land Owned other than Homestead Land in Rural Bangladesh') and Table DIII ('Landlessness in Rural Bangladesh') in F. Tomasson Jannuzi and James T. Peach, *Report on the Hierarchy of Interests in Land in Bangladesh, based on the 1977 Land Occupancy Survey of Rural Bangladesh* (Washington, D.C., U.S. Agency for International Development, September 1977), xxi, xxii.

stead land. Thus about 41 per cent of rural people in Bangladesh are functionally landless.

The percentage of landless people (owning no land excepting homestead land) in rural Bangladesh has risen rapidly since the 1950s. According to Census Reports, the figure stood at 14.4 per cent in 1951; by 1961 it was 18.9, and in 1974 24.9.[35] In 1977, the percentage was as high as 27.10.[36]

There are many factors which contribute to this increase in landlessness. Demographic conditions, the sluggish growth of the economy's non-agricultural sector and a population growth of 2–3 per cent per annum diminish the availability of land. Rural unemployment increased and *per capita* agricultural production declined. As a result the real wages of agricultural labour fell. And the situation was further compounded by the dislocations caused by the Independence struggle and the new Government's administrative inexperience. By 1975 real agricultural wages were the lowest since 1949. In rural Bangladesh, the landless and functionally landless people as well as farmers with uneconomic holdings depend on some kind of employment. These groups constitute 70 per cent of the rural population (see Table 1). As a consequence the decline in the real wage of agricultural labour affected the incomes of a majority of the rural population. Distress sales of land and other assets became frequent, and the ranks of the landless and functionally landless grew rapidly.[37]

The drop in *per capita* agricultural production and in the real wages of agricultural labour had an unequal impact on the lower strata of rural society. The real income of the upper 20 per cent kept increasing, becoming more pronounced after liberation. On the other hand, the real incomes of the lower groups plummeted.[38] The net redistribution of income made the rich richer and the poor poorer.

Many reasons could be attributed to the wide disparity in income levels. First, successive governments since 1947 failed to effect the necessary land reforms consistent with their proclaimed goals of greater production and less inequalities. In 1950, the East Bengal Assembly passed the East Bengal State Acquisition and Tenancy Act, abolishing all intermediary tenure and bringing the cultivator directly under the state. The Act also put a ceiling of 100 *bighas* (33 acres) on land ownership in respect of each family. Big landowners however evaded the law, largely because political leadership and its support bases were mainly from the landed classes. In 1961, the Ayub Khan regime blatantly raised the ceiling to 375 *bighas* (125 acres) per family 'on the plea of giving succour to the middle classes'.[39]

Through its Bangladesh Landholding (Limitation) Order, 1972, Sheikh Mujib's Government reimposed the ceiling of 100 *bighas* (33 acres) per family. This ceiling was high to begin with, for the average farm holding was only 2.6 acres. But even with this high ceiling, the Government came under pressure from large landowners; it amended the Presidential Order and relaxed the definition of family. Thereafter, the Government kept changing the dates for the submission of returns for excess lands, thereby providing an opportunity for such landholders to transfer proprietary rights in respect of parts of their lands to their near relations. No effort was made to ensure the accuracy of statements regarding land holdings. Hence by January 1975, the state had acquired only 20,317 of the expected 300,000 to 400,000 acres.[40] As Jannuzi and Peace reported, 'the current ceiling on the size of holdings is not strictly enforced and . . . many thousands of acres of land are retained illegally by owners.'[41] Even the acquired lands were improperly redistributed.[42]

The Zia government too was slow in introducing land reforms until late 1979 when it considered dropping the ceiling on landholdings to 50 *bighas* (about 17 acres), giving occupancy rights to share croppers and banning the sale and transfer of agricultural land to private individuals. Many members of parliament who either belonged to the landed class or had connections with it resisted the proposed reforms.[43] As a consequence, economic cleavages were perpetuated. At the same time successive governments widened the inequities by following strategies of agricultural growth which aimed at achieving a capitalist revolution by transforming the rich peasants into modern agricultural entrepreneurs. Governments provided easy loans from specially-created credit institutions, machinery for mechanising cultivation and modern seed-fertiliser irrigation technology at subsidized rates. Even by 1979 Bangladesh agriculture had still not achieved its capitalist breakthrough despite the fact that the 'green revolution' had begun in the 1960s. Only 11 per cent of the nation's cultivated land was under modern irrigation, and 0.45 per cent under mechanised cultivation.[44]

The attempted transformation of rich peasants into agricultural capitalists failed for two reasons. The state apparatus failed to educate the peasants in the use of new technology; the state was also not prompt in meeting the demand for improved machinery and other inputs. But of greater relevance were the impediments and constraints inherent in the nation's rural economic and social structures. The fragmented and dispersed nature of 90 per cent of landholdings, rural society's propensity towards horizontal expansion of land-possessions rather than intensive cropping, the profitability of land as a source for rentier income, higher and less uncertain earnings from distributory, usurious and speculative activities as opposed to investment in agriculture impeded fundamental changes in the mode of production in Bangladesh agriculture.[45]

As with all semi-planned and truncated processes of modernisation, the government's strategy in the area of agriculture brought only distorted growth. With government loans restricted to farmers owning 3 acres or more, only the upper landed class derived maximum benefit from government credit institutions. Again, rich peasants dominated the co-operatives formed for efficient use of mechanised irrigational facilities and other inputs. Thus the seed-fertiliser-irrigation technology could be fully introduced in only 7 to 8 per cent of cultivable land, and then only for the further enrichment of the already prosperous farmers. The partial application of the new technology was a little more popular among the peasants. For example, chemical fertilisers could be used in 14 per cent of tilled land. Yet once again, despite the subsidies only the surplus farmers[46] could individually afford their use. Occasional favourable terms of trade for agriculture and price-guarantee measures by the government for agricultural products also enhanced the profits of surplus farmers. Even so, the government developed no mechanism to mobilise the economic surplus of the rural rich.

Moreover, the same rich men stifled an attempt in 1973 to introduce a progressive agricultural income tax.[47]

Failing to become rural capitalists, the surplus farmers used their added resources to exploit the landless and poor peasants. Devices they used included hoarding foodgrains during crop seasons, selling them in times of scarcity, black-marketing agricultural inputs and relief goods (as members of co-operative societies and local bodies), lending money at usurious rates, and taking advantage of distress sales of property. Increasing inflationary pressures on the economy after 1972, mainly due to a general rise in prices in the international market, further worsened the plight of the lower-income rural groups.

Thus, the resulting pauperisation led to 'an unprecedented concentration of extreme poverty' in rural Bangladesh. According to one estimate, back in 1963/4, about 40 per cent of the rural population lived below the absolute poverty line. By 1974/5, the percentage had risen to 62 per cent. About 5 per cent of rural people were below the extreme poverty line in 1963/4, but the percentage had risen to 40 by 1974/5.[48]

Do these deepening antagonisms between peasantry, surplus farmers and the many impoverished semi-landless and landless people presage a social revolution in Bangladesh? Mao Tse-tung's successful revolution in the world's largest peasant society had many practitioners and students of social revolution to argue that the future of other states with peasant economies lay in their countrysides, not in their cities. The Chinese became the model for Eastern revolutions. Unlike Western revolutions, which are city-based and dominated by the urban proletariat, Eastern revolutions begin from rural bases, spread out over the countryside recruiting to the ranks poor peasants in ever-increasing numbers, and finally encompassing and overwhelming the cities.[49] Many have insisted that only with radical land reforms, which can create many new owner-cultivators, could other Asian states prevent Chinese-style revolutions.[50]

We have already seen how superficial were the attempts at land reform in Bangladesh, with ceilings of 33 acres on landholdings in contrast to the 7.5 acres in the more advanced and technologically-oriented societies of Japan and Taiwan. Bangladesh even failed to preserve the high ceiling it had prescribed. Nor was the Zia regime too enthusiastic. It dropped its land reform proposals at the first sign of opposition from the landed interests.

Is rural revolution, then, inevitable in this most rural of the world's largest agricultural economies?[51] Increasing poverty does not automatically create revolutions: awareness of their poverty and deprivation is needed to motivate people to rise against the system. Instilling this sense of deprivation in poor peasants is particularly difficult for political parties in an authoritarian regime. Because of their total dependence on landowners, small farmers become servile. This peasant 'idiocy' led classical Marxists to regard the peasant proletariat as essentially incapable of playing a leading role in revolution. And they were right. In Russia the peasant proletariat supported the revolution only after the urban revolutionaries had won political power.[52]

Nevertheless, the Chinese example has shown that when the right preconditions for mobilising poor peasants arise, the peasantry can play a crucial revolutionary role. Prolonged disorder creating a perpetual sense of insecurity; direct and open exploitation making it easy to identify the exploiting class; the growth of a rival political force promising the defeat of the 'enemies of the people'; the presence of a foreign power and its support of the rich class to inject nationalist fervour in the class war — all these are preconditions for revolutionising a rural proletariat. In China, for example, a revolutionary situation was created by a decade of social disorder and political corruption before 1927 and blatant oppression by warlords and government tax officers. Then first a revolutionary army and later the Red Army with its successive victories against the forces of reaction as well as the success of the Chinese Communist Party in presenting their war as an anti-imperialist, nationalist people's struggle gave them final victory. China's poor peasantry had no hesitation in joining the revolution.[53]

None of these conditions appears to be present in Bangladesh. True, a spurt of Leftist revolutionary activity came in the years just before Independence.[54] Radical ideas spawned by the 1971 guerrilla war spread dramatically among university and college students. They affected some of the Army. Cadres of the leftist revolutionaries, mostly students, who had acquired arms and ammunition during the Liberation War, fanned out into the rural areas, establishing bases for operations against security forces. They had some success. Rural people gave them at least tacit support, for they provided a countervailing force to Rakkhi Bahini, Sheikh Mujib's special security force that went about terrorising the country. The leftists also won popular support with their vigorous anti-Indian sloganeering after Sheikh Mujib had transformed Bangladesh into a virtual Indian satellite.[55]

But with the fall of the Sheikh Mujib government, the dismantling of its instruments of terror, and the consolidation of the new military regime, the innate conservatism of Bangladesh reasserted itself. During their two- to three-year stay in the rural areas the urban professional revolutionaries succeeded in revolutionising the poor peasantry only in a few isolated areas. When the peasants stopped sheltering them after Sheikh Mujib's overthrow, most of the revolutionaries returned to the cities. Thereafter, struck by a sense of ineffectiveness, they began occupying themselves with theoretical polemics, and this in turn affected the cohesion and unity of each of the revolutionary groups.

Several Leftist revolutionaries active in the rural areas told the author of their utter frustration in trying to radicalise the lower rural classes. Poor peasants fail to understand that landowners are exploiting them; they see land as a personal possession and believe its ownership to be legitimate and sacrosanct. The Left-wing slogan 'land to the tillers' gets no response.

Something else impeded the radicalising forces. The poor peasants of Bangladesh are anything but rootless people, alienated from rural social structures. Their relationships are many and intimate. One, for example, is the client-patron relationship between the poor peasants and the landed class. As is well-known, the dominant trait of the peasant community is its concern for immediate issues. The immediate problems of the poor peasants of Bangladesh relate to their daily food and shelter, protection against encroachment of their small landholdings, need for mediators for contacting government officials and ensuring their share in government reliefs and subsidies, and the like. These immediate needs of the peasants can be served only by the members of the local landed class.

Upper-class people, in turn, need the loyalty and support of poor peasants to increase their political and economic power both with government officials and against their rivals. Thus from the reciprocal needs of both the lower strata and upper classes of rural peasantry grow vertical formations undercutting the economic cleavages in the rural society. Resource allocation in rural politics tends to be in terms of these formations. For example, if one particular formation gains dominance and wins a seat in local government, the whole group might have a better share in a vast range of government reliefs and grants, jobs under rural development programmes, or even allotment of *khash* (public) land. Thus, although such formations may not help lower-class peasants gain upward mobility, they do help them in their immediate concerns. So it is that Bangladesh's revolutionaries have a hard task weaning poor peasants away from these formations and organizing them along class lines.[56]

One may well ask how it is that East Bengal's peasantry, so prone to rebellion in the past, are so passive now. This raises the question of what should be the crucial condition for a peasant revolution. Hitherto peasants rebelled against foreign rulers, Hindus and Muslims from Central India, the British and their surrogates — the Calcutta-based Hindus, and those from Karachi and Rawalpindi. Only nationalist appeals could inspire East Bengal peasants to rebel. So also Chinese and Vietnamese peasants could only join in social revolution when it merged with nationalist upheaval. As Huntington says, 'it is possible, as in the United States, to have a nationalist war of independence which is not also a social revolution. But it is impossible to have a social revolution which is not also a nationalist revolution.'[57] In the absence of any palpable foreign enemy the rural Bangladesh people are not able to find a suitable scapegoat. Consequently Communists now find it extremely difficult to arouse passive peasants into revolutionary action.

Urban inequality and urban-rural cleavage

Precise information about inequality of wealth in urban areas is unavailable. Even so, that inequality exists. There are large income differences between various categories of government servants, between managerial staff and wage workers in the industrial sector, between affluent trading and professional groups and slum dwellers. The present Government's strategy on industrial development serves only to accentuate the inequalities.

As already stated, this strategy helps only to foster a new industrial class. Prospective entrepreneurs first invest huge sums of capital, made available to them through B.S.B. and B.S.R.S., in speculative ventures; then, often enough, they earn huge profits even before starting work on the proposed projects. Dealing secretly with foreign businessmen, they also accumulate foreign-currency income by over-invoicing the cost of imported machinery. Moreover, they usually overrun the original estimates on their projects and, with industrial installations partly built, force the lending institutions to provide them with additional loans. They extract 'unearned income' for these new loans too in the ways mentioned above. Thus, by utilising public money, prospective industrialists get rich even before starting their new industries.[58]

Another group making easy money in Bangladesh is that engaged in the 'indenting trade'. Acting as agents and contractors of foreign aid and foreign business organisations, they get commissions for their services in foreign exchange. The friends and relatives of 200,000 Bangladeshis living abroad also make easy money. They do so through the 'Wage Earners' scheme under which they can import, without tax, foreign goods by utilising their earnings abroad. The result of all these activities is the growth of what Franda calls 'a small, affluent upper-middle class that is as conspicuous and as willing to engage in ostentatious living as any such class anywhere in the world'.[59]

But even the emergence of this new class has failed to agitate the industrial workers of Bangladesh, who now number about 300,000.

Industrial workers in Bangladesh are not truly a proletariat. Too many of them have rural connections; with homes in their native villages, they keep their families there, and moreover, by rural standards industrial workers are well-off. Saving from their wages, they buy plots of lands in their villages and thereby develop a stake in the *status quo*. Also, to avoid getting swallowed up in the urban mass society, they form parochial groups with other workers from their district or region instead of joining trade unions. Moreover, as some trade union leaders argue, religion and Bangladesh nationalism appeal so powerfully to the workers that making them class-conscious is extremely difficult.[60] The workers are thus more interested in immediate raises in wages than in the overthrow of the total system. In this context, no radical movement is likely, at least in the immediate future, to catch on with Bangladesh's urban workers.

Inequality in Bangladesh exists not only in class terms but also in the distribution of wealth between urban and rural areas. In 1969–70 per capita income in urban areas was about five times higher than in rural areas. The urban-rural inequality widened further during the post-liberation period. Despite the continuing governmental rhetoric about priority in agriculture, governmental funds continue to go to industry and the urban infrastructure. Although agriculture brings in more than 90 per cent of export earnings, provides 77 per cent of employment and 54 per cent of the GDP, agriculture gets only between 10 and 15 per cent of the annual development budgets. Even if one figures items like rural development programmes and flood and water control, which indirectly benefit agriculture, the rural sector's share hardly amounts to 30 per cent. Predominantly urban-oriented sectors like industry, power and natural resources, transport and communication each get bigger allocations than agriculture. As for allocations in fields such as physical planning and housing, education and health, only small portions are spent in rural areas.

The 'ration system' offers another striking example of government discrimination against rural people. Under this system, the government sells rice, wheat, and other foodstuffs at roughly half their open market prices. Of the entire ration offtake, two-thirds goes to residents of the six largest cities and to 'priority' groups like defence force personnel, police, civilian government employees, industrial workers, and students living in hostels. The remaining one-third is meant for the country people. But because of widespread corruption among the system's officials and distributors, only about 10 per cent of the total ration offtake actually reaches the rural inhabitants. Costing between 2.3 to 5.2 million Taka annually, the system is obviously designed to reduce discontent among the politically volatile urban groups whose support is crucial for any government's survival.[61]

Theoretically, the enormous disparity in wealth and privileges between urban and rural people should lead to a Maoist revolution among the Bangladesh peasants, inciting them to encircle the cities and take over the state power. We have already seen why they lack revolutionary consciousness and are hard to mobilise politically. But another important force too stands in the way of urban-rural conflict. This is the increasing convergence of the political and economic interests of the urban and rural élites. Most members of urban professional classes are also landowners; and by the same token more and more of the sons of landed families go to universities and other institutions of higher education, join defence and civilian services, and work in urban business and professional groups.

About 71 per cent of the Members of the 1970 legislative assembly and 75 per cent of those in the 1973 assembly belonged to the upper landed class. Each of these Members owned over 6.5 acres. More significantly, many members of the two assemblies had two or three occupations, law, business and farming being the three most common combinations.[62] The occupational backgrounds of the Members of the 1979 assembly are roughly similar to those of the Members of the preceding two assemblies.[63] Thus political leadership that so obviously and uniformly represents the vested urban interests can hardly be expected to reverse the present urban-rural relationship. Yet only a drastic change in this relationship can end the chronic economic stagnation of rural Bangladesh.

The middle-class political culture

Since, as we have argued, there is no immediate possibility of any social revolution and change in the dominant political position of urban regions, the future of politics in Bangladesh lies in the hands of powerful urban groups. These groups include members of various professions, civilian government employees, university and college students, the trading classes, the small but growing industrial entrepreneurial class, members of defence forces, and the like. These groups have been the dominant factor in the politics of the area since the 1920s and they may be conveniently and collectively termed as the middle class. The type of politics that Bangladesh will have in the immediate future will be determined by the political culture of this urban middle class.

The political culture of this middle class has been consistently manifested in its tendencies towards over-politicisation, in its lack of organisational skills and discipline, and in factionalism and ideological rhetoric. While the Indian Congress became the dominant political party in most areas of British India in the 1920s, the Bengal middle-class politicians remained divided into several smaller groups — Congressites, Muslim Leaguers, *Krishak Prajas* (members of the Peasants' and Tenants' Party) and the like. The factional character of Muslim politicians revealed itself more clearly in the parliamentary politics of United Bengal from 1937 to 1945. The various groups of Muslim legislators failed to accommodate each other. Several Ministries were formed and collapsed, the assembly often ending in uproar.[64] What was even worse was the phenomenon of parliamentary parties in the East Bengal legislature during the period 1947–58 continuously splitting and splintering into numerous mutually hostile groups of legislators. Chronic political instability and a rapid turnover of ineffective governments was the invariable result.[65]

The Bangladeshi middle-class propensity to political factionalism was heightened by the disruptive forces released during the Liberation War. Only a year after liberation, both the Awami League which had led the nationalist movement and the bureaucracy became factionalised.[66] The radical ideas generated by the Liberation War no doubt led to the formation of a new revolutionary political party and the strengthening and merger of several older revolutionary groups of pre-independence days. But the leaders of the revolutionary parties, were also drawn from the urban middle class. They could not overcome for long the limitations of middle-class political culture. Furthermore, this middle-class political culture was able to put the whole Left movement of Bangladesh into disarray because of the latter's tendency to doctrinal disunity.

Over-politicisation, factionalism and a fondness for ideological rhetoric constitute only one aspect of Bangladesh political culture. Another significant aspect is the proclivity for giving mass support to a single great leader, especially when a momentous issue affecting the national fate has to be decided. In the 1937 elections, the issue was economic freedom from the *zamindars* (landlords) and *mahajans* (money-lenders). The leader was A. K. Fazlul Huq. In 1946, the issue was Pakistan and the people of East Bengal rallied behind M. A. Jinnah. In 1954, the crucial issue was autonomy for East Bengal and the people voted decisively for A. K. Fazlul Huq as the upholder of their cause. Again in 1970, Bangladeshis displayed unprecedented unity under the leadership of Sheikh Mujibur Rahman. They gave him their undivided support on the Six-Point programme of autonomy for Bangladesh. And again, fearing Indian intervention, they showed a unique sense of solidarity on 7 November 1975, under the leadership of General Ziaur Rahman, in asserting national sovereignty. The Bangladeshi political character thus combines seemingly incompatible elements. Bangladeshis have an unexpressed desire for discipline, a great leader and great issues. Even so, they also relish opposing and belittling all types of leadership, raising storms over nuances of political issues and defying organisational discipline of any kind. The first set of characteristics helps them to turn crises into national triumphs. The second set incapacitates them from working in an organised way to deal with the enormous social, economic and political problems their country faces. This failure, in turn, perpetuates underdevelopment and stagnation and, if continued for long, could well erode all national self-confidence.

Naturally, some factionalism is common to all organisations, even in developed democratic countries. But the crucial variable is the matter of degree. All experienced observers of the Bangladesh scene agree that the extreme and tendentious degree to which Bangladesh factionalism drives itself has proved dysfunctional to her development efforts.[67]

The fractious nature of Bangladesh political culture can, in part, be attributed to the long struggle in which Bangladeshis were involved through battling for independence. The long centuries of struggle against alien rulers fostered an oppositional mentality, and even with independence Bangladeshis have not been able to shed that mentality. The problem has been aggravated, moreover, by the high stakes involved in all types of competition. A political party's capture of power, for example, opens up big economic opportunities for its leaders and supporters. Still more, the highly unfavourable resource-population ratio makes political competition all the more intense. In Bangladesh, the game is winner-take-all. There is no reward for loyal opposition. Nor is factionalism present only in politics. As social, economic and voluntary organisations get involved in the allocation of certain resources, fierce factionalism becomes endemic in these bodies too. Management is made difficult for sheer demographic reasons. There are 'so many people in such a small piece of land that they cannot sort out their relationships with one another in any productive way.'[68]

Zia's politics

Eventually, of course, Bangladeshis will acquire the 'art of associating together.' But recently the politics of fragmentation have been paramount. The nation's largest political party, the Awami League, displayed its factionalism in 1981–2. Two factions of the Muslim League broke away, one joining the new political party launched by Zia and the other forming a separate party. The larger faction, however, kept the party's original name. Even the fanatically ideological Jamaat-i-Islami party split along its organisational and parliamentary wings. The pro-Chinese Leftist parties now number about a dozen. The pro-Moscow Communists and their sympathisers were, by early 1981, divided into three parties. The two Leftist parties, most active in the post-Independence years, were Purbo Bangla Sarbohara (East Bengal Communist Party) and Jatio Samajtantric Dal (National Socialist Party or J.S.D.). The first one began factionalising after its leader, Siraj Sikdar, died in custody in January 1975. Ultimately it split into two organisations, both losing the organisational and fighting capacities of the original party.

In the days of Sheikh Mujib, J.S.D. looked like the party of the future with its massive appeal to students, and further more it kept its unity intact until recently. But the Zia Government's prolonged detention of its principal leaders and the diminishing appeal of its socialist slogans reduced J.S.D.'s importance as a major contender for power. Its failure to capture power gave its leadership a sense of inadequacy, and as a result, ideological polemics, which destroyed the unity of previous leftist groups, have seized it too. From their prison cells, J.S.D.'s top leaders are urging their comrades outside to modify the party platform on 'immediate social revolution'. They urge the party's rank and file to work instead for a 'democratic national government' by collaborating with 'bourgeois' political parties (including the two Awami Leagues). They argue that in the existing 'historical stage' of Bangladesh's development, direct socialist revolution cannot be achieved. Establishment of a 'democratic national government', according to them, would be a necessary intermediate stage towards preparing the ground for an ultimate socialist revolution. Many of the party's rank and file interpret the new move of their top leaders' as a ploy to get out of prison. These leaders cannot go free unless the Army Government is toppled, and this can be effected only by the joint efforts of the major political parties of the Left as well as of the Right. Many J.S.D. activists think that the new thesis of the gaoled leaders is a mere rationalisation for effecting a coalition between the Rightist and Leftist forces in order to dislodge the Army. They considered the move a betrayal of the socialist cause. So J.S.D. also faced a split with increased organisational ineffectiveness.[69]

With the growing ineffectiveness and fragmentation of opposition political parties, the shape of Bangladesh politics in the near future will be determined by developments in the Army regime's two main props — the Bangladesh Army and the Bangladesh Nationalist Party (B.N.P.) — and now on General Ershad's own qualities of leadership. Compared to India and Pakistan, Bangladesh has a small army, with a total strength of about 100,000. Its top echelons consist of one lieutenant-general, twelve major-generals and about fifty brigadiers. The officer corps as a whole numbers about 4,000, mostly 'repatriates' — who were trapped in West Pakistan during the 1971 war, coming back to Bangladesh after Independence. As for repatriated *jawans* (privates), they number about 35,000, and freedom fighters (participants in the Liberation War) amount to about 15,000. After the August 1975 coup, about 20,000 Rakkhi Bahini were absorbed into the Army. Recently the Army has added several thousand fresh recruits.

Army morale reached a low point during Sheikh Mujib's regime because of inadequate pay and accommodation and a lack of weapons and training facilities. The Freedom Fighters especially became highly politicised, linking up with various revolutionary parties. Some officers even retired or defected to join these radical groups. As there have been about a dozen attempted coups since 7 November 1975, clearly the Army has yet to achieve much cohesion.

But certainly matters have improved since the time of Sheikh Mujib. The Zia Government invested between 20 to 30 per cent (in contrast to 15–16 per cent under the Sheikh Mujib regime) of the annual revenue budget in defence. According to some informed sources, a major portion of expenditure under civilian heads like housing and construction, roads and highways in the development budget was also spent on housing and road construction in cantonment areas. The Army also appears to be better equipped; it was provided with improved training facilities. A military academy and a staff college were established and British advisers helped to train officers in both institutions. Increasingly officers are being sent abroad for training. The purges that took place in the Army after each attempted coup may have weeded out most of its politicised elements. Generally the Army has a conservative, anti-Indian and pro-Islamic world orientation. Although it has yet to become a fully integrated institution, it is now a strong organisation.

Zia showed his farsightedness by 'civilianising' his regime through free, contested elections and restoring constitutional politics. But his dependence on Army support was clear. He formally resigned from active Army service after having been democratically elected President; but he did not move out of the cantonment to the President's House in Dacca. Having enjoyed the exercise of power during the period of martial law, Army officers demanded a share in civil administration. The thirty-member Cabinet headed by Zia contained six retired army officers including Zia himself.[70] The officers of the armed forces were particularly keen to occupy lucrative positions in public corporations. Army officers headed ten major public corporations, boards and authorities, and officers held important posts in several other corporations. Eight Army officers held senior posts in the secretariat, and fourteen who were first inducted as Additional Superintendents of Police were raised to the rank of Superintendent of Police.[71] About 500 retired Army officers all but took over the fields of industry, indenting business, foreign trade and supply and contracts under the active patronage of Zia's Government. Zia's critics argued that he was consciously following the Indonesian model of 'partnership between military and civilian forces, civilians being the junior partners'.

But, as scholars working on the problems of military disengagement from politics argue, abrupt and swift withdrawal of the military from politics after its initial intervention is dysfunctional to the process of 'civilianisation'.[72] A slow and gradual process of military withdrawal and the simultaneous development of effective civilian institutions — particularly a broad-based political party — might ultimately bring in an era of uninterrupted civilian rule.

Thus much may depend in the long term on the development of the Bangladesh Nationalist Party (B.N.P.), which Zia founded in September 1978. The B.N.P. is a conglomeration of diverse political groupings — a section of the pro-Chinese National Awami Party, a faction of another pro-Chinese United Peoples Party, a dissident group of the Muslim League, a sprinkling of the Awami League, a few trade union leaders, a number of retired Army officers, a section of the landed class, and almost the whole industrial and trading interests of the country. There are reports of continuous factional feuds among the ideologically diverse groups in the B.N.P. Zia's opponents contended that lack of ideological unity within the party would hinder its growth into a well-knit organisation and that it would disintegrate with the fall of Zia.

Some of the former ministers in Zia's Cabinet argued that as a former military officer Zia had certain constraints which hindered him from building a democratic organisation. According to them, he was not able to comprehend the importance of political workers and political competition in building a political party. His 'democratic' critics within the B.N.P. pointed to the nominated character of the two highest bodies of the party — the National Standing Committee and National Executive Committee.[73] Critics of Zia within the B.N.P. also argued that his dependence on local officials rather than on local branches of the party to implement his otherwise laudable programmes, like canal-digging for irrigation through voluntary labour or eradicating mass illiteracy, clearly showed his preference for an administrative rather than a democratic model of development, as well as his distrust of political workers. They also pointed to Zia's inability to perceive that the B.N.P. could be turned into a grassroots organisation if B.N.P. members were allowed to take the lead and create a mass interest in these nation-building activities. They held further that such party-led efforts alone could have created conditions for sustained development efforts. These views held by Zia's opponents within the B.N.P. clearly had some merit.

What characterised Zia's rule was his ability to learn governmental skills as he went along, and right up until his fatal last trip to Chittagong in May 1981, where he met his death, the range of his skills seemed to outpace the narrow boundary of his military professionalism. It had seemed possible that he could outmanoeuvre his 'democratic' opponents by adopting their programmes. Besides, he has used the most effective force in Bangladesh politics — Bangladesh Nationalism — to increase his personal appeal and the appeal of his party to his countrymen.

Ultimately, however, his weakness, as earlier the foundation of his strength, lay in the Army. He was killed by mutinous Army officers who refused to accept his disciplinary authority when he visited them in Chittagong. The mutineers probably reasoned that with Zia dead they would easily be able to assume power before long in Dacca and the whole country. If this was so, they were wrong. At first, Zia's Vice-President, Abdus Sattar, ensured a relatively smooth succession, and then was elected President, comfortably defeating his chief challenger Dr Kamel Hossain of the Awami League. President Sattar's victory proved to be rather pyrrhic. Within weeks, the unease of the armed forces with the apparent indecisiveness and continuing factionalism of the government and of virtually all Bangladesh's leading politicians, led to General Ershad's coup and the re-imposition of military rule and martial law early in 1982.

The transition from military to civilian rule is always an arduous process. Military intervention followed by a civilian interlude followed again by military intervention is endemic in most developing countries which have once been under military rule. Given the weaknesses in the civilian political sector, the Bangladesh Army is always likely to play a decisive role in times of political crisis. Moreover, any future government of Bangladesh would probably have to face a 'Ghana-style amenities coup' if it decided to curtail the privileges of the Army officers.[74] Given the Army's overall political orientation — its conservatism, anti-Indianism and pro-Muslim world sympathy — it may not look with equanimity upon the prospect of a radical party like J.S.D. or the allegedly pro-Indian Awami League winning power.

Conclusion

We have shown how Bangladesh nationalism developed over the centuries. The memories of the struggle of the Bengalis against alien rulers, the sufferings they had undergone, and the aspirations they had shared — all these bound them together into a solid nation. The problems posed by a psychologically insecure Hindu minority, by a disaffected tribal group and by the uneven pattern of growth in the

Northwest and Eastern regions have still to be dealt with. The history of Bangladesh clearly provides the answer to the question whether Bangladeshis are Bangladeshis or Muslims first. Historically the Bangladeshis have tended to prefer their collective national interests. To ensure these, they have fought against Hindus, Christians and even their Muslim co-religionists. It is this nationalism that could ensure the perpetuity of the Bangladesh nation-state.

The involvement of the masses in the upheavals in the former East Pakistan in the late 1960s and in the guerrilla war of 1971 and the consequent processes of radicalisation led many observers to believe that Bangladesh would be the first South Asian country to undergo a social revolution. The political economy of Bangladesh indicates the existence of glaring inequalities between different classes both in the urban and rural areas. There is tremendous poverty in rural Bangladesh. However the presence of numerous intimate and informal cross-cutting class relationships based on client and patron in the rural areas has arrested the growth of class-consciousness among the poor peasants. Thus while the peasantry responded during the independence struggle to the nationalistic appeals of the urban élites, they are not now greatly affected by the radical slogans of urban revolutionaries. Furthermore, the urban industrial workers are still tied to traditional patterns of rural life and seek their identity in informal groups based on region rather than in a common militant workers' movement. A solid phalanx of workers is thus not available to the revolutionary leaders. There is also the fact that there has not been any significant penetration of modernising forces into Bangladesh society; also the War of Liberation was too short to affect the traditional social and economic structure of the country. A social revolution in Bangladesh for the present seems a remote prospect. However the development strategies pursued by successive governments could accentuate inequalities among the classes and between the urban and rural areas.

Thus the absence of an effective radical movement results in the urban middle class dominating politics as it has done since the beginning of the century. The politics of opposition and agitation over a long period of time has caused this urban middle class to develop a culture of over-politicisation, factionalism and dedication to ideology. Such a political culture is not able to cope with the strategy of large-scale organisations, a necessary condition for political stability and steady economic growth. High expectations, acute scarcity and rising prices consequently create an atmosphere of unrest. The Army has therefore by 1982 already felt compelled to intervene several times — and has also tried to effect a gradual disengagement of the Army from politics, without much success. It seems therefore that for the foreseeable future Bangladesh will be characterised by political instability, slow economic growth and periodic military intervention in politics.

NOTES

1. The population of Bangladesh was 71,478,000 (Census of Population, 1974). The United Nations' population projection studies estimated the population to be over 84 million in 1980. See *Statistical Year Book of Bangladesh, 1979* (Dacca: Bangladesh Bureau of Statistics, Government of the People's Republic of Bangladesh, 1979), 76. All demographic data is derived from the *Year Book* referred to.
2. In Japan, the yield per acre of rice is four times higher than that of Bangladesh.
3. Quoted in A.M.A. Muhith, *Bangladesh: Emergence of a Nation* (Dacca: Bangladesh Books International, 1978), 1.
4. Roger Reville, 'Possible Futures for Bangladesh', *Asia*, 29 (Spring 1973), 34. The phrase 'international basket case' became a widely quoted phrase for describing Bangladesh after Henry Kissinger used the term 'to tilt the balance' against Bangladesh at the height of the Bangladesh crisis in 1971.
5. In the early 1950s South Korea had only 5 million arable acres of land for 30 million people as against Bangladesh's 23 million acres for 70 million people in 1971. See Reville, op.cit., 51–4.
6. See Myron Weiner, 'The Politics of South Asia', in Gabriel A. Ahmond and James S. Coleman, *The Politics of Developing Areas* (Princeton University Press, 1960), 158. (Table 2).
7. A controversy still exists in political and intellectual circles in Bangladesh as to whether the peole of Bangladesh should be called 'Bengalis' or 'Bangladeshis'. Throughout this article the term 'Bangladeshis' has been used so as to differentiate them clearly from the people of West Bengal in the Republic of India who also call themselves Bengalis. The term 'Bangladeshis' has also been applied to the people of East Bengal in pre-Bangladesh Pakistan and to the people of East Bengal before the creation of Pakistan.
8. Jadunath Sarker, 'Transformation of Bengal Under Mughal Rule', in Jadunath Sarker (ed.), *The History of Bengal* (University of Dacca, 1948), II, 227.
9. See ch. II, 'Bangladesh Nationalism', in M. Anisuzzaman, *Bangladesh Public Administration and Society* (Dacca: Bangladesh Books International, 1979), 18–19, 31–2; Kamruddin Ahmad, *A Socio-Political History of Bengal and the Birth of Bangladesh* (Dacca: Inside Library, 1975), xv-xvi.
10. Op.cit., xxi-xxiv.
11. The Muslim rulers called the *Vanga* people *Bangalah* and the *Gauda* people *Bangali*. It was during the reign of the independent Muslim Sultan,

Shams-Uddin Ilyas (1342–57), who established his rule over both parts of Bengal that the terms *Bangalah* and *Bangali* were extended to include the territories and peoples of the West Bengal region. See M. A. Rahim, *Social and Cultural History of Bengal*, II (1576–1757) (Karachi: Pakistan Publishing House, 1967), 40–1.

12. For a discussion of the *Bara Bhuyians* see Rahim, op. cit., 187–202. Literally the term *Bara Bhuyians* means twelve landlords, but *Bara* was used in a colloquial sense to mean a large number. Most of the landlords opposing Mughal rule were Muslims and were from East Bengal.
13. For a detailed study of armed peasant revolts in East Bengal against British rule in the eighteenth and nineteenth centuries, see Sirajul Islam, 'British Birodhi Sasastra Sangram' (Armed Revolts Against the British) in M. A. Rahim *et al, Bangladesher Itihas* (History of Bangladesh), (Dacca: Nowroj Kitabistan, 1980).
14. See J. H. Broomfield, *Elite Conflict in a Plural Society: Twentieth Century Bengal* (Berkeley: University of California Press, 1968), 25–7.
15. Op.cit., 291–5, 308–15, 326–8.
16. In June 1947, the Bengal legislators met in two sections to decide the question of the partition of Bengal. The Caste Hindu legislators voted in favour of partition. The Muslim legislators and many of the Scheduled Caste Hindu legislators voted against partition. Even before the meeting of the legislators the Bengal Congress and the Bengal Hindu Mahasabha demanded partition. Op.cit., 312–13.
17. For a discussion of East Bengal's lack of share in power in Pakistan, see Rounaq Jahan, *Pakistan: Failure in National Integration* (Dacca: Oxford University Press, 1973), 9–66.
18. For a detailed study of the various mass movements in East Bengal and the implications of the 1954 and 1970 elections for East Bengal's demand for self-determination see Talukder Maniruzzaman, *The Bangladesh Revolution and Its Aftermath* (Dacca: Bangladesh Books International, 1980).
19. Op.cit., chs. V and VI, for a detailed analysis of the various phases of the liberation war.
20. Ibid.
21. Loc.cit.
22. The percentage distribution of the total population of Bangladesh by religious communities, according to the 1974 census, is as follows: Muslim 85.39, Caste Hindus 6.89, Scheduled Caste Hindus 6.64, Buddhists 0.61, Christians 0.31, others 0.15. See *Statistical Year book of Bangladesh, 1979*, 49.
23. *Census of Pakistan, 1951, Population According to Religion (Table 6), Census Bulletin no. 2* (Karachi: Government of Pakistan, Ministry of Interior, 1951), 1.
24. *Population Census of Pakistan, 1961, Bulletin no. 2* (Karachi: Ministry of Home and Kashmir Affairs, Home Affairs Division), 19.
25. Declining trends in the Hindu population of Bangladesh started long ago. The decennial censuses since 1901 show that the percentage of Hindus decreased by about one per cent in every ten years. See 'Statement 2-D',

Census of Pakistan, 1951, vol. I, (Karachi, Government of Pakistan), 27. The 1951 Census showed a decline of 6 per cent in the Hindu population as between 1941 and 1951 (loc.cit.). The rate of decline has continued to be high to date.

26. The rest of the tribal population of Bangladesh (totalling 211,993) is spread over eight Districts on the plains. The tribals in these Districts are too few to cause any big social or political problem. For a District-wise distribution of the tribals, see *Statistical Year book of Bangladesh, 1979*, 67.
27. The discussion on the *Santi Bahini* war against the Bangladesh government is based mainly on interviews with several persons well-informed on recent developments in the Hill Tract areas. The interviewees prefer to remain anonymous.
28. Emajuddin Ahmad, 'Development Strategy in Bangladesh: Probable Political Consequences', *Asian Survey*, XVIII, Nov. 1978, 1175.
29. A poster recently published by the *Committee for the Removal of Disparity Between Northern and Eastern Regions* and stuck on walls and buildings in Northern Bangladesh gave the following figures of disparity between Northern and Eastern Bengal:

	Eastern Region	*Northern Region*
Electricity producing capacity	490 megawatts	100 megawatts
Employees in government service	96%	4%
Employees in semi-autonomous bodies	98%	2%
Development expenditure	90%	10%
Bank advances	5631.8 m. Taka	900.1 m. Taka
Number of industrial enterprises	5,313	549
Metalled roads	2,310 miles	500 miles

30. During the First Five-year Plan (1973–8) and the Two-Year Plan (1978–80) periods a total of 2382 such industrial units were sanctioned by the NEC. See Wahiduddin Mahmud, 'Private Investment during the First Five-Year Plan (1973–1978) and the Two Year Plan (1978–1980), (Planning Commission, General Economic Division, January 1980, mimeo), 5.
31. The various incentives offered to prospective entrepreneurs by the Zia Government in Bangladesh are listed in Mahmud, op.cit., 4.
32. The figures are derived from Appendix 14, *Bangladesh Shilpa Bank Annual Report, 1977–1978* (Dacca: Bangladesh Shilpa Bank), 40–1.
33. The figures are derived from *Bangladesh Shilpa Rin Sangstha, Annual Report, 1974–75, 1975–76, 1976–77, 1977–78* (Dacca: Bangladesh Shilpa Rin Sangstha).
34. Sheikh Mujibur Rahman, who had been the effective head of the Government of Bangladesh from January 1972 to August 1975 came from Eastern Bangladesh, and Ziaur Rahman from Northwest Bangladesh.
35. See Table 14, *Census of Pakistan, 1951, Vol. 3, East Bengal, Report and Tables* 14–2; Table 44, *Population Census of Bangladesh 1974, National Volume, Report and Tables* (Dacca: Bureau of Statistics, Ministry of Planning, Bangladesh, 1977), 44.

36. See, Table DIII, F. Tomasson Jannuzi and T. Peach, James, *Report on the Hierarchy of Interests in Land in Bangladesh* (Washington, D.C.: USAID, 1977), xxii.
37. For a quantitative analysis of the decline of real wages in argicultural labour and increasing landlessness in rural Bangladesh, see Azizur Rahman Khan, 'Poverty and Inequality in Rural Bangladesh', in *Poverty and Landlessness in Rural Asia* (I.L.O., AWEP study, Geneva, 1977); see also Edward J. Clay, 'Institutional Change and Agricultural Wages in Bangladesh'. Staff Paper 76-5 (New York: Agricultural Development Council, 1979).
38. See Khan, op.cit., 153-4.
39. Kamal Siddiqui, 'The Political Economy of Land Reforms in Bangladesh', *Journal of Social Studies*, 6 (1969) 9.
40. For an incisive discussion of land reforms in Bangladesh during the Sheikh Mujib regime, see N. Mukherji, 'Agrarian Reforms in Bangladesh', *Asian Survey*, XVI, 5 (1976), 452-64.
41. Jannuzi and Peach, op.cit., p. 76.
42. Siddiqui, op.cit., 17-18.
43. See the statement of Shah Azizur Rahman, Prime Minister, Government of Bangladesh in *The Bangladesh Times* (Dacca), 17 October, 1979; Hossain Khasru, 'Vested Interests Score ''Revolution'' ', *Holiday* (Dacca), 25 November, 1979; 'Land Reforms — Facts or Fictions', *The New Nation* (Dacca), 18 November, 1979.
44. The percentages are derived from figures in Government of the People's Republic of Bangladesh, Ministry of Finance, Economic Advisers' Wing, *Bangladesh Economic Survey 1978-1979* (Dacca, May 1979).
45. See Shapan Adnan and Hussain Zillur Rahman, 'Peasant classes and Land Mobility: Structural Reproduction and Change in Rural Bangladesh', *Studies in Rural History* (Dacca: Bangladesh Itihas Samiti, 1979), 106-11; see also Jannuzi and Peach, op.cit., 66.
46. I have used the terms 'rich peasants', 'surplus farmers' and 'upper landed class' synonymously, meaning farmers who have at least some annual excess of agricultural products after meeting their consumption needs.
47. There now exist a number of studies showing how the agricultural development strategy followed in Bangladesh has led to the enrichment of surplus farmers: e.g. Henry W. Blair, *The Illusiveness of Equity: Institutional Approaches to Rural Development in Bangladesh* (Ithaca: Centre for International Studies, Cornell University, 1974); Abdullah, *et al.*, 'Agrarian Structure and the IDDP: Preliminary Consideration', *The Bangladesh Development Studies*, IV, 2 (April 1976), 231-44; Mohiuddin Alamgir, 'Some Aspects of Bangladesh Agriculture: Review of Performance and Policies', *The Bangladesh Development Studies*, III, 3 (July 1975), 261-300; M. Asaduzzaman and Mahboob Hossain, *Some Aspects of Agricultural Credit in Bangladesh* (Research Report (New Series), 19, Bangladesh Institute of Development Studies, 1975.
48. See Tables 45 and 48 in Khan, op.cit., 140, 147. Khan defines the poverty line as 'income inadequate to ensure a minimum diet'. The

minimum requirement for calories estimated by F.A.O. for the population of Bangladesh is about 2,150 per person per day. Khan defines a person having 90 per cent of this recommended calorie intake or less as absolutely poor and a person having no more than 80 per cent of the recommended calorie intake as extremely poor (pp. 139–41).

49. See Samuel P. Huntington, *Political Order in Changing Societies* (New Haven: Yale University Press, 1969), 266–74.
50. Werner Klatt, 'The Agrarian Question in Asia in the Light of Communist and Non-Communist Experience', in Richard Lowenthal (ed.), *Issues in the Future of Asia: Communist and Non-Communist Alternatives*, (New York: Frederick A. Praeger, 1969), 27–96; Huntington, op.cit., 374–96.
51. From the criterion of number of people dependent on agriculture, the largest agricultural countries are China, India, Indonesia and Bangladesh. In terms of proportion of population living in rural areas and depending on agriculture for a living, Bangladesh comes first. While 91 per cent of the Bangladesh population live in rural areas, the percentages of rural people in China, India, and Indonesia are 85, 80 and 82 respectively.
52. See Lenin's statement quoted in Hamza Alavi, 'Peasants and Revolution', in Kathleen Gough and Hari P. Sharma (ed.), *Imperialism and Revolution in South Asia* (New York: Monthly Review Press, 1973), 304.
53. Ibid., 304–16.
54. See Talukder Maniruzzaman, *Radical Politics and the Emergence of Bangladesh* (Dacca: Bangladesh Books International, 1975).
55. See Talukder Maniruzzaman, 'Bangladesh: An Unfinished Revolution?', *Journal of Asian Studies*, V XXXIV, 4 (August 1975), 891–911.
56. For a discussion on these vertical formations and their role in preventing the growth of 'classes-for-themselves' position among the poor peasants in Bangladesh, see Adnan and Rahman, op.cit., 100–3.
57. Huntington, op.cit., 304.
58. This paragraph is based on interviews with the officials of the B.S.B. and B.S.R.S. in February 1980. Prospective entrepreneurs make their purchases with government conniving at their irregularities; in turn they contribute liberally to government party funds.
59. Marcus Franda, 'Ziaur Rahman's Bangladesh Part II: Poverty and Discontent', *American Universities Field Staff Reports*, 26 (1979), Asia, 6.
60. See the proceedings of the seminar on trade unions in Bangladesh, *Ittefaq* (Dacca), 20 January, 1980.
61. For more on urban-rural disparity see de Vylder, 'Urban Bias in Development: Bangladesh', *Journal of Social Studies*, 4 (July 1979), 1–14.
62. See Rounaq Jahan, 'Members of Parliament in Bangladesh', *Legislative Studies Quarterly*, I, 3 (August 1976), 339–61.
63. See Mustafa Haroon, *Who's Who in the Parliament*, (Dacca: Showkhin Prakasani, 1979).
64. See Khalid Bin Sayeed, *Pakistan: the Formative Phase* (Karachi: Pakistan Publishing House, 1960), 230–2.
65. See Najma Choudhury, 'The Politics and Functioning of the East Bengal

Legislature, 1947–1958' (unpubl. Ph.D. thesis, University of London, 1972).

66. See Rounaq Jahan, 'Bangladesh in 1973: Management of Factional Politics', *Asian Survey*, XIV, 2, 125–35.
67. See Marcus F. Franda, 'Moral Implications of Bangladesh', *Asia* Supplement I (Fall 1974), 49; Keville, op.cit., 54.
68. Franda, op.cit., 49.
69. This paragraph is based on interviews with several J.S.D. activists in February 1980.
70. The Cabinet also includes a retired naval officer.
71. As it happened in all other countries which came under military domination, the Army in Bangladesh chose the police as their junior partner in administration, and the police personnel got increases in pay and privileges. Police officers secured even a larger share of jobs in the policy-making secretariat than Army officers. At present about half the forty-two posts of Secretaries, Additional Secretaries and Joint Secretaries are held by police officers, nine occupying at the level of Secretary.
72. See Claude E. Welch, 'The Dilemmas of Military Withdrawal from Politics: Some Considerations from Tropical Africa', *African Studies Review*, April 1974, 213–27; Gabriel Ben-Dor, 'Civilianization of Military Regimes in the Arab World', in Henry Biemen and David Morrell (ed.), *Political Participation under Military Regimes* (Beverly Hills: Sage Publications, 1976), 39–49. See also the last chapter in Claude E. Welch, Jr. (ed.), *Civilian Control of the Military: Theory and Cases from Developing Countries* (Albany: State University of New York Press, 1976).
73. All the 120 members of the National Executive Committee and eleven members of the National Standing Committee of the B.N.P. were appointed by the president of the party, i.e. by Zia himself. See *The Constitution of the Bangladesh Nationalist Party* (in Bengali), (Dacca: B.N.P.) n.d., 8–9.
74. In January 1972, K.A. Busia's civilian government in Ghana was overthrown by an army coup. The coup leaders themselves stated that the main reason for their takeover was the curtailment of many of their 'amenities' under Busia's 'austerity budget' of July 1971. Busia dubbed the coup as an 'amenities coup'. See Valerie Plave Bennett, 'Epilogue: Malcontents in Uniform — The 1972 Coup d'Etat' in Dennis Austin and Robin Luckham (ed.), *Politicians and Soldiers in Ghana 1966–1972*, (London: Frank Cass), 1975, 300–12.
75. Bangladesh has a small Navy and a small Air Force. The Navy has so far avoided involvement in politics, but the Air Force became involved in several attempted coups. According to opposition political circles, the officer corps of the Air Force is greatly depleted: some officers were killed in coup bids and many others were purged later. The Air Force is now functionally non-existent.

SRI LANKA AND ITS FUTURE: SINHALESE VERSUS TAMILS

A. Jeyaratnam Wilson

Within the next few decades the Tamil problem in Sri Lanka will determine whether the island is destined to be involved in the continuing haemorrhage of a Lebanon- or Ulster-style internecine civil war, or whether it might end up dividing itself into two separate mini-states. Solutions will depend largely on the attitudes of the élites, inclusive of their leadership among the Sinhalese ethnic majority. There might be a willingness on their part to effect the necessary accommodation but it may be the case of 'too little too late'. And a solution acceptable some ten to fifteen years ago could now be jibbed at by the Sri Lankan Tamils (hereinafter called the Tamils).

Had the leaders of the Indian National Congress been a little less inflexible, Pakistan might not have emerged in its present form. Even the last-minute formula produced by the resourceful C. Rajagopalachari could, by a hair's breadth, have deflected the Muslim demand for separate statehood.[1] It could certainly have been refined and adjusted to produce a working arrangement. But it was a case of concessions being made at a stage when they had lost their grace.

What the leaders of the Indian National Congress tried belatedly to accomplish with the Muslim League in India and the kind of accommodation in Sri Lanka that Sinhalese and Tamil leaders have sought to arrive at conforms to Arendt Lijphart's theory of 'overarching accommodation',[2] but with a significant difference. The Indian National Congress leaders, as representatives of the major groups, and drawn as they were from the bourgeois layers of society, refrained as best they could from mobilising the masses in their campaign of opposition to Muslim claims. The Muslims for their part did not seek to call on mass support from their own people in a situation that was fraught with explosive consequences until a point had been reached at which they felt that the 'high command' of Congress was being far too intransigent. Up to that point there was the possibility of the kind of inter-élite accommodation referred to by Lijphart; but once that point was passed, the possibility for peaceful settlement just fell to the ground.

Mohamed Ali Jinnah demanded that the British should 'divide and quit'; he spurned C. Rajagopalachari's formula on the score that it provided for a 'maimed, moth-eaten and truncated Pakistan',[3] and called for a 'direct action day' in which his fellow-Muslims were exhorted to resort to violence against their Hindu adversaries. But in the Hindu-Muslim situation in India, there was one variable which helped to make the surgery uncomplicated: the imperial power, Britain, was anxious to withdraw. The two groups left to themselves would probably have waged an interminable war. It was in the interests of the peace, stability and security of the region for the Indian National Congress leaders to be persuaded to accept the *fact* of Pakistan, and Britain, the departing power, in the person of her Viceroy Lord Mountbatten, was able to perform the role in as amicable a manner because the Congress high command trusted Mountbatten's good intentions. That variable is not present in every situation.

Strangely enough that same variable was not available to Sri Lanka at the time when negotiations for independence were going on in 1946–8. In these negotiations four key men were involved. On the Sri Lankan side, there were the leading Sinhalese statesman, Don Stephen Senanayake (1888–1952), later to become the island's first prime minister (1947–52), and his closest aide, Oliver Goonetileke (1888–1974). Acting as a constitutional adviser, but also with an eye to British interests, was Sir Ivor Jennings, then Vice-Chancellor of the University of Ceylon. On the British side was Oliver Stanley, Secretary of State for the Colonies in the Conservative Government of the time, to be succeeded in 1945 by Labour's G. F. S. Hall. Towards the end, the British Governor of the island, Sir Henry Monck-Mason-Moore came down heavily on the side of D. S. Senanayake. The British Government preferred to transfer power to the conservative leaders of the Sinhalese ethnic majority; it did very little for the minorities. In 1944 it appointed a Royal Commission of Inquiry headed by Lord Soulbury and two others. The Commission's findings favoured Senanayake's position;[4] it recommended territorial representation as against the demand for balanced representation (half the seats in the legislature for the ethnic majority, the other half for the minorities) which had been advanced by the foremost Tamil leader of this phase, G. G. Ponnambalam, and his powerful political organisation, the All-Ceylon Tamil Congress. It suggested a few safeguards for the ethnic and religious minorities, but little evidence was shown of a willingness to enforce them, and they were all to go by the board in the years to come. In effect Britain was prepared to leave the question of a fair deal for the ethnic minorities to the good intentions of the ethnic majority leaders. Britain accepted their expressions of goodwill at their face value.

The Tamil argument *vis-à-vis* the British withdrawal from Sri Lanka had some bearing on Britain's attitude to the maharajahs, nawabs, princes and princelings of their lost Indian empire. When Britain withdrew from India, her paramountcy over these potentates lapsed. The Nizam of Hyderabad took his legal cue from the constitutional vacuum thus created, and sought, with the aid of the eminent British lawyer, Sir Walter Monckton, to establish his claim as an independent sovereign ruler upon the withdrawal of British sovereignty. He argued persuasively that that sovereignty had lapsed and not found repose on the successor-government of independent India.[5] But before the Nizam could carry his arguments any further, the new Government of India 'engineered' the police action which ended with the incorporation of Hyderabad into Indian territory. The Nizam could probably have justified himself in a court of international law; but it was by now too late.

The Tamil argument in Sri Lanka proceeds on somewhat similar lines. Before the advent of the Westerner, in particular the Portuguese in 1505, there existed a Tamil kingdom in the north of the island which was ultimately conquered by the Portuguese in 1618. In addition to that kingdom, there were several vassal chiefs in close proximity who paid obeisance and acknowledged the overlordship of the Tamil king. A fair section of the island was in that respect under Tamil rule. The Dutch and the British brought the island under their sway, and so it remained until Britain transferred power in February 1948. Britain also provided a constitutional framework which it was hoped would safeguard the rights of the minorities;[6] but according to the Tamil argument, that Constitution was rejected by the Tamil people at the general election of 1948; at any rate, their leadership insist that they were not party to the framework it provided. Nor have they (the recognised leadership) participated in any of the subsequent efforts at constitution-making — in 1972 or 1977–8. In effect the Tamil claim is that Britain's paramountcy lapsed with the transfer of power in 1948; that power, they insist, could not be transferred to the Sinhalese ethnic majority only, but was transferred to *all* the people of the island. Once that power was transferred, they say, it was left to the élites of the different groups to meet in solemn constituent assembly and frame a system for which there was consensus. The Tamil argument is that none of that consensus was forthcoming or evident in 1948, 1972 or 1977–8, and that therefore they cannot be ruled without their consent by a constitution which has been imposed upon them. They hold to the position that with the lapse of British sovereignty they as a nation and a sovereign kingdom in their own right should have reverted to their situation as it was before the Portuguese subdued them in 1618. Therein lie the springs of Tamil nationalism, the theory of the Tamil national homeland, the demand for a federated united states of Sri

Lanka and in recent times the escalation of that demand for the creation of a separate sovereign state of *Eelam* for the Tamils in the north and east of the island.

The comparison between Britain and the Indian subcontinent does not end there. When Britain withdrew from the subcontinent, the desire was to provide for a stable situation. When she left Sri Lanka, it seemed on the surface that there would be peace, order and good government, but the Bandaranaike Governments of 1956–65 and 1970–7 enacted changes with far-reaching consequences. Even before 1956, a section of the Tamil leadership established the separatist Tamil Federal Party in 1949; the party was angered by the legislation of 1948 and 1949 which disfranchised and decitizenised overwhelming numbers of the domiciled Indian Tamil minority in Sri Lanka. The new party joined issue with the then Government, headed by D. S. Senanayake, over its attempts to settle Sinhalese colonists in state-aided agricultural settlements in the traditional Tamil homeland areas of the country. The new party, soon to become the leading political instrument of the Tamils, was in effect arguing the case for a constituent assembly and expressing its opposition to the unilateral imposition of a constitution on the Tamil-speaking peoples. The Federal Party sought to represent the Sri Lankan Tamils, the Indian Tamils and the Tamil-speaking Muslims; however, they failed to get active support from the Muslim minority.

Sri Lanka is consequently faced with a secessionist movement of serious proportions. There is genuine and widespread feeling that the two races can never live as partners in a united island — a fact which the political élites of the ethnic Sinhalese majority are unwilling to acknowledge. As we will show, they have used various strategies to bring the Tamils into the mainstream of politics, but actions have failed to match declared good intentions. The historic enmities and rivalries are deeply embedded, and there is little or no change of heart on either side. It is not realised that if each ethnic group feels free and equal within the confines of a single state, the chances for national consolidation are better than if the groups are involved in internecine warfare.

The Tamils of Sri Lanka who came to the island several centuries ago as invaders and settlers (approximately 11.1 per cent of the total population according to the 1971 census) are culturally similar but economically different from the Tamils of recent Indian origin (*ca.* 9.4 per cent, hereafter referred to as Indian Tamils) brought in by the British plantocracy in the nineteenth century. The Sri Lankan Tamils occupy a contiguous territorial area in the northern and eastern sectors of the island; large numbers of Indian Tamils live in labour housing in the plantations situated in the central and southwest parts. A fair proportion of the Sri Lankan Tamils are essentially middle-class in their orientation regarding ambitions in the professions and the administration; others are either *kulak*-type or small peasant farmers.

Therefore, the outlook of the Sri Lankan Tamils is in many respects conservative in character, and hitherto they have had leadership from the traditional sectors of society, especially professional men and sometimes landlord interests. A further contradiction arises in that many Sri Lankan Tamils live outside the northern and eastern provinces which are their traditional homelands. They are engaged in the professions, administration and entrepreneurial activities in the Sinhalese-majority districts. In the last two decades numbers of them, professional and otherwise, have migrated to Australia, the Middle East, Western Europe and North America. Without much statistical evidence to prove or disprove the contention, it is said that all these non-resident Tamils (the expatriates and those living in the seven Sinhalese-majority provinces outside the Tamil-inhabited traditional homelands) send home a fair proportion of their income. This may be a significant component of the homeland economy, but the thrifty industrious Tamil farmer also earns as well from the rewarding prices that he obtains for his paddy, chillies, potatoes and vegetables in the Sri Lanka market. There is, besides, a fair number of Sri Lankan Tamils engaged in fishing, which also brings in sizeable yields. The points being made here are three: first, a goodly proportion of the Sri Lankan Tamil population is middle-class-oriented and, if not, looks in that direction; secondly, a large section of Sri Lankan Tamils live and earn their living outside the homeland; and thirdly, a significant share of the income earned is sent back to dependents in the homeland.

An important question arises. Will the Tamil (Sri Lankan and Indian) population in the seven Sinhalese provinces be left in their professions and occupations if two separate states emerge? The answer is that they will not. The Sinhalese majority will be infuriated, having held strenuously to the view through the ages that Sri Lanka is *Dhammadipa* (the island of the *Dhamma*, the Buddhist scriptural text), that it is 'one and indivisible'; and that if they have been so 'unfortunate' as to have in their midst Tamils whom many look on as invaders, interlopers and traditional foes, and whom some of their élites regard as rivals and competitors in the trades, professions and the public services, they should and can only be accommodated not as equals but as a minority and a nuisance which must be 'forced' to accept its proper place in a hierarchically patterned social and political order.

Therein lies the dilemma of the Sri Lankan Tamils: whether to retain access to the whole island or to effect the amputation, which will result in a massacre of the Tamils in the seven Sinhalese provinces, accompanied, by a mass transfer of wealth from the Tamils in these areas to the Sinhalese as the result of rioting and disruption. The same process could take place in the two Tamil-speaking provinces but in one of these, the Eastern province, the population consists in nearly equal proportions between Sinhalese, Tamils and Tamil-speaking Muslims; nevertheless the Tamils and Muslims in the northeast sector of the Eastern province live in clusters and could therefore be a source of discomfort to the Sinhalese. If this operation ever succeeded, there would result a Bangladesh-type broken-backed state which will perforce be compelled to become the client or satellite of one or other of the super-powers, or of the Republic of India or the People's Republic of China. Alternatively, it could seek admission to the Commonwealth.

A second question follows. Can a rebellious ethnic minority, without any army and weaponry to call its own, seize power and declare its independence unilaterally against the armed might of the state, or rather the Sinhalese-dominated military forces? The answer is only too obvious. The costs that are likely to be incurred by the Tamils in such an operation would far outweigh the international sympathy accruing from publicity in the media on outrages and pogroms perpetrated. A pertinent third question is whether the super-powers and India, China and for that matter Britain, France and West Germany would permit a situation so unpredictable in its consequences to arise, especially in the context of alleged Soviet ambitions in the Indian Ocean, and with the Indian Ocean increasingly becoming a nuclear zone where the super-powers and the French and West German Navies are involved. One probability is that the opposing sides would supply arms and even forces to the rival combatants in the island. Sri Lanka would in that event pass into a confrontational situation similar to East and West Germany or North and South Korea.

A fourth possibility is that the Government of India will permit none of this, and that the moment there is evidence of the situation going out of control, troops will enter and take possession of the whole island. Presumably, except for the People's Republic of China, all the powers involved — and this would include the Soviet Union because of its good relations with India — will wink at such 'police action'. The Tamil militants do not rule out any of these possibilities. In fact they would prefer the witches' cauldron to be kept at boiling point.

There is however still another option available to the Tamil militants, namely that of slow strangulation of the political economy of the Sinhalese-dominated island. This could take the form of effective international propaganda. There are militant Tamil expatriate groups in India, West Germany, Britain, Canada and the United States, and they have achieved a measure of success. Their principal tactics are to expose discrimination by successive Sinhalese-dominated governments against the Tamils in Sri Lanka, bring to the world's attention violations of the Tamils' human rights, lobby governments and international lending agencies against providing economic aid to Sri Lanka, invite the attention of foreign investors and tourists to the political instability in the island[7] and popularise the cause of *Eelam*. A second tactic is to destabilise the internal political situation. Political murders, acts of sabotage, and inflammatory and provocative speeches are the established forms, and these have been tried. The Sinhalese masses and their lower-level ethnic leadership are needled by such acts and urge their rank and file to take retaliatory action. Nothing is more satisfying to the Tamil militants. A third strategy is to use the bogey of Tamil Nad in South India. The Sinhalese ethnic militants used this as a carrot to attract the Sinhalese electorate into supporting their stances for privileges for the Sinhalese language and Sinhalese Buddhism. The tactic succeeded at the general elections of 1956 and 1970, but in time it became a self-fulfilling prophecy and boomeranged on the Sinhalese. Increasing numbers of Tamil militants established hideouts on the South Indian coast. The Tamil nationalist parties established contacts with the South Indian nationalist D.M.K.s (Dravida Munnethra Kazhagam = Dravidian Progressive Front), originally one body but, since a schism, led respectively by M. Karunanidhi, former Chief Minister of Tamil Nad, and M. G. Ramachandran, the Chief Minister of Tamil Nad who has won two provincial elections. Consequently there has been built up in Tamil Nad a fund of support for the Tamil nationalist movement in Sri Lanka. Anti-Tamil riots in Sri Lanka have repercussions in Madras, the capital city of Tamil Nad. In August 1979, Tamil underground militants fled to their hideouts in the South Indian coast when a state of emergency was declared in the Tamil Northern province for the specific purpose of winnowing them out. Anti-Tamil riots in Sri Lanka are not specifically directed against Sri Lankan Tamils; when violence is widespread, the attackers make no distinction between Sri Lankan Tamils and Indian Tamils. The latter have attachments in Tamil Nad, and indeed, because since the status of large numbers of them has still to be finalised, the Government of India is invariably brought into an otherwise domestic conflict.

The situation is also complicated by the different positions taken by the various Indian Governments since Independence. Nehru's governments up to the time of his death refused to get embroiled, satisfying Indian opinion by declaring the vast majority of Indian Tamils in Sri Lanka to be 'stateless', a baffling problem in international law. Nehru's successor Lal Bahadur Shastri, presumably because of India's problems with Pakistan and the People's Republic of China, preferred to maintain good neighbourly relations with Sri Lanka and in 1964 concluded an agreement whereby a little over 54 per cent (i.e. 525,000 of the 975,000 Indians in Sri Lanka without citizenship rights) of the Indian Tamils in Sri Lanka and their natural increase would be repatriated to India over a fifteen-year period while Sri Lanka for her part would grant citizenship rights to some 32.4 per cent of the resident citizenless Indian population (300,000 Indians). The future of the remaining ± 13 per cent (approximately 150,000) was left undecided. In 1974 Mrs Gandhi's Government agreed with Mrs Bandaranaike's 1970–7 Government to split this remaining number fifty-fifty. The process of registration of Indian Tamil residents in Sri Lanka as citizens of either India or Sri Lanka has not worked according to the fifteen-year timetable, with the result that the Indian presence in the central heartlands of Sri Lanka remains a clearly visible one.

The complication is further compounded by the differing attitudes of Sri Lankan governments. In 1948 and 1949 a sovereign Sri Lanka (then Ceylon) disfranchised and decitizenised the overwhelming  majority of resident Indians who had had the franchise before Independence, provoking the Nehru Government to label these people as 'stateless'. The nationalist Sinhalese view has been that the resident Indians constitute a threat to the Sinhalese population — this for many reasons. In the highlands it is insisted that they have no permanent abiding interest in the land of their adoption. Indians have deprived the Sinhalese of employment opportunities in the tea and rubber plantations, and those of them who are traders drain profits to India and being more astute than the indigenous entrepreneurs, compete successfully with them. But, more important, the Sinhalese nationalists fear the Indian residents as a political threat. They could in various ways link up with Sri Lankan Tamil political organisations, and have indeed done so. This too has been a self-fulfilling prophecy. Where previously the resident Indians worked through their own political instruments, they have, particularly in the post-1956 years (when Sinhalese was made the only official language) tended to work in concert with Ceylon Tamil nationalist parties despite divergences of opinion on some fundamental questions such as the Sri Lankan Tamil demand for a federated Sri Lanka (1949–72) in which a Tamil homeland in the Northern and Eastern provinces would be recognised as an integral unit; or since 1972 when the agitation crystallised into the demand for a separate Tamil state of *Eelam*. There has also been objection by the Sinhalese to the representation of Indians in the legislature; after the 1947 general election, there were seven Indian members in a parliament of 101 members, but with the disfranchisement laws of 1948 and 1949, their number was reduced to nil; however, in spite of this reduction, and worse from the Sinhalese viewpoint, is the fact that Indian voters, since some of them regained the franchise, are able to influence the result in twenty or more constituencies.

The Sinhalese reaction to the Indian problem manifests itself in three ways. An oft-tried method, which has not been unsuccessful, is to create rifts between the Sri Lankan Tamil and Indian Tamil political leaderships. The majority section of the All Ceylon Tamil Congress, which was the dominant Sri Lankan Tamil party between 1947 and 1956, was persuaded by the then prime minister, D. S. Senanayake, to countenance the legislation in 1948 and 1949 against the resident Indians. This attitude greatly embittered both the resident Indian political and social élites and their leadership at various levels. From 1956 to 1977, the Tamil Federal Party and its successor umbrella organisation comprising the main Tamil parties (the Federal Party, the Tamil Congress and the Ceylon Workers' Congress) formed the Tamil United Liberation Front (T.U.L.F.). The Sri Lanka Tamil component of the T.U.L.F. worked in close liaison with the principal Indian Tamil organisation, the Ceylon Workers' Congress and its leader S. Thondaman. However after the general election of 1977, the newly-elected United National Party government led by J. R. Jayewardene persuaded Thondaman to join its ranks. Thondaman had up to this time been one of the presidents of the Tamil United Liberation Front. A second strategy, just as successful, was to persuade and/or pressure the Government of India to agree to the repatriation of a majority of the Indian resident population. A third, the outcome of which is still a matter for conjecture, is to seek to assimilate the remaining resident Indians who obtain Sri Lankan citizenship under the agreements of 1964 and 1974. The expectation is that in this way the proportion of the Sri Lankan Tamil population to the ethnic Sinhalese majority will be kept at present levels. The process of assimilation can be facilitated by the fact that the Indian Tamils live in the middle of the Sinhalese heartland, and not in areas contiguous to those of the Sri Lankan Tamils; and the schools in the plantation areas can therefore be made to provide instruction only in Sinhalese.

The political strategy of the Sri Lankan Tamil leadership has been to concentrate on creating strong bonds with the resident Indian Tamils. One of the problems of the former is that their population is not adequate to people the traditional homeland of the Northern and Eastern provinces. Consequently Indian Tamils in the plantation areas have been encouraged to found settlements in the border areas of these provinces, especially the northern province. In fact the Dudley Senanayake/Chelvanayakam Pact of March 1965 stipulated that in land settlement schemes in the Tamil homeland provinces, preference should be given to the people of these provinces, and next to Sri Lankan Tamils resident in other parts of the island, and if a sufficient number of Sri Lankan Tamils were not available, the overflow of Indian Tamils in the plantation areas should be given opportunities. The Ceylon Tamil Federal Party made a weak attempt in the 1960s to establish its own trade unions among Indian labour in the Sinhalese heartland. Since 1949, it has included citizenship and franchise rights for the resident Indian Tamils as an important plank in its political platform, and in its civil disobedience campaigns against the governments of Solomon Bandaranaike (1956–9) and Sirima Bandaranaike (1960–5), it endeavoured to secure the support of the two main Indian Tamil organisations, the more powerful Ceylon Workers' Congress and the Democratic Workers' Congress. The intention in all these strategies has been to mobilise a larger Tamil population in non-violent struggles against pro-Sinhala governments, and by various pressure tactics compel the Government of India to take note of the Tamil situation in Sri Lanka. The latter strategy was pursued with greater vigour in the post-1972 period. The leaders of the Ceylon Tamil United Liberation Front and activists from expatriate Sri Lankan Tamil nationalist organisations paid political visits to Indian leaders, in both government and opposition, in New Delhi and Tamil Nad with a view to advancing their cause.

India's national political leaders for their part have expressed ambivalent attitudes to the claims of the T.U.L.F. for a separate state. Their position is in a way influenced by the political complexion of the government in office as well as by the person at the helm in Sri Lanka. Mrs Gandhi was generally sympathetic to Mrs Sirima Bandaranaike and her centrist domestic and non-aligned foreign policies, but is cold towards President J. R. Jayewardene and his right-of-centre pro-West government (1977-). Morarji Desai, when prime minister, was close to President Jayewardene but, while discussing the Tamil situation with the Liberation Front leader Appapillai Amirthalingam and offering his good offices towards bringing President Jayewardene and the Front to the negotiating table, he decried the notion of a separate sovereign state. On the other hand regional leaders like those of the two DMKs in Tamil Nad, including their chief ministers the late C. N. Annadurai and his successors M. Karunanidhi and M. G. Ramachandran, while not specifically backing the agitation for a separate state, have nonetheless consistently supported the claims of the Tamils (Sri Lankan and Indian) for their due rights. They have been known to exercise pressure on New Delhi, and they have provided support to anti-Sri Lankan government demonstrations in Madras city. They have winked at Sri Lankan Tamil militants securing refuge in the Tamil mainland, and have not tried to interfere with the traffic in arms and men across the straits separating the South Indian coast and the northern coasts of Sri Lanka; these northern coastal areas are inhabited by Sri Lankan Tamils.

In various ways we have drawn attention to the centrifugal forces operating in an island which could, in the proper circumstances, have worked in the direction of a natural unity. No doubt attempts have been made to strengthen the centripetal tendencies. But these at times have been counter-productive, more because of mass involvement at the expense of the essential 'overarching élite co-operation'. At Independence some weightage in representation was provided for those sparsely populated areas in the island normally inhabited by members of the minority groups. But the advantages of increased representation for the minority groups were reversed by the disfranchisement and decitizenisation of Indian Tamils in 1948 and 1949, hardly a year later. Again, up to 1955, it was the policy of the major Sinhalese political parties to provide for the recognition of the Sinhalese and Tamil languages as official languages of the island. In 1955–6 the two major Sinhalese parties that mattered reversed their position to one of Sinhalese as the only official language, thereby giving an extra boost to the forces of Tamil separatism.

In 1957, the prime minister Solomon Bandaranaike, with a view to undoing the dangerous consequences of the Official Language Act of 1956, concluded an agreement with the Tamil Federal Party leader S. J. V. Chelvanayakam, providing for the control of land settlement schemes in the Tamil homelands and for a measure of official recognition for the Tamil language. The agreement had the support of the majority of Bandaranaike's cabinet and of the Federal Party.[8] It had however to be abrogated in May 1957 due to pressure exerted on the prime minister by politically involved Buddhist monks. In August 1958, the same prime minister had the Tamil Language (Special Provisions) Act enacted by Parliament. His objective was to contain the forces of Tamil separatism.

His widow Mrs Sirima Bandaranaike, who was prime minister during 1960–5, followed a policy of drift; she also permitted some of her ministers to pursue objectives that were antagonistic to the Tamils. The situation would have worsened considerably but for the return to power of the United National Party and its liberal democratic leader, Dudley Senanayake, who was premier from 1965 till 1970. The new prime minister came to an agreement with the Tamil Federal Party leader S. J. V. Chelvanayakam on lines similar to those of the agreement of 1957. The agreement was not honoured in full, but the Senanayake Government had parliament legislate regulations which made Tamil and Sinhalese the official languages in the Tamil homeland provinces (Northern and Eastern). It will be seen that the period

1956–70 was one in which Sinhalese leadership sought accommodation with the Tamils; but they were thwarted by their rank and file. The nation was however prevented from breaking up because the hope remained that liberal elements among the Sinhalese political élites would prevent the situation from going out of control.

Mrs Bandaranaike's second term as prime minister, in 1970–7, was the occasion for a well articulated pronouncement on the Tamil claim for sovereign statehood. Her Government wished to frame a new constitution. Again the Tamil leadership presaged a situation that went back to what they felt was the twilight period after Britain's withdrawal in 1948 and the consequent lapse of paramountcy over the island. But neither Mrs Bandaranaike nor her nationalistic Sinhalese Buddhist Cabinet was willing to allow the constituent assembly summoned to frame a new republican constitution to consider the Tamil claim for Tamil language rights and for a Tamil homeland which would be federated to the rest of the island. There were other acts which also alienated the Tamil minority. A scheme for the standardisation of marks for admission of students to the universities was directed towards reducing the intake of Tamil-medium students; and hardly any employment was provided that would enable Tamils to enter the public or private sectors. The beginnings of a Tamil underground movement comprising militant youth elements began to make itself felt, and in consequence the Tamil provinces were placed under military occupation and emergency rule. The time when the attitude of the Sinhalese élite alternated between carrot and stick had ended. It was now merely a question of employing military repression to counter the threat of inter-ethnic collision. It was thus when all else had failed after over a quarter of a century of agitation for a peaceful resolution or a negotiated settlement of the questions at issue that a now united front of the major Tamil political parties, the Tamil United Liberation Front, met in convention at Vaddukoddai, a town in the Tamil-inhabited Jaffna peninsula in the north of Sri Lanka on 14 May 1976 under the chairmanship of its charismatic father-figure S. J. V. Chelvanayakam, and resolved that 'a separate, free, secular, sovereign, socialist state of Tamil *Eelam*' should be established. At the 1977 general election, the Front sought a mandate for *Eelam* from the Tamil electors in the Tamil homeland provinces. It received convincing evidence of support for such a course of action.

An important question arises in the context of this move towards the politics of secession. The debates on human and language rights, equal opportunities, a separate Tamil identity, and the preservation of the Tamil homeland had been the great issues from the mid-1950s to the mid-1970s. The rationale seemed to be that there were liberal elements among the Sinhalese élites who could persuade their constituencies to agree to the necessary accommodation in order to maintain the island as a single entity. Did the year 1976, and what came to be known as the Vaddukoddai Resolution, imply that the Tamils had decided to step into a different epoch?

A precise answer is impossible, but there was little doubt that the situation had reached crisis proportions, and some of the major Sinhalese political parties were forced to take serious note of the rapid deterioration. The United National Party Government which came into power in 1977 raised the issue in its manifesto for the 1977 general election — at a time when it was still in opposition. It made specific reference to the Tamil demand for a separate state. The traditional Left (the Trotskyist Lanka Sama Samaja Party and the Moscow-oriented Communist Party), which had collaborated with Mrs Bandaranaike's 1970–7 Government, spoke broadly in terms of granting the Tamils the right of self-determination in a socialist system (only the uninitiated would have taken such a pronouncement literally). But of greater significance were the implications which the changed situation spelled out for the Tamil minority both in Sri Lanka and abroad. Up to 1976, the Tamil parties had contained the forces of Tamil separatism within the island's confines in the hope that the Sinhalese leadership could be pressured in to agreeing on various constitutional formulae which could preserve the Tamil language and culture, the Tamil identity and the Tamil homeland. Now for the first time these parties resolved to throw these hopes overboard as vain. Very deliberately they abandoned separatism for secession, in the process unleashing the forces of Tamil nationalism. They reminded the Tamil people that they had constituted a separate kingdom until the Portuguese, Dutch and British took possession of their territories, and exhorted them not to become 'a slave nation ruled by the new colonial masters, the Sinhalese'. It must be said that the effect in some Tamil quarters was electric. It opened up new vistas: new élites among the Tamils would find their due place in an independent Tamil *Eelam*. The fact of the matter was that the necessary indicators for the creation and fulfilment of a separate political identity were present. All that it needed was a clarion call from a hesitant leadership to a nation whose weaker élites were unable on their own to articulate ambitions for separate sovereign statehood with the required resoluteness.

With the return of the United National Party to power in July 1977, there was some hope that Tamil expectations would be met by the new leadership. But there were four factors which stymied these expectations. The T.U.L.F. claimed that it had obtained a mandate for the setting up of a separate state of Tamil *Eelam*. The mandate that was asked for was specific and left no room for doubt:[9]

There is only one alternative and that is to proclaim with the stamp of finality and fortitude that we alone shall rule over our homeland that our forefathers ruled. Sinhalese imperialism shall quit our homeland. The Tamil United Liberation Front regards the general election of 1977 as a means of proclaiming to the Sinhalese government this resolve of the Tamil nation . . . . Hence the Tamil United Liberation Front seeks in the General Election, a mandate from the Tamil nation to establish an independent sovereign, secular, socialist state of Tamil *Eelam* that includes all the geographically contiguous areas that have been the traditional homeland of the Tamil speaking people in the country.

The Tamil claim for separate statehood seemed to be bolstered by the fact that for the first time in Sri Lanka's parliament, a Tamil, and the leader of the T.U.L.F.'s parliamentary group at that, had become the official Leader of the Opposition. The Tamil nationalist view was that the office presented an opportunity for the Front's leader to bring the problem of the Tamil people to the attention of the world; and he was not slow to exploit the office to the advantage of his party.

Sinhalese-Tamil clashes throughout the island, which followed in the wake of the July 1977 general election in the months of August-September further widened the gap between the new Government and Tamil nationalist elements. The latter held the view that the Government had not hurried to suppress the rioting, but the Government pleaded, unofficially, that the police and armed forces had been infiltrated by the recruits and nominees of the preceding 1970–7 Sri Lanka Freedom Party Government to such an extent that it was not in an effective position to command the forces of law and order.

Finally the T.U.L.F. expected the new government to make tangible concessions to its demand for statehood. It expected at least a measure of regional autonomy to be written into the new constitution that was being formulated. But although important provisions were made for the use of the Tamil language and the protection of human rights, the expected autonomy failed to materialise.

These four factors contributed to a widespread internationalisation of the Tamil question. Tamil expatriates, many of them members of the educated and professional élites assisted by T.U.L.F. members of parliament, organised movements and campaigns in the important capitals and cities of the world to explain to governments and the media the problems of the Tamil people. The main objective was to influence aid-giving organisations so that they would ensure that any assistance was distributed equitably, and not utilised for the development of river valley schemes which could make inroads into the Tamil homelands. The Government in time began to feel the pressure, and took propaganda counter-measures, the effectiveness of which cannot easily be assessed. The Government, presumably to save its face, vehemently denied that foreign governments had begun to ask awkward questions and were slowing down their aid programmes.

The tension created by Tamil propaganda and apparent governmental indifference to Tamil demands for statehood began to have their effects on the domestic situation. The build-up of resentment between Sinhalese and Tamils at all levels, including that of the élites, where previously many Sinhalese had tended to be protective of their Tamil counterparts, almost reached flashpoint in June, July and early August 1979. It was at this point that an intermediary in the person of the present author offered his good offices to the Executive President of the Republic with a view to bringing the T.U.L.F. and Government spokesmen together to the negotiating table.

President J. R. Jayewardene accepted the arguments that this intermediary proffered against the convening of a roundtable conference. Such a conference was widely advocated; but it could have led opposed parties to adopt inflexible stances for public consumption. In such an atmosphere compromises or concessions could not have been made. A second alternative was for a cabinet committee to come up with proposals, but again the T.U.L.F. would not have had any representatives on it; and such a committee would have taken months before coming up with any concrete suggestions. The need of the hour was for speedy action. A third alternative could very well have been a directly negotiated settlement between the Executive President and the T.U.L.F. leaders — settlements such as those arrived at in the past between the Tamil leader S. J. V. Chelvanayakam and the prime minister of the day (Solomon Bandaranaike in 1958 and Dudley Senanayake in 1965). But then it would have been alleged that either too much was given away, or that the other parties involved had not been brought into the discussions, or, as had been said in the past, that concessions were extracted from a prime minister placed in a difficult if not perilous situation. Hence the idea suggested by the author to the President for a commission of experts appealed to the President; this would enable parties to negotiate, as it were, by proxy. They would not have to be riveted to their positions for fear of being subjected to pressure from groups and lobbies. It was just possible that a formula acceptable to the parties that mattered could be produced by such a commission, and the author persuaded the T.U.L.F. to accept the scheme. Sections of the Sri Lanka Freedom Party were not averse, but in the end the party's politbureau decided not to co-operate. The traditional Left declined to get involved. In the end the commission comprised representatives of the Government, the Muslim community, a representative from the T.U.L.F. and three academics including the present writer. It was headed by a former chief justice.

The appointment of the commission in early August 1979 was

intended to allay Tamil fears, indeed to raise Tamil expectations, for the commission's terms of reference had been agreed to by the T.U.L.F. and by the President; it called, among other things, for recommendations for the decentralisation of the administration and the devolution of subordinate law-making powers to district legislative bodies to be named district development councils. Simultaneously the Government also declared a state of emergency in early August 1979. There had been some twenty political assassinations in the Jaffna peninsula where a large percentage of the Ceylon Tamil population resides, and this, coupled with the persistent Tamil propaganda in Sri Lanka and abroad for a separate state, were leading towards an explosion. The state of emergency succeeded in controlling the dangerous situation.

Because of the urgent need to defuse what has been called the Tamil powder-keg, the President hoped that the commission would issue its report by the end of September (1979) so that he could have the necessary legislation enacted the following month,[10] but in both matters he was to be disappointed. The commission lingered on till the end of February 1980 when it finally came out with recommendations that were not in keeping with the President's formula to solve the Tamil deadlock. In the end the President and his Government had no alternative to sidestepping most of the commission's recommendations, although it used some of them as a basis for framing legislation that could possibly meet Tamil expectations, at least for the time being.

Briefly the legislation enacted in August 1980 provided for the establishment of district development councils in each of the island's twenty-four administrative districts. The members of parliament for a district were to be *ex-officio* members. A certain number of members would be elected to each council on the list system of proportional representation, but the number of elected members would not outnumber the members of parliament for the district except in those districts where the number of M.P.s was five or less than five; there the number of members elected would be fixed by Presidential order. Each council would have an elected chairman and an executive committee of not more than three or four members inclusive of the chairman and the District Minister. The members of the executive committee would be assigned a quota of subjects from among those devolved to the council by the central government and in terms of the legislation referred to, the determination of the membership of the executive committee and the assigning of subjects to each member being the responsibility of the District Minister who would have to act in consultation with the chairman of the Council. The District Minister would, in most situations, be chosen from the government parliamentary group. Finances are assigned to each council by the central government on the basis of a district development plan which the executive committee and the council would devise. Each council would also have limited taxing powers. The councils would further have the right to raise loans internally and abroad with the permission of the Minister of Finance.[11]

The T.U.L.F. accepted the legislation, but it did not abandon its goal of a separate sovereign state of Tamil *Eelam*.[12] Extreme Sinhalese militant groups have not accepted the legislation; nor has the Sri Lanka Freedom Party, whose consent to it could have helped to contain the demand for *Eelam*. There are yet other variables which will determine the direction that Tamil politics will take in the future. Much will depend on the kind of District Ministers appointed to the Tamil districts and, even more so, on the way in which the legislation will be implemented by Sinhalese bureaucrats.

In effect there are two points at issue. President J. R. Jayewardene will wish the system to function smoothly, but will his officials go along with him? And how will his successor view the scheme? And what if his successor should be the leader of the Sri Lanka Freedom Party? There is yet another serious imponderable: has the Sinhalese mind come round to the view that the present compromise is the most satisfactory in the circumstances? Apart from the fact that President Jayewardene seeks to work the scheme in the proper spirit, the answers to our other questions are either negative or in doubt. There is little evidence that there has been a change of heart among important sections of the Sinhalese élites. The prospects therefore do not appear favourable.

And what of the Tamils? There is deep-rooted suspicion among their intelligentsia and élites that their Sinhalese counterparts will not allow the system to work in the way they expect it should — as a quasi-federal set-up. The activists and militants for *Eelam* do not even look on it as a first step towards their objective; indeed they fear that it is a setback because the Government will now claim that it has effected a reconciliation. They allege that the T.U.L.F. has miscalculated in accepting the settlement even though the Front refuses to give up its objective of a separate state. The ranks of the Tamils are therefore just as divided as those of the Sinhalese. Social and ethnic peace has been legislated for, but the law will find it difficult to change the hostility to the Tamils among sections of the Sinhalese and the fear and suspicion of the Sinhalese felt in general by the Tamils. The situation is compounded by inflation and a declining economy with the attendant problems of limited wealth to share out. Looking into the future, the Tamil problem will defy a lasting solution unless the changes outlined above do actually take place.

NOTES

1. Larry Collins and Dominique Lapierre, *Freedom at Midnight* (New York, 1975), 124.
2. See his *Democracy in Plural Societies* (New Haven, 1977), especially 81–3.
3. Collins and Lapierre, op.cit.
4. *Ceylon: Report of the Commission on Constitutional Reform, Command 6677* (London, reprinted 1955).
5. See W. H. Morris-Jones, *The Government and Politics of India* (London, Hutchinson University Library, 1964), 75–8.
6. For the details and exposition of this constitution, see Sir Ivor Jennings, *The Constitution of Ceylon* (3rd edn, Bombay, 1953).
7. See for example 'The Tamil powder keg', *Financial Times*, 31 May 1978.
8. A. Jeyaratnam Wilson, *Politics in Sri Lanka, 1947–1979* (2nd edn, London, 1979), 42; also W. Howard Wriggins, *Ceylon: Dilemmas of a New Nation* (Princeton, N.J., 1960), 265–7.
9. Tamil United Liberation Front, Manifesto for the General Elections of 1977 (translation), 16.
10. See the interview given by the President of the Republic to the *Tribune*, 18 August 1979, 12.
11. For further details on the district development councils bill, see the speech of the Honourable R. Premadasa, Prime Minister of Sri Lanka in *Parliamentary Debates* (*Hansard*) vol. 11, no. 6, cols 396–434; also Sessional Paper No. V — 1980, *Report of the Presidential Commission on Development Councils* (Colombo, Government Publications Bureau, 1980).

SOUTH ASIA AND THE OUTSIDE WORLD

Leo E. Rose

The perspectives of South Asian states on the external environment since the withdrawal of the British from the subcontinent have varied widely over time, but there has been a considerable degree of consistency in their respective responses to the involvement of outside powers in the subcontinent. While this has been determined primarily by the specific circumstances surrounding both regional and extra-regional developments, there is also a wide variety of historical and cultural traditions that continue to influence policies and attitudes on foreign policy and security issues in the polities and subpolities in South Asia.

Geopolitical factors, of course, have always been critical in defining the worldview of the political élites in various parts of the subcontinent. In what is now Pakistan, Afghanistan and northern India, the 'North West Frontier' has usually been the critical security area as far as external threats are concerned, whether the time reference is to the Gupta, Moghul or British imperial period in South Asian history. There are, however, subtle but important differences in their respective perceptions on security issues. For northern Indian élites, the historical problem has been to attain and maintain regional unity in the face of aggression from the north-west. Balance of power strategies usually made little sense in such situations; Kautilya's fundamental principle that your neighbor was your natural enemy and your neighbor's neighbor on the other side your natural ally may have worked well in South Asia itself but was generally inapplicable to threats from outside the region. Even the British rulers of India could not apply balance of power strategies very effectively in their efforts to contain Russian expansion toward their Indian empire, but had to confront it through the subordination of the region to their imperial control and the creation of buffer areas. For the political élite in what is now Pakistan and in Afghanistan, however, the traditional power politics game has generally been interpreted quite differently. For polities in these areas, external security threats came from the subcontinent as well as from the north and west. Their normal response was to use balance of power politics — at least in those situations in which there were powers on two or more sides that could be balanced against each other.

Thus, quite different perspectives on security issues underlie the theoretical principles of the foreign policies of India, Pakistan, and Afghanistan. The latter two states have used balance of power strategies as the basis of their foreign policy when circumstances permitted (obviously, the Soviet occupation of Afghanistan in 1979–80 seriously inhibited that state from using such strategies — for the nonce). India, however, strongly rejects the very concept of balance of power in theory, although in actual practice it has used the principle quite effectively on several occasions.

For the Himalayan region, from Ladakh to Bhutan, the geostrategic situation has generally been similar to that on the North West Frontier of the subcontinent — i.e. the polities there faced threats from both the north and the south and had to adjust policies accordingly. There were, in general terms, three options available to them: (1) the maximum isolation of the area — or more generally one small part of the area — from the external world; (2) an accommodation with the dominant power to the north or south on the best possible terms; and (3) the employment of balance of power politics when feasible — e.g. when the external powers to both the north and south could be used to counteract each other. All three policies have been employed in the past by Himalayan area polities which have a long history of adroit adjustments to external political realities, shifting back and forth between policy options as circumstances dictated. This capacity for sensitive responses to *realpolitik* demands is still evident in the foreign policies of Nepal and Bhutan, now the only independent states in the Himalayas.

The Indian Ocean has been the principle strategic factor in the foreign policies of Sri Lanka and the littoral states in southern India, a very different brand of security issue from that which has preoccupied the attention of the rest of the subcontinent. At times the Ocean has been a barrier to interaction with the outside world, but more frequently it has been an avenue for political, economic and/or cultural expansionism. Over the past two millenia, for instance, Sri Lanka has been the target of Sinhala, Tamil, Muslim, Portuguese, Dutch, and British invaders, while Indian commercial and cultural 'imperialists' were very active in both insular and mainland Southeast Asia. This probably explains why Sri Lanka sponsored the proposal in the United Nations to make the Indian Ocean a 'zone of peace'. While it is doubtful that this serves contemporary Sri Lankan security interests in the region, since it would leave the Indian Navy — the only potential threat to Sri Lanka these days — as the principal military force in the waters around the island, it does fit nicely into the traditional Sri Lankan worldview on security issues.

One would also have expected that the British conquest of India from the sea would have made the post-1947 Indian political élite very sensitive to the strategic importance of the Indian Ocean, but by and large this was not the case. The explanation for this may be that much of the Indian decision-making élite on foreign policy issues was north Indian in origin and had a north Indian perspective on security issues. They only turned their attention seaward when developments there assumed dangerous proportions. The post-Independence Indian Government, for instance, virtually ignored the Indian Ocean (and the Indian Navy) until the early 1960s when a tacit working arrangement between China, Indonesia and Pakistan, combined with a substantial withdrawal of British naval power, raised the possibility of the Indian Ocean being dominated by unfriendly neighboring states.[1]

The diversity in contemporary South Asian foreign policies is also in part the consequence of some basic cultural factors in the region. The Muslim élite in Pakistan, by definition, prefers to stress ties with the Southwest Asian Islamic states rather than with the subcontinent. Pakistan can only do this to a limited extent, of course, since it has substantial political, economic and security interests in South Asia. There is, moreover, the large Muslim minority in India and the Islamic state of Bangladesh in the northeast for which the Pakistani élite still feels a residue of responsibility. On balance, nevertheless, Pakistan feels much more comfortable in its relations with the states to the west, and after the 1971 Indo-Pak war over Bangladesh it tended to project a self-identification as part of Southwest Asia rather than South Asia. The developments in Iran and Afghanistan in 1978–80 made this more difficult and less rewarding, and Islamabad has been compelled to turn back to South Asia — primarily India — to bolster its security interests. But when (and if) the crisis in these two neighboring Islamic states is resolved, Pakistan may well be inclined to renew its efforts to opt out of the regional system in the subcontinent as far as possible, again emphasising its membership in the Islamic bloc of states. Similarly, Bangladesh on the opposite side of the subcontinent has some elements in its élite which project identification with South and/or Southeast Asia and prefer to stress the Islamic character of their state. This is far less feasible for Bangladesh than for Pakistan in terms of geopolitical and economic realities, but it has had some impact on Bangladesh foreign policy since the overthrow of the Awami League regime in 1975.

Nepal's high-caste Hindu élite, which is an extension through intermarriage of equivalent caste groups in India, has been the principal determinant of the national Nepali worldview. Kathmandu has become quite adept at playing a variety of foreign policy games at particular points in time — e.g. using China as a counterbalance to India in both the nineteenth and twentieth centuries — but there is no question that the ultimate Nepali identification is with India for cultural as well as geostrategic reasons. The Sinhala Buddhist élite in Sri Lanka has also gone through the motions on occasion of trying to develop a closer relationship, mainly economic, with Buddhist societies in Southeast Asia (as well as with the Islamic states of Indonesia and Malaysia and Sinic Singapore) as an alternative to its regional ties with India. This never got very far in basic geostrategic terms, but it is one other instance in which cultural factors in the subcontinent constitute an important obstacle to the growth of a regional South Asia worldview.

South Asian foreign policies in the post-1947 period

One of the obvious characteristics of post-Independence South Asia is the importance of the British Indian heritage in defining the basic principle of foreign policy. This is not particularly surprising since the British Government of India had a classic South Asian perspective on security and strategic issues which were reflected in the long history of disagreements between London and Calcutta/New Delhi on certain key issues — primarily on how to handle Russian and Chinese threats to the Raj and on the role of British India in British imperial policy in other areas of Asia. The critical foreign policy decision-making élite in both India and Pakistan had imbibed these policy principles either through direct involvement in the administration (e.g. Girja Bajpai in India and Zafrullah Khan in Pakistan) or through osmosis (e.g. Nehru in India and Jinnah in Pakistan, both of whom were the products of British political *and* intellectual traditions).

There have been significant differences in the foreign policies of the major South Asian states — i.e. India's advocacy of nonalignment and zones of peace in contrast to Pakistan's acceptance of the need for alignment with external power(s) and balance of power politics. Nevertheless, the major foreign policy decisions by both powers that affected the subcontinent were strongly influenced by British Indian conceptual parameters. There has been, for instance, a basic continuity in Indian policy toward the Himalayan principalities (Nepal, Sikkim, Bhutan and Kashmir) in the British and post-Independence periods which the change in rulers in New Delhi has scarcely affected. Nehru's policy toward China was also classically British both in the 1950s, when he tried to develop a working relationship with Peking, and after the 1962 Sino-Indian war, when New Delhi sought to counterbalance the reassertion of Chinese influence in the Himalayan border area. Pakistan's policy toward Iran and Afghanistan was also derived from British experience, with Iran defined primarily as a support base (against India as well as Russia) and Afghanistan as an area of potential contention and confrontation.

While the conceptual models that underlay Indian and Pakistan foreign policy decision-making in the post-Independence period were not too dissimilar, there were important distinctions between their respective capacities to implement foreign policies. In 1947, India had a small but very effective political élite group with reasonably well-defined views on foreign policy issues and some capacity to deal with an intrusive outside world. Pakistan lacked this kind of expertise. Its political élite had been almost exclusively concerned with regional issues — that is, the establishment of an Islamic state in South Asia. There had been no consideration given to foreign policy issues before Independence, and there was nothing remotely resembling a consensus on the subject. The nominal 'Islamic' character of the new state defined its early foreign policy, primarily an effort to evolve a common policy with the Islamic states of Southwest Asia. This proved to be a formula for failure since there was nothing even remotely resembling a consensus on international issues among the states of the region at that time; but it was not until 1950 that Pakistan began seriously to consider alternative foreign policy options.

Nepal had what was probably the most experienced and pragmatic foreign policy élite in the whole of South Asia in 1947. While it regretted the British withdrawal from the subcontinent, it quickly adjusted to the new circumstances. Kathmandu's policy response was to establish essentially the same working relationship with New Delhi as had worked so well for Nepal during the British period — that is, to exchange acceptance of Government of India 'guidance' on Nepal's international relations and on security issues in exchange for almost total autonomy in internal matters. The treaty signed between India and Nepal in early 1950 was based upon these principles; but two developments later that year — the Chinese invasion of Tibet and internal disorders in Nepal — changed the situation drastically. The old regime in Nepal was replaced by a new political élite that had been largely socialised into politics in the Indian nationalist movement and was heavily dependent, both psychologically and materially, on Indian support. It was nearly a decade before foreign policy decision-making in Nepal was again based upon perceptions of the country's interests and role in the Himalayan region; and, as might have been expected, with an exaggerated reaction to anything that could be classified as acceptance of Indian leadership and guidance.

Some Indian leaders have demonstrated considerable difficulty in responding sensitively to Nepali concerns, usually defining as 'pro-Chinese' anything that Kathmandu saw as 'nationalist'. While there is no doubt that China has sought to complicate India's relationship with

Nepal in any way that it could, or that Nepal has often responded with some enthusiasm to Peking's efforts to provide a counterbalance to India, China's *capacity* to compete successfully with India in the sub-Himalayan region has been exaggerated in India. Despite the great advantages that India enjoys in economic, political, social, intellectual, and psychological relations with Nepal, there has been a propensity for Indian opinion — encouraged by Soviet-financed publications and intellectuals in India — to denounce every Sino-Nepali interaction as evidence that Nepal is a Chinese 'puppet'.

The subtle changes that took place in Chinese policy in South Asia in the late 1970s, reflected in a much reduced interest in encouraging anti-Indian elements in the subcontinent, is finally getting through to Indian élites beyond the official level, but the strong suspicions and hostility towards China's role in the Himalayan area is still readily evident to the public. The standard response is still to define anything the Chinese do in South Asia, and particularly in the Himalayas, as being motivated by anti-Indian objectives. Nepal has been one of the victims of this sentiment in respect of its giant neighbor to the south, as there have been occasions on which New Delhi has adopted a hardline position on Indo-Nepali relations in response to developments in Sino-Nepali relations. While Kathmandu's excessive enthusiasm and gratitude for what are often little more than token gestures of support from Peking certainly stimulates the Indian response, it was only in the mid-1970s that a more balanced reaction in New Delhi became evident.

Bhutan has had a high level of continuity in its political system and élite since 1947. Thus, the changes that have taken place in its foreign policy are changes in perception of the country's geopolitical environment. Bhutan followed its traditional isolationist policy until the early 1960s when Chinese involvement in Tibet began to appear threatening. Thimphu responded by accepting an accommodation with India which, in effect, made it part of the Indian security system on international issues, as well as a recipient of substantial Indian economic assistance for developmental programs. New Delhi has responded in a carefully generous way to Bhutan's interest in expanding its international relations, with results that have been reasonably satisfactory to both governments overall. Again there are politically motivated elements in India that occasionally raise the 'China threat' motif on developments in Bhutan, but this is now ludicrous enough not to elicit much response from even the more paranoiac (on the China issue) elements of the Indian public.

There has also been a substantial degree of continuity in the political élite and foreign policy in Sri Lanka despite the periodic changes in the party that controls the government. Sri Lanka's principles of international relations were established early and maintained at least until the late 1970s. These included: (1) keeping all kinds of contacts with South Asia — e.g. India — to the necessary minimum; (2) the maximum diversification of relations with nonregional powers; and (3) limited involvement in international disputes except on a rather harmless rhetorical level that did not alienate anybody important.[2] India has not always been particularly happy with Sri Lankan policy, particularly in periods when Colombo's relations with Peking have been interpreted by New Delhi as too close. But for the most part India has preferred to accommodate Sri Lankan 'demands' on issues in dispute between the two countries as these did not seriously affect basic Indian interests while a more hardline approach was potentially expensive.

Afghanistan has emerged in the 1980s as the buffer area between South Asia and the outside world in the most difficult and dangerous position. Since 1947 it has faced a continuing border dispute with Pakistan that has defied resolution because it is critical to the political system and security of both states. There has been a similar, if much less public and critical, problem in Iran-Afghan relations. In both cases, the principal issue in dispute is not so much the definition of a boundary alignment as it is control over the various communities — Pakhtoon, Baluchi, Shia Muslim — that straddle the borders of these three countries. Afghanistan has also faced persistent Soviet pressure of the type that could not be effectively countered in policy terms, but was dependent upon Soviet forbearance in intervening directly in Afghanistan — a forbearance that disappeared in 1979. Thus, Afghanistan's independence has been at best tentative since the mid-1950s, dependent upon the capacity of the government in Kabul to maintain a delicate balance based on the acceptance of the priority of Soviet interests but some diversification of Afghani international contacts.

The United States and, to a less extent, China were participants in Afghanistan's balance of power politics, but in the 1970s India and Iran assumed the more significant role. The 1980s began with massive Soviet intervention in Afghanistan in ways that made the survival of this ancient polity (if we can use that term to describe a system as decentralised as that of Afghanistan) very doubtful. The critical role of South Asia, and in particular India and Pakistan, in these developments is obvious, but there is no assurance that the South Asian states are capable of responding effectively to the challenge posed by Soviet intervention or that they can deter Moscow from pushing through whatever policy it should decide upon for its troublesome neighbor.

Foreign policy strategies

The differences between India and the other South Asian states is not confined to certain aspects of foreign policy principles, but extend to the strategies and tactics employed to achieve policy goals. For India, the primary objective since Independence has been to exclude the major external powers from any significant influence or role in the subcontinent, an intrinsic if usually unstated aspect of Nehru's nonalignment policy. Since this has not often been possible for a variety of reasons, New Delhi has instead sought to manipulate and limit the involvement of these external powers in the region to ways that serve Indian objectives and interests. When one or more of the major powers would not co-operate, India has then invited the involvement of the other(s) as a counter — in other words, it has used balance of power politics despite New Delhi's rhetorical aversion to the principle.

The other South Asian states in most instances have perceived the external powers in terms of their own relationship with India, and thus in very different ways from New Delhi. The concept of an 'equal relationship' with India is one that has seemed unrealistic, indeed utopian, and it has been the general assumption that New Delhi would never be satisfied with anything less than a hegemonic status in the region. Even a regional system in which all the South Asian states would be involved was not attractive, because such a system would inevitably be dominated by India. Only recently have some of the élite in the smaller states seen possible advantages in dealing with India on political, economic and security issues through a multilateral system rather than on the present bilateral basis, but the advantages and disadvantages of both are being carefully weighed before anything substantive is proposed.

Given the general view of India as their principal foreign policy problem, the other South Asian states have usually actively sought to involve external powers in South Asia on terms that improved their bargaining position with New Delhi and contributed to their security in other ways as well. There were some serious problems with this approach, however; New Delhi of course views such policies as 'anti-Indian' and as a threat to peace and security in the subcontinent, and the normal Indian response has been to become even more hardline in bilateral relations with its neighbors. Moreover, while the major external powers have been prepared at times to serve as a counter to India when this served their policy and strategic interests, more often they have been unenthusiastic about assuming such a role. When they have agreed to an involvement in the subcontinent, they have demanded a price — and on occasion a high price — for their co-operation with regional state policies. This is most evident in

Pakistan's relationship with the United States in the 1950s and 1960s and Nepal's with China in the 1960s and 1970s; but it was also integral to the Indian relationship with the Soviet Union in the 1960s when Moscow made some expensive demands upon New Delhi which the Government of India was not always able to reject. Thus, more often than not, the South Asian states which have invited the intervention of external powers in the region to serve their specific policy interests have had at best indifferent success (except possibly the Indo-Soviet relationship) in this endeavor, and have had to pay a high price in terms of their interactions with both external and regional powers.

Major power intervention and South Asian responses

The major powers capable of intervention in South Asia are the Soviet Union, China, the United States, and the Islamic states of Southwest Asia — particularly Iran (up to 1979) but the Arab League 'bloc' as well in some situations. India has had the most success in manipulating the involvement of these states in South Asia to its own advantage. From the mid-1950s to 1979, at least, the Soviet Union had been quite responsive to Indian wishes, as Moscow has usually defined its role in the subcontinent in ways that either served Indian interests or at least were not strongly opposed to them. There have been some important exceptions to this general rule: Moscow's ambiguous position on the Sino-Indian border dispute until 1963; the Soviet arms aid program to Pakistan in 1968–9; and the quiet but rather serious competition between India and the Soviet Union for the role of the most influential foreign power in Bangladesh in the 1972–5 period. But it has been the Soviet support of Leftist puppet regimes in Afghanistan in the late 1970s, culminating in direct Soviet military intervention in December 1979, that has posed the greatest dilemma for New Delhi, since this violates all the basic principles of Indian policy toward the role of external powers in South Asia.

Indian policy toward the Soviet Union since the mid-1950s has been consistent. New Delhi has been very appreciative of Soviet support on a wide range of issues in South Asia, and in particular its balancing role in the broader geostrategic environment in which the United States, China, and the Islamic states have often been perceived as following policies that ran counter to Indian interests. Even in those instances in which New Delhi was unhappy with Soviet policy, either in the region or outside, the policy has been to avoid public criticism of Moscow but, when necessary, to make the Indian positions clear through private discussions with the Soviet authorities. While this has at times raised doubts about India's claim to be nonaligned (given its predilection for loud public criticisms of almost anything that the United States or Chinese Government does), it has seemed a sensible approach to New Delhi and one that has had positive results overall. And while the Government of India has generally viewed the Soviet Union as a positive factor in South Asia, most of the responsible officials in New Delhi have understood that this was not necessarily eternal. The Indian response to Soviet military intervention in Afghanistan in 1980, for instance, has followed the pattern described above, but it is also evident that New Delhi is fully aware that a major change in the nature of the Soviet role in South Asia is occurring and that this may eventually require painful but unavoidable modifications in Indian policy or even more painful redefinitions of India's regional status as the 'dominant power'.

The Indian relationship with the People's Republic of China started out on approximately the same terms as that with the Soviet Union, but it has developed quite differently. There was a brief period of rather substantial Sino-Indian co-operation and even collaboration in the 1950s, both on South Asian and broader international issues. This was completely reversed by both sides after the outbreak of the Sino-Indian border dispute in 1959 and the brief border hostilities between the two powers in 1962. From the early 1960s through the mid-1970s, the basic principle of Chinese policy in South Asia was directed at organizing the other states in the region against India, or at least in doing everything possible to complicate New Delhi's relations with these states. China had considerable success with Pakistan and Nepal, both of which were responsive to Peking's overtures in this respect as these seemed to serve their own policy objectives as well.[3] China also sought to support internal dissident forces in India, particularly in the troubled northeastern area, by providing military assistance and training as well as ideological guidance to a variety of 'revolutionary' movements. There was a period in the late 1960s when the 'Great Thoughts of Chairman Mao' were spouted with almost as little comprehension in Calcutta as in Shanghai.

The 1971 Indo-Pakistan war and the major changes that followed in South Asian geopolitics led to some subtle but significant changes in Chinese policy toward the region. These coincided with modifications of Indian policy in the direction of a more 'balanced relationship' with the external powers, and led in 1975 to the 'normalization' of Sino-Indian diplomatic relations through an exchange of ambassadors — the first since 1962. While China retained its useful ties with the other South Asian states, it also redefined its role in the region in some interesting ways — primarily by shifting away from the policy of encouraging these states to assume anti-Indian positions to one where they were quietly encouraged — on some occasions, at least — to improve their relations with New Delhi. In any case, since 1975 Chinese policy in South Asia has been less threatening to India — and less of a complication — than at any time since the late 1950s.

Obviously this is the consequence of new postures and policies by both sides as New Delhi has also modified some of its policies (e.g. toward Pakistan) in ways that meet with approval in Peking. The two largest Asian powers are also cautiously discussing a resolution of their own disagreements, if with limited success. Peking, for instance, reportedly no longer provides support to dissident forces in India's northeast, apparently even resisting the temptation to seek some advantages out of the major confrontation between the Government of India and the state governments and political movements in Assam and other smaller northeast Indian states in 1979–80. India, in turn, has moderated its support of Tibetan rebel groups based south of the Himalayas and has encouraged the Dalai Lama to come to terms with Peking — particularly if these should result in a Tibetan provincial government with limited autonomy. A border settlement in the Aksaichin area in the highly strategic Ladakh/Tibet/Sinkiang triangle seems unlikely since China cannot concede the area for strategic reasons and India cannot for political reasons. But there has been a *de facto* settlement of the border dispute which is mutually satisfactory in most respects and honored by both governments.

The modifications in China's Indian policy was primarily motivated by a desire to counter 'excessive' Soviet influence in India — as it was seen from Peking; improving relations with New Delhi was considered a better way to do this than a continuation of the confrontationist politics of 1960–75. New Delhi is equally interested in improving relations with China, particularly if this can be accomplished in ways that serve India's regional interests. Soviet adventurism in Afghanistan in 1980 could also well have a positive impact on Sino-Indian relations. There are substantial differences between New Delhi's and Peking's interpretations of this event, as well as in their proposed responses to Soviet aggression; but it is also the case that both Governments view this development as a serious threat to their respective interests and consider it essential that Soviet military forces be withdrawn from Afghanistan. Open co-operation between the two powers for the achievement of this goal is not feasible for a number of reasons. But China has been very careful in defining its own role in this crisis in ways that are patently not threatening to India; New Delhi has generally responded in kind, if indirectly, through its efforts to improve relations with Pakistan without demanding a diminution in the strong Sino-Pakistani ties. Thus, while the 1980s are not likely to see a restoration of the tacit Sino-Indian alliance that existed in the

1950s, the confrontationist politics that characterized their relationship in the 1960–75 period may well be much less evident in the policies pursued by both Governments subsequently.

Since the mid-1950s, the United States has probably been the major power that has induced the greatest degree of anxiety, bewilderment and frustration in the Governments in the subcontinent. In contrast to the Soviet Union and China, the objectives and strategies adopted by Washington in South Asia have fluctuated widely over time, and not infrequently in ways that defied comprehension in the region. One consequence has been that the United States has a reputation in the subcontinent for being unpredictable and thus unreliable as a source of support — or, for that matter, opposition. This would not matter too much if the United States were an incidental factor in South Asian developments but — unfortunately, as far as the South Asian states are concerned — that is not the case.

There are several explanations for the inconsistencies in U.S. policies toward the subcontinent, including changes in administration in Washington that have on occasion led to revisions in the basic principles underlying American foreign policy. Another factor has been the relatively low priority attached to South Asia, as a general rule, by foreign policy decision-makers in Washington. There have been exceptions — e.g. the period between the 1962 Sino-Indian war and the 1965 Indo-Pakistan war, or the emerging crisis in Afghanistan in 1979–80. But for the most part South Asia has been considered peripheral to more important policy objectives elsewhere in Asia, and Washington has usually been prepared to sacrifice American interests in the subcontinent if this was seen as serving U.S. interests elsewhere.[4] In 1962, for instance, the United States sent the aircraft-carrier *Enterprise* into the Bay of Bengal in response to an Indian appeal for support in its hostilities with China as this was viewed in Washington as a contribution to the 'containment of China' policy. In 1971 the *Enterprise* was again sent into the Bay of Bengal during the Indo-Pakistan war over Bangladesh, but on that occasion as a token demonstration to Peking that the rapprochement between the United States and China then underway could also be used to support Chinese policy interests in South Asia.[5] The overt action taken by Washington on these two occasions may have been similar, but the objectives of U.S. policy were basically different. The eventual result throughout South Asia (and possibly in China) was to persuade the political élites in the region that it was a mistake to place any reliance upon Washington in a crisis.

It can be argued that the United States has proved to be much less subject to manipulation by South Asian states than either the Soviet Union or China because of its low level of involvement, and that

Washington is less bound by burdensome commitments in the region. More questionable, however, is whether this 'flexibility' has served and advanced American interests, not only in South Asia but elsewhere in Asia. The tendency in Washington to place a low priority on South Asia has seriously undermined the capacity of the United States to influence the course of developments there even when this has been considered necessary — e.g. the unresponsiveness of Pakistan to American aid offers in the context of the Afghanistan crisis in 1980. Washington has pursued what is, in essence, a 'no win' policy in South Asia, and the results have been what should have been expected.

India has probably been the primary beneficiary of the low-profile policy adopted by the United States in South Asia since the mid-1960s, but there have been few expressions of appreciation even from this quarter. Indeed, New Delhi would probably prefer a greater degree of continuity in the substance and objectives of U.S. policy in the region, since it is the unpredictability of the American response in crisis situations that seriously complicates decision-making in India. The Government of India, as well as the other states in South Asia, would prefer to define their own policies with some sense of confidence in Washington's likely response, but that sense is exactly what has been lacking in most instances. Thus, in the 1980s Washington may well pay a high price in the whole of southern Asia for its careless and casual attitude toward the subcontinent over the past two decades.

The Islamic states of Southwest Asia have also constituted an important factor in the politics of the subcontinent over three decades, and particularly in the foreign policies of Pakistan and India. The conflicts and disputes that accompanied the partition of British India in 1947 encouraged a beleaguered Pakistan Government to turn for support to its Islamic neighbors to the west, and later in the mid-1950s to join an alliance system — sponsored by the United States as part of its containment of Communism policy — which included the Southwest Asian states of Iran, Turkey, and (until the overthrow of the monarchy in 1958) Iraq. To counter this perceived 'threat', India sought to construct a close relationship with several other Islamic states in the region, primarily Egypt and Syria, as well as with the Soviet Union. New Delhi's objective was to prevent the emergence of a unified Islamic bloc supportive of Pakistan in its recurrent disputes with India, and the Indians were reasonably successful in this endeavor. During the Indo-Pakistani wars of 1965 and 1971, most of the Islamic states adopted positions publicly sympathetic to Pakistan, but only Pakistan's two allies, Iran and Turkey, actually provided small amounts of material assistance.

The capacity of the Southwest Asian states to wield a broad influence in the subcontinent has grown considerably since the 'oil crisis' of

1974, because South Asia is heavily dependent upon oil imports and, more recently, upon investments and other forms of indirect aid from neighboring OPEC countries. But this enhanced ability to intervene in South Asia has been accompanied by a generally more non-partisan position on Indo-Pakistani issues in Southwest Asia. In the 1974–8 period, for instance, Iran under the Shah sought to maintain a security relationship with Pakistan directed at the Soviet Union while, in effect, opting out of its earlier position of support for Pakistan in its disputes with India.

The so-called 'revivalist Islamic political movements' that have engineered the overthrow of the Shah in Iran and the smaller-scale upheavals in some other Southwest Asian states and Afghanistan pose potentially serious problems for South Asia — including Pakistan. What is occurring, of course, is a fundamental redefinition of relations among all the states of South and Southwest Asia, as well as between them and the Soviet Union, China, and the United States. The 1980s are certain to be a turbulent period for the entire southern Asian region from Indochina to the Horn of Africa, and the process of decision-making for the states in this area is undoubtedly more complex and danger-ridden now than at any time since the Second World War.

Obviously, the policies adopted by the Soviet Union, the United States, and China will have a substantial impact on developments in southern Asia and thus cannot be safely ignored. But it is possible that the capacities of these external powers to determine the course of developments — often greatly exaggerated even in the past — has diminished in the 1970s. They can use direct military force — e.g. the Soviets in Afghanistan and the Chinese in Indochina — but it is still unclear whether this enhances or compromises their powers and influence in the region. At the beginning of the 1980s, the Governments in South Asia appeared less responsive to the views of the major external powers than at any time since 1947. While this could be a brief interim, given the greatly expanded direct involvement of the three major external powers in southern Asia, it would seem more likely to be a portent of the future for the subcontinent.

NOTES

1. In the late 1950s, Indonesia was the recipient of substantial military assistance, including naval vessels, from the Soviet Union and was then the major regional naval power in the eastern Indian Ocean. The Soviet Union, of course, was as unhappy as India with the China-Indonesia-Pakistan 'alliance'. While there was not much that Moscow could do in the

short run to counter the consequences of its earlier Indonesian aid program, the Soviets were responsive to India's requests for assistance in developing its own naval forces. After the 1965 'coup' in Indonesia culminated in a total break in Sino-Indonesian relations, the strategic situation in the Indian Ocean shifted in India's favor. But the gradual expansion of Soviet, U.S., and French naval commitments to the Indian Ocean since the late 1960s has encouraged New Delhi to maintain its program for the expansion of its own naval capacities.

2. On assuming the prime ministership of a coalition government in Sri Lanka in 1970, Mrs Bandaranaike took a few blatantly 'anti-American' positions, reportedly to please her Leftist coalition partners — e.g. derecognition of Israel and South Vietnam and the expulsion of the Asia Foundation, a private U.S. aid organization. But at the same time she renewed the agreement with the United States under which the 'Voice of America' is allowed to broadcast from Sri Lanka — a much more important and positive decision as far as Washington was concerned.
3. It has been argued that in the 1960–80 period Pakistan was as successful in manipulating China's involvement in South Asia as India had been with the Soviet Union. One important difference, however, is that New Delhi has been able to exploit Soviet support to attain India's regional objectives while Islamabad has generally been less successful in using Peking for similar purposes. This was clearly demonstrated in both the 1965 and 1971 Indo-Pakistan wars.
4. This tendency to ignore southern Asia in U.S. official circles is also reflected in the products of the 'think tanks' that serve as advisory bodies to the U.S. government. For instance a report on Asian security in the 1980s prepared by the Rand Corporation for the Office of the Assistant Secretary of Defense, International Security Affairs, contained no discussion of South Asia and only two short papers on Southeast Asia, both contributed by Southeast Asian participants in the conference held on this subject. The publication date of the report was November 1979, more than a year after Iran and Afghanistan had become critical areas for U.S. security. See Richard H. Solomon (ed.), *Asian Security in the 1980s: Problems and Policies for a Time of Transition* (Santa Monica, Calif.: Rand Corporation), November 1979.
5. For an authoritative analysis of U.S. policy in the 1971 'Bangladesh war' that emphasizes the importance of the rapprochement with China in U.S. decision-making in this crisis, see Henry Kissinger, *The White House Years* (Boston: Little, Brown and Co., 1979), xxi, 842–918.

THE PUBLISHED WORKS OF W.H. MORRIS-JONES: AN ANNOTATED BIBLIOGRAPHY

Susili Wilson

Note: When Professor Morris-Jones began his academic career, he seemed to want to move into the realm of political philosophy and political theory. For a while he showed an interest even in the politics of the military, but then he became an interpreter of Indian politics and India's political mind. He also moved into the wider realm of Commonwealth affairs as the occupant of the chair in that field in the University of London and as the joint editor of the *Journal of Commonwealth Political Studies* and later as editor of the same journal which took a new title, *Journal of Commonwealth and Comparative Politics*.

BOOKS, BOOKLETS AND BOOKS EDITED

Socialism and bureaucracy. London: Fabian Publications, 1949. 29 p.

Parliament in India. London: Longmans, 1957; American ed. Philadelphia: University of Pennsylvania Press, 1957; reprinted Westport, Conn.: Greenwood Press, 1975. 417 p. Discusses Indian political behaviour after the inauguration of the new constitution in 1950.

Taste and principle in political theory. Inaugural lecture delivered 23 October 1956. Durham: University of Durham, 1957. 24 p. Probes the contemporary significance of political theory, and seeks to establish that objectivity can be achieved in political studies, as in the natural sciences, and that the standards applicable to political evaluation are similar to those of ethics.

Government and politics of India. London: Hutchinson, 1964; 2nd edn 1967; 3rd edn 1971. American paperback ed. New York: Doubleday, 1967. Indian edn New Delhi: B I. Publications, 1974. 239 p. Hindi language edn 1977. A compressed analytical framework of the Indian political system.

Patterns and trends in Indian politics: an ecological analysis of aggregate data on society and elections, editor with Biplab Dasgupta. Bombay: Allied Publishers, 1975. 364 p. A critical investigation of political participation in India.

The making of politicians: studies from Asia and Africa, editor and contributor. London: Althone Press, University of London, 1976. 249 p. Papers presented during 1972–4 at a seminar on comparative politics at the Institute of Commonwealth Studies. The author examines the problems of the political bibliographer.

Australia and Britain: studies in a changing relationship, editor with A. F. Madden; foreword by Kenneth Wheare. London: Cass in association with Institute of Commonwealth Studies, University of London, 1980, 195 p.

Decolonisation and after: the British and French experience, editor with

George Fischer. London: Cass, 1980. 369 p. Papers from a colloquium held in Paris, 6–8 May 1976. British and French scholars compare their countries' experiences with the processes of decolonisation.

Politics mainly Indian. Bombay: Orient Longman; Columbia, Mo.: South Asia Books, 1978. 392 p. The author uses the standard of liberal democracy to determine whether India has succeeded in her experiment in institution-building.

From Rhodesia to Zimbabwe: behind and beyond Lancaster House, editor. London: Cass, 1980. 123 p. Provides background information on the events leading up to the birth of Zimbabwe.

CONTRIBUTIONS TO BOOKS

'India's political idioms', in Philips, C. H. (ed.), *Politics and society in India*. New York: Praeger, 1962; London: Geo. Allen & Unwin, 1963. A survey in which the language and idiom of Indian politics is identified as 'modern', 'traditional' and 'saintly'.

'Behaviour and ideas in political India', in Spann, R. N. (ed.), *Constitutionalism in Asia*. Bombay: Asia Publishing House, 1963. Seminar on constitutionalism in Asia, Canberra, Australia, 1960. Deals with the importance of the provincial members of the legislative assemblies in the political education of the electors in the traditional areas of Indian politics.

'Stability and change in Indian politics', in Rose, S. (ed.), *Politics in Southern Asia*. London: Macmillan, 1963. A symposium held at St. Antony's College, Oxford, 1961. A general examination of Indian politics referring also to the civil service.

'Political institutions in New Commonwealth states', in Hamilton, W. B.; Robinson, K.; Goodwin, C. D. (eds.), *A decade of the Commonwealth, 1955–1964*. Durham, N.C.: Duke University Press, 1966. Considers the future of parliamentary institutions in the new states of the Commonwealth and emphasises the importance of leadership roles and administrative skills in the maintenance of parliamentary democracy.

'Language and region within the Indian Union', in Mason, Philip (ed.), *India and Ceylon: unity and diversity*. London: Oxford University Press for Institute of Race Relations, 1967. Interprets political developments in India in the context of the change from English to the regional languages.

'Political recruitment and political change', in Leys, Colin (ed.), *Politics and change in developing countries: studies in the theory and practice of development*. London: Cambridge University Press, 1969. Originally presented at a conference held at the University of Sussex. Studies the concept and utility of political development by an examination of the kinds of members recruited to the Parliament and state legislative assemblies of India.

'Candidate selection: the ordeal of Congress, 1966–1967', in Rajan, M. S. (ed.), *Studies in politics: national and international*, prepared in honour of Dr A. Appadorai. Foreword by Zakir Husain. Delhi: Vikas Publications, 1971.

'Power and inequality: in general and in South Asia', in Sharma, S. K. (ed.), *Dynamics of development: an international perspective*. Delhi: Concept Pub. Co., 1978. Essays in honour of J. N. Khosla.

ARTICLES

'Political rights of civil servants', *Political Quarterly*, 20(4), 1949. A critical examination of the Report of the Committee on the Political Activities of Civil Servants (Cmnd. 7718).

'The Indian elections', *Political Quarterly*, 23(3), 1952. Describes the expansion of the post-independence electoral network with the franchise being made universal after its previous restriction.

'Politicians and generals', *Cambridge Journal*, 6(1), 1952. Delineates the civil and military power in the political structure of the Western state with special reference to the United States, Britain, France and Germany.

'In defence of apathy: some doubts on the duty to vote', *Political Studies* 2(1), 1954. On democratic indifference and its incompatibility with compulsory voting.

'Experience of independence: India and Pakistan', *Political Quarterly*, 29(3), 1958. Deals with the role of the Congress Party, the personality of Nehru and other factors in India and compares them with the unfavourable situation in Pakistan.

'Recent political developments in India', *Parliamentary Affairs*, 11(4), 1958. The first instalment of a study containing a sympathetic analysis of the seven constitutional changes effected in the Indian constitution in a period of nine years.

'Recent political developments in India: II', *Parliamentary Affairs*, 12(1), 1959. A discussion of the parliamentary and ministerial consequences resulting from the report of the Inquiry Commission on the Affairs of the Life Insurance Corporation of India.

'The exploration of Indian political life', *Pacific Affairs*, 32(4), 1959. A critical review of eight books, the main themes examined being the impact of West on East and the tradition-modernity syndrome.

'Mahatma Gandhi: political philosopher?', *Political Studies*, 8(1), 1960, reprinted in *Politico*, 25(4), 1960. The possibility of a philosophy of politics in Gandhi's teachings on *satyagraha*, civil disobedience and non-cooperation is examined.

'Towards a new Commonwealth', *Foreign Policy Reports* (*Delhi*), 9(5), May 1960.

'Civil-military relations in the modern state', *International Social Science Journal*, 12(2), 1960. A summary of a conference organised by the International Political Science Association in Opatija, Yugoslavia, in September 1959 on the relationship between the armed forces and governments.

'The unhappy utopia', *Economic Weekly*, June 25 1960. A critical analysis of contemporary Indian political thinking as represented in the ideas of J. P. Narayan.

'A third Commonwealth', *Socialist Commentary*, September 1960.

'Military power in politics', *Durham University Journal, New Series*, 21(3), June 1961. There are two prominent contemporary political problems, an inseparable defence and foreign policy and the spread of various types of military regimes, both being aspects of the fundamental question of civil-military relations.

'Democratic decentralisation: some political consequences', *Economic Weekly*, July 1962. Deals with the local framework that developed from the Indian government's community development programme.

'The emergent countries', *Political Quarterly*, 34(3), 1963. Examines the problems of political development in new states especially those created despite territorial and cultural diversities.

'Political power in India', *New Society*. 19 March 1964.

'Parliament and dominant party: Indian experience', *Parliamentary Affairs*, 17, 1964. Defines the democratic nature of the one-dominant-party (Congress) which monopolises government in India.

'India: under new management, business as usual', *Asian Survey*, 5(2), February 1965. A survey of the political scene in India in 1964 following the death of Nehru and the emergence of the Shastri-Kamaraj combine.

'A communication on "constitutionalism" ', *American Political Science Review*, 59(2), 1965. General agreement is expressed in favour of Giovanni Sartori's 'Constitutionalism: a preliminary discussion' which appeared in the *American Political Science Review*, 56(2), 1962.

'India: the end of the beginning', *Political Studies*, 13(2), 1965. Critical observations on various political aspects of the subcontinental scene based on reviews of fourteen books on India and one on Pakistan.

'Dominance and dissent: their inter-relations in the Indian party system', *Government and Opposition*, 1(4), August 1966. An explanation of the one-party-dominance model as represented in the monopoly over government that the Indian National Congress exercises in India.

'India's political miracle', *Australian Journal of Politics and History*, 12(2), August 1966. An examination on the eve of India's fourth general election (1967) of the way in which the Indian political system works and the prospects for its continuing viability.

'The Indian Congress Party: a dilemma of dominance', *Modern Asian Studies*, 1(2), 1967. An observation of the shape of things to come with the death of Nehru. The Indian National Congress could become a tightly knit organisation with greater control of the periphery. Such a transformation could well mean 'political suicide', accompanied however by a rebirth.

'India: will the shock treatment work?', *Sunday Times*, 19 March 1967. A reflection as to possibilities with the decline of Congress after the general election of 1967.

'The Indian elections: how much has changed?', *The Round Table*, 57, 1967. Anticipates the consequences of the Congress debacle at the 1967 general elections and concludes that the politics of containment and quasi-federalism will give way to 'an era of full-blooded politics in a thoroughly federal society'.

'From monopoly to competition in India's politics', *Asian Review*, 1(1), November 1967. The split in Congress has caused a breakdown in the one-party-dominance model, but the ensuing competition between the rivals in the dominant party can be healthy for Indian democracy.

'Fourth general election in Madhya Pradesh' (with Biplab Dasgupta), *Economic and Political Weekly*, January 1968. A statistical investigation and explanation of the fortunes of the leading contenders in one of the more important units of the Indian federation.

'India's political areas: interim report on an ecological electoral investigation' (with Biplab Dasgupta), *Asian Survey*, 9(6), June 1969. A statistical investigation of the Indian general elections of 1957, 1962 and 1967 based on defined political and socio-economic variables with a view to explaining party vote-shares and electoral swings.

'Congress, dead or alive', *Pacific Affairs*, 42(2), Summer 1969. A review article in which questions are asked about the nature of the Indian National Congress and of its impact on the Indian political scene based on a critical review of Stanley A. Kochanek's (1967) and Myron Weiner's (1968) books on the Indian National Congress.

'A commonwealth of learning: a common professional culture' (with T. J. Johnson), *The Round Table*, 60, October 1970. The main themes outlined here are the influence of universities in Britain and in some of the countries of the Commonwealth on higher learning in other Commonwealth states.

'The road to Indian independence: official documents', *Political Quarterly*, 42(1), 1971. Critical observations on the compilation of selected documents on India's road to independence during the period January April 1942 by N. Mansergh and E. W. R. Lumby (eds), *The transfer of power, 1942–7*: vol. 1, *The Cripps Mission, January-April 1942*, 1970.

'Mrs Gandhi's new politics', *Spectator*, 20 March 1971. Two despatches, one from Calcutta and the other from Delhi, are written against the background of the Indian general election of 1971 when Mrs Gandhi's Congress scored a resounding victory.

'India elects for change and stability', *Asian Survey*, 11(8), August 1971. The general election of March 1971 restored the one-party-dominance system in India. The author speculates that voter behaviour could possibly have changed to some extent but not as much as remarked by some observers.

'Press performance on election forecasts', *Economic and Political Weekly*, 6(30–32), July 1971. Comments based on clippings from four Delhi newspapers — *Times of India, Statesman, Hindustan Times* and *Indian Express* — and on limited clippings of their non-Delhi editions sent from Delhi to the states from January to March 1971, the view being that the projections were off the mark as they tended to rely too heavily on the local correspondents of these newspapers rather than on a sample of ordinary voters.

'Pakistan post-mortem and the roots of Bangladesh', *Political Quarterly*, 43(2), April 1972. An analysis of the civil and military factors which in 1972 led to the emergence of Bangladesh.

'India: the one and the many', *Art International*, 18(3), 20 March 1974.

'Not a safari, just a stopover', *Lugano Review*, 3, 1975. A discussion of some of the political, economic and nationalistic problems that beset the three countries, Uganda, Kenya and Tanzania, which constituted the East African Community.

'Whose emergency — India's or Indira's?', *The World Today*, 31, November 1975. An examination of the events which led up to the declaration of a state of emergency on 26 June 1975 — the role of J. P. Narayan, Morarji Desai, various communalist elements and the Allahabad judgement of Justice Sinha in which Mrs Gandhi was found guilty of two election malpractices.

'The bamboo ballot-box', *Times Literary Supplement*, 19 December 1975. A critical review of N. D. Palmer's *Elections and political development: the South Asian experience* (1975) and A. Jeyaratnam Wilson's *Electoral politics in an emergent state: the Ceylon general election of May 1970* (1975) in which the author concludes that 'at opposite ends of the spectrum, Nepal and Sri Lanka seem the safest bets for the least movement'.

'The parliamentary politician in Asia', *Legislative Studies Quarterly*, 1(3), August 1976. Introduction to a special issue of the journal where, as guest editor, the author summarises the similarities and differences apparent from individual contributions on the behaviour of legislators in India, Bangladesh, Malaysia and Singapore.

'Creeping but uneasy authoritarianism: India 1975–6', *Government and Opposition*, 12(1), 1977. The mechanisms of emergency rule are scrutinised and an estimate made of their becoming permanently incorporated into the body politic in the form of a 'coded democracy' as a prelude to the holding of elections necessary to institutionalise the authoritarian structures set up by Mrs Gandhi.

'India discards dictatorship', *The World Today*, 33, May 1977. An initial analysis of India's sixth general election (1977) which resulted in Mrs Gandhi's defeat and victory for the Janata coalition.

'The Indian elections and their aftermath', *Asian Affairs*, 8(3), October 1977. An examination of the factors that produced the victory for Mrs Gandhi at the general election of 1977.

'Theories of development and dependence', *American Political Science Review*, 72(12), 1978. A communication. The character of work and research at the Institute of Commonwealth Studies, University of London, explained to refute criticisms of its empirical and 'hostile to theory' ethos made by Dr V. Berman in his review of Edward Brett's *Colonialism and Underdevelopment in East Africa* which appeared in the *American Political Science Review*, 70(3), 1976.

'The study of political science in the universities of Bangladesh', *Minerva*, 16(3), 1978. A descriptive analysis of the unhappy state of political science in the universities in Bangladesh with particular reference to teaching, linguistic difficulties, research and other factors.

'The West and the Third World: whose democracy, whose development?', *Third World Quarterly*, 1(3), July 1979. The author takes issue with B. K. Nehru's thesis in *Third World Quarterly*, 1(2), that liberal democracy is unsuitable to deal with the problems of underdevelopment and development.

'The transfer of power: a view from the sidelines', *Modern Asian Studies*, 16(1), 1982. The author explains how, as constitutional adviser to Lord Mountbatten, he had to wrestle with the most difficult problems that followed the British withdrawal from India.

INDEX